PERSPECTIVES IN EDUCATION, RELIGION, AND THE ARTS

CONTEMPORARY PHILOSOPHIC THOUGHT

The International Philosophy Year Conferences At Brockport

PERSPECTIVES IN EDUCATION, RELIGION, AND THE ARTS

Edited by Howard E. Kiefer and Milton K. Munitz

STATE UNIVERSITY OF NEW YORK PRESS

ALBANY

PUBLISHED BY STATE UNIVERSITY OF NEW YORK PRESS

THURLOW TERRACE, ALBANY, NEW YORK 12201

© 1970 BY STATE UNIVERSITY OF NEW YORK,
ALBANY, NEW YORK. ALL RIGHTS RESERVED

LIBRARY OF CONGRESS CATALOG CARD NUMBER 69-14641
STANDARD BOOK NUMBER 87395-053-4
MANUFACTURED IN THE UNITED STATES OF AMERICA

DESIGNER: RHODA C. CURLEY

CONTENTS

PREFACE

Education, religion, and the arts have been of lasting interest to philosophers, not only because they are areas of human activity which are of perennial human concern, but also because the philosophical problems they pose place interesting demands on the exercise of philosophic inquiry. Few topics seem to be more subject to individual critical analysis or, therefore, more apt to excite controversial interpretation. Not unexpectedly, some practitioners in these areas consider the expertise of the practicing specialist as essential to a proper understanding of the issues involved. On the other hand, some interested laymen seem to hold to the opposite view, often on grounds which call to mind Clemenceau's caveat about war and generals. Both practicing specialists and interested laymen may look with suspicion on the role which the professed philosopher plays in addressing himself to their problems and concerns. The reader may expect to find some of these differences illustrated by the views expressed in this volume.

Educator and lecturer Harold Taylor begins by questioning the current relevance of the academic philosophical enterprise to educational problems in the second half of the twentieth century, particularly with regard to the special problems of societal change and the volatile issues which have found expression both in the public schools and in higher education. Professor William Frankena concerns himself specifically with the problem of characterizing the dispositions which an individual needs in order to lead the best life of which he is capable. He argues that the good life can be considered as requiring two overlapping elements: activities and experiences that are enjoyable (including pleasure, beatitude, and contentment), and activities and experiences that involve the achievement of excellence (as judged by standards intrinsic to the activity). He criticizes existing views which de-emphasize excellence and enjoyment in order to substitute such things as self-expression, committment, authenticity, or even anxiety, although he agrees that the good life will be better if lived in certain ways or frames of mind rather than others. Professor Henry David Aiken objects to the form of rationalism he finds in education which seems to encourage the consideration of science as more important than other branches of learning, in a way which narrows the proper range of human knowledge. He argues that there is much more to the life of the mind than this, and emphasizes the role and function of natural language in providing an essential basis for knowledge of matters of fact, of logic, and of those forms of knowledge concerned with conduct and action. He contends that an education should be a philosophical education, in order to cultivate free men with free minds for a free society. Professor Marvin Farber contends that the existing and emerging needs of any particular society should be met without major disruption of the educational system. He suggests that one necessary condition to accomplish this would require colleges and universities to maintain flexible curricula which would allow for all interests, and which would provide the basis for needed change. He argues that the aims of an educational system that seeks to further the interests of mankind must provide both for specialization and for general knowledge or training, and that these are not mutually exclusive and do not necessarily oppose or preclude each other. Chancellor Samuel B. Gould emphasizes the point that the university must be a place where dedicated scholars may continue to search for truth but also points out that the university must be a place where man comes to recognize his inner self. He suggests that the university must rely heavily on philosophy and philosophers, not only to give today's generation their own perception of their moral and intellectual goals, but also to preserve the university as an institution which nurtures both the spirit and the intellect.

In the section on Religion, Professors John Macquarrie and Kai Nielsen focus on the problem of theism and atheism, by discussing what "talk about God" means. Professor Macquarrie holds that clarification of what is meant by the word "God" is essential to clarifying the dispute between theism and atheism, and he argues that the word "God" may be explained in terms of three concepts: the context of the meaning of human existence; "Being;" and the form of the world. Professor Nielsen, on the other hand, contends that the concept of God is incoherent. Like Macquarrie, he is not concerned with the believer who has an anthropomorphic conception of God; such a person, he holds, simply has false, superstitious beliefs. Professor Nielsen argues that no identifiable state of affairs can be characterized which would make any putative religious statements true, and intelligible directions are lacking which would suitably identify the supposed reference for the word "God." In addition to the two major papers of Professors Macquarrie and Nielsen, their direct responses are also included in this volume. Professor Winfield Nagley discusses the importance of the concept of the Archimedean point to Kierkegaard's philosophical views, especially those on religion.

In opening the discussion on the Arts, Professor Morris Weitz argues that whereas genre is an open concept, style is a concept that is irreducibly vague. He traces the way in which mannerism as a style concept is used by art historians and critics, coming to the conclusion that each has used different criteria in speaking of mannerism. He concludes that since at least one style concept is vague (and this vagueness is the fundamental logical feature of the concept), it would be false to claim that all style concepts are logically closed. Professor Monroe Beardsley suggests that the aesthetic point of view finds its place in mediating disputes, in estimating the aesthetic value of an art object, and in providing a broad concept of art that might be helpful for certain purposes. He argues that to take an aesthetic point of view toward an art object or event is to take an interest in whatever aesthetic value it may possess in any particular experience of it when it is correctly experienced. But he points out that this seems to leave us with a dilemma, so far as aesthetic education is concerned; that is, we are torn between conflicting ways of redirecting taste, for there seem to be occasions when it would be clearly wrong to adopt a particular aesthetic point of view, when at the same time it is not wrong *per se* to consider *any* object or event from an aesthetic point of view. Professor William Kennick suggests that the concept of creativity is not a psychological one, by distinguishing between creative acts and creative processes, contending that it is a logically necessary condition for a work of art that it has been created by a person. He adds that this does not mean, however, that anything need be known about the psychology of the artist. If a work of art is creative, then the artist who created it is creative. Thus, if the concept of a work of art is not a psychological concept, then neither is the concept of creativity itself. In responding to Professor Kennick, Professor Jack Glickman distinguishes between creating and making, noting that particulars can be made, but only types can be created. He contends that creating is neither an activity nor a process, for if it were either, one could decide to create; that is, one could create at will. He argues that creating is not an isolable activity that can be done without also doing something else; rather, he suggests that "create" is an achievement verb, and "creating" like "winning," a kind of achievement. Professor Jerome Stolnitz argues against two forms of what he calls "the Identity Thesis," which may be taken to mean that whatever is (or should be) apprehended by the audience of a work of art, is (or should be) identical with what the artist knowingly created. He suggests that there ought to be a new approach to aesthetics arising from the interaction between the concepts of art and aesthetic, in that art objects are not the source of things that invite narrow interpretations, but rather require permissive conditions for the encouragement of novel aesthetic delights. Art historian Horst Janson addresses himself to some of the issues raised above, and provides critical commentary. He claims that it is the aesthetician, rather than the artist or critic, who formulates theories of art. Recognizing that the art historian does make judgments, as exemplified by changes in the style of art history over the years, he suggests that the art historian's values are molded by the contemporary artist, rather than by the aesthetician.

The topic of Communications and the Arts (the plural of both terms is intentional) is introduced by encyclopaedist and author Clifton Fadiman, who discusses the impact of mass communications on patterns of rhetoric and the effect of the development of technical sophistication of a medium on the personality of the communicators. He holds that through multiplicity and diffusion, some art forms are lost, some rediscovered, and some invented as a result of the activity of the media through which they are viewed. Professor Richard McKeon observes that the philosophic arts of discourse and making have been transformed into the arts of rhetoric or communications, and grammar or construction. In turn, the arts of communication construction must establish and use principles which function not unlike the ordering principles of metaphysics, and must develop and formulate methods of discourse that are adapted to facts and to statements of relations among facts. He contends that the arts of communication and construction are arts of language and action, and are both universal and particular. When, in addition, the philosophic arts are viewed as arts of communication and construction, rhetoric, the art of persuasion and debate, is made into a universal and architectonic art. Professor H. W. Johnstone, Jr., addresses himself to the relationship of communication in philosophy as it is concerned with rhetoric, and points out that important aspects of contemporary philosophy recognize the function of philosophy to be fundamentally a rhetorical enterprise. He discusses the views of Wittgenstein and Heidegger as they relate to this thesis, and argues that philosophy has always had this function. Taking issue with Professor Johnstone, Professor George Stack claims that one cannot conclude that rhetoric is communication just because communication employs rhetorical devices, or because communication and rhetoric produce a coincidence of effect. He holds that rhetoric does have a communicative effect insofar as it communicates attitudes, beliefs, and values, but unlike philosophic communication, rhetoric is not concerned with the direct transmission of factual knowledge. Professor Harold Zyskind claims that rhetoric can function as a language game; that is to say, that it is in the context of language usage that rhetoric clearly exhibits its proper philosophical role. Rhetoric viewed in this way reveals basic principles (which are really incomplete actions) in their most literal form. In response to his views, Professor Harold Greenstein cautions against a too readily accepted reconciliation between the separate concepts of philosophy and rhetoric. He argues that the eloquence of an argument or the psychology of its author says nothing about the argument's logical points; that is to say, the medium through which the message is sent must not be taken as the message itself. Poet and author Kenneth Burke concerns himself with what he calls "entelechial principles," principles revealing a type of symbolic action that is characteristic only of man. He holds that the philosophy which can best warn us of the limitations found in communication is the one which pays attention to the "Rhetorical Situation"—the one that pays attention to persuasion as well as to purely symbolic aspects of communication.

The papers contained in the four volumes of this anthology were drawn from the fourteen conferences of the International Philosophy Year program of 1967–1968, held on the Brockport Campus of State University of New York. The conference sessions on Philosophy of Education and Philosophy of Religion provided the papers contained in the corresponding sections of this volume, while two conference sessions (Aesthetics and Philosophy of Communications and the Arts) provided the papers contained in the Arts section, which accounts for the substantially larger size of that section.

H. E. K.

EDUCATION

PHILOSOPHY AND CULTURAL CHANGE

Harold Taylor

The relation between philosophy and education has grown more and more tenuous as the practitioners of each have become separated from each other by interests which have become mutually exclusive. The educators have been busy with buildings, budgets, organization charts, equipment, innovations and expansions, with no compelling idea of the philosophical foundations on which their activities rest or the direction in which education should go. The philosophers have organized themselves, within the academy, into academic enclaves which are insulated from the practical problems of the social order—including the problems of education. When they do turn to education it is in the spirit of the professional academician, with the intent of turning education into an academic subject, while neither the educator nor the philosopher thinks of teaching as the task in which each should be most deeply engaged.

Among the four books capable of arousing national discussion of educational issues over the past ten years, one was by a labor economist and labor mediator turned university president, Clark Kerr of the University of California; another was by a foundation executive, also a university president, James Perkins of Cornell; a third, by a former university president, scientist, and diplomat, James Conant; and the fourth by a professor of sociology, Daniel Bell of Columbia University. None of the authors was, by training or inclination, a philosopher. Not one was a trained scholar in the field of education. The fact that the books themselves lacked the depth and range of philosophical insight which could help to give imaginative direction to contemporary society and its educational institutions is less attributable to the authors' not having been trained in the philosophical disciplines than to their not being philosophically-minded. This is a useful distinction to make, since it applies not only to many contemporary writers on education but to a

3

large sector of academic philosophers who are too little accustomed to dealing with the intricate relation between their ideas and the cultural context in which the ideas occur. There is apparent an inverse ratio between the ability to deal in depth with the problems of education and cultural change and the study and/or practice of philosophy within the American university. Those who now teach, study, and profess philosophy in the university have too little to say that is interesting, useful, or important except to other professors of philosophy.

I was struck by the title of a recent piece in *The Listener,* "Philosophy and Madness," by Stuart Hampshire—who is one of the exceptions to what I have been saying—and I regretted for a moment that I had not thought of it as a title for this evening's address. It is a title most useful to describe a situation in which we face a world full of the young in search of teachers and in search of a direction for their lives, while the university professionals in the field of philosophy, the humanities, the arts and sciences of society deliberately organize themselves into bands of professionals the better to pursue their careers in a chosen field. What troubles me most is not merely the absence of powerful and enlightened teaching, by persons trained in the philosophical and social disciplines, teaching which can move the younger generation into a new mood of intellectual and cultural concern, but that under the present circumstances the school, the college, and the university are losing their capacity to influence the lives and commitments of young people.

The young seek, wherever they can find it, the kind of teaching that does have an effect on their lives and if they cannot find it in the schools, colleges, and universities they will find it elsewhere, and among themselves. "If the university does not educate, others will," says William Arrowsmith in his rousing, devastating, and beautiful statement about teaching in America. "Education," says Arrowsmith, "will pass, as it is passing now, to the artist, to the intellectual, to the gurus of the mass media, to the charismatic charlatans and sages, and to the whole immense range of secular and religious street corner fakes and saints. . . . What matters is the integration of significant life and knowledge, of compassionate study and informed conduct." In Mr. Arrowsmith we have a passionate advocate of the philosopher as teacher, of the philosopher who wishes to engage himself with the issues of his own culture, the person who feels that his role as a teacher is not to disseminate ideas about systems of philosophy, but as one to whom the young can turn for some kind of intellectual manifestation and some kind of intellectual satisfaction.

This is what matters to the young, and has mattered in every age.

There are many who have already begun to question the relevance of their education to their own lives and to the things which they hope to achieve in their lives. Among them are those who have already become involved in social action, who cannot stay tranquil while the big injustices perpetuate themselves. The path they can take into a larger understanding of the world and to an understanding of how best to act in it to secure its welfare does not lie through the orderly syllabus of general education, or in the arid land of the philosophy courses. It lies through the informed experience which the student may have with cultures which surround him in his own society.

What the academic man does not understand is that to educate students is to change the culture and the society. It is to educate persons who can understand the world in which they are living and can talk and act honestly in it. Before students can understand their own world, they must become sensitive to the character of their own lives and their own beliefs. Otherwise the student has no way of understanding the nature of anyone else's life. It is like trying to explain modern art to someone who has never seen a modern painting.

I would, therefore, make one generalization about the present state of the education of teachers: What is presently lacking among educators —whether they be called philosophers of education or members of philosophy departments or academic faculty members or whatever term one wishes to use for them—is a concern for the commitment young people are capable of making to changing the culture in which they live. Students of education are not simply persons who are coming to college in order to enter a profession or to start a career—they are persons capable of acts of devotion to the cause of learning and to the welfare of children and young adults.

If the students see around them daily, in the colleges and universities, the cynicism of teachers who care little for the art of teaching, whose own lives are lived elsewhere than in a commitment to humane learning, or whose talents ill equip them for the task they have accepted and for which they are paid, the young are unable to respond and unlikely to create their own conceptions of what it means to be a teacher and a scholar. If the young do not foresee in the four college-years ahead of them, wide horizons, anticipations of delight, promises of an opening up of their lives, if they see only duties to be borne and trivial tasks to undertake, they are unlikely to find energies within themselves through which to infuse their own education with a sense of purpose.

The curriculum—whatever it is—in philosophy, in the humanities, in the natural sciences, must start with the intention on the part of the educator to create a situation in which the student can honestly commit himself to what he is asked to do. If he is to be a teacher, what he is asked to do must in some way illuminate his understanding of what it means to be a teacher. His motivation for learning matters very much indeed, since it determines how he learns and whether he learns, and those who do not know how to arrange an education for teachers which makes them want to teach should not meddle with education.

This is the setting into which the teacher of philosophy comes. It may be worth noting that there are other characteristics of the culture of which the teacher of philosophy is a part. He belongs to a highly organized academic culture. If you look at the organization of the professional philosopher within the universities and colleges, you find that he is organized in a way more similar to that of the American Medical Association than of the Society for the Psychological Study of Social Issues. I recommend, as an invitation to intellectual disaster, a visit to the meetings of the American Philosophical Association in session. There the intellect does not survive the bureaucracy. The papers are, as I have already suggested, written for other philosophers about matters which are professionally interesting, and these do not include the matters I have been discussing up to now.

Those who are at all sensitive to the situation of the world at large, whether students, intellectuals, philosophers, or laymen concerned about mankind, can recognize the fact that we are in a situation in man's history in which every threat which has ever been made to the security of the human intellect and the human person is now rampant. When we calculate the number of deaths that could possibly be caused by simple shifts in political antagonisms between the Soviet Union and ourselves, we discover that we can demolish 60 to 70 million Russians and they can demolish the same number of Americans. When we are talking about this kind of philosophy we are not talking about abstract subjects to be embalmed in a curriculum, we are talking about the situation of mankind as it is now being dealt with in the political, cultural, and social problems of contemporary world history. The phenomena of the existential condition of mankind in the twentieth century have escaped the university professors of philosophy. They are unknown factors in the plans of curricula for the education of teachers.

I stand before you as one chastened by the experience of having been in sixty-seven different classes over this past year and a half, in the philosophy, history, foundations, and psychology of education, and a similar number of other classes in the humanities and social sciences. I have been engaged in a study of the education of teachers in America in the field of world affairs. Since I define world affairs as what happens in the world to persons, and I define education as what, in fact, happens in the experience of the individual, I have felt no constriction in the limits of my study. As I have gone to education classes I have taken notes with the other students. I have been lectured to in classes in the philosophy of education, in principles of secondary education, in principles of elementary school education, in methods of education, in surveys of Western civilization, and even in surveys of non-Western cultures.

I report to you as a fact, that the entire undergraduate curriculum for the embryo teacher for the American schools is a wasteland in which few things grow. The students are simply receiving academic information which is not very useful. As soon as they get it they are immediately examined, graded, and passed on to the next stage of information-gathering. The teachers of philosophy are giving stones when the students are asking for bread. In the entire field of undergraduate education, not very much that is intellectually exciting, spiritually nourishing, or factually important is being given to the American students. It is their good fortune that in this situation the students have their own resources about which I will speak in a moment.

I look at the university as an institution for the creation of cultural and social change. The university is the place where societies and individual lives can be imagined and where the existing reality of contemporary culture and world society can be analyzed and a measurement taken. Existing values and realities can be measured against imagined situations which it is the duty of the university to create for its students and for itself. Then we can have standards of comparison. The true university is an outpost of cultural and social change. It serves society and is served by society. Its policies are determined by changes in the society which demand a response.

The standard view of this relationship between the university and its society is presented by Mr. Clark Kerr, who, in his *Uses of the University*, speaks of the process of social change: "The process cannot be stopped, the results cannot be foreseen—it remains to adapt. . . . The universities able to adapt quickly and effectively will be the great universities of the future."

This I must deny at once. Greatness is not achieved by adaptation. It is achieved, if it is going to be achieved at all, by creation. The first step toward greatness in the case of any intellectual enterprise is not to adapt but to think; to assess critically and with vigor the character of the social and cultural forces, to oppose some and support others with enthusiasm, and to act as the critical and creative intelligence of the world. Otherwise the philosopher and the university have lost their central function. The university and its philosophers who fail to act in this style have little hope of achieving greatness.

In any event, consciously to seek after greatness is an ambition of arrogance. What is more important is to do those things from day to day which, in the life of the university and the lives of students and scholars, are intellectually and culturally valid in their own terms, with no particular insistence on their producing greatness, as long as they avoid being ignoble, pretentious, irrelevant, and anti-intellectual. By anti-intellectual I mean an attitude which encourages the purveying of ideas which do not nourish the intellect, as well as encouraging attacks on those who have ideas that incite active thought.

At its very best the university can be an intellectual, cultural, and social leader for its own society. When we talk about the aims of the university, whether it be this university, the whole state system of New York, or the entire system of universities in the United States, we must remind ourselves that there is no such thing as a university which has aims, or philosophers who express the aims of a university. There are only people who work together in a given set of buildings at particular tasks to which they are either assigned or to which they assign themselves.

In a fairly accurate description of the reality of the big university, Mr. Kerr has noted that the president of the big university is not a philosopher or a statesman of the intellect. He is a man who presides over a loosely held set of bureaucracies, all of them fighting each other. Among the usual witticisms of the contemporary discourse about higher education is one that asserts the university to be a collection of buildings held together by a parking lot. The duty of the university president, according to Mr. Kerr, is to mediate between the forces at work, to meet the demands of the interest groups, all of them equally legitimate: the faculty, the alumni, the community, the Federal government, the voters, industry, agriculture, science, society, and, of course, the students. Unfortunately they are there, they have to be dealt with.

The president, in Mr. Kerr's view, is therefore not an intellectual leader, not a philosopher of culture seeking new forms of thought and educational action, nor should he try to be. The faculty wouldn't like it. In any case, the president's duties in relation to real estate, business arrangements, management, and public relations prevent that kind of activity. In fact the trustees of most universities who are at work to find new university presidents as the old ones wear out and have to be replaced, would find the existence of intellectual interests in any high degree in a candidate a genuine handicap to his candidacy.

The president is generally considered to be a mediator of the forces within the university community and its surrounding society. He must have the opportunity to persuade those who are antagonistic toward each other to take a more moderate view than would otherwise be the case. "The president must find satisfaction in being equally distasteful to each of his constituencies," says Mr. Kerr. "He must reconcile himself to the harsh reality that successes are shrouded in silence while failures are spotlighted in notoriety."

Here we have the genteel cynicism of the American university, expressing in general the attitude of the professionally organized academic. I think the attitude is scandalous. Why not seize the best? Why not have within our institutions of education those who profess and hold a philosophy according to which they wish to be judged? Why be distasteful to all constituencies? Why be carried along on the wave of what exists? To yield to this kind of cynicism, to say bluntly that the welter of public demands and practical necessities prevents doing anything morally or educationally important is to create conditions under which it is perfectly natural for the students and all men of good will to revolt. Educational arrangements must, after all, be made from ideals and expectations of a higher sort than this. No wonder students are against the entire apparatus and against the practitioners of the knowledge industry and its branches in the universities. The university has become organized in such a way that competitive success by its members, including the members of the philosophy departments, is measured by the skill with which the professors do the particular things they are hired to do, that is, to produce and distribute academic knowledge.

The big universities have, in fact, changed in exactly the way Mr. Kerr has described. Within the universities the discipline of philosophy has become departmentalized and has become another corner of organized information, gathered together in textbooks and distributed to students. On the basis of direct observation of what is happening in undergraduate classes in the philosophy of education and in philosophy itself, I can testify that most of what is taught, for the reasons Mr. Kerr has described, has become irrelevant to the central interests and needs of the students themselves.

I do not see how the university president and the university faculty can back away from these problems. The problem, put as succinctly as possible, is that of relating what the faculty knows to what the students need to know. In the case of the natural sciences, and particularly the physical as against the biological sciences, there are certain things that those who wish to move ahead in the scientific community need to know. These things can, in a sense, be more specific than can those in the humanities and the social sciences. It is interesting to note that philosophy in some institutions is classified as a social science and in others as part of the humanities; in still other institutions it is bracketed with comparative religion. One hopes that in being transported from one area of human knowledge to another it will not be damaged in the process. We have forgotten that the study of philosophy is the inquiry into the entire enterprise of human values and into the question of how life can be understood and how a life should be lived. We have therefore been unable to contribute to the students in contemporary America the kind of insight for which they search.

The big universities have managed to organize the body of philosophical knowledge into one general system. It consists in surveying the ideas of the systematic philosophers. In the usual caricature of what philosophy truly is, the course rushes in fifteen weeks from the pre-Socratics to John Dewey in order to cover the material. In one philosophy class of this kind which I visited, I found that in fifty minutes, the teacher of philosophy provided us with a fast description of pragmatism, existentialism, and what he called traditionalism, mentioning in passing the names of philosophers attached to each of those movements. That was all those students were going to hear about those particular philosophical movements in their fifteen weeks. I believe we must have set a world record for getting through existentialism, pragmatism, and traditionalism. The extraordinary fact was that the students enjoyed it, and found the pace exhilarating. They knew they had been witnesses to a pedagogical triumph.

This approach to the teaching of philosophy is dominant in the American instutions where philosophy is considered to have some relationship to education—that is to say, where courses in the philosophy of education are taught. I refer you to one text which is widely used in the preparation of teachers, as an example of how education is explained to students when teachers forget that their students have spent all their lives in elementary schools and high schools before coming to college. This text produced for the consideration of the students a check list of the good teacher's attributes. Among the questions raised was: "Is your hair neatly arranged, and frequently combed? Are your nails carefully manicured and your skin free from blemishes? Do you have an upright posture and a free swinging walk?" These questions were being studied in a course entitled "The School and Society."

Other texts with similar lists ask the student teacher to decide whether or not he had an appropriate personality for the classroom, and to rate himself and other teachers on such items as sparkle, drive, vitality, warmth, and radiation, as if the teacher were a kind of fireworks, or source of nuclear energy. Another text in the same field, an "Introduction to Education," provides the information that "The modern library usually is housed in an attractive, well-constructed building and is so organized that readers can meet their needs effectively and with as little lost motion as possible."

The content of the curriculum in institutions where teachers are being educated consists of an undergraduate program of two years of general education—an academic major—and twenty to thirty units of professional courses. In about eight hundred such institutions, ninety percent of all our teachers in America are being educated. From my study of a cross-section of these institutions, the philosophy of education and what are called the foundations of education contain comparable materials. In one class in the philosophy of education I found a text in which within fifteen pages the students had been told something about the following topics: the Advance of Science and Technology (this was one paragraph), the Impact of Industrialization, the Growth of Nationalism, the Consequences of Imperialism, the Effects of Militarism, the Use of Progaganda, the Tragedy of the Great War, the Failure of the League of Nations, the Rise of Dictatorships in Totalitarian Countries, World War II and the United Nations (this was one page), the Threat of Russian Communism, and the Challenge to Education.

This is a textbook in use in courses in the philosophy of and introduction to education in the United States in 1967. I found in another text, which has fairly wide use, a chapter of nineteen pages containing short statements on Freedom of the Will, the Nature of Man, the Meaning of Metaphysics, followed by a description of the philosophy of education from Plato to Aquinas. Allow me to give you an example of how the text dealt with one philosopher. "Impatient with scholastic thought, Sir Francis Bacon urged men to discard the idols of thought and begin anew, by careful empirical observation of data and the treatment of these data by an inductive method." You can imagine a freshman who doesn't know what "inductive" means being told this about Sir Francis Bacon. The next sentence reads, "Hobbes, a materialist, believed in mind." Off we go again!

Enough of this. I would enjoy nothing more than leading us through the hilarious circuit of the other courses and texts I visited—but that would become counter-productive. If we are to regard intelligently the relation of philosophy as a discipline to education as a discipline—and that is not hard to do—one of the things we must consider is the content of courses in philosophy taught to the defenseless student of education who is imprisoned in the certification requirements and must take something with the title "philosophy" in it from whoever is teaching it. I submit to you that this too is a scandal, a national scandal.

I should now like to consider what to do with all this. I begin by noting one of the factors in the present situation—the all-university committee which makes policy for the education of teachers. The assumption behind the work of the all-university committee is that there is no separation between the practice of teaching and what are called the liberal arts and sciences. I am happy to affirm that assumption, but with some concern about whether the committee which is based on it knows what it is doing. What happens is that faculty representatives from every sector of the departmental system, from the natural sciences to the social sciences, the humanities, and foreign languages, are appointed or elected to the all-university committee. This simply means that departmental interests demand that certain areas of subject-matter must be required as part of the general curriculum for preparing teachers. The qualifications for committee membership include a knowledge of the subject-matter of the department represented, political suitability in representing that area of the curriculum, and a concern for the academic respectability of the curriculum which finally evolves. This means in practice that the committee discussions have mainly to do with how many credits of what kind of subject matter should be put before the potential teacher as he moves through to his certificate in teaching in the public schools.

When we look at another sector of teacher preparation—the graduate school—we find that few institutions in the graduate field have an interest in education for teaching, and that the separation between expert scholarship and the art of teaching has become almost complete. This can be explained not only by the conventional reasons having to do with the career line of the academic professional through reasearch and publication, but by the definition of education and teaching as the production and dissemination of bodies of knowledge. When the graduate school separates the student from a direct relation with teaching, it does so in apparent ignorance of the fact that one's own scholarship is immensely enriched by the act of teaching what one knows to others. I assert the private view, which I hope may eventually grow in public acceptance and force in the years ahead, that one of the best ways to nourish the growth of humane scholarship is to put it to the test by teaching it to young people. Otherwise, the scholar is likely to fall into the same trap as novelists and playwrights who begin to write novels and plays about other writers or about the problems of writers in trying to write, or become members of an intellectual community which reduces itself to writing only about other writers and their works.

The major thrust of the graduate schools is against teaching and against the undergraduate. When a young man with serious philosophical and intellectual interests raises the question, Where can I find a graduate school in which I can work at questions in philosophy which trouble me and learn how to teach in the field of philosophy, there are too few answers which can honestly be given. Where are the philosophers who are concerned for the development of imaginative thinking among undergraduates? From what quarter do we receive that infusion of intellectual energy we have a right to expect from philosophers and the exponents of humane learning, through which the culture is enriched and the values of society are seen in new perspectives?

There are particular ways in which changes happen in any society and in any culture. They happen, for example, when a society organizes itself from the top, and develops an educational system to sustain its own organization. The graduate school is then a training institute for staffing the organization. That is what we have had over the years in the European societies and their university systems. All the philosophical issues having to do with social structure and social values are settled in advance, and the curriculum, modes of instruction, and general pedagogy are already decided by those among the educational elite who are in charge of the universities. The pace of cultural change is therefore very slow, since the resistance to the established intellectual order is minimal, having been contained by the power of the universities to control admission, graduation, and instruction without reference either to the views and interests of students or to changes in the society at large.

Another way in which cultural change occurs is by what could be called, in a short-hand phrase, the land-grant philosophy, originally invoked in the United States to ensure the development of the sciences and technologies of agriculture and industry, and put into wider use as the citizens of this country expanded their needs into the fields of the natural and social sciences, the humanities and the arts. The university was then asked to respond to the needs of the citizens in all the dimensions of their lives, from the need for education in social and political action to the need for education in theatre, dance, music, the visual arts, and literature.

If education is considered to be a way in which the needs of the citizens are fulfilled, and the teacher of philosophy is asked to share in that fulfillment, the first necessity is that the teacher turn his attention directly to the intellectual needs and resources of the students. They are the link between himself and the existing cultural order. The difficulty is that at the present time, the collective faculty body, including that part of the body inhabited by the practitioners of philosophy, is one of the most conservative forces now operating in the educational system. Against those forces are arranged the energies and resources of the American student-body. Having been disciplined and rendered sensitive to philosophical issues by experience in the society—mainly through the anti-war and civil rights movements—a minority of the students have begun to turn their attention to the reform of the universities, and through them, to the reform of the society and its multiple cultures.

The degree of student concern and cultural energy varies from one institution to another. There are universities and colleges in which nothing very much is happening at all. I have visited campuses in which students, having heard of revolts, protests, and alarms in other institutions, regret that they have no issues around which their own intellectual and personal energies could be organized. Some of them have asked if there were not some issues I could leave with them before going away, so that they too could become excited, to which I have replied that the time was too short to develop the kind of revolt which would do justice to my views.

Allowing for variations from campus to campus, it is possible to calculate with a fair degree of accuracy, that of the six and one half million students in the 2300 colleges and universities in the United States, approximately one half million are in some degree of tension with the existing social order and its educational agencies. These would include the quarter million students who are tutoring children in the slums, both urban and rural; the thirty to forty thousand each year who apply to the Peace Corps; the VISTA volunteers; the candidates for the National Teacher Corps; the members of Students for a Democratic Society; the social activists with religious affiliations; and the others who are active in projects having to do with the reform of their universities. Among them are those who have deliberately set out to change the society by what they do, and who have in mind an image of the society they would like to create. A small minority has no image of this kind and refuses to admit to one, preferring first the destruction of what exists.

Who would have predicted five years ago that a twenty-three-year-old philosophy student in the University of California would have been surrounded by upwards of three hundred television, radio, magazine, and newspaper reporters whenever he stood up to make pronouncements on educational philosophy and practice? Yet that is what happened in the case of Mario Savio, following the educational events in

Berkeley, California of 1964 and 1965. Who would have predicted even three years ago that a twenty-four-year-old student educated in New York and at Howard University could command a national and international audience when he stood up to make his statements on social change and the role of the Negro in bringing about that change? Yet that is what happened in the case of Stokely Carmichael.

I cite these two young men as examples of a new element in the political and cultural life of the United States, with careers in public life made possible by the agencies of the mass media and the development of social movements within the younger generation. If the educators are wise, they will take the movement seriously, and consider it to be one of the most potent and important sources of desirable change now available for the reform of the American educational system. To look at it from an opposite point of view, as a threat to the stability of the existing cultural order, is to cultivate disaster and regression.

It is no longer possible for the philosopher, whether he is considered to be a social scientist, a humanist scholar, or a speculative metaphysician, to remain aloof from the reality of the society which surrounds him or of a new culture now in the process of being created by young intellectuals, artists, activists, and educational reformers. It does little good to stand on the dignity of the philosophical tradition and assert the eternal verities. The young do not consider the verities to be either eternal or in the possession of the academic philosophers. In the view of the new generation, what truths there are will be found through their own experience with the ideas and values of contemporary society. The moral and social questions are being raised for philosophical scrutiny in the context of genuine problems embedded in the fabric of contemporary history. To ignore the problems in favor of academic abstractions is to lose touch with the students as well as with the problems.

The new generation of youth has accepted one proposition in common—that they are no longer responsible to an older generation which in the past has assumed control of their political and social lives. Having created a gap between themselves and their elders, they intend to stay on their side of the gap, and to make changes in the educational and social system to which society will be compelled to adapt. That is the present situation.

In this situation, the philosophers of education, the teachers of philosophy, the members of departments of philosophy, and all those in that loosely held dominion of the philosophically minded, can do one of two things. They can ignore the young and the society in which they are operating, write students off as "students," transients in the world of the mind who can simply take what they get from those appointed to teach them. Or they can pay attention to the moral and philosophical issues the students are raising, and recognize in them the source of philosophical insight and controversy with which philosophy and education must come to terms. Until now, the philosophers and teachers of philosophy in the academies have chosen the former course. The universities and the society have begun to pay the price of that choice.

EDUCATING FOR THE GOOD LIFE

William K. Frankena

Before I begin, some words of explanation concerning my title would seem necessary. To begin with, there are two kinds of good life: the one that is "led" and the one that is "had." When we say of a man that he *led* a good life, we mean that he led a morally good life or was a good man; we do not necessarily mean that he was a happy man or had a good life. We may even think that he did not have as good a life as he deserved. Is the good man the happy man?, and, Is virtue profitable? are not pointless questions, and, He was too good for his own good, is not a selfcontradictory remark. Again, when we say of a man that he *had* a good life, we mean that he had a happy or desirable one; we do not necessarily mean that he was a morally good man. A person looking back, can say, Well, it's been a good life, I would do it again, without claiming to have been very virtuous morally; he is in a sense approving of his life, but not necessarily in a moral sense or from a moral point of view. We must, therefore, distinguish the moral or morally good life from the happy or otherwise (nonmorally) good life, and it is the latter to which I refer here as the good life, a way of speaking that is close enough to ordinary speech not to be misleading, once it has been explained.

In making and insisting upon this distinction between the good and the moral life, I do not mean to imply that they may not coincide. Like Plato, Kant, and many other moral philosophers, I am in fact inclined to believe that they do in some sense coincide, though I have my moments of Hesiodic worry or even Sophistic doubt. I mean that their coincidence should not be taken for granted; it is something to be shown by argument or evidence or postulated by an act of faith. It is not, so far as I can see, a conceptual truth that a way of living simply cannot be morally good if it is not for the good of the liver. The moral and the good lives will indeed coincide if the morally good life is defined as that which is conducive to one's own happiness or welfare, but such a definition strikes me as clearly mistaken, as it did Butler and Kant. They will also coincide if it is true that no man is an island and that all bells toll for everyone, but this poetic thesis must be argued for or taken on faith; it is not analytic or so much as self-evident.

It follows that we should also distinguish, at least prima facie, between two kinds or parts of education: moral education or "educating the good man," and nonmoral education or "educating for the good life." Having tried my hand briefly at saying something about the first,[1] I shall now seek to put down some thoughts concerning the second. But first I must make a few more introductory remarks.

(1) Education for the good life has not done its job in the case of an individual if it has not done all that education can do to make his life, not only a good one, but the best he is capable of having. In other words, the goal of such education is not just a good life but the best life.

(2) Clearly education cannot by itself alone realize this end; it must, as the Greeks saw, have an assist from fortune in the form of food supply, climate, native endowment, and the like. This elementary fact must not be lost sight of, even though it is true that education can equip us to do something about such matters. As Kant might have put it, education must fail if nature is too unkind a stepmother.

(3) If being morally good is a necessary and sufficient condition of having the best life one is capable of, then the educator (oneself or another) needs to concern himself only with moral education, since the rest—the good life—will then be added unto him, and a separate discussion of nonmoral education will be gratuitous. As I have indicated, however, it is not yet certain that the moral life is also the best life, and we must therefore still think of education as having to promote *both* the moral and the good lives.

(4) If, and insofar as the moral and the good lives do not coincide, it is at least possible that moral and nonmoral education should sometimes conflict with and limit one another.

(5) It may, however, also be that moral virtue and morally right action are among the things that belong to the good life, as Plato and many others have thought, and if this is so, then any full discussion of education for the good life must include

something about moral education. I believe that it is so, and hence will touch on this point again, but, for the rest, I shall endeavor to deal with education for the good life in abstraction from any consideration of the moral life.

(6) It used to be usual to distinguish and contrast moral or "character" education and intellectual education, and this distinction between two kinds of education bears some resemblance to mine. In my opinion, however, moral education is at least partly intellectual, and, on the other hand, as I shall try to show, education for the good life involves fostering not only certain dispositions of the intellect, but also certain traits of character, will, and emotion.

(7) Today it is usual to talk about the teaching and acquisition of "values" or of "moral and spiritual values." I shall for the most part avoid talking in this fuzzy way, but, in these terms, my concern is to distinguish two kinds of values, moral ones and nonmoral ones, and to say something about the teaching of nonmoral values, leaving aside, except for the point mentioned in (5), the teaching of moral ones.

There are four things a philosopher might do in dealing with my topic: (a) carry on a conceptual or meta-ethical inquiry, asking about the meaning or use of expressions such as "good," "knowledge," "teach," etc., and about the methods of justifying the various sorts of statements in which they occur; (b) make and defend normative judgments about what the good life is, or what activities or experiences are good, better, and best; (c) answer educational questions about the dispositions to be fostered in educating for the good life and the methods to be used in doing so; (d) make and defend factual statements bearing on such questions. Some philosophers of education would limit themselves on principle to the first of these four things, leaving the others to moralists, educational practitioners, and scientists, for example, D. J. O'Connor, C. D. Hardie, and R. S. Peters. This position may be the better part of valor and must be respected, but, as for me and my house, we will serve the Lord (or the lords of the Establishment) more generously and more dangerously. Indeed, I shall do very little more of the first kind of thing here than I have already done, and rather more of the other three, though, being a philosopher, I shall play matters safely by sticking to quite general points. For, when Dewey said that philosophy is the most general theory of education, he implied that only the most general theory of education is philosophy. I assume, of course, that a philosopher can say something of some use to educators on at least some points of general theory, even though there is a great deal that he must leave to educators and educational scientists (as more purely analytical philosophers insist). After all, he is or may be an authority on one thing involved in education for the good life, namely the teaching of philosophy, and perhaps this, if nothing else, entitles him to a hearing on some more general matters.

I

In order to make some progress within the bounds of a single paper, I shall also make some more substantive assumptions. The first is that the notion of intrinsic value and the distinction between ends and means are in some sense valid, in spite of the attack made on them by some writers on education and value.[2] The second is that we may also use a distinction, which is not so usual and which I shall not do much to clarify, between the content of the good life and its form. The third is that the *content* of the good life consists primarily of what Aristotle calls *energeiai* or exercises of the soul—that is, conscious activities and experiences—that are good in themselves or as ends, though they may also be good as means, and secondarily of activities that are good at least in an instrumental sense or even in what C. I. Lewis calls a contributive one,[3] that is, in the sense of contributing to the intrinsic value of the wholes of which they are parts without themselves having intrinsic value separately. That is, the good life consists of actualizations, not of potentialities, and is not something one can have when asleep or unconscious but only when conscious and awake, even though one cannot have it if one never allows sleep to knit the ravelled sleeves of care. This assumption can be admitted by those who believe, as Plato and G. E. Moore did (at least sometimes), that other things besides activities and experiences can be intrinsically good, for even they must allow that the good *life* can consist only of activities and experiences. As for its *form*, let us assume that the good life must be informed by some kind of pattern, as Plato thought, both at a given time and through time, and also that it must be governed by certain attitudes or frames of mind. I do not assume that this content or form must be the same for everyone; in fact, I believe that the kind of life that is best for one kind of person will differ in important ways from the kinds of lives that are best for other kinds of individuals, even though I also hold that there are enough generic truths about human nature to make a science of educational psychology possible and a paper like this worthwhile.

The fifth assumption is that the activities and experiences that make up the content of the good life for an individual, as well as those that manifest its form, are actualizations of certain capacities, skills, character traits, habits, etc., all of which will here be called "dispositions," using this term to cover the various kinds of states of the self that Aristotle would put under potentiality, and not only to refer to things like "sunny" dispositions. For human beings, if not for God, the good life is conditioned and underpinned by these dispositions or excellences (*aretai*), but it does not consist of them, since, as Aristotle pointed out, we may have them when we are asleep or unconscious, though it may, of course, include a consciousness of having them. One need not assume here any particular metaphysical theory about the soul, its activities, and its dispositions, or about the relations to one another of the things referred to by these terms. For the most part, such metaphysical theories make no educational differences. It does matter educationally whether the self is immortal or not, but otherwise, so far as I can see, it does not matter educationally whether it is material or spiritual; whether its dispositions are states of the body or not; or whether or not they are reducible to (logical constructions out of) its experiences and activities. What matters educationally is only what is relevant to the questions, Which dispositions is education to foster? and How, when and why is it to foster them? It is a corollary of this fifth assumption that what some educators have called "growth" must be understood as the acquisition of dispositions, that is, of the dispositions that underlie the good (and the moral) life. Otherwise one can only say, as some educators have seemed to do, that growth is what leads to more growth, which is what leads to still more growth, and so on without end—to which one can only reply that a rose is a rose is a rose and by any other name would smell as sweet.

The last assumption has to do with the question raised at the opening of Plato's *Meno*, asked, not about the dispositions involved in the moral life, but about those involved in the good life (which may, of course, overlap with the others). The question is: How does or how may one acquire these dispositions? We must assume that they are not all, in their final forms at least, innate or automatically acquired, and that they cannot all be acquired merely by some act of seeing, remembering, or choosing that requires no deliberate or thoughtful preparation, nor by a purely animal process of adjustmanship to the world. Innate capacities, automatic acquisitions, animal adjustments, and untutored acts of seeing, remembering, and deciding may be involved, but, if they are sufficient to give us the dispositions required for the good life, then there can be no need for anything properly called education in connection with those dispositions, though it may still be needed in connection with the moral life. For example, on the Gaspé Peninsula there are (1967) signs saying simply, "Souviens-toi. Remember." If nothing more is to be done, then there is no call for what is known as education. Even Plato, who held that learning is recollection, believed that this recollecting presupposes some kind of teaching, namely, the asking of questions by oneself or by someone else, and preferably by Socrates. Again, if we need only make an authentic but unguided or arbitrary choice, or take LSD, then, once more, any educational effort will be gratuitous.

The task of anything properly called education for the good life, then, whether it is carried on by oneself or by another, is to foster the dispositions whose actualization in conscious, waking life will issue in the person's concerned having the best life he is capable of, at least if he so wishes and fortune is willing. When speaking here of the task of education, I refer to education as a whole, not just to formal education or to the schools. Much of the task actually is and should be performed by informal processes of education and by agencies other than schools— certainly by agencies other than the public schools. What processes are properly called education, we need not seek to determine here. The main point for us is that their proximate aim must be to engender the dispositions that eventuate in the actualization of the good or rather best life, which is their ultimate aim. The question is, What dispositions is education for the good life to seek to engender, and how and when is it to do so?

II

It would seem obvious, prima facie, that the answer to the question or group of questions discussed above, depends at least in part on one's conception of the form and content of the good life. Consider two philosophies of the good life recently contrasted in an interesting little book by C. H. and W. M. Whiteley called *The Permissive Morality*.[4] According to one—the "soft" view let us call it—the good life consists entirely in a sequence of pleasures, enjoyments, satisfactions, and the like, simple or complex, ordered or unordered, but involving no aspiration, no skill, no attainment or effort to attain anything like excellence as judged by some standard. According to the other—or "hard" view— the good life is not a matter of pleasure or enjoyment at all (or only incidentally); it consists wholly of what Aristotle calls excellent activities carried on for their own sake, in some beautiful pattern, and in a spirit of classical love of perfection or perhaps of romantic excelsiorism, or even of Nietzschean will to "power." It is clear that these two conceptions of the good life, taken in their pure forms, will entail very different educational conclusions about the dispositions to be promoted and the methods to be used, whether they are associated with a permissive or with a nonpermissive view of the *moral* life. Which view comes closest to that of Dewey or to that which prevails in American education, I shall not try to determine.

It must not, however, simply be taken for granted that different philosophical theories about the good and the good life necessarily imply different views about educational matters. Suppose that A holds, as a hedonist does, that the good is pleasure; B, much as Aristotle did, that it is excellent activity; C that it is the fulfillment of one's potentialities; and D that it is the satisfaction of one's desires. These are in an important sense four very different conceptions of the good life. It does not follow, however, that A, B, C, and D, must come to very different conclusions about the proximate aims and methods of education. For A, C, and D, might, on further enquiry, respectively come to believe, that a life of excellent activity such as B advocates is in fact precisely the life that gives the most pleasure, that most fully realizes our potentialities, and that most completely fulfills our desires. Then they would all four draw the same conclusions about the dispositions education is to promote: their educational conclusions would be the same although their rationales for these conclusions would be different. In fact, a philosopher might argue that the good = happiness = excellent activity = the realization of potentiality = the satisfaction of desire = what gives the most pleasure. Aristotle is almost in accord with this argument, as are Brand Blanshard and A. C. Garnett, and possibly even the Whiteleys. Notice, incidentally, that a hedonist like A need not espouse the "soft" view of the good life, since he may hold that the most pleasant life is a life of rather strenuous activity of the soul in accordance with excellence, and thereby agree with B in maintaining the "hard" view. The hedonistic and the "energistic" or perfectionist theories so nicely opposed to one another by Eudoxus and Aristotle or later by G. von Gizycki and Friedrich Paulsen do not necessarily lead to different ways of living in practice. Whether they do or do not depends entirely on what other premises their proponents accept.

III

The point made above suggests that it may be of interest to see if anything of educational significance can be said that will hold independently of all particular theories about the content or form of the good life or about the dispositions to be fostered in education for the good life. It seems to me that several relevant things may be said, most of them familiar. In the first place, we may notice that the dispositions involved in the good life will be of two kinds: means-dispositions and ends-dispositions. By a means-disposition I mean one whose actualization is an activity that is instrumentally but not intrinsically good, e.g.

the habit of brushing one's teeth. Into each good life some tasks must fall—and they must be prepared for, however much it may be insisted that education is life and not just a preparation for life. By an ends-disposition, then, I mean one whose actualization is an experience or action that is worthwhile in itself and finds its place in the good life primarily for that reason, e.g. the ability to appreciate music.

In the second place, looking at the dispositions involved in the good life in another perspective, we can see that they will be of several different sorts: abilities, habits, sensitivities, skills, and knowing-hows (in Ryle's sense), and various kinds of knowing-that. Educating for the good life will, then, include promoting dispositions of all these different sorts by the use of the appropriate methods. Will it also include the formation of character-traits, or will this belong entirely to the area of moral education? It seems clear that it will include some character formation: As writers from Plato to Dewey have been pointing out, such "virtues" as self-control and prudence are in some form or other as necessary for the good as for the moral life, though it should be added that some of our contemporary sub-cultures seem bent on rejecting this tradition along with all the others. The pursuit of goodness of life must include at least some minimal concern about the goodness of one's future life and hence some willingness and ability to restrain one's present impulses. Of course, one might reply that we are by nature completely prudent, that a concern for the goodness of our future lives is always present and dominant in us, so that, if we know what is good for us, we will invariably act accordingly. Then education for the good life, if not for the moral life, could concern itself only with the acquisition of knowledge, as Socrates thought. But this kind of psychological egoism is pretty plainly false; as Joseph Butler pointed out, we are not always that attentive to the futures of our own lives.

At the same time it should be remarked, for the benefit of those who talk as if character is the whole proximate aim of education—as Kant and even Dewey and Kilpatrick sometimes do—that this cannot be true of education for the good life, even if it is true of moral education, since education for the good life must also seek to foster other kinds of dispositions besides character and character traits. The talk in question could be correct only if the term "character" is taken to cover all relevant kinds of dispositions, and this usage is palpably misleading. One *can* so take the term "character," but one must remember that to have knowledge of the kings of Britain, is then, a quality of character, and not only such things as attentiveness, industry, and self-control (all probably needed for the acquisition of such knowledge). More generally, one must remember the differences between skills and virtues, so nicely illustrated by Socrates' comparison of musical proficiency and justice in Book I of the *Republic*.

Of course, it might still be that a certain agency or stage of education for the good life should concern itself only with the formation of character or only with the communication and pursuit of knowledge— for example, the schools, or the technical schools, or the church, or the university. My point is only that educating for the good life, taken as a whole, must have as its business the development of both kinds of disposition, and of others as well.

In the third place, since such different sorts of dispositions are involved in the good life in any view of what it may be, it seems plausible to hold that education for such a life will be partly negative and partly positive—or at least some of it will be relatively negative and some relatively positive. In other words, some of it will consist wholly or mainly in clearing the ground for seeing or enjoying something, or in undoing the results of earlier failures of education; and some of it will consist in more positive actions of instruction or initiation. How much of it will be positive and how much negative, will depend on one's view about the extent to which the dispositions needed for the good life are "natural" (innate or automatically acquired if society and the external world do not admit impediments to progress of true minds) or "artificial" (culturally conditioned). In other words, it depends on how Rousseauist (or how Summerhillish) one is.[5] This issue cannot be resolved here, but I must at least point out that it is not entirely settled merely by arguing, quite correctly, that our minds would get nowhere in the direction of the good life without the social gift of language. What is really crucial is the question of what other additional gifts are needed.

In the fourth place, while I am, to some extent, in sympathy with those who disparage the newer learning by doing in favor of the older method of learning by being told or instructed and/or reading, I do wish to express general agreement with R. S. Peters' conception of education as initiation into worthwhile activities.[6] Aristotle justly remarked that we become just only by doing just acts; but by contrasting the moral with the intellectual virtues in this respect, he was covering up the extent to which the latter—and, indeed, all excellent dispositions—are likewise formed only by our engaging in an appropriate kind of activity. Here I refer, not only to the fact that one must at least listen and remember if one is to come to know the kings of Britain or to have the intellectual virtue called mathematics, but also to the fact that one can hardly be said to have these dispositions unless he has done some historical or mathematical thinking himself. Whether he must also have walked about the room instead of sitting quietly at a desk I shall not venture to decide.

Finally, it seems to me clear that, although we should not disregard what we have learned in the past about these matters, we must allow, whatever our view of the general nature of the good life, that there will always be a great deal of room for new experience, experiment, and discovery in connection with the content and the form of the good life, the dispositions to be fostered, and the kinds and methods of education needed. As I said, we should not forget whatever wisdom the past has given us—or simply blow our minds utterly clean as if it had given us none. But Plato was surely wrong when he thought that our only way to a knowledge of the good is through some kind of remembrance of things past. It is not likely, but it is at least possible, that when the day comes that we see the new Jerusalem we shall, indeed, find that it is all new. We cannot really know that a kind of activity, experience, or life is good, or how good it is, unless we are or have been acquainted with it, much as we cannot understand what blue is unless something has at least looked blue to us. In these matters learning is finally only by doing or perhaps by eating. And, while I believe that human beings have already been acquainted with much that is good, I also believe we must recognize that, when the day comes that we see what the good life really is, if ever, we may find that it is very different from any life that we have known, even if it is not *all* new (if it were all new, we could not even recognize it as good).

IV

Still, it remains true that, except for such general points as those just made, what one can say about education for the good life depends at least in part on one's views about what the good life is. If we are to proceed, I must formulate some more specific ideas about its content and form. In a recent comic picture a little boy says to his baby brother in the crib, You'd better shape up if you expect to join the great society! I have been saying, in effect, You'd better shape up if you expect to have a good life (the best life you are capable of)! Now I must make clearer what shapes we should take.

For what it is worth, I shall venture one meta-ethical remark as a preface to the rest of what is to come, and I am aware that it is less than the whole truth, namely, that the good activity, experience, or life is that which it is rational to desire, like, choose, or prefer, i.e., that which one would desire, like, choose, or prefer if one were reflective, clear-headed, and fully cognizant. But, to get quickly off this arid (but, I insist, not dry) mesa where I live so much of the time, along with so many other analytical philosophers, I shall first say something about the content of the good life and then about its form. There are many kinds of activities and experiences that seem to me rational to like or choose as *contents* of the good life, even if we consider only those it is rational to like or choose for their own sakes. I think, however, and this is one of the main hypotheses I wish to advance, that they can be reduced to two overlapping kinds.

(1) First, there are various sorts of pleasures, activities or experiences that are pleasant or enjoyable, long or short, simple or complex. I agree with the proponents of the "soft" view of the good life that such activities or experiences are or may be good in themselves even if they involve no skill or excellence, or, in other words, that one of the things that makes a stretch of time good is the mere fact that it is enjoyed or liked when had, like the taste of a dish or the smell of a flower. Most anti-hedonists have admitted this—for example, Plato, Aristotle, and Moore. Not long ago an advertisement claimed that drinking a certain whiskey is part of the good life. Without judging this claim, I would say that many kinds of experience belong to the good life merely or at least partly because they are agreeable or pleasant when we have them. In fact, I would go farther with the hedonist and add that an activity or experience is not intrinsically good unless it is as such on the whole agreeable or pleasant, though it may, of course, be extrinsically or contributively good anyway; and that a life is not good unless it is somehow as a whole a happy or at least contenting one, though, of course, it may be a "useful" or even a "full and useful" life even if it is not.

(2) In the *Philebus*, Plato rightly argues, however, that pleasure cannot be regarded as the only ingredient in the good life, or as the only intrinsically good-making feature of activities or experiences, citing knowledge as his prize counterexample of something else that is intrinsically good or good-making. But knowing is just one instance of an activity that is excellent by its own immanent standard (in this case, truth), and, following Aristotle, I suggest that it is not just cognition but excellence of activity as measured by an immanent standard that is the main factor—other than enjoyableness—that makes experiences good or worthwhile (or better or worse) in themselves: e.g., what makes playing the flute well intrinsically good is not just the pleasure involved but also the fact that it is excellent by the standard appropriate to flute-playing. It is not the fact that cognition is present that makes such playing good (for it is hard to see what one is cognizing except the presence of excellence) but the more general fact that excellence (in this case, beauty) is present.

Many kinds of activity, then, belong to the good life because, besides being enjoyable, they involve the achievement of or approach to excellence or perfection as judged by a standard intrinsic to the activity, e.g. dancing, loving, mathematics, and both teaching and learning, thank goodness. To quote,

> What good is like to this
> To do worthy the writing, and to write
> Worthy the reading, and the world's delight? [7]

Of course, a hedonist may reply that such activities are good in themselves only because and insofar as they are pleasant or enjoyable—I used to maintain this myself, though only in the semiprivacy of my classroom —but it now strikes me as just not true. It would be more plausible to contend, as J. S. Mill did, that such activities yield a different and higher kind of pleasure, though not necessarily a greater quantity of it, than more purely physical enjoyments, and that what makes them worthwhile or preferable as ends is always and only their pleasantness—its quality rather than its quantity—and never even in part their excellence as such (except indirectly by affecting the quality of the pleasure). Mill's contention, however, appears to be essentially a way of admitting the substance of my view without giving up the semblance of hedonism.

"What," it may be asked, "about Truth, Beauty, and Goodness, often regarded as the three ends of life?" The case of Goodness, by which is meant moral goodness, I shall take up later. Truth and Beauty, in my opinion, are not intrinsic goods or parts of the good life; rather, they are standards we try to achieve in some of our activities, and it is not they but these activities of knowing the truth or of enjoying and creating beauty that are worthwhile in themselves. If Truth and Beauty are themselves rightly said to be good, then they are what C. I. Lewis calls "inherent goods"—objects of which the contemplation is good in itself even though they are not.

"What," it may be asked again, "about suffering and tragedy? Is a good life of any profound kind possible without them, and, if not, must they not be included among intrinsic goods?" It is not in the least clear that suffering must be a part of the best life that anyone is capable of—I really doubt that it must—but it may be true that some people's lives are somehow made richer and better than they were before by an experience of tragedy. Notice that, for this to be true, it is not enough that their lives be made morally better or artistically more sensitive and productive; they must be made better in the same nonmoral sense in which the good life is good. Even if it is true, however, it follows only that pain and suffering may be instrumentally or even contributively good, not that they are in themselves desirable.

A more extreme antihedonist than I might maintain that all intrinsically worthwhile activities and experiences can be construed as involving the attainment of excellence as measured by some standard, and that the presence of excellence may therefore be regarded as the one and only intrinsically good-making factor in life. I doubt that this thesis can be sustained, say, in cases like enjoying a taste or a smell, though I suppose one could argue, using a point in Aristotle, that in such cases there is present an innate excellence of these senses which makes the *energeiai* in question good. If it can be plausibly sustained, however, I shall not be much exercized to dispute it.[8] There is at least some cogency in the lines painted on a summer cottage in the Engadine valley, not far from the one Nietzsche stayed in:

> Stil liegen und einsam sich sonnen
> Ist auch ein tapfere Kunst.

The "soft" view would pooh-pooh excellence and the "hard" view mere pleasure, but, if I am right, these views contain between them the truth about the content of the good life: All of the activities and experiences belonging to it can be accounted for under the two headings of the excellent and the enjoyable (or both), if the latter is taken in a wide sense as including pleasure, beatitude, contentment, etc.[9] There is abroad, however, another view, variously described as romantic, irrationalistic, voluntaristic, or existentialistic, which cries a plague on both excellence and enjoyment, perhaps even on the good life itself. Its proponents exalt such various things as struggle, striving, self-expression, creativity, freedom, autonomy, commitment, authenticity, decision, doing your own thing, being the captain of one's soul, believing even if it is absurd, having a sense of identity, even anxiety. They say or seem to say such things as:

A man's reach must exceed his grasp.
It is not whether you win or lose that matters, but how you play the game.
'Tis better to have loved and lost than never to have loved at all.
Choose authentically, no matter what.
Commit yourself, no matter to what.
Express yourself, create; all is permissible.
It matters not how strait the gate,

How charged with punishments the scroll,
I am the master of my fate,
I am the captain of my soul.

The idea is clear (more or less): It is not pleasure or excellence in accordance with standards that is important, but something of a very different kind, something that relates to *form* and not content. In rejecting pleasure the view is a hard one, in rejecting excellence and standards it has a kind of softness. Ultimately, in any pure or extreme form, it seems to me not to make sense if it does not finally bring in excellence or enjoyment. But the view does contain an important grain of truth. Abstracting from any moral claims it may be making, we may interpret it as saying that our lives will be better if we take them or live them in certain ways or frames of mind rather than others—if they have certain "subjective forms" or "styles," to use Whitehead's words. In other words, the *how* of our lives matters to their goodness as well as the *what*. This seems to me to be profoundly true, as long as it is not suggested that the *what* does not matter at all or very much, or that all we need attend to educationally or otherwise is the *how* and the rest will take care of itself, D. V. or not.

One can readily think of a number of attitudes or frames of mind that might be regarded as important to the good life, if not of cows and pigs then at least of human beings, though perhaps one must allow for some variation in the case of humans. Very tentatively I offer the following partial list, not all of them acceptable to those who hold the view I am teeing off from:

(1) There is what Dewey calls "the habit of reflective intelligence" or what Israel Scheffler calls "rationality," [10] and a whole family of related dispositions, for example, objectivity, impartiality, clearheadedness, responsibility, discipline, and examined living.

(2) There are virtues of the kind characteristically emphasized by existentialists, but also by others: [11] authenticity, honesty, courage, autonomy, commitment, decision, responsibility (once more), and fidelity. A Christian would want to add hope, but, of course, some existentialists would stress anxiety. Dewey would want to include cheerfulness and even what he calls "the religious," and Whitehead "reverence." I should myself wish to include a disposition to seek the best life one is capable of, or what one might call "prudence." O. F. Bollnow would

insist on including the antiexistential disposition of *Geborgen-heit*.[12]

(3) There is also love, so central in Christianity, and "relating to others," so central in "the new morality" (or, if you prefer, "the new immorality"). This should include the realization of the lives of others of which William James writes so well in *On a Certain Blindness in Human Beings.*

Many, if not all, of the things on this list would also be related to the moral life, but I am thinking of them here as related to the good life. Actually, they are all dispositions, not activities or experiences, and I conceive of them as somehow framing the good life, that is, not as being actualized in separate kinds of activity or experience (if they were they would provide its content and not its form), but as being actualized in the course of other activities and experiences—in the way in which we engage in or take them. For example, courage may be displayed in lives of very different content, as may devotion to God, love of neighbor, etc. These virtues, as it were, ride piggy-back for their actualization on the activities and experiences actualizing other more contentual dispositions, at least so far as the good life is concerned.[13]

There is, however, another sense in which a life may have a *form* besides that in which courage and the other dispositions just mentioned may serve to give it a form—what one might call its "objective" in contrast to its "subjective" form. When Plato asks about the good life in the *Philebus*, he mentions (a) pleasure, (b) knowledge, (c) *arete* or excellence [I should mention, instead, (a) pleasure, (b) excellent activities, including knowing, (c) the framing virtues just indicated.] He then adds (d) pattern, beauty, harmony, proportion—also pooh-poohed by the anticlassical position described a little while ago; and I want now to add them to my account as well. Like pictures, lives may, indeed must, have designs or patterns as well as frames, and, while I do not wish to assert that every good life must have the same pattern, I do think that something in the nature of pattern or formal structure must come in, as Plato tried to show in the *Gorgias*. Whatever pattern a life has affects its value and perhaps also that of its parts, for, if no life is an island, certainly no part of a life is. Thus, for example, Whitehead used to insist that a good life must include continuity and tradition (or, as some say, "roots"), as well as novelty and adventure, and D. H. Parker asserted that it must have such features as unity in variety, balance, rhythm, and hierarchy.[14] There must be some kind of economy of the good life, even if it turns out to be very different from that envisaged by any past generation—as different as the way out members of the "new" or "beat" generation seem to think it must be.

V

If this very schematic picture of the good life for man is anywhere near correct, then its realization involves the formation of four groups of dispositions, two relating to its *content* and two to its *form*.

A. Dispositions relating to the content of the good life [15]
    1. Those whose actualizations are pleasures or enjoyments, e.g. a liking for roast pig
    2. Those whose actualizations are excellent activities, e.g. abilities, skills, and knowledge
B. Dispositions relating to its form
    1. Those whose actualization shows itself in the way or spirit in which we engage in our activities or take our experiences— in *how* we do or take them, though not in *how well* we do them as judged by a standard (if one is relevant), e.g. courage, soul-captaincy, sense of identity, integrity
    2. Those whose actualization shows itself in the order or pattern of our lives, e.g. balance, putting first things first.

To complete my account of the good life, I should, of course, give a more definite list and description of all the dispositions involved and their actualizations—and an educator must have such a complete account from a philosopher of education—but I cannot help shying away from being so specific. Fortunately, time is also in short supply, so that I must limit myself to making some remarks about education in connection with each of these four types of dispositions. First, the fact that a disposition is necessary for or conducive to the good or best life does not mean that education must be concerned to foster it. It must do so only if the disposition is not innate, if it can be fostered by a process appropriately called education (and not every process that produces a disposition is appropriately called education) and if it cannot be better produced by some other process. Certainly, it does not mean that the disposition must be fostered by the schools or by a university. In particular, it seems clear that education need not concern itself with all of the dispositions under A-1, since many of them are either innate or automatically formed. In some cases, however, a kind of negative education may be needed to clear the way for a certain liking or sensitivity, or even a piece of psychoanalysis. It may even be that for one to have certain enjoyments some more positive education is needed to prepare his sensitivities, for example, one might have to read Wordsworth to learn natural piety or daffodil-watching. However, the disposition in question in that case should perhaps be put under A-2, for then it will probably entail some kind of skill or excellence, some kind of "tapfere Kunst." In any case, there will be a place in education for teaching children what experiences will bring pleasure or happiness, and for equipping them with knowledge enabling them to obtain, control, and enrich such experiences. But then, as Dewey saw, one is providing them with forms of knowledge, which are dispositions falling under A-2. In fact, it appears that most of the dispositions that education might foster in promoting the pursuit of enjoyment fall under A-2, since most enjoyments and satisfactions probably come to us only through the development of some kind of skill or excellence, e.g., the pleasure of dancing.[16]

It should be noted that teaching X that Y is an enjoyable kind of activity or experience may take several forms: (a) telling him that it is, with such evidence as one can marshall, (b) giving him an experience of that kind, (c) helping him to imagine someone's having such an experience, perhaps through the use of literature. It seems to me that all of these ways of teaching are acceptable, the second probably being the most effective, but not always available. Perhaps I should add that much of our concern in education relating to the pursuit of enjoyment is to teach restraint, discipline, and temperance, and quite rightly so. As Aristotle says, the right education is to bring up the youth to feel pleasure and pain at the right things. Much of this concern belongs to moral education, which is what Aristotle is talking about, but not all of it. For, as philosophers as different as Kant and Dewey have pointed out, an individual must learn self-control if he is to have the best life—even in terms of enjoyment alone—that he is capable of. Aristotle's remark also serves to remind us that human nature is not unmalleable, and that our training can lead us to find pleasure in one direction rather than another. This is a fact which educators should, at least on moral grounds, use carefully, but which they must keep in mind, if only because they might otherwise be using it inadvertently to impoverish people's lives.

To return to the matter of self-control in connection with the good life, it seems to me that this may be one point at which "straight" society may have something to say to the hippies we have all been reading about, even if it may let them learn the need for some kind of discipline the hard way (perhaps in this case, we could speak of learning by not-doing, or by undoing). This is not to imply that the hippies are only looking for the most enjoyable life—there appears to be a moral tenet in their creed too—but, on the whole, hippiedom does seem to be for the soft pad in life; it does not look as if there is much thought given to discipline, excellence, or consequences.

It should also be remarked here, that even insofar as the good life is a matter of enjoyment, it cannot be simply a matter of choice or decision about what one will be happy with. There may be an element of choice in the achievement of happiness, as Dewey implies when he says that one may make a voluntary choice of those objects that bring good to others and thus make one's desires such that his happiness can be complete only if others are happy too. Even so, what one will enjoy or be happy with is at least as much a matter for finding out as it is for creation or decision. Since it is so much a matter for discovery, it follows that there is here a great deal of room for exploration and experimentation, as Dewey has advocated, or as the hippies may be practicing. However, while stressing this need for exploration of sources of enjoyment, I must repeat that it is foolish to discard anything that has already been learned in the experience and reflection of mankind. Even a "do it yourself (because nobody else can)" kit for the good life must have some basis in previous discoveries. Here, I am inclined to think, Deweyans, existentialists, and "the new generation" alike are open to criticism. As bad as traditional education may have been, it had something, or it would not have lasted long enough to become traditional.

We come now to content-conditioning dispositions of the second kind: those whose actualizations take the form of activities that are excellent by some standard immanent in the activity, some standard other than the amount or kind of pleasure they give, e.g., the ability to dance, knowledge, and aesthetic creativity. Much could be said here, but I shall confine myself to five points. (1) Without disparaging the dispositions involved in knowing-how, I wish to underline those involved in knowing-that and having a true-opinion-that. Contemporary views of education and of the good life are too little concerned to foster the latter. As was indicated earlier, there is in some quarters a tendency to put a high value on sincere belief and utter commitment, as if mistaken belief or commitment is better than judicious caution or scepticism. However, the point of believing-that is, after all, to claim truth; mistaken belief, no matter how sincere, is a failure by its own standard. "He believed not wisely, but too well" is therefore more sensible than "he believed not wisely, but he believed well." Many, however, who would join me in decrying such trigger-happy fideism, themselves undervalue knowledge and truth. They insist on the value of inquiring and on the centrality of method, and they say over and over again that education in science, for example, should not aim at inculcating its conclusions but at communicating its spirit and method. But, again, the aim of inquiry and its method is to come as near to the truth as possible—the goal is knowledge wherever it is attainable. It is all very well to avoid dogmatism and fixity of belief, but it is not at all well to create the impression that knowledge and truth of belief are somehow unimportant, and that we may simply substitute "training-value for knowledge-value . . . mental gymnastics for truth, and being in fine fettle, for wisdom." [17] It is, in any case, a moral duty to know or believe and claim truth for some of the things on the basis of which one acts or votes, and not only to think acutely, logically, and suggestively about such matters. Furthermore, since we are here leaving moral considerations to one side, I shall claim also that one's life is less good, even if more pleasant, if one has only method and mental gymnastics than if one has both these and knowledge or true opinion too. May there not be method in one's thinking and yet madness also, as an old phrase implies? If sincerity is not enough,[18] then neither are method and intellectual initiative, let alone being in fine fettle.

Yet another—and perhaps the latest—form of the disparagement of knowing-and-believing-that is the move made by some analytical philosophers to reduce knowing-that to knowing-how, by arguing, for example, that knowing that something is the case may be regarded as knowing how to answer the question, Is it the case?, or as knowing how to prove it. In reply, one might say that such a move is a mere trick, but it is enough to point out that even if it is accepted, we may and should still insist that *this* kind of knowing-how is different from other kinds and that it is desirable and important to have it, and to communicate it to those who do not, whether by doing or by telling (with reasons, if possible).

(2) At the same time, I must also dispute the opinion that all of the dispositions to be cultivated under the second heading (A-2) are forms of knowledge-that, as Aristotle implies when he identifies happiness with contemplation. Some of them are certainly abilities, skills, or knowledge-hows, e.g. the ability to sail a boat. Much of what is involved in becoming a good mathematician, physicist, or classicist is itself a grasp of method, a kind of knowing-how not necessarily formulable in propositions that one has or can have consciously in mind. In fact, as Dewey, Bronowski, and others have often shown, there are also certain character-traits that are integral to the achievement of excellence in any intellectual enterprise.[19] All sorts of dispositions, therefore, must be taught or acquired in the course of educating or being educated for goodness of life, not just knowledge-that or true-opinion-that. One of them is a disposition to pursue knowledge-that, and this is not itself a piece of knowledge-that or even of knowing-how.

(3) There are, moreover, some areas in which the matter of

teaching-that must be approached with care, even though these areas are important for the value of life. It is essential to the good life that one have some view or attitude on ultimate questions. When someone saw poor and needy Johnny Jones sitting cheerfully on a fence by the side of the road, he asked Johnny how he could be so contented. "Because," said Johnny, "I've learned to cooperate with necessity." I do not mean to claim (or to deny) that some *religious* faith is necessary to the good life—that is another question and it is worth noting that there is nothing distinctively religious about Johnny's philosophy of life—but only that some basic view or feeling about life and the world is humanly needed, if only to maintain sanity. Now if one has such a view or feeling oneself, one will also have a strong impulse, perhaps even a sense of duty, to teach it to others as the truth, treating one's philosophical or theological beliefs just as one would treat the findings of history or chemistry.[20] However, while one may, in history and chemistry, rightly represent certain things as true and known, though not as infallibly so, and mark a student wrong or at least regard it as evidence of some kind of deficiency if he insists on putting down the opposite (even in public schools), the situation in philosophy and religion seems to me very different. In these fields, at least in public schools and colleges (for private ones do not have the same limitations, except by choice), the educator must confine himself to what may broadly be called history and method, showing the student what others have believed and lived by, what it is like so to believe and live, and how to think understandingly and intelligently about such beliefs and ways of living. He must scrupulously avoid seeming to put the weight of the state on one side or the other—even on the side of theism as opposed to atheism, naturalism, or God-is-deadism, whatever that is—leaving commitment on ultimate questions to other agencies and to the individual himself.

(4) Throughout the present topic, there arises the sticky question of teachers imposing beliefs, standards, and values on the student, and the student's autonomy in accepting or rejecting them. When I was a boy I read (I think in *The Youth's Companion*) a story about a Revolutionary War heroine who had a cow named "Free 'n' Equal." Today, it seems to me, some educators and students have a cow named "Free and Empty." Yet, if the good life includes excellent activities and if education for it includes the formation of dispositions to act in accordance with standards of excellence, then education for the good (as well as for the moral) life entails some kind of teaching and learning of standards, however much it may also aim at autonomy. Both educator and educated, who may be the same person, must see this from the beginning or come to see it. If one is going to "get with" the good life,

one had better shape up in some way, even if not in the same way in which others should shape up or in which one's parents did. The combination of autonomy with recognition of standards is possible and involves no difficulty in principle or even in practice (except for "authoritarian personalities" if there really are such things) in such fields as mathematics, science, history, philosophy—not to mention athletics—and perhaps also in the arts. There is, therefore, no irresolvable antimony or paradox of "freedom and authority" in education for the good life, as some seem to think, though it is not easy to find a nice formula with which to work in resolving the apparent tension between them.

Are the standards of excellence referred to wholly relative, subjective, up to the arbitrary if "creative" choice of the individual? A hippie guideline reads, "Do your own thing, wherever you have to do it and whenever you want." [21] Perhaps this is in a sense an action-guide, but it is also tantamount to saying that there are no standards, and hence no activities for which any kind of excellence can be claimed. Even if it is interpreted as saying that there are no standards except those of one's own choosing (if this means that one's choice of standards is entirely arbitrary) it is still in effect proclaiming that there are no standards. It may, of course, be replied that there are standards but that their validity is purely subjective and relative (one's own thing), but this contention is at least not true in all areas. There are standards of excellence that may fairly be claimed to be objective in matters of belief, cognition, and reasoning in such areas as history and science, for example, standards of logic and truth—also in athletics, and, for all that has been shown to the contrary, perhaps even in the arts, though here I must confess to some doubts after observing what is held to be art in certain circles. Actually, I am inclined to think that the most hopeful way to understand the philosophy of our hippie sub-culture (and of the larger movement of which it is symptomatic) is to view it as believing that there are standards of excellence for human living but that our "straight" society has not yet found them or even come near finding them. This is almost implied in another hippie guideline: "Blow the mind of every straight person you can reach. Turn them on, if not to drugs, then to beauty, love, honesty, fun." [22] This not only shows a morally creditable, if somewhat misguided, concern to do good to others, it also suggests a sense of having discerned, correctly or incorrectly, radically new standards of excellence in art and love, as well as new forms of enjoyment. Thus viewed, the movement has something healthy about it, even if it is too ready to assume that all our centuries of thought and experience have gone for nothing. There is also no reason for us to assume that the forms and standards of human good living have all been discovered even in their main outlines. There was at least some truth in the two lessons Lincoln Steffens tried to teach his son: nothing is known, definitely and for certain; and nothing has been done, finally or well.

(5) The question of the relation of the moral to the good life must also be raised here. By this I do not mean the question whether the morally good life is also the good or happy life, so much discussed by moral philosophers, but the more specific and less discussed question, whether morally excellent action should be counted as one of the kinds of excellent activity that make up so much of the content of the good life. As was indicated, Plato held virtue to be an ingredient in the good life, not just as a means to it but as a part of it; so did Kant and so does W. D. Ross. Whether Aristotle did or not depends on how one interprets him. In some passages he identifies *eudaimonia* (happiness or good life) with contemplation, in others he says that morally excellent activity constitutes a second-best kind of happiness. In no place, however, does he consider it to belong to the highest kind of happiness available to man, and it is not part of the happiness he ascribes to God, which consists entirely in contemplation.[23] Even hedonists have been of two minds in this matter. Mill allowed that moral virtue might, by association of ideas, come to be sought or prized for its own sake and so be a part of happiness (i.e. a direct source of pleasure) and not just a means to it. Henry Sidgwick, however, argued that ultimate good can only be conceived as pleasurable consciousness, including a consciousness of virtue as a part, but not virtue itself. Moore, though rejecting hedonism, agreed with Sidgwick: for him right action was good only as a means (though right categorically), and virtue, being a disposition which one can have when asleep, could not be intrinsically good. Only the feelings one has in being morally good or doing what is morally right could be good in themselves or parts of the good life, according to him. For a long time I followed Sidgwick and Moore on this point, but in accordance with my present view, morally excellent activities (better called "actions") are just as much parts of the content of the good life as cognitive or aesthetic activities are, provided, of course, that they are engaged in with pleasure or satisfaction of some kind. Now, "morally excellent action" is ambiguous: it may mean either "morally *right* action" or "morally *good* action." Aristotle remarked that a man may do what the just man does without doing it *as* the just man does it; for example, if he does it simply out of habit and not out of a sense of its justice. Then his action, morally considered, is right but not good or virtuous. Kant made a similar distinction, and so do we when we say of someone that he did the right thing from the wrong motive. Using this

distinction, I suggest that morally *right* acts are intrinsically good and parts of a good life when they are done with satisfaction and that morally *good* actions are always intrinsically good and parts of the good life because they are done with satisfaction. It is true that a man may do a right action out of a sense of duty but with a heavy heart, and then it would seem to be morally good but not to be good or desirable in itself. But then, I should think, although he is sad for other reasons at having to do it, he will still be glad to do it insofar as it is the right thing to do, and so it will be intrinsically good after all, though there are things connected with it that are not. As for virtue or moral goodness as a *disposition* of the self—I still agree with Aristotle, Sidgwick, and Moore in thinking that this would not be good in itself. It may, however, be an inherent good in Lewis' sense or, as has also been suggested, an object of judgments of "moral appreciation." [24]

Even if morally excellent action of either sort is among the contents of the good life, it does not necessarily follow that it must be a part of the best life one is capable of. It may be that Dennis the Menace is so constituted that he will have the best life he is capable of without ever doing anything morally right or good. It will, however, follow that moral goodness is generally to be regarded as one of the dispositions to be fostered, not only in educating the good man but also in educating for the good life. To this extent, moral education must be a part of education for goodness of life, independently of any proof or postulate to the effect that the moral life is a condition of or means to the good life. I shall not, however, spell out here what is involved in moral education, but only add one point to what I have said elsewhere. This is that the dispositions issuing in morally right action and those issuing in morally good action are not necessarily the same. An action is morally good if the agent is sincerely trying to see and to do what is right, even if he in fact fails in this. It is right only if he succeeds in seeing and doing what he should. For right action, then, he must have abilities and knowledge that are not required for him to be morally good. This is a point made by Russell in "The Harm that Good Men Do" and often used by Dewey in his attacks on Kant, though Kant could and probably would have agreed with it. It is also implied in Carlyle's blunt mot: "Obey your conscience, yes, but see to it that it is not the conscience of an ass."

VI

About dispositions connected with the *form* of the good life I shall not say much. In the case of those affecting its *how* (B-1) it is plausible to think there is more room for the kind of choice or decision of which existentialists speak, than there is in the case of dispositions relating to the content of the good life. This is not to say that we cannot choose the contents of our lives—we can and do—but only that it is not simply a matter for us to *decide* whether or not our choice of content is the best or even a good one. However, even if there is more room for choice in relation to the *how* of our lives than to their *what*, native endowment is also a factor here. I do not buy the existentialist thesis that we choose this too, except in the sense of accepting it as something one must live with (and here Carlyle might exclaim, "Gad, we'd better!"). Some people seem, for example, to be by constitution more cheerful than others (or would psychoanalysts deny this?), and some seem to need less freedom and less autonomy for happiness than others (even if their "escape from freedom" is somehow reprehensible on moral grounds). As for the matter of pattern (B-2), it is especially tempting to suppose that, even if the best life for everyone must include some enjoyments and some excellent activities of all the various kinds open to human beings (and it is not clear that this is the case), it need not include them in the same sequence or proportion. It would also seem that there could be a considerable place for choice, at least about the temporal order of our activities and experiences.

One more word about choice and its place in the good life and in educating for it: there must certainly be choice of a kind whenever doing one thing or having one experience precludes doing something else or having some other experience. This means that we must choose our lives, consciously or unconsciously, but it does not mean that we can make our lives good simply by choosing them. The man who says, "Evil, be thou my good!" chooses to pursue evil as his end, but he does not thereby make it good for him to do so. If one could make a life good by choosing it, there would be no place for anxiety, for anxiety has a place only if one's choice can somehow turn out to be mistaken or regrettable. In any case, however, whether a life is made good by being chosen or only found to be good (or bad) after being chosen, education will have the task of showing us, both vividly and veridically, what various kinds of lives are open to human beings and what they are like in the living, and of helping us to choose the best one for ourselves and to shape ourselves for it. Here it must enlist imaginative literature, comparative religion, philosophy, and all of the humanities, but also anthropology, psychology, and sociology.

VII

Many questions remain, some already alluded to and some not. What is the role in education for the good life of liberal education, vocational education, the public schools, the church, etc.? Does educating for the moral life impose any restrictions on educating for the good life? Must we distinguish between the dispositions required for the good life, those required for the moral life, and those required for citizenship or for democracy, and, if so, which are we to cultivate? To what extent can and should education itself *be* a good life instead of being a preparation for a good life? The main question left over, however, is this: What is the general nature of the education that will best foster the dispositions underpinning the good life as I have sketched them? Is it a "softer," more or less Summerhillian education that emphasizes the child, freedom, self-government, love, play, sincerity, and emotion, or is it a "harder," more or less traditional education that stresses the subject, discipline, direction, learning, culture, work, and intellect? [25] My insistence on excellence and its achievement, including knowing-that, as part of the good life suggests that it is the latter, but it is not actually a priori true that a Summerhillian education will foster the required dispositions less effectively than its opposite. Even as a philosopher I am tempted to say something about this matter.[26] However, once the nature of the good life and of the dispositions underlying it have been settled on (more definitely than has been done here), the question, what kind of an educational process will best promote them, is to such a large extent an empirical matter for educational scientists and practitioners to decide that a philosopher must not rush in, even if, not being an angel, he need not fear to tread. Anyway, for me, enough is enough, and, for you, I suspect, too little has already proved too much.

NOTES

1. See "Toward a Philosophy of Moral Education," *Harvard Educational Review*, XXVIII (1958), pp. 300–313. In "Public Education and the Good Life," *ibid.*, XXXI (1961), pp. 413–426, I distinguish the two kinds of good life and discuss the problems of public education with respect to both of them. *Cf.* also "A Point of View for the Future," in *Religion and the State University*, ed. by E. A. Walters (1958), pp. 295–309; "The Teaching of Religion: Some Guiding Principles," *Religious Education*, LIV (1959), pp. 108–109, 117. In "Educational Values and Goals," *Monist* 51 (1967), I make some suggestions about the dispositions to be fostered, with both the moral and the good life in mind.

2. *Cf.* e.g. M. C. Beardsley, "Intrinsic Value," *Philosophy and Phenomenological Research*, XXVI (1965), pp. 1–17.

3. See *Analysis of Knowledge and Valuation* (1946), p. 487.

4. Methuen and Co. Ltd. (1964). See esp. pp. 21–24, 98–102. The Whiteleys do not keep clear the distinction between hard and soft conceptions of the moral life and hard and soft conceptions of the good life.

5. *Cf.* A. S. Niell, *Summerhill* (1960), p. 4.

6. See *Education as Initiation* (University of London Institute of Education, 1964). Like Peters, I mean "initiation," not "invitation"; even *if* it is true that a teacher should only *invite* his pupils to engage in worthwhile activities, it is also true that they will receive no education until they have been initiated or at least initiate themselves into such activities.

7. Quoted by A. L. Rowse, *The England of Elizabeth* (1951), p. 533.

8. In any case, I should insist that an activity is not intrinsically good unless it is enjoyable, even if it is excellent.

9. In *Politics*, VII, 1, Aristotle remarks that men consider happiness to consist of enjoyment or excellence or both, and in VIII, 5, he seems himself to agree that it consists of both.

10. I do not mean here to settle on any one view of the nature of this disposition. For Scheffler's view, see "Concepts of Education," in *Guidance in American Education*, ed. by E. Landy and P. A. Berry, pp. 20–27.

11. *Cf.* J. D. Wild, *Existence and the World of Freedom* (1963), pp. 161–167; C. Smith, *Contemporary French Philosophy* (1964), p. 229.

12. *Cf. Neue Geborgenheit* (1960).

13. This may not be wholly true of devotion to God or love of neighbor.

14. For Parker see *Human Values* (1931), ch. IV; *The Philosophy of Value* (1957), ch. V, VII. When Whitehead speaks of "style" in *The Aims of Education* he may mean to include both pattern and subjective form (*Cf.* Mentor Books edition, 1929, p. 24).

15. Some dispositions may come under both A1 and A2.

16. One may "dance with joy" without first acquiring any special skill, but then the dancing is more an expression of joy than a source of it. What some call "peak experiences" and Dewey "consummatory experiences" are, I take it, joys that depend on some kind of excellence.

17. *Cf. Education at the Crossroads* (Yale, 1943), pp. 51–55.

18. *Cf.* Niell, *op. cit.*, p. 111.

19. *Cf.* e.g. J. Bronowski, *Science and Human Values* (1956).

20. As Cardinal Newman does in *The Scope and Nature of University Education* (1958).

21. *Time*, July 7, 1967, p. 20.

22. *Ibid.*

23. These remarks apply to his *Ethics*. In *Politics*, VII, 1, he seems to say that happiness consists of intellectually *and* morally excellent activities.

24. *Cf.* J. Margolis, "Moral Appreciation," *Journal of Philosophy*, LIX (1962), pp. 351–354.

25. I should put a Deweyan education somewhere between these two. See my *Three Historical Philosophies of Education* (1965), ch. 4.

26. It does look as if a "pursuit of excellence" in a society would involve the creation, through education and otherwise, of a climate in which its achievement in some form or other is both desired and expected, though it must also include a recognition that the forms and standards of excellence are not yet all fully known and, hence, a certain tolerance of deviant and exploratory ways of living and doing things.

REASON, HIGHER LEARNING, AND THE GOOD SOCIETY

Henry Aiken

The aim of this essay is critical and constructive. I mean, to attack views of education and of the good society widely prevalent in our culture, particularly in our institutions of so-called higher learning, i.e., the colleges and universities, and, more recently, the institutes for advanced study. But the point of view I shall call in question goes deeper and extends more widely. It involves a conception of higher learning, accepted by virtually the whole society in which we live and the civilization of which we are a part, and this in turn reflects conceptions of knowledge, of human nature, and of human values and attainments, to be found in the writings of formative thinkers of our entire western tradition as far back as Plato. In some considerable part, the break down of our civilization is evidence of the errors—I should call them philosophical—inherent in this point of view which I call "rationalism." Unlike some others, however, I do not believe that the whole aim of Educators concerned with liberal education is to try to shore up the ruins of the rationalist tradition. Here, in my judgment, we would do well to let the dead bury their dead. What is worthy of survival—and of course much is—in the West has developed in spite of and against the grain of the rationalist tradition. What should be saved must be set free from the bonds in which it has hitherto been tied. In fact, what is most worthy of survival belongs to an unofficial, almost an underground culture, that has grown up in spite of the attempts of rationalists to destroy or else to conceal it.

As these last sentences suggest, I shall not be merely critical, but shall offer in later sections some more positive suggestions about education and the good society. But the bases for them will emerge gradually through my dialectical oppositions to rationalism.

I. THE IDEOLOGY OF RATIONALISM

In speaking of the "ideology" of rationalism, I do not use the word "ideology" itself in a pejorative sense. Accordingly, I do not mean that rationalism is wicked or a form of "false consciousness," simply because it is an ideology; some ideologies, kept within bounds, may be quite benign. Nor does it seem to me possible for a society with continuous traditions, or a people with a sense of its own identity, to persist without some form of ideology. Ideologies, which are in part the products of philosophical ideas and points of view, are semi-systems of ideals, principles, standards, aspirations, along with their supporting over-beliefs about the world, the nature of man, his history and his destiny, his capacities and limitations, his institutions and forms of life. Such over-beliefs, moreover, may be either scientific or wildly speculative, explicit or implicit, literal-minded or figurative. What makes them ideological, as I use the term, are (a) their active social roles, and (b) the fact that their roles are social. The social roles of ideological attitudes and beliefs are active and practical in the sense that they serve as determinants and conditions of action, as mental sets, attitudes, presuppositions, assumptions that guide not only action but thought conceived as symbolic action and as a preparation for actions that are overt and explicit. As ideological, however, such roles are not selected by individuals at their own pleasure; rather, they are ingrained in the whole institutional life of a society or people or social class. And for a society, they form a large part of its lore, its prevailing intellectual and social history, what it conceives to be its traditions. Inevitably they are also ingrained in its basic educational practices and institutions; its teachers tend to follow it; its administrators expound it, its students assimilate it; and students and teachers who oppose "the system" are usually in one way or another opposed to its ideology. I am convinced that many of the so-called "drop-outs" from our own contemporary institutions of higher learning are in fact people disaffected with the ideology of rationalism. Hence, even if one wants merely to understand the sources of disquiet, of disaffection and revolt in our contemporary universities one must look to the rationalist ideology that animates much of our established culture.

Just because rationalism as an ideology is a pervasive set of social attitudes and beliefs, it cannot be ascribed *in toto* to any particular philosopher or even to a certain philosophical succession. Plato, I am persuaded, is preeminent among the philosophical progenitors of the rationalist ideology, but I do not, save for purposes of reference and illustration identify rationalism with Plato's philosophy. Likewise, the great succession of Continental rationalists, from Descartes to Leibniz, have also had considerable formative influence upon the ideology of rationalism. But they did not, so to say, write its constitution. And no doubt rationalism betrays, or caricatures the thought of these great thinkers at one point or another. Sometimes indeed it betrays some of their deeper intentions. Furthermore, one can find, as one would expect if my view of the matter is right, evidences of rationalism in the thought of many philosophers, historians, men of letters, who are, or think they are, opposed to major aspects of Plato's or Descartes' thought, or who are, or think they are, simply preoccupied with different questions. Although in the text books the theory of knowledge called "empiricism" is commonly set in opposition to rationalist theories of knowledge, many empiricists hold views about knowledge and its place in human affairs that are virtually paradigms of what I here understand by rationalism.

The following outline of rationalism as an ideology is intended merely as a rough, though I hope serviceable, sketch. Let us begin by noticing a fact or two about the term rationalism itself. As an *"ism"* word, rationalism in its ordinary use refers primarily to a cluster of attitudes, points of view, ways of taking things. It stands to reason and rationality as evolutionism stands to evolution or historicism to history. In short, it is not only a theory about reason and rationality, though it indeed involves such a theory, but also it is a perspective upon human experience and conduct which ascribes to reason and rationality a central and controlling place in our scheme of things. The rationalist, it is plain, not merely defends reason against its detractors: plenty of people, myself included, would wish to do this against irrationalists, mystagogues, and obscurantists. The rationalist also asserts the supremacy of reason as a human faculty, the fundamentality of its norms, and its sufficiency as an organon for thought and action. In Santayana's phrase, the rationalist is committed, symptomatically and above all else to something he envisages as "the life of reason."

But there is a second aspect of the use of the term "rationalism" in most quarters. Some "ism" words are mainly pejorative, or are conceived by people who employ them pejoratively. Thus "historicism" is, for most people, Karl Popper for instance, a bugaboo, a scapegoat, a kind of original sin philosophically and ideologically. In a primarily rationalist tradition and culture rationalism is, not unnaturally, a word with a halo around it, as one discovers when one attacks the points of view associated with it. And when one avows oneself to be an antirationalist, one automatically declares oneself to be a deviant, a kind of drop-out from the prevailing culture. So be it.

As here conceived, the principle doctrines or contentions of rationalism and rationalists are as follows: [1]

(1) First of all, rationalism is a doctrine about man and his cul-

ture. Man, for the rationalist, is par excellence the rational animal. It is rationality which distinguishes him from other creatures. And it is rationality which is his salient gift, his most precious faculty. The classical rationalists of course conceived of exercise of reason teleologically as man's own distinctive and proper end. But they also conceived it in quasi-administrative terms, as the faculty which properly coordinates and controls all other human faculties, activities, and affairs. It is, or ought to be, the master of the passions and emotions. If certain other ends are also inherent in human nature, reason not only discovers the means to their realization, but, where they conflict, it is empowered and entitled to reorient and harmonize them in various appropriate ways. Finally, not only is human rationality thus conceived immanent with human nature, so that all men, unless perverted or deprived in some way, strive, at first unconsciously, and then more and more consciously, to become rational animals; but also the principles of rationality are, both in thought and in action, to be regarded eternalistically as unamenable to change.[2] Its norms, whose paradigms of course are the norms of logic and exact science, are not only universalistic but universal rules of order to which every man is at all times beholden. Questions of genesis, history, social or psychological context, have nothing to do with and are always strictly irrelevant to questions of rationality. Nor is it merely that rational standards and claims are formulated ahistorically; it is also, and more saliently so, that no meta-descriptive account of them, which suggests that they are really subject to change, is acceptable. Such an account is not an account of rationality in history but only of fallible human meta-beliefs about it or else of vagaries in the practices of historical individuals and societies.

Certain important consequences concerning human nature follow at once. The rationalist views, or tends to view, man's faculties as forming a kind of hierarchy and, so to say, the internal political economy of a human life as properly a sort of aristocracy. Here, however, there is considerable room for variation within the rationalist tradition. In the view of some rationalists, rationality, though exhibited most saliently, in the work of the logician and scientist, may also be present in some implicit fashion in art and poetry, or in religious thought. In short, some rationalists are, as we may call them, "inclusivists" and informalists who seek to find in every sphere of activity redemptive and entitling evidences of rationality. From their point of view, although a poet may be a less perfect example of the rational animal than a logician, a rational poet is superior to a nonrational or irrational one. Others are "exclusivists" or rigorists who limit rationality strictly to logical and scientific thought. From their point of view, any activity, such as painting or sculpture, perhaps even morality and religion, which is found to be (from the preferred point of view) essentially nonrational, is *ipso facto* below the salt of essentially *human* aspiration. And poets, musicians, ministers, *et al.* are not in their characteristic work acting as human beings.

(2) Taking classical rationalism again as a preliminary point of reference, we are to view man's good as complex. His complete good consists in the fulfillment of his whole nature, including his basic appetitive and emotional drives. Usually the rationalists have envisaged man's complete good as a harmony. Each propensity or power being fulfilled only to the extent that it does not impair fulfillment of the rest. Such a harmony, however, is minimal, for it envisages nothing more than a mutual compatibility or consistency. Maximally, the fulfilled propensities would be a form of a kind of consortium, each of which provided a positive reinforcement or support for the rest. Thus a man whose hunger and whose sexual impulses are adequately satisfied is so far enabled to devote his energies more fully to his proper work as a rational being than one who is continually hungry or sexually deprived. Man's highest good, however, consists alone in the exercise of his rational faculty.

On this point, again, rationalists have not always taken precisely the same view of what this good involves. In part this is owing to variant theories of human cognition; in part also it is owing to different views about the degrees of worth to be ascribed to several objects or levels of knowledge; and finally, it is owing to different views about the diversity of intellectual capacity among men.

The following broad tendencies may be noted here. Among classical rationalists, who conceive of at least the higher forms of knowledge in terms of a direct intellectual intuition of the object known, the exercise of reason, in its higher, theoretical reaches, is essentially contemplative. However, among modern rationalist theories of knowledge, for which scientific knowledge serves as a paradigm, the cognitive role assigned to intuition has continually declined. Knowledge is now viewed in verificationist terms, and one who knows is one who is able to, or knows how to verify the propositions and theories that he is said to know. In another way, scientific knowledge which is now conceived in terms of controlled inquiry and explanation does not consist in intuitive perceptions of the thing known, but rather in an ability to offer satisfactory explanations of it. Thus, knowing that certain propositions are true or probable depends essentially upon skills necessary to knowing how to explain that which one knows, and this in particular involves both powers of logico-mathematical formulation and manipulation for the statement and organization of theories and skills required for the performance of controlled experiments and observations required for their verification.[3]

It is no accident that all forms of rationalism which view theoretical science as the paradigm of human knowledge also tend to assign to the most exact and certain of the sciences the place of highest intrinsic value in the hierarchy of cognitive disciplines. Correspondingly, the scientists who possess this knowledge and the skills pertaining thereto, are regarded as individuals of the highest dignity and authority among those who know. Such persons, moreover, tend to be viewed by rationalists as paradigms of human excellence generally, to be emulated wherever possible, to be deferred to where not. In classical times this meant that philosophers were the most exemplary of men, not just because they loved wisdom but because the knowledge they aspired to possess was the highest, most perfect of all. Such a view with some variations prevailed down through the time of Descartes and Spinoza. It is notable, however, that John Locke regarded his own philosophical activity in less exalted terms, and since Locke rationalists have tended to demote philosophy, at best, to a subordinate place in the hierarchy of cognitive disciplines. Nowadays, as we know, few professional philosophers love wisdom and those who do love it occupy an even lower place in the hierarchy than their colleagues.

In passing it is also worth remarking that so-called rational theology, which during the middle ages surpassed even philosophy as an intellectual discipline, has fallen to a position even lower than philosophy in the modern rationalist hierarchy. In fact the general view among rationalists, nowadays, appears to be that rational theology is a contradiction in terms, and that among theologians, semantical atheists who repudiate "God-talk" altogether are by all odds the most reputable. In mentioning the theologians, here, let me add, my aim is merely to remove a possible objection to this part of my synopsis of rationalism. Remembering Plato and Aristotle, as well as the Medieval philosophers and theologians, it is arguable that some thinkers who belong to the rationalist tradition have assigned priority to philosophy or theology, not only because it was considered to be the most exact and perfect of all forms of knowledge, but also because the object of philosophical or theological study is the highest of all forms of being. And certainly many rationalists have taken such a view. But this does not require a serious qualification of my account of rationalism as an ideology. On the contrary, it serves indirectly to reinforce that account. For upon discovering that knowledge of God or the good is neither clear nor exact, at least from a scientific point of view, rationalists do not conclude that there are forms of knowledge that surpass the sciences in value and authority, and knowers who possess a higher dignity than the scientists. On the contrary, they conclude that such forms of knowledge, if knowledge they be, are of much lower value, and those who profess it of much less distinction as knowers.

In our universities, at the present time, such is precisely the prevailing view. In general, the sciences most highly esteemed are mathematics and the exact physical sciences; and theologians who at least try to be rational in their investigations occupy places of far less intellectual prestige than their colleagues. And if, in some academic circles, philosophy has to some extent recouped its losses, this is due largely, or entirely, to the rise of mathematical logic and to its widespread use among analytical philosophers and in particular among philosophers of science.[4]

A word must now be said about the attitudes of rationalists regarding the abilities of men to achieve man's highest good. It is of course not enough simply to say that man's highest good consists in the possession of exact, scientific knowledge. For if there are men who have little scientific ability, and if therefore they are highly imperfect and inadequate rational animals (and indeed to that extent imperfect and inadequate human beings) then the conclusion likely to be drawn is that man's highest good is simply beyond their grasp, or else is available to them only in a diminished or diluted form. And if it is believed, as Plato and Aristotle for example plainly did believe, that such ability is relatively rare, or restricted to particular races or classes of men, then the basis for certain forms of elitism is already prepared.

Here again however, we must proceed with caution. And though, rationalism is, as I am convinced, inherently elitist, just to the extent that its view of the highest good is not accessible or else is accessible only in a diminished form to many, or most, men, it does not follow that rationalism is thereby committed, for example, to elitist political ideologies in the ordinary sense. There are many elites and accordingly many kinds of elitism, just as there are many views of the diversity of human abilities. Moreover, there are, within rationalist theories of knowledge, countervailing tendencies which to some extent offset its proneness to elitism.

Let me speak of the latter. In the first place, modern rationalists have increasingly stressed the public, objective, impersonal, and impartial character of scientific inquiry and knowledge. Such knowledge therefore is accessible in some degree to anyone who can master the skills required for scientific analysis, experimentation, and observation. Hence, questions of race, color, wealth, social class, or political power are wholly irrelevant to an individual's ability to share in the scientific enterprise or to enjoy the benefits of a scientific education. Indeed, it is commonly argued that the scientific community is a perfect democracy, a society of equals, each of whom is free to confute his fellow, if he can, and everyone is pledged to subordinate his judgment to the immanent consensus of qualified scientific observers or judges. But of course a scientific consensus is at best an ideal one, since no member of the scientific community, at any given time, has the time, energy, or relevant knowledge necessary to test the theories of his peers. And in fact the amount of faith actually required to keep the enterprise of empirical science going has become, in our time, exponential.

In brief, the equalitarian and democratic tendencies implied by modern rationalist doctrines of knowledge are both in principle and in fact restrictive. Perhaps the least misleading analogy here is the *institution* of science and the restrictive democracy of ancient Athens. In principle, anyone who possesses the necessary aptitudes and can acquire the requisite skills for performing the appropriate intellectual operations, is free to enter the scientific establishment. Even so, such a principle is by definition restrictive.[5] Here we shall discount restrictions that are owing to historical social factors, which are generally regarded by rationalists as accidental rather than essential. Even so it is impossible to ignore the great native differences in scientific aptitude. Bertrand Russell, himself a great liberal as well as a rationalist, has said somewhere that the difference in intellectual capacity between an Einstein and an ordinary man is hardly less great than the difference in this regard between an ordinary man and a chimpanzee. Russell has often been given to hyperboles, but I think we all get the point: A great number of human beings, even under optimum conditions, cannot be expected to understand clearly, not to say make contributions to, the most advanced forms of exact science. And if intellectual power, not to say rationality itself, is measured primarily in terms of the ability to do exact science, then it may be taken for granted that scientific institutions and especially those concerned with the so-called higher learning, provide little basis or support for principles of extensive human equality and general social or political democracy. And from the standpoint of society as a whole, any rationalist ideology preoccupied with the greatest possible realization of man's highest good, itself conceived essentially in terms of scientific understanding, is bound to that extent to be elitist and hence undemocratic.

No doubt such a conception of rationalism as a general ideology is too simplistic, though I think that it is well to have it in the record before its lines are softened. With this understanding, several important qualifications of it may now be introduced. From Plato on down, rationalists have generally emphasized that there should be equal opportunity among the members of society to receive as much intellectual training as possible, and so to fulfill whatever powers they may have for realizing man's distinctive or highest good. Secondly, many rationalists, including Plato, have argued that *high* intellectual capacity (again conceived in terms of rationalist assumptions) may not be required for the creditable performance of other jobs essential to any tolerable, not to say good, society. Moreover, such jobs both presuppose and realize some measure of intellectual power. In the performance of such jobs, imaginatively conceived and understood, men of relatively low intelligence (once more conceived in rationalist terms) thus realize their own limits of man's highest good. More important, however, rationalism need not ignore the common requirements for citizenship and, still more important, for moral respect. On these scores, rationalists often argue that the essential thing is not high intelligence but simply intelligence, not perfect rationality but essential rationality. Citizenship may be intellectually less demanding than set theory or nuclear physics, but every chump above the level of a chimp can qualify for the citizen's bit. So the basic forms of social and political life in a rationalist utopia (which as a utopia aspires only to the not-impossible) might still be conceived in quite broadly equalitarian and democratic terms. As for moral respect, which the rationalist is disposed to conceive—at least by analogy—in law-like terms, this is the respect due any individual in terms that are essentially "human." And all that being human requires, from this point of view, is a medium of the power to perform the operations essential to scientific understanding. What I must respect in the case of every featherless biped that can qualify as human is his essential rationality, not the degree of his brilliance as a potential mathematician or physicist or logician.

(3) We have now to consider, also only schematically, the rationalist approach to the ideal of the good society. Broadly speaking, it follows from the rationalist conceptions of man, his nature and good. I have already remarked upon rationalism's fundamental view concerning the moral relations among men. Something more must now be said about rationalist approaches to morality. This is a sticky wicket. To begin with, as I have said, the ground of *moral* rights and responsibilities for most rationalists is human rationality itself. But now this thesis must itself be qualified. Here we may distinguish a strong or exclusivist rationalism in ethics from a weaker or inclusivist rationalism. Strong or exclusivist rationalism maintains that the sole basis of moral regard or concern should be man's nature as a rational being. This may be taken to imply that the fundamental human right to respect for the rationality of the individual: his capacity, that is to say, for scientific understanding and judgment. All other human rights are derived from or justified in terms of this right. Thus, if the fundamental right is a right to respect for the

rational faculty of every individual who possesses it, it follows, since every faculty exists not simply to be possessed as a latent power but to be exercised in practice and in act, that each individual has a right (a) to respect for those opinions which are rationally arrived at and which therefore fall within the range of his intellectual competence and (b) to as much education as his natural powers permit. Other rights, accordingly, could be justified as conditions of these primary rights of rational beings as such. Thus, for example, the rights to life, security, the satisfaction of natural appetites or drives, liberty, and so on might be justified in terms of their utility in relation to the life of reason which is the life of knowledge. But it must be added at once, exclusivist rationalism does not acknowledge any independent human right to any of these other putative goods or satisfactions.

It is not clear that any great moral philosopher has been an exponent of exclusivist rationalism, though some Kantians appear to have come very close to such a view. However, Kant himself (as I understand him) contended that although each rational being has a right to be regarded as an end unto himself, he is, to himself, not merely a rational being but also one who desires happiness. And for present purposes this may be taken to include the satisfaction of his natural desires. Hence, it could be argued that Kant's own view implied that although the right to exercise and develop one's rational faculty is the absolutely unconditional and primary human right, there is another right, that is, the right to pursue one's happiness which, although secondary to the right to regard and respect as a rational being and conditional upon one's being a rational being (non-rational beings, that is, cannot claim a right to pursue happiness) is *not* dependent upon its utility as a means to the life of reason itself.

The Greeks generally talked less of rights and duties than of goods and virtues. However, a weak or inclusivist rationalism may be easily derived from the classical rationalist conception of man's complete good. From this inclusivist point of view, one could readily argue that although man's primary, or in cases of conflict, prior, rights pertain to his essential rationality, his other fundamental propensities provide the basis of rights which, as such, need not be defended on utilitarian grounds as causal conditions of the exercise and enjoyment of the rights of rational beings. These rights pertain only to *rational* beings, but, on this condition, though secondary or lower, they deserve respect. The rights pertaining to rationality always take precedence. But where no problem of conflict exists, they provide the basis of moral claims by individuals both upon society itself and upon its members.

There remains another position open to rationalists which is of considerable interest both on its own account and in the light of certain developments in the institutional life of modern science. The rationalist may begin by returning to the basic premise of his notion of the good life, namely, that man's highest good consists in the pursuit and enjoyment of knowledge, and that the exemplary form of human knowledge is exact positive science. He then may argue that the rights of men as functioning *rational* beings are not a result of their native endowment of judgment and understanding, which is virtually nil. Man is through and through a social being, and his rationality, both in potency and in act, is a social achievement. And the more exact and systematic human knowledge becomes, the more evident is this fact. Both the advancement of learning and its transmission through the educational process are increasingly products of corporate institutional activities. To be sure, the collective fund of human knowledge is acquired, saved, and transmitted through the work of men. Nevertheless, the individual scholar, scientist, and teacher of science, remains, so to say, the legatee and trustee of a corporate fund of knowledge. And his rights and his dignity as a rational animal derive entirely from his ability to fill these roles. In short, the scientists as such is a truly anonymous public servant whose goals, standards, and works belong entirely to the social institutions which he serves.

In times past, to be sure, the advancement of learning was, or appeared to be, largely the work of independent scholars and inquirers, and the transmission of the skills and powers essential to this advancement was a far more loosely organized social enterprise than it has become in our own time. Accordingly, the progress of human knowledge was intermittent, spotty, and uncertain. Now the reverse is true. The exponential enlargement of human learning is itself a direct function of the development of modern institutions of controlled experimental inquiry. These corporate bodies, with their own indispensable divisions of labor, involve sharply differentiated and stratified intellectual responsibilities and prerogatives. In the great scientific laboratories, for example, section heads, laboratory technicians, secretarial aides, and the rest are in practice organized in a quasi-platonic manner, under the direction of administrative "guardians" who at once set the goals for inquiry and determine the rights of various classes of scientific workers. And even in universities, where the organization is looser than in industrial research corporations, stratifications remain and individual freedom of inquiry, except among tenured professors, is severely limited. And the freedom of teachers to teach what they please, as they please, is perhaps even more restricted by departmental and university needs and by corporate standards of objectivity and truth.

If, then, the highest of human goods is the advancement of knowledge, then in the modern world that good must be regarded, progressively and ideally, as the collective achievement of a highly organized and stratified institution or hierarchy of institutions. And if the society of scientific inquirers and scholars is still viewed, as it commonly is by rationalists, as a paradigm of the rational and hence good society itself, then rationalism is to that extent increasingly committed to a corporatist, rather than an individualist or contractualist conception of the ideal social system. This suggests also that old-fashioned libertarian notions of free thought and inquiry should be radically qualified, if indeed not replaced altogether, in ways that take account of the real social conditions of scientific research. Indeed, one can readily imagine that, from a rationalist point of view, the free-lance inquirer who investigates whatever he pleases in accordance with whatever procedures and standards of truth and meaning he may consider appropriate is to be viewed as intellectually irresponsible and hence socially undesirable.

To a certain extent, in fact, such a view already prevails in practice within the universities and scientific institutes, if not yet in the society at large. This is evidenced by the fact that, as a number of leading sociologists, including Daniel Bell and Lewis Coser, have suggested, the old individualist ideal of the intellectual, along with those of his progenitors, the philosophe and the general man of letters, have now been replaced by those of the academician and the scholar. And though the free-floating intellectual still exists, he tends to be regarded by professional scholars as, at best, a "journalist," and at worst, as an incompetent meddler in affairs that are not his concern.

In sum, then, corporatist or institutionalist rationalism, as it may be called, tends increasingly to view the rights of men as rational beings as entirely a function of their potentialities as participants in the collective work of scientific research and education. The *fundamental* right, however, belongs to the enterprise of science itself and to the research and academic institutions to which that enterprise is entrusted. Accordingly, freedom of inquiry, so far as the individual is concerned, is a derivative freedom, at once justified in terms of his institutional roles and limited by the appropriate rules that govern them. The fundamental respect that is due man, the rational being, is thus a respect for the self-determining and the self-correcting corporate enterprise of science as a whole. Accordingly, the correlative rights of individual men, as rational beings, are essentially social rights which that enterprise, through its appropriate qualified representatives, should determine.

Modern rationalist ideologies, I believe, are increasingly a cross between what I have called inclusive rationalism and corporate rationalism. Undoubtedly this is responsible for some of the profound tensions which now exist within the primary institution concerned with the advancement and transmission of human knowledge in modern societies: the university itself. On the one side, there remains an ideal of a society of human individuals in whom certain inalienable rights to respect and nurture are invested. According to this ideal each individual is to be entirely free to inquire, to think, to express himself as he sees fit, subject only to the inner checks within his conscience of right reason. Because the multiversity, as Clark Kerr has dubbed it, is not only a "science factory," but also a kind of republic in its own right, complete with facilities that minister not only to the student's scientific development but also (if incidently) to his artistic, religious, and moral nurture, as well as his basic bodily needs for shelter, food, and sexual gratification, it can indeed be viewed to a certain extent, microcosmically, as an inclusive rationalist's modern paradigm of the good society itself.[6]

At the same time, there can be no doubt that the multiversity, however diversified its activities, however pluralistic its internal organization, remains a corporate institution which (with a qualification presently to be observed) not only seeks to advance and transmit knowledge but which, through its own governing bodies, its various departments and schools, its area studies and research projects, establishes the rules and principles in terms of which the advancement and transmission of knowledge are in practice to be understood. Here of course it is impossible to describe what all this means from the standpoints of the several groups which constitute the multiversity: the administration, the faculty, the student body, and the great miscellany of workers that perform the tasks necessary to the operation of the physical plant, the housekeeping and dining facilities, the stores, and the extracurricular facilities essential to the life of the institution and its communities. In his interesting book, *Bureaucracy in Higher Education*, Dean Herbert Stroup, himself a professional sociologist, has illuminatingly described the organization of offices in the modern American university as a cross between two systems or types of hierarchy: (a) the scalar, and (b) the functional.[7] From his account, it is clear that the hierarchical organization of the university itself cannot be understood in terms of simplistic analogies provided by the pyramidal hierarchies to be found in some military or business organizations (though even there, one suspects the hierarchies are not as simplistic as they may appear to the casual observer). Nonetheless, the importance of the integral hierarchies of the university, which also pervade its structures of formal instruction and research, cannot be minimized. One simple way of testing this fact is to compare the modern university with Paul Goodman's quasi-medieval ideal of a university as an anarchist community of more or less independent scholars and students who gather together, for the time being, for whatever intellectual and personal companionship and mutual illumination their friendly company may afford. Goodman's ideal, relative to what exists, is admittedly utopian. Nor is it a utopia to which modern academicians generally aspire. Only the so-called "free universities" that have sprung up in the shadows of the multiversity bear any analogy to the Goodmanian ideal. And from any modern rationalist's point of view, they are accordingly thoroughly subversive.

Before bringing this résumé of the drift of rationalism as an ideology to a close, two further points remain to be made. Both concern the institutions of education, and in particular the institutions of higher learning. In the first place, as Plato, the archetypal rationalist, long ago foresaw, the educational system is for the rationalist ideology the indispensable feeder institution to the good society or polis. In an era of advanced scientific technology such as our own, in which every other institution from industry to government, from business to the so-called media, from Madison Avenue image makers and advertisers to city planners, depends continually and essentially upon the achievements and products of modern science, there is scarcely a human activity that is not directly dependent upon or vitally affected by the educational system. Indeed, what is called "self-defense" is itself now largely dependent upon the establishments of scientific education. Modern national societies such as our own, have in this regard out-Platonized Plato himself.

But the Platonic analogy goes still deeper. For just as in the *Republic*, the state and the educational system are, in effect, one and the same, the educators serving as guardians and the guardians as educators, so in our own national society, the government and the educational system are similarly intertwined. Hence, as it now becomes impossible within the university to separate what President Perkins of Cornell calls the "missions" of research and teaching from that of public service—which in practice means primarily service in and to the federal government—so it becomes increasingly difficult, even in a formal congressional system like our own, to separate the "leaders" of the academy from those who at once implement and determine the working policies of the state. Without a cooperative educational system, including in particular the universities, the state quite simply could neither sustain nor defend itself. And without the interlocking ties to the state and its government, the whole educational system itself would disintegrate. To be sure, this need not mean that the proximate aims of the state are indistinguishable from those of the educational system, though in practice they overlap increasingly. Nor does it mean that the educational system, again including the universities in particular, is a mere pawn of the nation-state or of its government. Rather, it means, that the destinies of the state and the educational system, and in particular the university, conceived as the primary institution for the propagation and advancement of scientific learning, are mutually indispensable to one another.

The second main point concerns the role of the educational system generally, and the university in particular, in relation not simply to the concerns of the nation-state but to the society as a whole. Here I shall adopt for the sake of discussion the point of view of the inclusive rationalist who, while envisaging the corporate advancement of scientific knowledge as man's highest good, also accepts the notion of a common social good which includes satisfaction of the noncognitive propensities of men. In the *Republic* Plato does not always keep steadily in view the complete good of the community, and so he sometimes overstresses, or appears to overstress, the role of education in the polis as a whole. In a way Plato, its founder, fell in love with Academy. However, the enlightened rationalist acknowledges that the educational system, no matter how indispensable, is merely a necessary, not a sufficient institution for a tolerable, not to say, a good society. Furthermore, the inclusive rationalist insists on not only the necessity of ministering to the needs of all members of society (and not merely those which show promise of intellectual distinction and hence usefulness to the state), but of serving them all in depth, as whole men who have needs that cannot be the immediate concern of education, including educational institutions as far-flung in their activities and roles as the multiversity. Education, no matter how encompassing the activities of its own institutions may be, moves toward different goals than do government or economy. There are also many lower-order cultural activities that have different proximate goals from those of the educational system, no matter how broadly gauged. For example, art, literature, music, and dance, as well as the newer "media," as they are called, are intended in part at least not as contributions to learning but rather as sources of consummatory satisfaction or pleasure. Their aim, as Bernard Berenson used to say, is immediately "life-enhancing." And just because of this they must not be tied too closely to activities that are concerned with learning and teaching. The proper complaint against academic art is simply that it is a bore. And rationalists, no more than other people, are not obliged to approve of boredom. Thus, while the university should cultivate (in moderation) all of the arts, it should distinguish between the work of the teacher and the apprentice on the one side, and the mature, creative artist and his audience on the other, even though in practice both, or all, of these groups may in fact overlap.

The rationalist himself may be the first to insist that an educational system whose concern is with the advancement and propagation of knowledge cannot be all things to all men, however much the universities may tend to become miscrocosmic societies and social systems in their own right. Education cannot be all, because learning cannot be all. Man is indeed, as Ralph Barton Perry used to put it, the "docile" animal, by which he meant that animal that learns from his experience. However, docility is not manhood, only its condition. And when we become "men"—as, one may hope, we are always becoming from the moment of birth—we seek, rightly and rightfully, to use our acquired skills and abilities to make and form and act and do things which, as such, are not the learner's immediate business—nor yet, therefore, the teacher's. A society dominated by its teachers and learners is a society committed to the ideal that learning is man's only, or primary good. And this is not true. Such a society, ironically, makes a fetish of immaturity.

II

It is evident from the preceding remarks that we have been passing implicitly from the description of rationalism as an ideology, including its sense in its more inclusive forms of the role of education, toward its critique. Let us now bring that critique into the open.

I shall begin by saying something about the fundamental weaknesses of rationalism as an ideology, even at its best, and hence the radical errors to which, at that best, its view of man, society, and education are prone. This is also a critique of an ever more deeply ingrained tradition in our whole Western culture with which, in my judgment, it is necessary to make a final and radical break. Of necessity, I shall have to deal with these difficult matters in a very summary and superficial fashion which may make it appear that I am more dogmatic, as well as surer of my ground, than I am. The following remarks are thus to be viewed as challenges and as explorations, rather than as finished positions.

Bluntly: although rationality is indeed one essential dimension of a tolerable human nature, it is by no means the only propensity that on the one side distinguishes man from other creatures: nor does it form *the* basis of his highest good.

Consider how much is either left out or misconceived when man's rational faculty is viewed as his unique, controlling, and highest human endowment. For example, man is also uniquely the religious animal, the being capable of grasping his own mortality, and of making something beyond his own individual existence a matter of ultimate concern. This is something that escapes the rational animal as such. Secondly, (and here I am not interested in questions of priority or rank), man is the communal animal, capable of friendship, comradeship, and the forms of love sometimes grouped under the heading of agape. Man, if you will, is the animal that loves; he is therefore the animal that reciprocates and needs reciprocity. At the same time, man is also the self-perfecting, self-overcoming, and self-transcending being. And this, not only in the religious or social or intellectual dimension, but in the widest sense, in the ethical or moral dimension. Now, however, another ideal comes more distinctly into view: the ideal of self-determination, of self-control, of what Kant called "giving oneself the law." The very notion of morality is impossible apart from the ideal of the individual as an autonomous agent, who assumes responsibility for his own conduct, his own principles, his own comportment. In fact, apart from such a view of man, free personal relations among men, including above all the relations of contract and personal loyalty and love, can scarcely exist.

But the moment the word "person" is introduced, a whole dimension of human character comes into view which cannot be adequately comprehended by the notion of rationality. In fact rationality itself is but one of the forms which this dimension of character normally takes. Man is, inventively, the role-playing, the acting, and not merely the active animal. In large part his cultural and spiritual life, indeed his entire mental life itself is a matter of role-playing and of acting. Clearly role-playing involves the capacity to follow rules, and the attitudes attendant thereto. The role-playing requires the ability to subordinate his interests, feelings, indeed his whole "subjective" personality, as it is sometimes called, to the role itself. But it requires much more; in most cases it also requires the capacity for identification which is sometimes called empathy. And since the mode of identification is in this case freely imaginative, it is not something that can be fully understood in terms of rule-governed activities and practices: it is, in fact, to the latter what the actual, open-ended, dialogical and speculative use of language is to rules of grammar and of usage.

Summarily we may say that man is or should be distinctively the animal capable of living the life of the mind. This, among other things, means the power to turn or to transform every motion, every bodily change, every purely behavioral process into an action, a passion, an event, an occasion. Or if this sounds insufferably loose and romantic, we may say more exactly that man is the creature whose own bodily processes, changes, and motions have no *being* for him save in so far as he can relate them to mental events, developments, actions.

But such a conception of man is not adequately conveyed by the notion of the rational animal. In fact I should be prepared to argue that the rationalist misconceives the life of the mind, and that his reductivist view of knowledge is itself symptomatic of that misconception. His own fault, curiously, is itself a failure of understanding and of knowledge. In consequence he at once misconceives and misrepresents man's good, high as well as complete, and as a result the forms of social life and of education required for both endurable- and well-being. Worse, he has an inadequate understanding of rationality itself. Rationality in fact must be saved from the ideology of rationalism.

In saying this, let me add that I do not object to the view, which my friend Frankena (in conversation) considers very rationalistic indeed, that the task of education, as such, being concerned with learning is therefore concerned with knowledge. For I conceive the proximate aim of all learning to be some form of knowledge, and knowledge to be the achievement which learning, and hence education itself, can bestow. My objections to rationalism are (a) that it woefully narrows both the proper range of human knowledge and hence the proper forms of learning education, and (b) that even when that range is extended as far as it legitimately may be, there is still much more to the life of the mind than the idea of knowledge adequately comprehends.

To take the last point first, we want and ought to do more with our minds than seek knowledge. We want and ought, for one thing, simply to exercise them. Physical exercise is a pleasure, but so is mental exercise. Study, inquiry, analysis can be intrinsic goods even for those who do not succeed very far in advancing learning. But the point is more extensive. I am not proposing a bill of rights, educational or otherwise, for intellectual failures. The great romantics, however much they may have overstated or misrepresented their own aspirations, recognized above all the incomparable values and virtues of what they called the imagination. Every form of cultural and mental life yields satisfactions as well as achievements which are more and less than cognitive. And the value of these achievements is often mixed: it is intrinsic to the satisfaction or to the act as well as instrumental to other ends.

I am aware that many inclusive rationalists doubtless mean to do justice to the "lower" pleasures and to the satisfactions afforded by the body. I am not talking of them here, though the rationalist's hierarchies strike me as absurd. I am not, in short, talking about the plainly *mental* values inherent in sensory experience, or in the affective gratifications which sensation may yield, important as they may be. What is here in view is the entire incomparable life of the constructive imagination, whose aim at least in part, is not to inform us about what is or ought to be but to offer envisagements of what might be and to fashion symbolic forms to which questions of literal fact are not determining.

Nothing is more indispensable to the domains of literature and indeed of all art than the tropes, in which the mind finds a great part of its own inner life and happiness. Their loss, or worse their repudiation among literal-minded "cognitivists," concerned exclusively with describing or explaining what is the case, entails not only for themselves but for societies and educational systems which view them as exemplary, a terrible constriction of the whole life of the human spirit and a ghastly depletion of man's capacity for refreshment and self-renewal.

But if the rationalist misunderstands the mind he so greatly prizes, no less does he foolishly disenfranchise familiar ranges of human cognition. This is all the more perverse, since from his point of view, knowledge itself is the proper end and achievement of the human mind. Here, let me emphasize, I do not mean to dwell simply upon the nonempirical elements in scientific understanding itself: that is, its essential dependence upon mathematics and logic, its involvement in contra-factual or subjunctive modes of understanding, and the sophisticated perceptual and motor drills and skills required for experimental inquiries and confirmations. The issue now concerns forms of knowledge that are *not* merely dimensions or vehicles of scientific inquiry or conditions of the cognitive achievements which it affords.

In such a paper as this it is perhaps most useful to proceed by reference to domains of activity that the modern rationalist, at least, generally concedes to lie outside of the scope of positive science itself. Most important is the understanding of ordinary language and symbolic forms themselves. The rationalist often appears to take linguistic understanding for granted. And in fact the great rationalists have often treated language as little more than an auxiliary device for communicating ideas and beliefs, perceptions and understandings already acquired and possessed in some other way. Here I can do no more than remind you of a truth, tersely stated by one of the greatest of modern rationalists, C. S. Peirce, namely, that "thought and expression are one," and that without the intelligent use of language as well as other modes of expression there could be no thought and no knowledge of any sort. Language is essential not to communication only, but also to the very formation of scientific propositions, theories, and doctrines. It is also indispensable to that dialogue of the soul with itself in terms of which Socrates conceived self-knowledge. Without it, in fact, the life of the mind would shrivel virtually to nothing. But the knowledge achieved by anyone who knows how to use any natural language (together with its attendant symbolisms) properly and hence discriminately is a knowledge of an enormously varied range of forms of expression (and thought) that serve to articulate and to guide corresponding forms of life. To know how to read and to speak a natural language is automatically to know what it is to participate in all such correlative ways of life.

Of course such understandings may be jammed, confused, impoverished by a prevailing rationalist ideology or culture. But they cannot entirely be destroyed by it. Men who know what it means to love God may be hobbled by a misguided semantics or theory of knowledge, or an ontology beset by preconceptions about "what there is." But the language they learn, and the knowledge thereby acquired, permit no further hobbling. Likewise, those who know what is said when the moralist, or the poet, or the politician says his bit, know and learn more than any rationalist ideology can undo. If an atheist learns the King's English he automatically learns in spite of himself what it means to pray. And if a Platonist learns the marvelous language of his forebearers, he learns more than tendentious Plato could try to make him unlearn.

I need go no further. Knowledge of a natural language continues a basic human culture in its own right, an ability to achieve many things that the rationalist always misunderstands or falsifies. Let me be more specific. The person who learns how to read the Bible, knows also what it can be to know or love God. The person who knows how to read Hamlet knows what it is to understand and appreciate a work of art. The individual who knows what a "person" is knows at the same time what it means to assume or to be assigned a role, along with the responsibilities and rights that pertain thereto. And the person who knows how we address another as "you" or "thou," knows what communication and fraternity, what contract and community are. Overstating the point in order to make it, I say: language is all. Or if it is not (and it is not), a statement of what the knower of a language really knows suffices both to confute and to enlarge the understanding of anyone who fancies himself to be a rationalist.

Of course the knowledge of a language makes possible many forms of achievement that are *not* intrinsically cognitive. Thus, giving an order, though it indeed presupposes and involves a considerable range of cognitive skills—including knowing how to give an order—is not itself a cognitive achievement. Not everything we do with words, by a very long shot, is to articulate or communicate something we know, even in the very widest sense of the term. Nor is every successful verbal expression or communication intended to convey a cognition. Yet one of the major ranges (or system of ranges) of human utterance is indeed cognitive. And cognition, in one form or another, is the proximate goal of a very great part of human expression and thought. In fact, my main intention in mentioning the centrality of the knowledge required for the use of a natural language is not only to show what other things are presupposed by linguistic skills, but to first of all set the stage for a review of the gamut of essentially cognitive activities for which the knowledge of a natural language prepares us:

(A) Understanding of a (natural) language makes possible, and is essential to, all forms of theoretical knowledge which the rationalist himself most saliently emphasizes; that is to say, general knowledge of matters of fact, and, no less important, those systematic bodies of such knowledge which comprise a theory or, more broadly, a science.

(B) Furthermore, it makes possible the basic modes of the formal knowledge that comprise logic and mathematics. And because the conditions of this sort of knowledge are not exactly the same as those required for general factual knowledge, or of the sorts embodied in the empirical sciences, the adequate understanding of a language at least introduces the user to the differential conditions required for formal logical understanding and for empirical knowledge.

(C) Understanding the roles and functions of a natural language also enables us to grasp the forms of knowledge concerned with the life of conduct and of action. In so doing it introduces us to the principles and ranges of practical reason. Here I must simply state what I believe to be the truth, that although these forms of knowledge do indeed involve and presuppose empirical factual knowledge, practical understanding is not reducible to the latter. In fact one of the ways of bringing out the differences between the latter and the knowledge involved in matters of action is through the sorts of desultory linguistic study to which so-called ordinary language philosophers have so usefully devoted themselves since the Second World War.

(C₁) Among the forms of knowledge essential to the life of action are first of all those comprised under the headings of want, desire, and interest. Rational action would be impossible if individuals could not know, or come to know, *what* they desire. And I consider it a very grave error on the part of philosophers in the tradition of Hume to set human knowledge generally in contrast or opposition to those forms of deliberation and action that determine, inform, and issue from desire. Knowing what one wants is a distinctive and often difficult human achievement, rendered all the more difficult by philosophies which systematically deny it cognitive status as such. But knowing what one wants also presupposes another preliminary form of knowledge to which Stuart Hampshire, among others, has called attention in his recent book, *The Freedom of the Individual*. This is the knowledge of the kinds of possibility which I shall here call "human" in order to distinguish them from logical or physical possibilities. Here I have space only to mention the knowledge of possible objectives as well as possible lines of action which one could pursue, or institute, if one chose to do so. This sort of knowledge, let me add, is an indispensable phase of that range of human understanding we call self-knowledge.

(C₂) Of course knowing what one wants, or could do if one wanted to, is only a part of what one needs to know in order to understand oneself or in order to engage in rational action. Here we may simply follow Kant in making a general but indispensable distinction between the knowledge of what is wanted or desired and the knowledge of what is good and right, of what ought to be and to be done (including what *ought* to be affirmed and said). All the same, I believe Kant to be mistaken in certain fundamental particulars as to the nature of the latter forms of knowledge. But again there is space here only to set out the barest mention of what I take to be the correct view. First is the knowledge derived from and dependent upon the employment of public standards and grading systems. Participation in such routine collective enterprises as various as going to market, getting an academic degree, passing an examination, or returning a bad egg to the waiter, all essentially involve both the knowledge of standards and the ability to apply them. Knowing what is good and bad is in very large part knowledge of just this sort. But it should be stressed here that one has not learned all that is involved and required in distinguishing between the good and the bad unless one also knows what it is to be involved in a grading situation, to perform grading operations, and not least to establish *and to modify* the standards by which things may be graded. By analogical extension, we move by stages from the simple knowledge of grades and of things as graded, to the knowledge—also essentially public and impersonal—involved in the understanding of institutions and the forms of activity essential or proper to them. Here in particular I have in mind the knowledge of what particular institutions and forms of activity are for, the ends they serve—in terms of which alone they are distinguished from one another as institutions. Here indeed, at a distance, there is much to be learned from the classical rationalist, and especially Plato himself. Among such forms of activity are the various arts and crafts, and indeed all the various disciplines whose principles must be known if one is to engage in or to obtain a competence in them. In many instances, it may be added, such knowledge would be difficult or impossible to acquire without formal instruction of some sort. For, also involved in full knowledge of a discipline is the understanding of its various offices, and of the distinctive responsibilities and rights pertaining thereto. All this knowledge is also entirely public and impersonal, although it has aspects which again radically distinguish it from the sorts of knowledge that are usually called scientific. Where Plato and Aristotle went radically wrong is in supposing that institutions and hence their constitutions are unalterable. Full knowledge of an institution entails a grasp of its history and hence its possibilities and directions of change.

(C_3) But of course no man is merely a bundle of stations and duties, and only the mythological organization man has solved the problems about what he should do with himself when he knows the institutions, the activities, and the responsibilities and rights pertaining thereto, in which his life is entangled. And if we use the term "ethics" in referring to the codes of right action which such institutional activities involve, then let us reserve the term "moral," here, for responsibilities and problems of conduct not covered by such codes. This way of putting the matter, however, may be misleading, for I do not mean to suggest that morality is simply what is left over after, so to say, we have done our various ethical sums and received the grades we truly deserve. In particular there are problems of "personal relations," which I conceive of as distinctively and crucially *moral* problems, that cannot be settled by appeal to any institutional or disciplinary principles whatever. Nonetheless, for each individual there *is* such a thing as moral knowledge—that is to say, the knowledge of what "I" ought to aim at and to do. And, correlatively, there is an irreducibly first-personal knowledge of moral responsibilities or obligations. This knowledge, as I have argued elsewhere, may itself be (and be called) objective. But this, precisely, does not entail that such knowledge is of the sort acquired by following either the public routines of the positive sciences or the lines of activity which our public stations and duties impose upon us. Objectivity is *not* the special or exclusive prerogative of public or of institutional life, not to mention the form of institutional life of which "science" is the inadequate summary name.

(C_4) But it is essential now to say something about philosophical knowledge. As I conceive it, morality is concerned with problems of personal relations and hence with problems of conduct concerned essentially with what we, as human beings, ought to do in our dealings with persons (including ourselves). But if all of us, *as moral beings,* are more and less than systems of stations and duties, so also are we as individual human beings more than persons. Our selves encompass and are not encompassed by our various personae; we also encompass and are not encompassed by our personalities as moral agents. I agree with Professor Frankena, although for different reasons, that what he calls the good life includes more than the moral life. But from my point of view the moral life and the moral problems which it involves are an inalienable part of the good, or at least the tolerable, life. Nor, on the other hand, do I conceive the good or tolerable life in terms either of ends set by our interests or desires, or even of their harmonious or inclusive satisfaction. For a tolerable life would involve, among other things, living or trying to live up to one's moral responsibilities, being able, as we say suggestively, to live with oneself. But a good life encompasses more than a life both of satisfied desires and of good conscience in the moral sense. For a good life must, in principle, provide some fulfillment or satisfaction of every range and dimension of the self. And this includes the fulfillment of those responsibilities which one sets oneself, simply as such, but which go beyond the range of personal relations. Here, for purposes of discussion, let me invoke the useful Protestant notion of the vocation or calling. Thus conceived, an individual self becomes involved, by stages, in a *life* and in a destiny that is peculiarly and poignantly his own. And the knowledge or understanding of that life, and of the vocation or vocations it commits him to is achieved only by many stages, not all of them moral. No one, I should argue, can finally know my vocation but me (and God, if God there be). Others may offer advice, which may and doubtless should be gratefully listened to—on occasion. But the knowledge their advice is based on or may embody is not, as such, the knowledge of what I am finally to be and to become. For it remains general and impersonal, a knowledge of human character and human nature, which, again, is at once both more and much less than a knowledge of myself.

What has this to do with philosophy? In the end quite simply everything. For if morality concerns the problems of first-personal relations among self-determining persons, philosophy concerns the problems faced by the would-be self-governing self in its great confrontations with its total environment and in its developing and cumulative efforts to discover for itself those modes of self-identification out of which it can make a life. The philosopher, who by definition seeks not just the wisdom of life in general (if such there be) but the wisdom of and for his own life, is driven precisely to raise all the limiting questions which the establishmentarian, the bureaucrat, and the functionary do not answer because they have neither a need nor a duty to ask them. For the latter, in fact, such questions are precisely meaningless, without point, silly. For the philosopher (and, of course, in some fashion everyone of us is a philosopher) however, they and his efforts to answer them are in a way his very life. And, conversely, his life is a series of *agones*: struggles, or arguments with himself whose ever-unfinished and unfinishable end is precisely that positive freedom to which (among others) Socrates and Spinoza, the great idealists, and, in our time, the existentialists, have all in one way or another aspired. This is why the dialogical form adopted by Plato, and recurrently employed and readapted by many philosophers since his time, seems so naturally to be the classical literary genre for the presentation of philosophical problems. It is also why, at a certain stage, it becomes necessary for the philosopher to move, as Kant for one so conspicuously did, from analysis to dialectic. For analysis offers only the elucidation of a distinctive form of words or symbols and its corresponding form of activity and life. Dialectic, however, is required when one moves beyond the principles that govern it to their ever unstable places in one's own scheme of things and hence to the claims they may rightly make upon one's own encompassing being.

Thus conceived, there can be strictly no such thing as *the* philosophy of science, *the* philosophy of art, or *the* philosophy of education, but only philosophies of science, art, and education. And these themselves become philosophies, or rather partial philosophies, only when they are eventually brought into dialectical relation to the other "philosophies of x" which concern one's life.

The analytic stages of philosophical inquiry do, or can, yield bona fide public knowledge, though properly conceived this can never be a purely empirical knowledge, precisely because the "object" to be known is not a pattern of physical change but a form of thought and action, a system not of phenomena, but of principles, rules, methods. But the philosopher, again, can never content himself with analysis; for having discovered, as he thinks, what the principles governing a form of activity are, he must then go on to ask normative questions about them which in the final instance are essentially first-personal. And if the answers he comes to are illuminating to others, this is only because they have asked analogous questions for themselves and find themselves involved in corresponding predicaments of their own. But each of us must finally discover the "essential facts" for himself.

Much more would have to be said of course to turn this rude sketch into a convincing portrait. If I am right, however, philosophical knowledge or understanding, like moral knowledge, can never aspire to become part of the cumulative, public knowledge which the rationalist so exclusively prizes and indeed regards as the paradigm form of human knowledge itself. But this means that philosophy, like morality (let me now add), like religion, literature and the arts, and indeed like all the humanities, when they go to fundamentals, presents educational problems, and particularly for formal educational institutions such as the school, the college, and the university, which are essentially different from those presented by the sciences.[8]

But before saying anything about these problems by way of a conclusion, let me express my own commitment to the humanities, not just as indispensable parts of a liberal education and of a decent or free life, but also therefore, as inalienable activities of a decent, properly free society. Or, rather, it is just because they are, as I view them, inalienable functions of a free life and a free society, that any tolerable system of public education must make them central features of its curriculum. And indeed, it is only when the sciences themselves are taught and learned in a liberal and philosophical spirit that they themselves become proper parts of that liberal education which is indispensable to free men and a free society. I will go further: Until the humanities, properly conceived, are again regarded as the very heartland of such an education, and a humanistic spirit is made to prevail throughout the whole educational system—especially and increasingly throughout its institutions of higher learning—that system and those institutions will remain inadequate to their occasions. Worse, when, as now, they are regarded as incidental studies, cultural adornments to be satisfied mainly in the form of a meagre and haphazard distribution requirement, or else are viewed like the sciences themselves as specialties for a few unchosen spirits who haven't the wits to do proper science, the educational system becomes a positive impediment to personal and social freedom.

Nothing could be educationally more subversive from the standpoint of a free society than a system of higher learning dominated by the aspirations—wholly legitimate of course in their own way—of positive science and scientific technology, i.e., of the spirit of rationalism. And in fact it is precisely in the closed and totalitarian society that the institutions of higher learning become nothing but institutes of science and technology. Make no mistake: in the Soviet Union, for example, the exact physical sciences, and the forms of education that serve them flourish as well or better than they do in so-called free societies. It is the humanities, and philosophy in particular that must go underground, if they are to exist at all in the totalitarian state. I have no doubt that there are true philosophers in the Soviet Union, just as I have no doubt that there are true philosophers wherever individual men ask limiting questions, however secretly, about "the system." And just to the extent that philosophers exist, the system is already broken, whether its masters know it or not. In a tolerable society, however, the system is broken in public.

But now a word must be said about the problems which philosophy in particular and the humanities in general present to the educator and especially to the formal educational institution. One may ask whether philosophy, as I conceive it, can be taught at all. And if in some sense it can be taught, the question remains whether it can be properly taught within the university. Let me say at once that no problems of special difficulty arise—up to a point at least—so long as one confines oneself to the history of philosophy and to the analytical philosophical preliminaries and prolegomena. Intellectual history generally requires skills which are no doubt beyond the reach of the ordinary political or social historian. Still, formal courses in intellectual history and in the history of philosophy, conceived as a branch of intellectual history, are taught, and well taught—up to a point—in many contemporary universities. Similarly, excellent courses in so-called analytical and linguistic philosophy are given in many universities and colleges. And the same is true of other humanistic studies.

It is also arguable that the only way in which philosophy can be taught is through its history. And the same may be said of other humanistic studies, including literature, the arts, and religion. I should argue, however, that the historian as such can never finally penetrate the heart of a philosophical work, any more than he can penetrate the heart of a work of literature, a musical composition, or a bible. And the reason is simply this: the matters to which such a work addresses itself are philosophical problems, and that if one has no philosophical impulses of one's own one cannot understand finally what it is all about, any more than a musicologist with a tin ear can understand what a string quartet is all about. Understanding here presupposes the possibility of first-personal appreciation, which requires a direct individual engagement and involvement with the object. In the case of philosophy, however, there is in a sense no "object" at all, but only a series of meditations which the reader or listener is permitted, for his own edification and use, to overhear. Or, to vary the figure, it is only the internal dialogue which the reader carries on with the philosophical work which is the true philosophical object. And until the historian is ready and able to conduct such a dialogue with Spinoza or Hume or Hegel or Wittgenstein he is inadequate to the work he seeks to study and to understand as a work of *philosophy*.

In philosophy, as such, the following stages can be regarded in principle as forms of learning. First of all is the task of learning how to read a philosophical work. This requires a grasp of its intention as a search for clarification and self-control on the part of its author. And this means that one must come to know what such searches and what results are to be expected from them. Here one learns and comes to know only by doing, that is, by entering directly and freely into the philosophical enterprise itself. This involves, for the reader, impersonating the philosopher one reads or listens to by asking or coming to ask his questions and struggling toward the answers he seeks and sometimes finds. But to read philosophically requires not only impersonation but, as I have already suggested, a continuing dialogical relationship on the reader's part to the work, to its questions and answers: that is to say, a questioning of the point and significance of the questions themselves, a demand for their further clarification, and a continuing struggle to make the questions one's own, or else, as is sometimes the case, to see why one must repudiate them along with their answers. As Moore once said, A large part of learning philosophy is learning what questions to ask. Another large part consists in learning what questions not to ask, what are merely pseudo-questions or show-questions that have no significance for one's life. Said Peirce in one of his profoundest *dicta*, "Dismiss make-believe!" But dismissing make-believe often takes a bit of doing. Moreover, one sometimes finds, as I have done, that one begins by making believe and ends by asking in dead earnest. Each person must finally dismiss his own make-believe. There is a sense in which the playfulness of Socrates is an essential part of his ultimate seriousness. Just because philosophy is, in part, a search for significant questions, it requires a touch of the child's play at raising questions. The question, Why? begins as a game, and ends, sometimes, as the puzzle of a life-time.

No doubt philosophy can, by various forms of indirection, imitation, and emulation, be learned. And no doubt the philosopher is, and must be, a supreme example of the autodidact. The question rather is whether anyone else can teach a man philosophy but the man himself. Here the answers are of great difficulty and my suggestions are made with diffidence.

Confining myself now to the ultimate aspirations of philosophers, rather than to the analytical preliminaries, I think one must say, first of all, that all philosophical learning and hence teaching must be at once informal and dialogical. And if, on occasion, the philosophical teacher "lectures," as I am doing here, he must try to impersonate his pupils by trying to anticipate their questions, by raising their difficulties, and by conveying the sense of struggle—the agony, if you will—involved in all genuine philosophical reflection. Socrates remains, in my view, the archetypal philosophical teacher, that is, one who teaches by asking leading questions, and then by forcing his "pupils" to question and requestion their own successive answers. All philosophical teaching is indeed a kind of spiritual midwivery. The philosopher does not and cannot teach by telling or even, finally, by explaining. Or rather, all his tellings and explainings are at best leading and exemplary. But even these will misfire without a plentiful and continual dose of the irony, including the self-mockery, of which Socrates was so great a master.

Now I must bring these remarks to a head and close. I do not mean to suggest that Socrates is the ideal teacher; in many spheres of learning his way of teaching is either impossible or immensely inefficient. There is a place for the pedagogue who teaches by telling and explaining, by formal demonstrations, and the rest. What I do contend is that philosophical education and the forms of learning and teaching possible and proper to it, is an indispensable part of any education that pretends to be liberal and that aims at the cultivation of free men and free minds for a free society.

What does all this really come to? It means, I think, that there are not and can never be an "objective" paradigm case of the philosopher, or a philosophical problem, even, indeed, of a philosophical activity. Philosophy is not a science, but neither is it an art. Philosophers want discipline, but not entrance into a discipline. There are, and can be, no principles of philosophy, in the way that there are, say, principles of logic or of physics. Philosophical principles, like moral ones, are at best or worst first-personal precepts, even when, on occasion, the first person happens to be not singular but plural. Philosophy in short is the indispensable free activity of the liberal mind and the free man. Its possibility is also a condition and a token of the free or tolerable society. And philosophical education, accordingly, must be an indispensable ingredient in any system of higher education proper to a free society.

One may go a step further. The informality of philosophical study, and hence of philosophical learning and teaching; its playfulness and seriousness; its imitativeness and its refusal to put up with imitation; its exemplars and undercutting of all exemplars and leaders; and finally, its aspiration to go beyond study to mature acts of self-commitment and self-creation offers, not a model for the good society or the good life, but a necessary dimension or aspect of a tolerable society and an endurable human life. Accordingly, it is because rationalism so totally perverts the philosophical spirit and aspiration that it must be exorcised not only from academic philosophy itself, but also, and for deeper, more fundamental reasons, from the implicit ideologies both of the university and of our contemporary polis in America. Or it must be exorcised if the American university is to be a truly liberal institution of higher education and if the American polis is to be, or to aspire to be, a society fit for free men.

As it is, I am bound to say, it is entirely problematic whether American universities—deeply interpenetrated as they are by the spirit of rationalism and the American social system, and overwhelmed as the latter is by the cant and by all the status symbols of a rationalist ideology —are very much better fitted than their "totalitarian" counter-parts to be the objects of a philosopher's piety and love.

NOTES

1. From time to time I will mention variant forms of rationalism. My purpose in so doing is in part to make it clear that rationalism, like all living ideologies, is not a static but a historically developing point of view.

2. It is on this point of course that Hegel differs from ordinary rationalists, as it is, also, a major reason for their disdain for his philosophy.

3. Henceforth it is these latter conceptions of the powers essential to scientific thought and understanding which will be emphasized.

4. Let me add that in my opinion it is largely owing to the pervasive influence of rationalism as an ideology both within the universities generally and also within academic departments of philosophy that existentialism has had little or no impact upon professional philosophy, despite the great interest of students in it. For a similar reason, the so-called informalist linguistic and analytical philosophy that stems from the work of the later Wittgenstein may now be seen for what it always had been: a mere episode in the history of academic philosophy in the twentieth century.

5. In practice, of course, there are *de facto* limitations which always make such a principle still more restrictive. For apart from the question of native ability, there is the problem of utilizable ability—of what, in view of their early nurture or "background" (economic, social, educational, psychological), individuals can manage to accomplish. In any actual, historical society, the working abilities of men so far as potential scientific understanding is concerned, vary and doubtless will continue to vary enormously. Many, perhaps most, men in actual societies, and certainly in our own, would be unable to make use of the sort of training Plato envisaged for the philosophers (guardians in the *Republic*). And it is for this reason that scientifically oriented educators, such as James Bryant Conant, have argued that the ideal of a university education for everyone is impractical, even in a society which could afford it.

6. Let me emphasize that I am aware that important qualifications of such a conception would have to be made in any full account, since a multiversity is precisely not a complete polis, and doubtless should not be permitted to become one. Even for the rationalist it remains merely *one* highly complex and indispensable institution within a still more inclusive and complex social system. I am also aware that most rationalists would themselves insist that there are corporate responsibilities which the multiversity cannot, and doubtless should not, assume in relation either to its individual faculty members or to its students.

7. The former, exemplified in certain military and business organizations, is pyramidal, involving chains and levels of authority and responsibility, that begin with the trustees and run down through the various offices of the president, the deans, department heads, professors, assistants, and so on. The latter, or functional type, is a class structure whose rights and duties are established by various specific functions or roles essential to the activities and the work of the university as a whole. It is in terms of this structure that the familiar distinctions between students, faculty, and administration are conceived, as well as the divisions of the faculties themselves into schools and departments, and the so-called liberal arts departments are arranged in the well-known trivium of natural sciences, social sciences, and humanities.

8. Of course, this as it stands won't do either.

THE AIMS OF EDUCATION
IN A CHANGING WORLD

Marvin Farber

I. The Present "Crisis" and Its Meaning for Education

No period has been more subject to change, and to an increasing tempo of change, than the present. All phases of our cultural life are affected; and education feels its impact in important respects. On this there is general agreement.

To some who view events dramatically it has appeared that there is a crisis in American education. To be sure, there are "hot" and "cold" crises. If it is true that we are now living in an age of perpetual war, it may also be said that there is a perpetual crisis—i.e., that there are problems related to the far-reaching social and economic changes of our social order, with understandable anxiety on the part of all concerned.

More concretely, people usually have a number of challenging problems in mind when speaking of a crisis in education: (a) problems related to the coming space age; (b) the Soviet and the Chinese challenge; (c) the growing population and the demands on the schools; (d) the need for achieving higher standards while providing opportunities for all; (e) economic recessions and their consequences; (f) recurrent interference with academic freedom; (g) the precarious future of private institutions; (h) the dual educational system, secular and religious; (i) the dismaying prospect, to many, of really overcoming segregation and realizing our avowed democratic purposes. The further realization, if not the survival, of the ideal of democracy is at issue. All aspects of the awareness of change converge on this question.

Nothing could be more absurd or futile than protesting against change. The real point is to do something about directing its course. The evasion of change may be left to the imaginative arts. Attempts to establish the unreality of time or change, while sometimes profound, and always subtle, turn out to be merely interesting intellectual exercises, mistaken at their very basis because they violate the first facts of experience.

The tempo of change is most rapid in the social order; and that tempo has been accelerated beyond all previous expectations. The importance of research as a necessity for survival in our competitive economic system has added impetus to the process. As a result, there has been more progress in science and technology in the present century than in the entire historical past. The increase in scientific knowledge and the technological advances of recent years have been instrumental in bringing about the new conditions which affect us educationally.

Some persons profess to stand bewildered in the presence of the enormous scope of human achievement. There has been talk of the inability of the imagination, which was so effective in the progress of science, to give us an adequate idea of the consequences of scientific progress. This has been suggested in connection with the dangers of nuclear warfare. Granting that it may be difficult to imagine the effects of the new weapons of destruction in detail, there are surely ways of pointing them out, with the aid of the imagination. There are no assignable limits to intelligence, or to any mode of experience taken in cooperation with the resources of intelligence. The possibility of the destruction of mankind can be understood, and represented graphically. The sources of intelligence by which the present conditions and dangers were brought about must be adequate for the means to convert dangers and misuses into positive benefits for mankind. There never was anything wrong with the human mind, except its misuses or its insufficient development. *Per se* the mind is potentially capable of meeting all problems. That must be the answer to all anti-intellectualism.

It is easy enough to accept change as a universal and all-pervasive feature of existence. But it may be far less easy to face it in a very limited area, especially if it affects one's own interests and the immediate social environment. A great altruism in general may go along with a selfish accommodation to changing circumstances in particular.

Much attention has been directed to the differences in our mode of living in the present scientifically conditioned age; and to the new requirements for understanding it, participating in it, and influencing its further development. The increase of automation, and the resulting new industrial revolution, have resulted in shorter working hours and renewed problems of unemployment. The demands for security and its safeguards have gone forward unabated. The heightened industrial development has been greatly intensified by international competition and the effort to attain leadership in the economic realm. Educationally that has meant recognition of the greater technical and scientific requirements in the natural sciences. But it has also meant recognition of the importance of the social sciences and the humanities. For the functions of education include the understanding of man and society; preparation for the enjoyment of our cultural offerings as well as the creative addition to them; and also, as a condition for the realization of all values, the assurance of physical fitness.

One should not focus his attention unduly upon the horizon of space, in this coming space age. It should be remembered that the pressure outwards has been due to the successful working of our industrial processes. There are always problems in our immediate environment, and they are the root-problems for mankind.

Although the tempo of change has been increasing at an ever more rapid rate, educational forms are resistant to change. That is the case with all social forms, as illustrated by etiquette, and in general by moral patterns of conduct. There is a good side to such resistance, and a disadvantageous side. Adjustment to all change need not be prompt and total, for there is always much to be preserved. No positive values should be lost if that can be avoided, in a period of adjustment to new conditions. However, established forms and practices may tend to act in the manner of entrenched interests, with a tendency to preserve themselves in the face of changing conditions. The old required studies of selected subject matters are cases in point.

The importance, in principle, of physical science as the basic level of science was recognized in former years. But the truth of the principle of physical unity, or of physical monism, was of more remote theoretical interest. Today that truth is attested to in a variety of fields. The old and much disputed issue of the reducibility of the human and organic to the physical now appears to be an antiquated issue, and one more stage in the effort to restrict the scope of scientific inquiry. On the other hand, the idea of a social physics is of less interest as an objective. Although it is theoretically defensible, the problems and concepts of the social sciences are less in need of physical analysis than of understanding on the social level of discourse and inquiry. Such problems as poverty and war are not in need of clarification through a social physics. They are accessible on the social level.

Broad equipment in the various areas of science is desirable in any case—for the general understanding of scientific methods, and for specialized work in a limited area. Suggestions and patterns of possible inquiry may be obtained from widely divergent areas.

II. On the Aims of Education

The course of our thought shows that it is not possible to go very far without raising the question of the aims of education. For all questions of educational principle and policy depend upon the aims which are acknowledged. The title "The Aims of Education" suggests the existence of a valid set of aims which should command acceptance on the part of all sentient beings. We are still far removed from that happy—or potentially mischievous—condition. In past history there were the dominant aims of education in fourth-century B. C. Athens; the aims of education as conceived by the Church in thirteenth-century Europe; or as conceived in America in 1860, or in 1960—whereby numerous regional differences, and differences within one region, are to be noted; and, there are the aims of education in Soviet Russia.

A factual type of question is in order, and it is one which can be answered readily: What is the source, and what is the justification given, for the aims of education in each of the many historical examples that could be cited? The dominant group or party in each case impresses its ideas and preferences on the educational process. Thus, antecedently accepted preferences or articles of faith have dominated entire areas, with philosophical justification advanced in an apologetic fashion. A dualistic view of man, the alleged inferiority of worldly existence, and the preparation for a life of the spirit, were among the beliefs and practices which were prevalent for centuries. The development of scientific methods and their increasing use were characteristic of the modern period. But that did not include a scientifically prepared or justified set of aims for education. Educational processes continued to serve the established interests in a given region. In a monarchy, special privileges were taken for granted. The first concern of the educational process was to preserve the established order of society. It was never to disturb the dominant interests.

Political and economic events, in part made possible by scientific and technical advances, ushered in a new era. The modern democratic state, along with large-scale industrial production, required a high level of scientific achievement. The sciences of nature were developed first, but only after centuries of resistance. The sciences of man were the last to be introduced; and there the resistance still is intense, for political and economic as well as religious reasons. There are still many, including some professors of philosophy and of education, who hopefully appraise difficulties encountered by scientists, with the thought that science may be contained therewith, and a place secured for traditional beliefs and interests. That the very aims of education are at stake is seen clearly enough when controversial questions of policy are raised—e.g., whether religion and spiritual values have a place in education.

It is desirable to see the ways in which the aims of education responded to social influences in the past, so that present influences may be more readily recognized. It is always the present that is being served.

Interests retained from the past are still present interests. Although the present alone is real, it bears features of the past out of which it has grown; and it prepares the way toward a future, with the values to be achieved defined with reference to present interests.

The aims of education are not to be discerned intuitively, as though they were axioms, any more than they are to be snatched from the sky. The same terms (happiness, justice, etc.) may be used in different historical contexts, but they are really variables and not constants in their significance and reference. If this applies to past historical systems, which moved relatively slowly, it is seen much more forcefully in the present period.

The sciences are developing so rapidly that one will never expect to meet a mathematician who knows all of the established mathematics, or any exponent of a flourishing science who commands all the knowledge of his area of scholarship. The development is so rapid that many mature scholars may not be able to adjust satisfactorily to new technical requirements for research in areas in which they had already proved themselves competent according to past procedures and standards. Consider, for example, the progress in biological and medical research, with the growing prominence of physical chemistry and biophysics, and the greater requirements in mathematics. This indicates the need for a sufficiently broad and deep basic training to enable scholars to undertake research with a greater readiness for change. Education for change is indeed a fundamental aim of education.

That does not signify any sacrifice of stability, or of individuality. Strictly speaking, there are no constants in reality, so far as the things themselves are concerned. All real things are variable; they are passing events. A person is variable in that sense. The concept of character suggests something unchanging, but the real person, with a character, is variable, and is an event exhibiting a pattern of behavior. The requirements of character do not include rigidity, although there are examples of rigid character. A character, or a pattern of behavior according to principles, involves a plan, an organization of goals and purposes; and also the capacity to react to a variety of situations.

A pattern or plan organizes the more stable features of behavior. The pattern itself may be subject to some degree of variation in the course of experience. Thus, if gaining a master's degree is the dominant purpose, there are numerous possible avenues of approach. If one selects physics as the area, frustration in that case will lead to another choice. A readiness for alternatives is an important requirement of character. An unswerving firmness is to be reserved for adherence to the principles applying to ethical values.

The fundamental principles applying to values in a given system—

say for the ethics of democracy—depend in turn upon voluntary commitments of individuals. We choose to regard all human beings as having equal rights to the fulfillment of their interests. We also choose to regard a greater amount of interest-fulfillment as preferable to a lesser amount. There is nothing absolute in such principles. History records tensions and conflicts in which such choices were fought out in actual practice, and can point out the increase in satisfaction and in achievement if they are realized. Most people, but not all, favor such principles. There is no element of compulsion in them. An individual may decide to accept or reject them as a matter of choice, although not in fact if they are embodied in a system of laws. The choices of the majority of the people will be decisive in the long run.

The quantitative test is applicable socially, as well as individually, in determining life-plans and plans of shorter range. Educational thinking operates in the light of such principles.

Briefly, they are as follows: The process of education is directed toward the realization of human values; and human values are defined in terms of the fulfillment of interests, desires, or needs. But not all fulfillments are desirable, as seen from the larger perspective of an individual's entire life, or of social experience. The test of quantity means that more fulfillment is to be preferred to less fulfillment. In order to achieve a greater amount of value, if not the maximum possible value, a dominant life-plan is required, along with subordinated partial plans, and with concrete goals. It is not possible to draw the line of the most desirable course for all persons. There are individual and group differences. It is surely desirable to attend as much as possible to individual aptitudes, needs, and desires, insofar as the values of the social system will allow. There is no antithesis between the individual and the group. Neither one is real without the other. But there is a basic principle to be borne in mind in all thinking about the values of democracy, the principle of the finality of the individual. The structure of the whole is conditioned by what happens to the parts. All subordination or sacrifice of parts for the whole must be most seriously weighed and justified.

The determination and choice of an educational plan for an individual is thus an instance of the determination of value plans in general. This perspective connects decisions concerning the choice of courses and vocational or professional goals with the general process of realizing human values. Concentration in biology or psychology, or a program in medical technology, would involve value-systems in each case. There is the value system of the student, and there are the value systems of all concerned by his action, directly or indirectly. There is a value equivalent, in the sense of the fulfillment or frustration of interests, in the case of every educational decision, just as there is in scientific research, artistic activities, or industrial operations. Wherever interests are affected there is a value equivalent, however difficult or even impossible it may be to quantify it.

In extreme cases these considerations may be brought to light emphatically. As a rule they are glossed over, because so many choices do not seem to involve far-reaching differences of value. The youth who aspires to be a dentist or a physician may, for example, be just about equally suited for numerous other vocations. The particular decision might be largely a matter of indifference for society. In the case of a disturbing imbalance of trained personnel, however, it becomes necessary to attract students to vocations in need—nursing, physics, etc.—in the interest of social values, if not in the national interest. The good of the whole becomes the final criterion. It is prior to the good of the individual on quantitative grounds, assuming the principle of equality.

All of this is clear enough for well-chosen examples. There are, however, many cases in which the path is not at all clearly marked out. It is possible, as a matter of fact, that one is never really able to determine accurately the value equivalent of an educational decision. The difficulty may lie on the side of the judgment of the factors affecting the student's prospects: his aptitudes or capacities, his motivation and character, and all the conditions (family, economic, social, health) that bear upon his success. There are always possible alternatives to be considered, in connection with the needs of society, and vocational advantages and disadvantages. Who would presume to speak with complete assurance on any of these factors?

If it is true that empirical knowledge is at most probable, one may never hope to speak with certainty about the educational career of any individual. A second Beethoven—i.e., a person with traits and capacities like those of Beethoven—might well be stifled, if not eliminated as a nonconformist, in some conscientiously administered schools. There is little comfort in observing that genius or talent will be sure to emerge. Sometimes it does, in the face of all obstacles. But one may well suppose that far more talent is submerged. It is hazardous to judge aptitudes and capacities in the arts, literature, mathematics, and other areas. There will be little doubt about the existence of an entire spectrum of degrees and kinds of ability. But how is one to decide in a given case, once and for all, if special reasons might be assigned for backwardness, or for greater apparent fitness? For practical reasons, decisions must be made, of course, to the best of our knowledge and judgment.

It is pertinent to ask whether we are doing all that could be done in critical areas of educational development and scholarship. A vastly intensified effort, for example, to raise the level of mathematical education, would require not only the more widespread introduction of logical analysis and a logical approach, but also sustained attention to the problems of individual students from early life on to the stage of college study. Such an all-sided effort could be expected to show impressive results. The amount of loss must be reduced, and there must be fewer cases of unfulfilled capacities, in so basic an area as mathematics.

Mathematics, like logic, should be introduced early in the educational process, to a greater degree than heretofore. Besides being a language, mathematics is an instrument, a tool of inquiry, and the way to the formal structure of reality. All regions of reality have their mathematical (or logical) structure. That structure is determined progressively, with adjustment to the complexity of the subject matter. The mathematics of physical nature is relatively far advanced, as compared with the mathematics of human nature.

Many sciences, and ideally all sciences, require the understanding and control of an increasing amount of mathematics. With regard to the future, in which physical science is bound to play an ever greater role, the satisfaction of this need amounts to a primary aim of education. This is true for practical reasons alone, as students of chemistry, physiology, and social science already know so well. It is also important theoretically, in that it points the way to the conception of a unified science.

Logic provides the basic analysis which is so essential for mathematics as well as for science in general. Although much still remains to be done for educational pruposes, recent work in logic has become effective as an instrument for analysis, and as a theory of inquiry in the broadest sense of the term. It is the traditional function of logic to provide a critical theory of methods of inquiry, and it is well suited to serve as a unifying element in the curriculum. Despite its growing prominence, it must be said that the educational use of logic is still in its beginning stage.

In the democratic philosophy, equality means equality of right to the fulfillment of one's capacities and interests, insofar as that is possible on the basis of the social system. There is no denial of the existence of a great diversity of capacities, aptitudes, and interests. In the trend toward spreading democracy to include all persons who are willing to participate, attention should never be diverted from the smaller number of highly gifted students. The swinging pendulum of educational change is illustrated by the way in which emphasis is placed upon the superior student in one period, and is followed by the widespread effort to spread educational values as far as possible among the population. But the one does not exclude the other. Both objectives should be included in the aims of education. Honors programs should never be discouraged in favor of a general educational program, or for any reason connected with the realization of democracy. For democracy does not imply sameness of level of achievement; nor does it rest upon any dogma of equality of capacity.

The occurrence of such an easygoing dichotomy shows how difficult it can be to entertain two ideas at the same time. It seems to be either an elite group of preferred honors students, or democratic education of the great majority of the people, as though they were exclusive alternatives. The recognition of individual differences and ability levels does not signify the neglect of anyone. The greatest possible self-realization of individuals can only be achieved within the limits of a social system; and there is room for an endless diversity of capacities, subject only to the needs of the social system. Furthermore, the classification of types of ability is not to be represented by a straight line, or by a single line. It is much more complex, for a high rating in one area may go along with a low rating in other areas. In an abundant economy such as ours, intensified efforts toward the education of specialists in selected areas need not imply the neglect of nonspecialists. Nothing less than adequate attention to the needs of all students, and all people, will suffice for a democracy. The error of an easygoing dichotomy lies in its oversimplification, and in the implied mutual exclusiveness of the alternatives. The correction is achieved through the appraisal of the positive merits of each side. It is hardly necessary to point out that the general interests of society are best served by including special attention to the development of the most gifted students.

Viewed strictly, we have no choice but to serve the social order in which we live. That does not mean simply accepting any historically conditioned form, or, as may be, any dislocation of that order. The example of the rise of Nazi Germany in the place of the democratic state of the second *Reich* illustrates this point. What was called "Politische Wissenschaft" was intended to take the place of "objective science," i.e., science called "political" in the interest of Nazi Germany as conceived by a certain ill-fated group of individuals. To accept the aims of education in that way would bespeak blind fanaticism or intimidation, or at best a shortsighted opportunism.

If the passive acceptance of aims from a dominant group, whether insurrectionists or gradual emergents, is to be justified, it is necessary to consider value principles. The basic conception of democracy, viewed philosophically, must itself be justified. It can be justified in terms of experience, in terms of its consequences, and in terms of the voluntary commitments of the great majority of the people. The important thing to be noted is that nothing may be taken for granted implicitly. To paraphrase John Locke, no value principle may be cited, for which a man may not rightly demand a reason. This applies to all the aims of education. Nothing short of an ethical and social philosophy of education, logically presented and implemented, will be satisfactory. It must be a philosophy that will stand the test of experience, of all the consequences for society and for individuals. The maximum of fulfillment and the minimum of frustration will be borne in mind as general criteria in the judgment of value systems.

The aim to prepare individuals to fit into a social order is thus in need of qualification. Students must be helped to become dynamic members of society, capable of participating intelligently in constructive movements toward the improvement of society. The democratic framework is only a general structure providing for the preservation of society and for the possibility of improvement. The problem of the realization of the values of democracy is a never-ending one. At no time can it be said to be complete.

This, then, falls to the aims of education: not only to preserve or to serve our social order, but to continue the process of change in a way that will lead to the realization of the greatest possible amount of value. Education has not only a conservative function. It also functions for progressive reform, which in the course of time may accomplish far-reaching change.

If individuals could determine with finality all that they need or desire, or the things in which they may be interested, a convenient yardstick for measurement could be constructed. The fact is, however, that needs, desires, and interests are variables in more than one way. Some desires increase as they are satisfied, such as the desire for drink, whereas others suffer from satiety. What a person needs will vary in different circumstances. In a simple economy, on the proverbial desert island, food, water, shelter, and basic security are the primary needs. In an economy such as ours, the need may be for mink, or a Rolls Royce, or it may be for the enjoyment of music by Chopin. The problem of setting up workable criteria is not hopeless, however, for one can operate with statistical knowledge of normal desires and needs in a given social system, as viewed with the aid of experts in the relevant fields of knowledge. A complete system of needs or desires is out of the question, and is really unnecessary. One can operate initially with needs that are present in every culture system, such as the need for food, or for security, even though such needs are construed differently on different levels of technological development.

It is possible to portray what would seem to be the maximum of satisfaction of needs in a given historical period. The existing social relations are always somewhat removed from that ideal, sometimes far removed from it. One thinks of "what should be" on the basis of "what is." Norms, ideal goals, or ends, are read out of existing conditions, and are projected into the future as aims. The aims of education are rooted in present conditions. They must also be forwardlooking, and concerned with the greater realization of human values.

Current interest in the aims of education is influenced by new international conditions, as well as by scientific and technical progress. Never has the goal of the maximum achievement of value been so close as at present; and never has the possibility of the extinction of mankind been more real. An aim underlying all other aims must be the restoration and preservation of peace as a necessary condition for all human activities.

Finally, some mention should be made of synthesis as an educational aim. It is important to insure a significant common denominator for all mankind, while allowing for flexibility and change. That must include a broad view of all world cultures, attending to their peculiar differences as well as to their common elements. Unity plus diversity is, in short, the goal. Above all, a twentieth-century synthesis must be methodological in character. The main principles of inquiry must be imparted in a concrete as well as in a general form. These principles of procedure are to apply to all phases of the synthesis, just as they do to all phases of science and experience.

For practical reasons alone, it would be too much to expect to have a convenient synthesis outlined for the educational process. Every synthesis is "dated," and has its own time. In any case, the student must undertake studies in the various divisions of scholarship, and become acquainted with their methods of inquiry.

There is no unanimity of opinion concerning methodology. There is, rather, warfare to be noted among the various schools of thought; and there is usually no lack of internecine strife in any group. Complicating the scene are idealists, dialecticians, positivists, phenomenologists, existentialists, fideists, and naturalists of various types. It is, nevertheless, true that the logic of scientific method suggested by the actual procedures of the sciences is sufficiently established to meet the needs of education. Diversions and confusions of antiscientific writers can readily be met by logical analysis.

III. On Education for Democracy

It is pertinent to recall the work of a Presidential Commission on Higher Education,[1] which was concerned with bringing, to all the people of the nation, "education for a fuller realization of democracy in every phase of living; education for international understanding and co-operation; and education for the application of creative imagination and trained intelligence to the solution of social problems and the administration of public affairs." The welfare of the people was taken to be the criterion; and the improvement of our democracy was taken to be "one of today's urgent objectives for higher education." Instead of leaving "education for democratic living" to courses in history and political science, it was proposed that it become the primary aim of all classroom teaching and of every phase of campus life. In education for democracy, the first goal was regarded as the full, rounded, and continuing development of the person. The discovery, training, and utilization of an individual's talents was declared to be of fundamental importance in a free society, and the furtherance of individual self-realization was called the greatest glory of democracy. Our colleges and universities were called upon to aim at graduating individuals who have learned how to be free. That requires the development of self-discipline, and ethical principles as a guide for conduct. Sensitivity to injustice and inequality, and high social aims, were to be combined with specialized information and technical skill. In short, "teaching and learning must be invested with public purpose."

It is necessary to render such ideas concrete, in terms of the social realities and economic facts. There should be actual mention of the types of injustice and inequality that present problems in our social order. It must be admitted that authoritarian regimes have known how to perfume themselves with highsounding generalities, with eulogistic language. The term "high" is sometimes one of those terms. It may mean exactly what the *status quo* in a given country would have it mean.

Certainly the Presidential Commission's work was significant in emphasizing education for democracy and for international understanding, and in urging that patterns of education be devised that will prepare people more effectively for responsible roles in modern society. Colleges were admonished to find the "right relationship" between specialized training and the transmission of a common cultural heritage toward a common citizenship. That relationship could not be fixed for all purposes and times. Neither could it be something concrete, as a stable item in the curriculum. It would have to be expressed in terms of variables, so that adjustment could be made to changing conditions in scholarship, and with respect to the needs of society.

In general, the Presidential Commission touched upon crucial matters, although they were characteristically abstract or general in their formulation. They can only be applied to the extent to which society is ready for them. In their extreme form, conceived as fully realized, they constitute a regulative program, a set of directives or ideals. The emphasis is upon "the person," upon freedom of thought and action, upon the use of intelligence and knowledge for problems of human relations, just as they are used for problems of the physical world: [2] this emphasis has a ringing appeal and causes no misgivings, so long as it remains abstract and general. If applied concretely to social issues, however, there will surely be strong repercussions as vested interests are affected.

The idealism of the Presidential Commission was, however, tempered by reference to the abilities and capacities of students. A question to be answered was, How many have the ability for mathematics, or physics, or logic, etc.? The Commission believed that at least 49% of our population has the mental ability to complete fourteen years of schooling; and at least 32% of our population has the mental ability to complete an advanced liberal or specialized professional education.

Care must be taken in all group estimates, and in the firm judgment of an individual case. Teaching methods must be considered. The premium usually goes to those who are quick to learn at a given stage in their development, especially in the sciences. A slower period of preparation might salvage many students with a sufficient potentiality. As in the case of the arts, some take to their studies quickly, whereas others will be slow, plodding, and experimental. There are cases of genius that might never have emerged if an early selection of students had been enforced. Biographies of persons of great achievement will give ample evidence for that statement. They include writers, philosophers, and political leaders. Informed flexibility should be the aim, and a sufficient basis for multiple choices should be provided.

IV. On Organized Education: The Curriculum

No discussion of educational objectives would be considered complete without at least mention of the liberalizing effect of the educational process. All studies in the curriculum may contribute toward broadening the view of students, and are in that sense liberal.

It is sufficient to look back to the recent past, to be reminded of the enormous changes that have occurred. Harvard College in 1860 will do very well for that purpose. Professor George Herbert Palmer gave an account of Harvard education as it was, when, in 1860, he entered as a student:

Harvard education reached its lowest point during my college course . . . Nearly all its studies were prescribed, and these were chiefly Greek, Latin, and Mathematics. There was one course in Modern History, one in Philosophy, a half course in Economics. There was no English literature, but in the

Sophomore year three hours a week were required in Anglo-Saxon. A feeble course or two in modern languages was allowed to those who wished it. There were two or three courses in Natural Science, taught without laboratory work. All courses were taught from textbooks and by recitations. Though lectures were announced in several subjects, among them English literature, not more than half a dozen of these were given in a year. Professor Cooke, it is true, lectured to the Sophomores an hour each week on Chemistry. But though we were all required to attend, there was no examination. All teaching was of a low order . . . Such a curriculum—and it was no worse than in other colleges—would seem to have been arranged by a lunatic and to be valuable only as preparing the way for an Eliot. . . .[3]

The way was prepared, of course, not only for Eliot, but for the Lowell plan of concentration and distribution and the later emphasis on general education.

In American education generally there has been evidence of a kind of swinging pendulum: from a "frozen" curriculum reflecting traditional conceptions of higher education, there was a gradual development of freedom of election, with recognition of individual interests and differences. Carried through to its logical outcome, that meant recognition of self-realization as a goal for an individual, and social realization as the goal for society. Certainly there was only a very partial approach to that objective. The emphasis on a common core-curriculum for the realization of social aims served to correct the shortcomings of an individualistic emphasis. Any notion of relative fixity or stability of a core-curriculum was soon to be corrected in accordance with the needs generated by the competitive position of America in recent world developments. Whatever remains of sameness in the curriculum becomes sameness of pattern, with differences in most details.

The curriculum must be not only comprehensive, but always responsive to the growth of knowledge and the needs to be met. But a narrow conception of utility might be dangerous. It is understandable that national interests lead to the support of projects promising practical results. What is at issue is not the desirability of practical results, but rather an enlightened, as opposed to a narrow, view of the practical, the point being that pure inquiry may unexpectedly have concrete results. The implication for educational policy is obvious. To the extent that an educational system can afford it, there should be unrestricted opportunities for research and training in all fields, including so-called pure scholarship. It is sufficient that a scholar be interested in a line of inquiry to justify its pursuit (to be sure, after immediate needs have been met). There is bound to be a waste of effort in many cases. Like vivisection, where not every sacrifice of animal life may be justified by results, much pure scholarship may well be deposited in the unused archives of human effort. I recall the case of a Ph. D. candidate, whose thesis was finally accepted with the observation that he had succeeded, with great pains and diligence, in proving something that interested nobody. That was of course true at the time, and not necessarily true for the future.

A large degree of freedom is needed in the election of courses if the aims of research are to be met. But more than that, the peculiar interests of students should be recognized as much as possible, within the frame of educational planning. It is important to insure understanding and training in a wide distribution of areas—from Egyptology to Chinese history; from ornithology to musicology; etc. Correspondingly, there must be offerings of courses and tutorial instruction in the greatest possible number of areas, to keep alive the skills and continued scholarship that may be necessary for national and international interests.

It is the function of a college or university to retain from the tradition, to serve all possible interests of the present, and to help to lay the basis for change, leading to unknown conditions in the future. Just as it would be impossible to anticipate all future needs, it would be unreasonable to seek to impose all the lines for future change in society. The complex function of institutions of higher education, integrated with the elementary and secondary schools, requires a great diversity of offerings, and the encouragement of widespread selective interest in them.

As is well known, the desirability of students doing useful work for society as a proper part of their educational experience has been advocated in America, and in Russia as well. The educational value of such experience will be granted. In a country in which more and more can be produced in less and less time, as in the United States, there is surely no need for the productive efforts of students, unlike a backward country, or one less highly developed industrially. But the educational argument remains. It is for the good of the student, to participate in constructive activities for the sake of society; and that means ultimately, for the good of society.

A similar consideration applies to social and political activities. Closer contact with the organized forces and movements of society would be desirable in the process of education for citizenship. The classroom would thus be brought into direct relationship with social realities.

So long as one speaks of society and the student in abstraction, all of this is very good. If one makes application to Nazi Germany, or to Perón's Argentina, however, the contact with social and political movements takes on another form, a form that would surely put an end to all that is envisaged when one speaks the language of democracy. But it is also fair to point out that social and political experience with unpopular minority groups in America would not be likely to be generally approved by educators, or by representatives of well established interests.

V. On Plans and Program Making in Organized Education

Adjustment is extolled by many as an educational aim. A passive acquiescence to all conditions could hardly be meant, however. It is inviting to suggest that adjustment be assimilated to direction as the aim. But empty generalities should not be made to be slogans, purporting to be guidance indicators. Concrete cases and facts are called for. Under some conditions, maladjustment would be defensible if not imperative, as in the case of neglected interests reacting against special privileges. Viewed constructively, if one is not to accept conditions in which there is needless frustration and loss of value, his interest must be in a program of action, in direction.

In the process of organized education, a plan or program is of central importance. The alternative would be aimlessness in the extreme form, or at least the danger of lesser achievement in the absence of intelligent reflection. Aimlessness, whether complete or partial, and directed organization are the alternatives.

The fundamental importance of having a plan was recognized by Aristotle in his ethical philosophy. A "logos" or plan was necessary for the development of character. Organization is always directed toward an end, which may change. There may be a dominant end, with some elements of choice; or there may be organization toward an end with almost total absorption, and with suppression of diverting interests. Some plans are determinate in the light of an accepted philosophy, for example other-worldly, or Aristotelian (the "vita contemplativa"). Most pertinent are the variable plans, flexible as far as possible, and always subject to alteration. There are, however, practical limits to the degree of experimentation that is possible, for individual and social reasons. An excessive number of changes of objectives, or of means, might result in failure.

A plan should be justifiable in terms of the needs and values of society. A social system with a relatively great degree of technical mastery over nature can afford to allow greater freedom to individuals. This is expressed abstractly and ideally. In reality there are economic and social forces that restrict the range of planning of most individuals. But one may nevertheless ask for the ideal justification of any plan of action in terms of the values of society, on the basis of the democratic principle of equality.

The fitness of an individual for a given plan is another matter. An individual may have the necessary aptitude, and may also desire the goal in question; or there may be aptitude without desire; or desire without aptitude. The remaining case of the absence of aptitude and desire may be neglected, even though it is not without exemplification.

There are difficulties in all directions. It is often impossible to determine the appropriate plan and goal for practical or factual reasons. But it is necessary to approach a determination as closely as possible. The answers to questions involved can only have a probability value, although that will be sufficient in most cases. If it is admitted that all empirical knowledge is more or less probable, one cannot expect to rise above probability in this context of problems. Dogmatism and unfounded assurance must be ruled out, although firm decisions must be made if anything is to be accomplished.

Practitioners in advisement must have patterns and principles for guidance. It is similar to psychiatric or psychological advisement: the normal and the desirable are considered in relationship to the human material involved, and the social demands and opportunities. Although each case of advisement is an individual one, in the last analysis, the study and judgment of individual cases must always be based upon group knowledge and the nature of social needs.

A plan may be dominated by one direction of interest, in one of the areas of organized knowledge; or the goal may be economic success, or a career as a writer. The specialized absorption so prominently illustrated in music is at one extreme (the narrow Paganini type, or the Wagner type, requiring broader training). At the other extreme are those without a dominant direction of interest. The burden is placed therewith on a broad program of education, to allow for future choices.

There are relatively constant and variable factors in program making. A common denominator is always indicated, as a minimum, in logic and mathematics, the sciences, and the humanities. If there is any unity, it must be the type of unity which characterizes science in general—*collective unity*.

The selection of a dominant, over-all educational plan reflects national interests. This is clearly seen in the case of Soviet Russia. Soviet Russian is contrasted with American education in Korol's book on Soviet Education.[4] In America in 1956, a year used for comparison, there were 17 college students per 1,000 population. In Russia there were fewer than 7 per 1,000. But for engineering students the ratio was 2:1 in favor of the Russians. The latter also trained a greater number of students in science and technology and in some other professional fields. Except for political "Party" work in Russia, there is no desirable alternative to professional work, because of the prestige and economic advantage involved. Korol suggests that there is a preference in Russia to encourage study "in a politically neutral direction," in "politically safe disciplines such as mathematics and the physical sciences." But surely the centralized national encouragement of the study of mathematics, physical science, and engineering is sufficient to account for the great upsurge of students in those areas. Whatever Russia was to accomplish industrially had to be achieved quickly; and that motive was reinforced by military and tactical considerations.

Fears have been expressed [5] that "we have almost lost the battle for scientific manpower" (Benjamin Fine, quoting Dean Dunning of Columbia University's School of Engineering), and that, in the words of Dr. Edward Teller, ten years from now the best scientists will be found in Russia. No doubt the purpose of such judgments is to stimulate greater scientific activity.

It may be reassuring to reflect that vocational skill is not "true" education: [6] If, as Faust expressed it,[7] "it is the fundamental purpose of education to develop as fully as possible the range of . . . reflection upon our beliefs and ideals," spokesmen for the educational systems of all other countries would be likely to claim that they are doing just that. The appeal must then be to objective analysis, which faces the difficulties of empirical knowledge as well as the dangers of one-sidedness and bias.

In the selection of students in the various special fields, positive motivation should be relied upon as far as possible, and compulsion reduced to the minimum that may be unavoidable. Complete freedom is an empty ideal. But complete compulsion would be worse. It is convenient to speak of the greatest possible amount of freedom, as judged in the light of social needs. But one must make clear the nature of the social needs, since society is not an undifferentiated unity. In short, we must talk about concrete social realities, and all criteria must be clarified and justified. The criteria cannot be simply read out of existing dominant preferences. For the preferences must themselves be justified, or at least critically examined.

What is an acute need at one time—say a shortage of engineers—may be met quickly by strenuous measures. The same holds true for other cases of a shortage of professional workers. But a flourishing society could not be made up of technical workers alone. There is really a shortage of effective workers and scholars in all fields. A highly developed and complex society needs a great diversity of specialists. It also needs the greatest possible number of people to be grounded in a broad distribution of areas of training and scholarship, to help to meet future needs. No areas should be neglected. There should be no "lost" arts, sciences, or skills. A way should always be open, through adequately trained scholars, to the cultural traditions of the past and cultural movements of the present. The capacity to react successfully to changing conditions is enhanced by breadth of education, as well as by specialized training. Engineers are indeed necessary. But broadly informed engineers are preferable to narrowly trained specialists, i.e., engineers capable of further study, inquiry, and adaptation; and also possessing a grasp of social problems, and a logical approach to human values.

What has been said about engineers, who can be increased in number when the need arises, could also be said about botanists, linguists, or psychologists. Such needs may be met without throwing the entire social and educational system off balance, provided that there is the necessary depth and breadth of training in enough cases. Temporary imbalances could thus be corrected by diverting persons toward the fulfillment of new needs.

In short, specialization does not necessarily oppose or preclude generality of knowledge, insight, and training.

VI. Underlying Philosophies of Man

A philosophy of man is presupposed in all talk of values and education. It is obviously a science-oriented philosophy of man that has been prominent in the present discussion.

On the other hand, one-sided philosophies of man have abounded. It will only be possible to indicate one type. That current complex of many strands, popularly called existentialism—a name that will suit practically any purpose—brings together motives of faith and reason as well as idealism and realism, with a conspicuous element of anti-intellectualism. Prominent in the literature of existentialism is a marked anti-scientific tendency, manifested through hostility to a naturalistic philosophy of human existence. The sciences have presumably missed some highly important things, which are to be corrected readily, regardless of the scientific competence of the philosopher concerned. Thus in the drive toward specialization man was divided among the various sciences, so that parts of man were treated without regard to the whole man. Whole man specialists appeared to be called for and, presto, there was a rapidly increasing number of existentialists. Publications purporting to be existentialist education have begun to appear. My recent books on Naturalism and Subjectivism [8] and Phenomenology and Existence [9] took account of the philosophical aspects and background of existentialism. It will only be possible to appraise existentialist educational thought when it is carried through in terms of a philosophy of values and human society. An early example of the existentialist approach is seen in Ulich's Fundamentals of Democratic Education (1940), with its talk of mystery and the limits of science. The existentialist tendency proves to be the historical successor of the old-line idealists and anti-intellectualists, opposing above all the scientific view of the world as the basis of a philosophy. But the prestige of the sciences is not to be undermined by writers sniping at their admitted incompleteness and their cautious, qualified claims.

VII. Consequences of Change and the Challenge to Education

By way of summary, but with some concluding formulations, a final glance at the consequences brought about by the new "space age" will now be in order.

(a) There has been a tremendous extension of our spatial boundaries, with the impact being felt increasingly in numerous contexts—scientific, philosophical, economic, and educational.

(b) The vestiges of anthropocentrism have received a further and perhaps final blow.

(c) There is now a new perspective for viewing human concerns.

(d) There are, along with the opening up of unlimited horizons and the solution of problems arising therewith, further steps in the solution of problems regarding the preservation of life on this earth—medical, scientific (physical and biological science), technological, social and political, and psychological.

What had begun to look like a shrinking, contracting economy has speedily shown frontiers of boundless expansion. The old mode of staking claims has been changed. The old way would now appear ridiculous. Philosophers of the traditional school of speculative idealism placed themselves firmly on the "ego" and sought to account for the world. If the evolutionary perspective opened up by 19th century science did not succeed in fully disposing of that view, 20th century advancements have succeeded in doing so with finality. Man, the risen animal of evolution, is engaged in increasing his homeland indefinitely. He knows that no matter how far he proceeds, he will still be indefinitely removed from a vision of all existence. He will always be a finite part of an infinite—or indefinitely great—whole.

(e) The smallness of man, as a minute part of existence gradually extending his horizons, is counteracted by the recognition of the remarkable achievements that have so greatly improved his position in the cosmos, with promise of vastly more to come. The smallness of man, and his greatness—especially his potential greatness—are two themes that can be argued equally with truth.

(f) Science is the key to the problems now opening up more fully. More science, much more, is needed. The ideal would be the elaboration of a true *mathesis universalis* or a universal science realizing the ideals of the great rationalists of the modern period. That is an endless task. The completion of science is as unthinkable for us as would be the closure of time and space.

(g) There is nothing wrong with science *per se*. Neither has scientific progress occurred too rapidly in recent time, as some have feared. Man need not tremble in the presence of his own creations. All man-made problems should be capable on principle of being solved by man. This emphasizes the need for greater attention to the social sciences, as well as the humanities. For their proper development, the social sciences and humanities must be accorded the degree of freedom of inquiry now given to the natural sciences in so many places.

(h) Scientific progress presents unlimited opportunities for human value. But science is construed too narrowly if all aspects of human activity, and all forms of knowledge, are not included. All the sciences are unified by means of the concept of inquiry: natural, social, formal, and philosophical.

(i) The motivation for education is always derived from a historically conditioned social system. Its forms and processes are further developments of what has been inherited from the past. Even its strong reactions against inherited forms are indebted to those forms. What education is, and what it can accomplish, depend upon the prevailing scientific level. It is vitally dependent upon a scientifically oriented conception of man, and is bound to be adversely affected by reactionary, antiscientific beliefs. The generalized scientific philosophy that is indicated therewith extends all the way to the philosophy of values, as well as to the determination and justification of the aims of education.

(j) No matter what happens in the recesses of space, the human individual remains the social unit for the realization of value. All criteria are directed to the individual, in the last analysis. A society is a collection of individuals and groups of individuals, with behavior traits peculiar to the collection. Individuals remain the units of reference, although their behavior patterns involve the whole complexity of a social order. To further the interests of mankind is the ultimate aim of education. Everything that can be said about the potentialities and hazards of the new scientific age must be assessed in the light of this aim. All talk of the maximum achievement of value, of the justification for pure research, and of multiple educational offerings, derives meaning from this principle. The "substance" of human value is at the same time the "substance" of the educational process.

(k) A final consequence of the rapidity of cultural change may be noted, and it is easily one of the most important. It is clearly impossible to provide the educational basis for future change, including the requirements of scientific and technical progress, in one brief period of formal education. There must be a continuing process of education. Opportunities must be provided for review, as well as courses to assist more mature students to assimilate newer techniques and scientific advances in all fields. Furthermore, research work of an advanced grade must be encouraged, whether beyond the Ph.D. or its equivalent in achievement, or simply in response to problems at any stage of a person's development. College education is thus only an early stage of a long-continuing educational process. Surely there can no longer be any patience with superficiality in college education. There must be an effective understanding of the basic sciences, to be followed by a never-ending study of the progress of science and technology. That study should always be enlightened by the understanding of the social consequences of scientific progress and the long-range aims of education. Nothing less than that will be sufficient to meet the challenge presented by our changing world. To state that challenge in educational terms is at the same time to point the way to a constructive answer.

NOTES

1. Gail Kennedy, editor, *Education for Democracy* (Boston, D. C. Heath and Co., 1952).

2. T. R. McConnell, in, *Education for Democracy*, p. 109.

3. G. H. Palmer, in his "Introduction," in *Contemporary American Philosophy* (New York, The Macmillan Co., 1930), V. I, p. 20.

4. Alexander G. Korol, *Soviet Education for Science and Technology* (New York, John Wiley and Sons, Inc., 1957), pp. 398 ff.

5. *Cf.* Korol, *op. cit.*, p. 408.

6. Clarence Faust, quoted by Korol, *op. cit.*, p. 406.

7. *Ibid.*

8. M. Farber, *Naturalism and Subjectivism* (Albany, State University of New York Press, 1968). *Phenomenology and Existence* (New York, Harper and Row Torchbooks, 1967).

A LOOK AT EDUCATIONAL PHILOSOPHY

Samuel B. Gould

To paraphrase Adlai Stevenson, I am occasionally given to believe that an educator is a philosopher who approaches every question with an open mouth. While I might agree that this human condition plagues more of us than we generally concede, I would hope that no educator or university administrator comes to his tasks empty-handed in terms of philosophic substance. Without it, he is indeed not an educator at all. He becomes—to steal a term from our pop-culture—a "noneducator."

The whole educative process must begin with certain basic assumptions, the first of these being self-knowledge. Those who are truly educated find the experience not only exhilarating, but also come to it with enormous humility. Two thousand years ago, Epictetus asked the question: "What is the first business of one who studies philosophy? To part with self-conceit. For it is impossible for anyone to begin to learn what he thinks he already knows."

As Aristotle said, learning is always accompanied by pain, and if there is anything I as a practitioner of education can bring to this forum, it is to reaffirm that to both the taught and the teacher, the act of acquiring an education in the true humanist sense has rarely been more painful than it is today. Why this should be so is not too difficult to see. One of the fundamental philosophic assumptions in American education is the perfectability of man. It proscribes an attitude of the mind and the spirit, of what Whitehead called "the climate of thought." Much of education today is the product of Jacksonian rather than Hamiltonian thought, and its philosophic milestones are Franklin and Jefferson, Barnard, Mann and Dewey, and the social reformers of the early twentieth century.

But do these traditional philosophic assumptions about the purposes of American education still hold? Does the possibility of the per-

95

fectability of man still inspire us to believe in the perfectability of society? It is a cruel fact of the twentieth century, I think, that the first no longer assures the second. Education, Aristotle said, must first of all serve the purpose of preserving the state: "That which contributes most to the permanence of constitutions, is the adaptation of education to the form of government." One of the primary and pressing obligations of educators in the present day must be the constant questioning of this basic assumption, whether the socializing of the young does indeed still lead to the preservation of the present society. Surely, we have arrived at a time when the complexities of our total environment force upon each individual a kind of philosophic self-reliance, without which the lot of men and women in the twenty-first century may become quite unbearable. One of the causes of student discontent is the philosophic schism between what they perceive to be themselves and their view of society over which they have little or no control.

I think Richard Goodwin described this philosophic dilemma very well. "There is one central cause to our condition," he said. "It is the fear of the individual that he has become meaningless in the great human enterprise. Decisions of peace and war, life and death, are made by a handful of men beyond his reach. Cities and factories grow and spread seemingly powered by a force beyond the control of man. Our science describes our world in terms we cannot understand, reaching past the limits of ordinary understanding. Computers and marvelous machines," Goodwin continues, "seem to make man unnecessary—even in his oldest stronghold—his work."

If we regard the end of education as more important than the means—a view adhered to by educators and philosophers alike—what then does modern education prepare us for? Will self-knowledge alienate the student still further from life as it is really led, or will he discover the kind of philosophic and intellectual assimilation which often goes these days by the name of "educational relevance." Take, for example, Plato's concepts of the curriculum, and match these against the pressing and cold realities of the present day: Speaking of the study of dialectic, Plato said that "when a person starts in the discovery of the absolute by the light of reason only, and without any assistance of sense, and perseveres until by pure intelligence he arrives at the perception of the absolute good, he at last finds himself at the end of the intellectual world."

It is questionable just how many of our young men and women finally arrive at Plato's "perception of absolute good." But some do. What do we as educators have to say to them about the fruits of their having searched for—the truth? For our present generation, does truth indeed make them free, or does it merely isolate and cause retreat and withdrawal? Is it surprising that in many of our nation's colleges the philosophic curricula and the classics are run on threadbare budgets? Nor is there a great stampede of students to classes on Aristotelian logic. No fat government funds flow into the coffers of departments of philosophy. But perhaps philosophy thrives best on poverty.

And yet, having stated the worst, I believe that philosophy contains at the same time the very seed of a new vitality and relevance to learning. The purity of dialectic thought must always stand as a fortress against the compromises and arrangements of modern life. Rarely has there been a time when the humanizing of each and every individual acquired a higher priority on the scale of human survival.

Man, in the isolation of his human condition, must have that buttress of philosophical continuity. All else may otherwise be lost. If the teaching of philosophy to our present generation is to take on meaning, it must succeed in giving the young their own perception of their moral and intellectual goals, goals which reach far beyond the turmoil of the present, and which must in fact lead straight to the continuity of man and to his civilized spirit.

Viktor Frank, speaking of his experiences in a Nazi concentration camp, writes about this very philosophic cornerstone: "Any attempt to restore man's inner strength in the camp has first to succeed in showing him some future goals." Nietzsche's words, "He who has a *why* to live for can bear almost any *how*" could be the guiding motto for all psychotherapeutic and psychohygienic efforts regarding prisoners. Whenever there was an opportunity for it, one had to be given a *why*—an aim—for their lives, in order to strengthen them to bear the terrible *how* of their existence. Woe to him who saw no more sense in his life, no aim, no purpose, and therefore no point in carrying on. He was soon lost."

There continue to be other forms of concentration camps. There continue to be all kinds of lost men, unprepared and unarmed because their spirit resides in a philosophic vacuum. Plato's account of educated man's ascent from the cave into the sunlight is perhaps too simplistic a view today. There are now too many caves, and too many openings leading to Truth. It is up to us as educators to interconnect the caves and unite the openings which lead to the light.

The university is one of the few places left on earth in which this search continues. A university must be a citadel of both mind and soul. When it forgets or is diverted from either of these two elements, an incompleteness results that damages the future of all who come under its influence and therefore the future of the world. It is the only place where ideas can be born and nurtured honestly, impartially, frankly, un-equivocally; it is similarly one of the few places where matters of the spirit can be sustained and given strength. Unless great minds are accompanied by great hearts in the academic leadership, the university can easily become mechanistic in its outlook and oblivious to human needs. It must be a place where new intellectual vistas are opened and exciting discoveries emerge from dedicated scholarship; simultaneously it must be a place where man learns to recognize his inner and better self, and to use that better self as an instrument for the shaping of an enlightened society.

These two elements within this citadel are particularly important to the undergraduate student in the university. Unless he has food for both mind and soul, he emerges from his experience inadequately equipped for his next steps of specialization. He runs the danger of being powerful in intellect and yet puny in understanding. He runs the danger of never having grasped the importance of undergirding knowledge with appreciations and aesthetic sensitivities.

The development or lack of development of individuality in youth has had its share of attention as education has been criticized. A great cry has been that we must beware the perils of conformity, and I would agree that real dangers lie in this direction. But equally real dangers lie in the development of an incompleted or arrested kind of individuality —the kind that never gets beyond the consideration of one's self. Education can take part of the blame for this, but not all. The family can be given a share, too, in its frequent inability to establish values in early life which will withstand the tests and challenges of time. This is, after all, a primary function of family life. But it has more and more been shunted off on the educational system, which was intended to test and strengthen values, not to originate them. Too many young people arrive near the end of college life, therefore, with an interpretation of individuality that has little relevance to life outside themselves. Even when we realize that such absolutist views will give way in time, we still wonder at how little our educational system seems to have achieved for these young people in leaving them so far short of wisdom. What sorts of personalities have touched them, and with what irrelevancies have they been concerned? Henry Murray, Harvard professor of clinical psychology, has much to offer on this point:

To tell the truth, individuality as a value, as a boast, as a stead for pride, strikes me, in certain moods as naive, shallow, and pretentious. It lacks the depth dimension. As an ideal it plays a strategic role, no doubt, during those years in a young man's life when he must discover his own nature, select a vocation appropriate to his talents, and, in so doing, grow in a differentiated way out of the family husk in which he was imbedded and out of the collodial matrix of his adolescent peer group. But, beyond that, it is too apt to lead on to illusory self-inflations, false poses, and counterfeit aggrandizements, tumors of the ego. The individualist says 'I' with a special stress and accent. 'I did this,' 'I did that,' always 'I,' as if he had never come upon the fact that he could not do any of these things without the participation of nature and also, in most cases, of other people. It does not seem that he has ever humbly acknowledged that he is pretty nearly powerless vis-à-vis his own body and vis-à-vis the greater part of his personality and mind. He is not able to decide that the heart shall keep on beating. He is not able to decide that a plentiful supply of energy and enthusiasm will be available next morning. He is not able to decide to fall in love. He is not able to decide that fresh and significant ideas shall spring to mind to enliven his conversation or to advance his thought. He cannot choose to choose what he will choose. From first to last he is utterly dependent for his being, for the capacity to sense, feel, think, and act, for the delight of living, upon the perfect orchestration of billions of uncontrollable, irreversible, and inscrutable goings on within him. And yet his objective knowledge of these facts does not bring him round to wisdom. He takes it all for granted: accepts it without reverence, without gratitude, and without grace. The fault, as I see it, lies in a kind of hydrocephalus of the ego. The ego shouts 'I am the master of my fate!' and a minute later one tiny embolus slits the thin-spun life and puts an end to all that nonsense.[1]

Murray remarks that in the past individuality was based on a "commitment to an ideal bigger than itself, whereas today it is founded on the refusal to accept the yoke of any such commitment." He goes on in a more positive vein to say that individuality is something to be built for the sake of something else. It is a structure of potential energies for expenditure in the service of an idea, a cultural endeavor, the betterment of man, an emergent value. "Individual self is made only to be lost— that is, only to pledge itself to some enterprise that is in league with a good future, and thereby find itself once more, but this time as the actor of a living myth, an instrument of culture."

The point is, therefore, that one necessary experience on the pathway to a mature felicity and to a full-grown individuality is full acknowledgment of our utterable and unutterable dependence upon nature and all that it contains, and upon each other. Acknowledgment of this in one's very marrow gives rise to wonder, awe, reverence, gratitude, and hope. Individuality emerges as an ideal only after one has acquired conscience, character, and the habits of consideration and seriousness. An educational philosophy that encourages such individuality and the creativeness it engenders is to me a proper one for America, but one that ignores this or misinterprets it can do infinite harm.

We know that in the pattern of educational diversity we follow in America, a university can be many things to many people, things good and things bad. It can be a center for sociable activity or a center for social consciousness; it can be a hunting ground for a husband, a deterrent to military service, a convenient headquarters for doing nothing; it can also be a proving ground for effective living, a setting for meditative thinking, a fountainhead of wisdom; it can be an encourager of skepticism or a bulwark of denominationalism; it can make monsters or it can make men; it can reconcile and strengthen values or it can destroy them; it can develop pseudo-individualists or it can nurture the free, creative mind mature enough to see that its freedom and creativity must inevitably be directed toward society as a whole rather than toward an inward and egotistic satisfaction.

The citadel of learning we try to build must have room for both the intellect and the spirit. Man's achievements are charted by carefully reasoned plans and logical discoveries; they are consummated with the most far-reaching consequences, however, when reason and logic are stimulated and inspired by deep and even tremendous emotional forces, forces that stem from the inner yearnings and transcendent dreams of the individual. I fervently hope that in the future of the American university there will be a new awakening to this realization.

Whatever else can be said about the present condition of the university, it is certain that the future of the university is very much wrapped up in the future of philosophy as a continuously relevant intellectual concern. At this very moment, we suffer in American intellectual life from a new kind of philosophic disorientation. The gap between the ideology of modern man and his actuality widens even further. We need to build the bridges. And if the liberal arts are in disrepair, can the sciences be far behind? We must put our intellectual house in order because, as the Israelis discovered during their recent six-day war, the alternative to victory is oblivion. It is the kind of secret weapon which may work for us all. If an educator as a practitioner has anything to say to philosophers these days, it is that we cannot allow philosophy to be entombed. It must be interwoven into the educational process all along the line.

Here we may learn something from history. Many times in human affairs new and powerful forces emerge at the very time they seem destined to descend into oblivion. I am reminded of a quote by Alfred North Whitehead when he said that "we might as well have had the Industrial Age in the time of Archimedes; everything necessary was known; the only things lacking were tea and coffee. That fact so affected the habits of the people that the Industrial Age had to wait centuries until people in Scotland watched their kettles boil and so invented the steam engine."

We need not remind ourselves that the kettle boils today as it has never done before. Out of it may emerge another kind of steam engine, an engine of new philosophic thrust for the twentieth century, resounding throughout our house of intellect, and bringing sense and direction and peace to a strange and unrelenting world.

NOTES

1. Henry A. Murray, "The Meaning and Content of Individuality in Contemporary America," *Daedalus*, 87, No. 2 (1958), 39.

RELIGION

ON GODS AND GARDENERS

John Macquarrie

The title of this paper contains an obvious allusion to John Wisdom's well-known essay, "Gods".[1] That essay considers whether the existence of God can today be considered as an experimental issue, and the issue is proposed in terms of a parable: "Two people return to their long neglected garden and find among the weeds a few of the old plants surprisingly vigorous. One says to the other, 'It must be that a gardener has been coming and doing something about these plants.' Upon inquiry, they find that no neighbour has ever seen anyone at work in their garden. The first man says to the other, 'He must have worked while people slept.' The other says, 'No, someone would have heard him, and besides, anyone who cared about the plants would have kept down these weeds.' "[2]

Most of us are familiar with this opening part of John Wisdom's argument, and we regard it as a useful parable for elucidating the traditional argument between the theist and the atheist. This argument took the form: "Is there or isn't there a being beyond the world who laid it out in the first place and still cares for it?"—just as a gardener might lay out a garden and then continue to maintain it in an orderly form. But what we less readily notice is that the dispute between the two men, as Wisdom reports it, takes two fairly distinct forms. They begin by returning to their neglected garden, and the question at issue is whether or not a gardener comes to tend it. But only a page further on, the argument is presented differently, for now the one man says to the other, "You still think the world's a garden and not a wilderness." [3] Now the argument is not about a gardener who may or may not come and tend the plot of ground, but about the character of this plot of ground itself —whether or not it is a garden. As the argument proceeds, it seems to me that it assumes increasingly the second form. It is less and less an argument as to whether there is a gardener, and it becomes more and more an argument as to whether the world displays such a character as would permit us to call it a garden or whether it must be reckoned a wilderness.

Furthermore, it seems to me that this change of ground that takes place in Wisdom's argument is very much like the change of ground that has come about historically in the disputes between theists and atheists. There was a time when the dispute concerned the existence or nonexistence of a being external to and independent of the world, but a being who had nevertheless started off the world in the first place and still looked after it. But nowadays, at least among the more sophisticated theologians and philosophers, the issue is different. It is a question whether the world has one character or another, represented in Wisdom's parable by the images of the "garden" and the "wilderness."

Does this mean then that the atheist has triumphed in the dispute? I think we have to recognize here that atheism has many forms, and that any particular form of atheism is relative to some form of theism. The earliest form of belief in a God or gods was mythological, that is to say, the god was supposed to be a kind of magnified person who might appear bodily in the world. We read that Adam and Eve "heard the sound of the Lord God walking in the garden in the cool of the day." [4] But nowadays none of us would expect to find that kind of evidence of God. We have all become atheists as far as gods who walk in the garden in the cool of the day are concerned. It is worth remembering that, according to St. Justin, some of the early Christians were accused by the authorities of atheism, and they were indeed atheists from the point of view of those who believed in the gods of classical mythology. Of course, the traces of mythology in the oldest parts of the Hebrew scriptures were in course of time superseded by more sophisticated notions of God, and the great Hebrew prophets would have utterly denied that one could see or hear God in any direct or literal fashion. In the philosophical Judaism of Philo of Alexandria, we are told that "God can be grasped only through the powers that are subsequent to his being, for these powers do not present his essence but only his existence from the effects resulting from it." [5]

Philo is in effect saying that there is no point in waiting around in the hope that some day you may see the gardener. There is no gardener of that sort. Our attention is directed instead to the garden itself, and there, Philo claims, we will see features which point to the existence of the gardener. But this gardener is very different from the old mythological gods. The new gardener is rather the God of metaphysical theism. He was conceived as another being, out there beyond the world, sovereign and self-contained, so that most theologians have argued that he either could have made the world or refrained from making it, and that the creation is thus external to him. It was this second kind of gardener, the God of classical theism, whose existence was debated in the disputes of recent times between theists and atheists. But now this kind of gardener too seems to have become an unnecessary hypothesis, and the earlier, elaborate natural theology is universally acknowledged to have fallen into great difficulties, if it has not indeed become completely disintegrated.

But the dispute has not ended. People still go on arguing about the character of the world, even if they no longer wish to infer from this character to the existence or nonexistence of some being beyond the world. The two men in Wisdom's parable go on tracing their conflicting patterns, even after they have given up supposing that any argument can establish the existence of a gardener. It seems to me that this argument concerning the character of the garden itself is a new phase of the old argument, and that we may rightly regard it as the continuation of the dispute of theism versus atheism, though both of these positions have undergone major transformations in the course of history, first from the mythological way of thinking to the metaphysical, and more recently from the metaphysical to what we may call the "ontological," as it is a question about "the way things are."

Classical theists, of course, always spoke of the immanence of God as well as of his transcendence, though indeed it was his transcendence that was usually stressed and a bias toward immanence was suspect as pantheism. It seems obvious that if one abandons the thought of God as another being out there somewhere, then the stress must be much more on his immanence. Yet this would not necessarily lead to the abandonment of some idea of transcendence, though a transcendence that appears as a dimension within the world or within history.

It would seem that differences of belief about the character of the world or about "the way things are" can be quite meaningful and can be in sharp opposition to one another. At the one extreme there is the view that the world is essentially absurd and frustrating. An absurd world is indeed a godless world. This position has probably found its most powerful expression in recent times from some of the French existentialist writers, such as Sartre and Camus, and we might regard this as the classic form of contemporary atheism. The opposite extreme holds that the world makes sense, that it is going somewhere, that it is not indifferent to human aspirations, and perhaps some such beliefs as these constitute the core of a contemporary theism. This seems to be approximately the meaning of Schubert Ogden's claim that "the primary use or function of the word 'God' is to refer to the objective ground in reality itself of our ineradicable confidence in the final worth of our existence. It lies in the nature of this basic confidence to affirm that the real whole of which we experience ourselves to be parts is such as to be worthy of, and thus itself to evoke, that very confidence." [6]

When the difference between theism and atheism is presented in this way, it becomes clear also that there would be many intermediate opinions between the extremes, some tending toward atheism, some toward theism. If we think of a thoroughgoing atheism as meaning that one regards the world as totally absurd (godless) and as utterly frustrating man's quest for reasonableness and value, then perhaps very few people have held to this view—indeed, it is hard to see how one could live with it for long. Perhaps Camus and Sartre came near to it, but we see in both of these writers a tendency to move away from extreme assertions of the meaninglessness, oppressiveness and pointlessness of the world. This does not mean that they cease to be atheists, but it does seem to indicate, as indeed Camus himself stated, that we try to break out of nihilism and look for at least some limited areas of meaning that will make human life more supportable and hopeful. But at the opposite end of the scale, there must be equally few people whose confidence in "the way things are" is complete and unshakeable. The naïve optimism of a Browning—"God's in his heaven, All's right with the world"—strikes us not only as credulous but even more as insensitive in a world where there is so much suffering and waste. The view of Leibniz, that this is "the best of all possible worlds," is not easy to believe, and if one were to believe it, it might induce a complacency and lack of sensitivity that would be just as paralyzing to moral effort as the despair of one who believed in the sheer unrelieved absurdity of the world.

Actually, most people are between these extremes, and it is on this spectrum that the conflicts of faith and doubt take place. Faith is not knowledge, while doubt is less than sheer denial. Certainly, one could not simply draw a dividing line through the mass of humanity, with theists on one side and atheists on the other. There are atheistic elements in belief, and certainly in Biblical faith with its powerful abhorrence of idolatry; but likewise there are elements of belief in atheism.

Where, for instance, would one place the Marxist on the spectrum of which I am speaking? In so far as he believes in a dialectic of history constituting an objective pattern of events and in so far as he entertains eschatological expectations concerning a goal toward which history is moving, his position is very distinct from that of the extreme atheism which denies any meaningful patterns in history. Yet, on the other hand, since the Marxist thinks of the historical process as determined by subpersonal factors, whether material or socio-economic, his position is also very different from that of the religious believer, who holds to belief in a providential ordering of history that cannot be understood in less than personal terms.

There are many relativisms, and theism and atheism do not present us with an absolute disjunction. We have always to ask: What kind of theism, or what kind of atheism is intended? Yet the words "theism" and "atheism" are meant to point to a genuine distinction, and while this distinction may not be so clear-cut as it was supposed to be when people held more naive ideas of what is meant by the word "God," the distinction is a real and important one, and it should not be blurred but it needs rather to be clarified. Thus I think we ought to dissociate ourselves from the tendency nowadays for one side to try to annex the other. In a well-known article, Alastair McIntyre began by saying about the Bishop of Woolwich's book, *Honest to God:* "What is striking about Dr. Robinson's book is first and foremost that he is an atheist." [7] He then went on to claim that Tillich, Barth and most other contemporary theologians are all really atheists. The opposite tendency can be seen in writers like John Baillie, who claimed that atheists are really believers at heart, and in Karl Rahner who seems ready to bestow the honorary title of "anonymous Christian" on just about anybody! But there are real differences among these people, and our business is to try to see what the differences are. It is not helpful to assert that the other side really believes the same as you do, but is too confused to see this.

I expressly say that there are "real" differences here, and by that I intend to rule out the explanation that all we have here is a difference in the way people *feel* about the world. Wisdom, of course, makes the same point. The two men in his parable do in fact feel differently about the plot of ground, but he insists that this difference goes beyond the way they feel. Although both men see the same garden, they see different patterns or absences of patterns, and they continue to dispute about these.

If we are to clarify what the dispute is about and how the difference between theism and atheism is nowadays to be understood, then it seems we can do this only by saying more clearly what we mean by the word "God." So far we have quoted Ogden's statement that the word "God" is used to refer to the objective ground of our confidence in the final worth of existence. This statement makes it clear that there are two fairly distinct semantic poles in the word "God"—I might call them an "axiological" pole and an "ontological" pole. The axiological pole has to do with the notion of worth. The word "God" is not a purely descriptive term. It carries with it an evaluation. Language about God is therefore self-involving, and this is one reason why such language is colored by our feelings much more than language about some quite neutral and more or less indifferent fact. To argue about the existence or nonexistence of God is much more self-involving than to argue, let us say, about the existence or nonexistence of plant life on Mars. But then, I say that the word "God" has also an ontological pole of meaning. It does not just point to some highest value, but claims that this is somehow rooted in the way things are, in the objective structures of reality. Actually, the atheist and the believer may sometimes be committed to very similar values. Where they differ is in their beliefs about the ontological status of these values. So we come back to the point that the difference between them is deeper than just a difference about the way they feel toward the world. Perhaps we should add further that it is more than just a verbal difference. It is not simply that some people use the word "God" to integrate and organize some of their experiences and aspirations, while other people use a different language. The person who uses God-language is convinced that this language expresses a belief about reality, and that this belief could be right or wrong.

It is obviously this ontological pole of the meaning of the word "God" that stands most in need of clarification. What "real" difference, if any, is implied in the theistic as opposed to the atheistic view of the world?

Since we have already said that God does not seem to be some *other* entity, beyond or above or outside the world, then have we perhaps conceded that there is no real difference between the theist and the atheist at all? Or can we develop more intelligibly the suggestion whether by "God" we don't mean a gardener but rather something about the garden itself—that which constitutes it a garden rather than a wilderness? What would this be? And could we consider it a difference in *reality* if it is not another thing or person or distinct entity?

Perhaps we should first of all make a reservation. If God is real and if God-language is a meaningful language, then this reality of God is unique and cannot be subsumed under any of the ordinary categories of thought. Theologians have usually, in principle if not in practice, recognized this, and acknowledged that their concepts must fall short of what they are trying to talk about, so that their language has an oblique character. The theologian agrees with the positivist in recognizing that there are limits to language. Julian Casserley has recently written of positivism that it is "a kind of baffled mysticism." [8] However, while the theologian admits that our language is incapable of making direct literal statements about God, he would hold that we can find images and concepts which light up something of the mystery of God, so that we are not reduced to complete silence about him. Thus when we take up the task of trying to clarify the meaning of the word "God" in its ontological sense, perhaps the best we can do is to adduce certain concepts and analogues which, we may hope, tell us something of the meaning of God language, but certainly could not yield a concept of God comparable in clarity to, let us say, our concept of a tree or any other entity that we can examine within the world.

Could we get some clarification from thinking of God as the *form* of the world? I am using the word "form" here in something like its Aristotelian sense. I do not mean just a static shape or configuration, but, as it were, an active *Gestalt* that expresses itself in the world-process. Traditional philosophy has sometimes talked of the soul as the form of the body, and it would be in an analogous way that we might think of God as the form of the world. Of course, we immediately notice that this is no more than an analogy, for the physical world is certainly very different from the human body. Nevertheless, religious imagery has in fact very often pictured God as "spirit" or "life", and these are not substances or independently existing entities, but rather forms in the sense in which we have used this world.

To use the notion of the form of the world as an explanatory model for thinking of God would certainly depart, I suppose, from the notion that God is completely independent of the world and that he created it at will. We are acknowledging in fact that God is inseparable from the world, that he is not a gardener who can come and go but is rather the form of the garden. Yet we are not on the other hand simply identifying God with the world in a kind of pantheism. To speak of him as the form of the world is to combine the notions of transcendence and immanence, and again the soul-body analogy may be helpful.

Let me now turn to a second concept that may help in clarifying the nature of belief in God. This is the concept of *meaning*. To believe in God is to believe that human existence is set within a wider context of meaning. Of course, the concept of meaning is itself a highly complex one, and we use the word "meaning" in a variety of senses. When I talk of a "context of meaning," I have in mind something that makes sense, some ordered unity or whole that also confers significance on all its constituent parts. The opposite case would be an absurdity, a chaos, something without any *rationale* or directedness.

Of course, as we noted already, perhaps no one could get along believing in the sheer absurdity of the world. He would look for at least some limited areas of meaning, or he would try to create these. Here again we seem to strike a difference between the atheist and the believer. The atheist would say that such limited areas of meaning as there are, he has himself constructed, whereas the theist would claim that he discovers meaning that is already there and has a ground independent of him.

We must notice too that when we talk of discovering meaning, we must be intending something more than just the regularities of physical nature (though perhaps these raise a question of their own). Alfred J. Ayer was surely correct when he wrote: "If the sentence 'God exists' entails no more than that certain types of phenomena occur in certain sequences, then to assert the existence of a God will be simply equivalent to asserting that there is the requisite regularity in nature; and no religious man would admit that this is all he intended to assert in asserting the existence of a God." [9] The reason that no *religious* man would allow that this level of meaning alone could be properly designated "God" is, of course, that the word "God" has also its axiological pole. God is called "God" only if he is worshipful. Hence the context of meaning that one has in mind would need to be on the personal and historical level, as well as on the merely natural. Bishop Robinson expresses the point by saying: "He can trust the universe not only at the level of certain mathematical regularities, but at the level of utterly personal reliability." [10] Matthew Arnold's way of speaking of God is worth pondering: "[A] power not ourselves making for righteousness." This, in turn, is perhaps close to the thought of God that finds expression in the Hebrew scriptures—a directedness in history that by and large supports man's moral development and enhances the meaning and dignity of human life, yet in no simple or unambiguous way, as the Book of Job so clearly reminds us.

A third concept that helps to clarify what we mean by God is the concept of *Being*. God and Being have long been closely connected in philosophy and theology. I am well aware that persons of nominalist tendency find this word "Being" of doubtful validity. It seems to me that the difficulty is compounded by the sheer accident that in English we have only one word, "being", to stand both for the present participle and the verbal noun of the verb "to be," whereas many other languages have two quite distinct forms. Latin distinguishes *esse*, Being as the act or power of existing, from *entia*, the beings or the things that actually are. Similarly Greek distinguishes *to einai* and *ta onta*, and German *das Sein* and *das Seiende*. God, as we have repeatedly said, does not seem to be another being; but is he not rightly described (as St. Thomas thought) as Being, that power or principle of existing that is exemplified or manifested in all the beings, the things that are? The notion of God, or of Being in this fundamental sense, arises in response to the question: "Why beings rather than just nothing?" The words "God" or "Being" do not indeed *answer* this question as a question of fact might be answered. But these words do point us to an awareness of the mystery— the "wonder of wonders," as Heidegger calls it—that there are beings and not just nothing. Even if all the questions of science were answered, we might still raise a question about the world itself. This is what Wittgenstein had in mind in his famous utterance: "Not *how* the world is, is the mystical, but *that* it is." [11]

We may note there the close connection between mysticism and positivism. Our language seems to be fitted for talking about the *how* of the world, about the beings, but can we do anything other than remain silent about the *that* of the world, the mystery of Being itself? Julian Casserley has described positivism as "a baffled mysticism," as we noted earlier. But mystical theology often seems itself to be a baffled positivism. I refer especially to the negative theology. Since Being or God does not fall under any of the categories applicable to things in the world, it might seem that we can say only what they are *not*. We can say that Being is *not* a being; that it is *not* a property; that it is *not* a class; that it is *not* the sum of beings. It cannot indeed "be" any of these things if it is unique, and answers an entirely different kind of question from the "how" questions concerning the beings within the world.

But does the negative theology do any more than establish the "otherness" of that which we designate by the word "Being"? Does it afford any real clarification of what we are trying to talk about, or does it not make it plain that "Being" is an empty word?

In practice, theologians have never been content with the *via negativa* alone. If Being is indeed wholly other to the beings (and in this sense transcendent) one must also assert that Being is known only as it is exemplified and manifested in the beings (and in this sense, it has immanence). On the basis of the immanence of Being in the beings, the various kinds of symbolic and analogical language have been constructed. The theologican claims that of these analogies, the most adequate is that of a self or person, though this would remain an analogy. The self is not another thing or substance added to the body (as the old-fashioned substantial soul was sometimes supposed to be) but is rather another dimension for existence that constitutes a new kind of unity and meaning. Similarly we may say that God is not another substantial being in addition to the world, but is rather that depth of the world's existence that lets it stand out from nothing, that lets it be, that confronts us with a world rather than just nothing.

But the description of God as Being requires the same kind of reservations as we made in exploring the concepts of form and meaning. "Being" is itself a neutral word. Sartre can talk very well of the meaning of Being, and indeed he provides a classic elucidation or evocation of what is meant by "l'être" in his novel, *La Nausée*.[12] But Being, as it is disclosed in that novel, is undifferentiated, massive, oppressive sheer "is-ness," that could not possibly be called God. It might rather be called demonic. Once again we have to note that the word "God" is an eval-uating word, adding to the notion of Being, the further notion of that which elicits worship and commitment.

If we allow that such notions as form, meaning, Being, help to clarify what is intended when one speaks of a theistic or atheistic view of the world, we have still to ask about the way in which people come to hold the one view or the other. The later part of Wisdom's essay indi-cates—rightly, I believe—that the difference is one of interpretation. Neither the theist nor the atheist has access to additional facts that are hidden from the other, but they pattern their facts in different ways, so that one sees the world *as* a garden, the other sees it *as* a wilderness. To see something *as* something depends on the way the various items in what we see are configured and interrelated in the way we see it.

But it seems obvious too that the theistic or atheistic stance is not reached as the result of a kind of calculus, whereby we balance against each other connections and lack of connections supporting the one view or the other, and finally accept one or the other. The truth is that the world always remains ambiguous, and although people can argue as long as they like, tracing their rival patterns, they will never establish conclu-sively the case for one interpretation or the other. For this reason, the religious believer talks of faith. He has committed himself to a way of understanding himself and his world, and he may think this is a reason-able way and that there are evidences to support it, but he will also ac-knowledge that there is a leap beyond the evidences and that faith is not a guaranteed certitude. He will also say, however, that man's finitude demands precisely that we must commit ourselves beyond what can be certainly known, and that we are doing this all the time, for instance, in our moral choices.

The two friends in Wisdom's parable have taken up their respective stances before they begin their argument. How then did they arrive at them? It seems to me that what usually happens is that some limited pattern of events or facts impresses itself upon us so strongly that we take it as a paradigm for the whole and try to interpret the whole in terms of it. This, I think, is what is pointed to in the believer's talk of "revelation." The revelation may be a historical event or a person or something else exhibiting a certain character which, the believer be-comes convinced, is illuminating for the character of the whole. Basil Mitchell's parable of the resistance fighter and the stranger [13] expresses this side of the matter very well, and adds a very important dimension to Wisdom's account of the logic of religious belief. Furthermore, it seems that the atheist too often reaches his stance because some particular pattern of events so strongly impresses him that it becomes a paradigm for interpreting other events. In some cases, one could speak of a "negative revelation." This is very clear in the case of Sartre's novel, to which I made reference earlier. Sitting on the park bench among the chestnut trees, the hero of that novel is suddenly seized of the alien and oppressive character of Being, in an experience that has all the formal characteristics of a revelation. One may recall also how events like the Lisbon earthquake and, more recently, the tragedy of Auschwitz, have so profoundly impressed some people, perhaps even whole generations of people, so that these events have been assigned a major role in the interpretation of experience as a whole.

It is widely recognized among contemporary theologians that the traditional natural theology is not really a *prolegmonenon* to faith but is subsequent to faith. It is rational reflection on the affirmations of faith, a weighing of the arguments for and against. I have suggested that in an ambiguous world, no conclusive evidence will be forthcoming. Nevertheless, this kind of procedure is needed if faith is not to be mere superstition but is to be a reasonable faith. Likewise, the denial of faith must submit itself to the same kind of reflective examination. Are we right in taking some events or some patterns rather than others as guidelines for the attitudes that we take up toward the world as a whole? Perhaps the only kind of test is to ask whether, as we go along, our interpretative principles show themselves capable of embracing increasingly wider areas of experience, or whether they break down in the face of interactable data.

I have suggested that both a naive supernaturalistic theism at the one extreme and the thoroughgoing atheistic assertion of the absurd at the other extreme do in fact soon break down, and my purpose has been to clarify the options of faith and doubt that lie between these extremes.

NOTES

1. *Philosophy and Psychoanalysis* (Oxford, Blackwell, 1953), pp. 149–68.
2. *Loc. cit.*, pp. 154–5.
3. *Loc. cit.*, p. 155.
4. Genesis 3:8.

5. *Opera* (Berlin, 1896), Vol. ii, p. 237.
6. *The Reality of God* (New York, Harper & Row, 1966), p. 37. Press, 1963), p. 215.
7. D. L. Edwards, ed., *Honest to God Debate*, (Philadelphia, Westminster)
8. *The Death of Man* (New York, Morehouse-Barlow, 1967), p. 117.
9. *Language, Truth and Logic*, 2nd ed. (London, V. Gollancz, 1946), p. 115.
10. *Exploration into God* (Stanford, Calif., Stanford University Press, 1967), p. 68.
11. *Tractatus Logico-Philosophicus* (London, Kegan Paul, 1922), p. 187.
12. (Paris, Gallimard, 1938).
13. Cf. *New Essays in Philosophical Theology*, A. Flew and A. MacIntyre, ed. (London, SCM Press, 1955), pp. 103–5.

ON WASTE AND WASTELANDS

(A RESPONSE)

Kai Nielsen

I

Professor Macquarrie has written about a vast array of conflicting traditions and philosophical and theological approaches with impressive knowledge and a breadth of sympathy. While his own deepest sympathies are clearly with the existentialist tradition, he has been willing to dine with the analytic philosophers, secularist and non-secularist, and to try to meet them on their own grounds. His "On Gods and Gardeners" is another attempt to do just that and I hope that I shall not be thought ungrateful and a prickly upstart if I contend that he has failed—that he has not correctly distinguished the crucial differences between theism and atheism or given a coherent account of the concept of God. It will be the burden of my critical remarks to establish that this is so. But, since I so fundamentally disagree with Professor Macquarrie both about specific points of analysis and about basic philosophical methodology, let me commence, so we can put these points aside, by stating some important respects in which we do agree.

1. I agree that the specific criticisms that an atheist will make of theism will or at least should depend on the kind of theism that is being advocated.

2. I also agree with Macquarrie that the distinction between atheism and theism or atheism and Judaism and Christianity "is a real and important one." Alasdair MacIntyre was indeed muddled when he called Bishop Robinson an atheist. Any man who can speak of God as the ultimate reality, the ground of the world, in which Being is revealed as gracious, is most certainly not an atheist. In remarking that Bishop Robinson is hardly "guilty of anything more than a considerable confusion of thought," Father Mascall was being far more perceptive than Mac-

Intyre.[1] In the same vein, I would agree with Macquarrie that when theologians like Tillich and Baillie try to turn Ludwig Feuerbach, Bertrand Russell, Jean-Paul Sartre and Sigmund Freud into religious believers by stipulative redefinition, they are only playing with words and confusing the issue. But granted that there is a genuine difference between atheists and theists what exactly is this difference and how is it to be adjudicated? Here we get very little help from Macquarrie. I shall return to this point.

3. I also agree with Professor Macquarrie that the difference between an atheist, on the one hand, and a Jew or Christian, on the other, is not *just* in how people feel about the world. Indeed, since religious discourse is self-involving, atheists and theists characteristically have different commitments. But what is more to the present point is to recognize, as Macquarrie puts it, that the difference between atheism and theism "is not simply that some people use the word 'God' to integrate and organize some of their experiences and aspirations, while other people use a different language."

4. I also agree that "God," as it occurs in Jewish and Christian discourses, is *not* a purely descriptive term; it also carries a normative or evaluative force. In the jargon of philosophers "God is worthy of worship" is analytic.

II

So far, all has been sweetness and perhaps even light; so far Macquarrie and I agree, but with his characterization of atheism and theism dispute breaks out. Let us turn to his characterization.

Sophisticated atheists and theists, Macquarrie tells us, no longer dispute whether there is a reality called "God," transcendent to the world and independent of the world—a reality which is somehow the cause of the world. Rather, the dispute is about the character of the world. But this is a spurious dichotomy. Father Copleston, Father Mascall and Professor I. M. Crombie clearly count as sophisticated theists if anyone does, and Bertrand Russell, Antony Flew and Ronald Hepburn count as sophisticated skeptics if anyone does. But the dispute between these believers and skeptics is about whether the world has the character of being dependent such that it can be said to have a transcendent ground or cause. So we have here a dispute about the character of the world which is *at the same time* a dispute about the reality of a Being transcendent to the world, whose being is not dependent on the existence of the world. Since this is so, Macquarrie's dichotomy is plainly a spurious one.

Let us pass on to a new point. Macquarrie rightly stresses that as

Judaism and Christianity have changed, they have come to have partially new conceptions of God. There has been an accentuation of this in the twentieth century so that we are now living in a time of theological upheaval. We are coming to conceptualize God in new ways and this in turn restructures the debate between atheism and theism. As Macquarrie sees it, in our theological situation the really crucial dispute between atheism and theism is about the character of the world. The crucial dispute is not about what, if anything, creates, sustains or is the ground of the world, but about the world itself. Is it a garden or a wasteland? This, according to him, is the nub of the difference between the atheist and the theist. Unfortunately, Macquarrie identifies atheism with one of its rather romantic and incoherent species and consequently blurs the crucial differences between atheism and theism. He takes as his paradigm of an atheist, the nihilist who believes that the world is essentially absurd and frustrating. For Macquarrie "a thoroughgoing atheism" is a world-view in which the world is regarded "as totally absurd (godless) and as utterly frustrating man's quest for reasonableness and value . . . ." But this is a most unfair and most idiosyncratic characterization of atheism. Indeed, there have been atheists with such nihilistic attitudes, but there have also been many who have not had such attitudes and, as we shall see in a moment, there is nothing in the root idea of atheism that commits one to such attitudes. Feuerbach, Marx, Santayana, George Eliot, Antony Flew, Ernest Nagel and my colleague Sidney Hook are all atheists and yet they certainly do not think that the world is totally absurd. The utterance "There is no God, but love, companionship, human solidarity, and reasonableness are still possible" is not self-contradictory, logically odd, or a deviation from a linguistic regularity. Given Macquarrie's views, such a statement should be self-contradictory, but, on the contrary, he has not given us the slightest reason to think it false, let alone self-contradictory or incoherent. And Macquarrie apart, as far as I can see there is no good reason to think such a statement is false. God or no God, the napalming of children is evil; God or no God the social policies of a Dag Hammarskjöld are superior to the social policies of an Adolf Hitler. Moreover, the recognition of and the justification of such claims is quite independent of the issue between atheism and theism.

In a similar vein, Macquarrie's characterization of a theist or a believer in God is not adequate to distinguish atheists from religious believers. "God," we are told, refers to the "objective ground in reality itself of our ineradicable confidence in the final worth of our existence." Such a characterization by stipulative redefinition makes Spinoza, Feuerbach, Marx and Dewey into believers in God. Macquarrie chided

Tillich and Baillie for such linguistic legerdemain, but he has unwittingly followed the same path himself. G. E. Moore was an atheist but he was also an ethical objectivist. If an optimistic atheist were an ethical objectivist and, unlike Moore, given to talking in a rather inflated idiom and/or to indulging, after the fashion of Tillich, in bombastic redescription, he could quite consistently affirm his confidence "that the real whole of which we experience ourselves to be parts is such to be worthy of, and thus itself to evoke, that very confidence." Thus this is no way to distinguish a theist from an atheist.

Let me return to Macquarrie's characterization of atheism. *Given such a characterization,* it is evident enough 1) why atheism appears to be an absurd position and 2) that there are many alternative positions between the extremes. But this is Macquarrie versus a strawman. Macquarrie wants to clarify what he takes to be a real and important distinction between atheism and theism, but as far as I can see, he only succeeds in spreading confusion in this conceptual area.

III

How then should the difference between the atheist and the theist be drawn. Traditionally atheists have been said to be people who maintain that it is false or probably false that there is a God. But many contemporary atheists would surely accept Charles Bradlaugh's remark in his *Plea for Atheism:* "The atheist does not say 'There is no God,' but he says 'I know not what you mean by God; I am without idea of God; the word 'God' is to me a sound conveying no clear or distinct affirmation . . . .'" Rather than say atheism is the belief that the sentence 'There is a God' expresses a false assertion, it should be formulated as follows: an atheist *rejects* belief in God or what is taken to be belief in God, for, depending on how God is conceived, one of the following reasons: 1) because it is false or probably false that there is a God, 2) because the concept of God is either meaningless, unintelligible, contradictory or incoherent or 3) because the concept of God in question is such that it merely masks an atheistic substance, e.g., "God" is a symbolic term for moral ideals.

I like to think of myself as an atheist and I take the first position toward an anthropomorphic God like Thor or Zeus or the concept of God which is most prominent in the Bible, the second position toward the various conceptions of God of mainstream Judaism and Christianity, and the third position toward Spinoza's, Dewey's, Hare's or Braithwaite's God.

Traditionally, Jews and Christians have characterized God as a supreme personal being, the all-powerful, loving, just and perfectly good

creator or ground of the world. Where we try to take these terms literally we get an *anthropomorphic* God but—and I take it that here Macquarrie agrees with me—such a God most surely does not exist and to
believe in such a God is to worship an idol and to be caught in a superstition. Macquarrie, however, feels that sophisticated believers have long
ago discarded such an idol. In the present mainstream of Judeo-Christian thought, God is not such an idol but is thought to have a unique
kind of existence. God, for such nonanthropomorphites, is taken to have
a necessary existence which contrasts with finite, dependent, contingent
existence. God is taken to be a completely independent being (a being
who depends on no being or group of beings), a being that is not a
being among other beings but an eternal, non-spatio-temporal, infinite
Pure Spirit which has no sufficient conditions and is transcendent to the
world. This is the most central conception of God in the Jewish-Christian tradition. And in the dispute between atheism and theism the crucial question is 1) over whether this conception of God is sufficiently
coherent to be believable and 2) over whether, even if it has this degree
of coherency, there is such a Divine reality. These issues are at the very
heart of a nonevasive philosophical scrutiny of religion. It is over such
considerations that the central cleavages between atheism and theism,
between unbelief and belief, develop. But Macquarrie's characterization
of atheism and theism obscures these really crucial issues.

IV

It is evident enough that Macquarrie is in varying degrees dissatis-
fied with traditional conceptions of God—including, of course, the
characterization I have just given above. And he well might be, for it is
far from evident that such traditional conceptions are coherent. But instead of becoming an atheist or an agnostic, Macquarrie gives us a new
conception of God. I shall now try to show that his own attempt at a
replacement and a new conceptualization of the deity is incoherent and
should be rejected. His new model for God, his new image of God,
simply substitutes an unfamiliar incoherency for a familiar one.

Macquarrie appropriately enough tells us that in talking about God
we are not just talking about some highest value but we are trying to
make a unique claim about how things are, about the objective ground
of our confidence in the final worth of existence. Macquarrie wants to
assert the reality of God, but he does not want to say that God is some
independent reality transcendent to the world. He seems to regard that
traditional notion as something that cannot justifiably be believed in. In
its stead, we get the claim that *God is the form of the world*. God, we
are told, is "an active Gestalt that expresses itself in the world-process."

And explicating the obscure and problematical with something nearly as obscure and problematical, he compares "God as the form of the world" with "the soul as the form of the body." Since he conceives of form in a rather Aristotelian manner, he is allegedly talking of the "structure of the world," though presumably this is an "active structure." But what is crucial to note is that given this Aristotelian conception of form, there can be no forms without matter. In short, there could be no God if there were no world. Macquarrie does not conceive of God as a completely independent reality upon whom all other realities depend but who depends on no other realities. God, in fine, is no longer conceived of as having *aseity* (self-existence) but God is believed to be dependent upon the world. If there were no world, there would be no God, just as for Aristotle there would be no forms if there were no sensible things.

Quite apart from the obscurities of this doctrine, take note of what you would be buying if you were to accept it. Recognize how very much Christianity and Judaism would indeed change if such beliefs were to be accepted. The feeling of gratitude for one's very existence is at the very heart of such religions. For a Jew or a Christian, God is his Creator to whom everything is owed. But on Macquarrie's view, God can no longer consistently be thought of as the creator or sustainer of the world. The world can no longer be thought of as dependent on God. If such a conception of God came to have firm and universal acceptance, the key passages in *Job* would not only lose their religious force, but also there could be no appropriate sense of awe at a Creator who laid the foundations of the earth and before whom one is as dust and ashes.

Since, however, many of us may be quite uninterested in plugging the leaky vessel of Christianity, let us also note the obscurities of Macquarrie's formulation. When we speak of the form of a basketball—its being oval, say—or the form of a man, those characteristics which all and only men have, we understand what we are talking about. But what is it to speak of *the form* of the world? Surely language is idling here. In other words, we literally do not know what we are talking about when we speak of "the form of the world." Is the world a kind of "big thing" or "gigantic process" that could have a form? Surely not. Is it a totality? Well, what kind of totality? It could hardly be a class or a group. It could hardly be a group, for then it would have members and this would imply that there could be several worlds or universes, but this is surely nonsense. If instead we say the universe is a class we need to know its defining characteristics. But no such characteristics have been given or could be given unless (and Macquarrie is unwilling to do this) we could intelligibly speak of a necessary being distinct from the world with defining characteristics which are *contrastable* with the defining characteristics of the world. But Macquarrie with his concept of God as the form of the world cannot treat God as a necessary being which transcends the world. Excluding the concept of a being or a reality independent of or distinct from the world, there is nothing that the universe is contrastable with such that it could have distinguishing characteristics and be a class or totality. Well, "the universe" or "the world" may be just umbrella terms for all the things, processes, events that there are. But if this is so, the universe or the world could not be a class, group, or totality and there would be no way of speaking of its structure or form.

We can speak of the form of a garden but no sense has been given to "the form of the world." It may not appear, as "the color of heat," to wear its unintelligibility on its sleeve. Perhaps it is more like "4 P.M. on the sun"—a bit of disguised incoherence. We come to see, as Wittgenstein pointed out, the unintelligibility of "It is 4 P.M. on the sun," when we come to recognize that nothing counts for or against its truth. If someone tries to assert it, we have no idea at all what would have to transpire in order for it to be known to be so or even probably so. The same thing is true for "The world has a form." If I were foolish enough to try to deny that the world has a form and Macquarrie countered and reasserted that the world has a form, what could conceivably count for or against either of our putative claims? What conceivable evidence could either of us bring to show that either assertion was true or false or probably true or false? Macquarrie has not shown what could so count and I submit that nothing could. But do not take my above arguments as evidence for the falsity of "The universe has a form." They were designed rather to show that "The universe has a form" could not possibly be true, for it is not sufficiently intelligible to be true or false. If nothing could count as evidence for or against the putative factual utterance "The world has a form" there is no way of knowing what Macquarrie is claiming or what I would be denying if I were so befuddled as to try to deny such a putative claim. But of course I do not deny it; rather I reject it because I believe it is an *Erzatz* claim which, as "It is 4 P.M. on the sun," is so indeterminate that those who utter it have no understanding of what they are claiming. If we go around saying things like "God is the form of the world," or "View God as the form of the world," we are simply using words in an irresponsible manner. But since "There is a God" means for Macquarrie "There is a form of the world," exactly the same must be said for "There is a God," given Macquarrie's use of "God." The atheist should not say that in believing in God, Macquarrie believes in something which is not so. He should rather say that what Macquarrie thinks he believes in is so incoherent that his belief could not possibly be true, that it could not possibly even be a genuine belief.

V

Macquarrie moves from incoherence to misleading platitude. The second concept he uses to elucidate "the nature of belief in God" is the claim, as he puts it, that "to believe in God is to believe that human existence is set within a wider context of meaning." But surely this confuses what is perhaps a necessary condition with a sufficient condition. In talking about "a wider context of meaning," he is talking about "a wider context of significance." But an atheist or agnostic, not to mention a Buddhist or some other religious person who does not believe in God, could also find a wider significance to human existence. A Marxist humanist, for example—say a man like Régis Debray or Isaac Deutscher —who was thoroughly and even iconoclastically atheistical, could well discover significance in the revolutionary struggle to create for the toiling and exploited masses a new quality of life and a new image of man. Together with people in the movement and in relation to the exploited, he could very well discover a wider context of significance. Macquarrie has given us no grounds at all for thinking that we need a theistic or even a religious *Weltanschauung* to find such a wider context of significance.

VI

Macquarrie's talk of Being is mystifying. It is indeed true that we may come to feel a sense of awe when we take to heart the fact that there might have been nothing at all. That is, to put the matter differently, to avoid the impression that I am reifying and taking "nothing" to be a name, we may feel awe when we reflect that as far as mere *logical* possibilities are concerned all affirmative existential statements might be false. But that this might be so is at best a mere *logical* possibility. It does not show that the world is contingent, rather it only reflects the putative conceptual truth that no existential statement is logically necessary. Of course, if by "the world is contingent" we simply mean that no existential statement is logically necessary, then we will have given "the world is contingent" a sense, though a very Pickwickian sense. But now the theologian's claim is simply a truism. Talk of the "mystery of being" is quite gratuitous and unnecessary. Moreover, to speak either of the self or of Being as "another dimension of existence" is completely unhelpful until we know what sort of "dimension" we are talking about, until we have been given some key as to what we are referring to when we use such an expression. All we know from Macquarrie's account is that Being is not *a* being, a property, a class, a sum of things. But what then are we talking about? If we say "a power or principle of existing," or "a dimension of existence," the question still remains what, after all, is this? Is this even an intelligible collection of words? To the philosophically unwary talk of "a dimension of existence" may sound profound, but it actually tells us nothing. We know what we are talking about when we speak of "a power of attorney" or "the power of electricity," but unless "X has the power of existing" is just a moderately bombastic redescription of "There are no X's now but there might be some later," it is very unclear what it could possibly mean. Moreover, the variable "X" could, given the above sensible interpretation, hardly have as its value God or Being for then we could be saying that there is no God or Being now but there may very well be such a Being or God at some later time. But this is clearly not how Macquarrie wants to use "God" and it is clearly not how anyone who wants to remain even remotely faithful to the Jewish-Christian tradition will use "God." But if "power of existing" does not mean *that*, pray tell what *does* it mean? Moreover, does something just have the power of existing, but not as a thing, process, event or a characteristic of things, processes, events? No intelligible use has been given to such a phrase so the nonevasive, perplexed person can come to know whether there is or is not or probably is or probably is not such a "principle of existing" or "dimension of existence." Again, language has gone on a holiday.

Macquarrie would no doubt reply that we are perplexed in this manner because, after all, we are talking about a mystery. But if we cannot even in principle find out whether there is or is not such a "principle of Being" or "dimension of existence" then what we are talking about is utterly incomprehensible. And what is utterly incomprehensible cannot be known or even believed in or even grasped by a leap of faith, for only if we understand what *P* means can we believe in or have faith in *P*. Unless we have some understanding of what *P means* we cannot know what it is we are to take on faith. With all the good will in the world, we cannot take something on trust if we do not understand what it is we are to take on trust.[2]

Putting anthropomorphism aside, it is not that there is an atheistic interpretation of the world and a theistic interpretation of the world and somehow, in a "world which always remains ambiguous," we must choose—perhaps just opt in a Jamesian fashion—between them. Rather, a Macquarrie-type theist has given us no intelligible interpretation of the world at all. The atheist should not reject it as a rival interpretation of the world; rather he should reject Macquarrie's putative claims on the grounds of their very incoherence. It is not, as Macquarrie would have it, that we lack "conclusive evidence" for theistic claims—that has long been tolerable to the fideist—but that we do not even know what would count as "evidence" here. Just for a moment think literally, honestly and nonevasively about two of Macquarrie's central claims:

1) The world is going somewhere.
2) God is the depth of the world's existence that lets it stand out from nothing.

If, on the one hand, these are metaphors, pray tell what are they metaphors of, what literal paraphrases do they have? If, on the other hand, they are literal statements, what indeed do they mean, what is it that Macquarrie is asserting, what kind of evidence would give us the slightest reason to think these utterances might possibly be true or false? Until, or unless, Professor Macquarrie can answer such questions he has not given us insights into a profound mystery but has merely burdened us with some muddles decked out as insights.

NOTES

1. I have tried to give substance to such claims about Bishop Robinson in my "Language and the Concept of God," *Question* 2 (January, 1969), pp. 36–40 and in the second chapter of my *Quest For God*, forthcoming.

2. This needs further elucidation and some slight qualification. See my "Can Faith Validate God-talk?" in *Philosophy and Religion: Some Contemporary Perspectives*, Jerry A. Gill, ed., (Minneapolis, Minnesota, 1968), pp. 233–246.

IN DEFENSE OF ATHEISM

Kai Nielsen

Unsinn ist das höchste Wesen der Theologie . . . Ludwig Feuerbach

I

Jews, Christians and Moslems do not and cannot take their religion to be simply their fundamental conceptual framework or metaphysical system. Fundamental human commitments and attitudes are an essential part of being religious. The feeling of gratitude for one's very existence no matter what the quality or condition of that existence is at the very heart of religion. To be religious consists fundamentally in living in a certain way, in holding a certain set of convictions, in the having of certain attitudes and in being a member of a distinctive confessional group.

Religious discourse reflects this. Religious utterances express our basic sense of security in life and our gratitude for being alive. Jews, Christians and Moslems pray, and engage in rituals and ceremonies in the doing of which they use language in a distinctive way. In religious discourse, we give voice to our deepest and most pervasive hopes, ideals and wishes concerning what we should try to be and what expectations we may entertain. If we really are religious and do not regard religion simply as "moral poetry" but use religious discourse seriously to make distinctively religious claims, we commit ourselves to what we as believers take to be a certain general view about "the ultimate basis of the universe." This is exhibited in the very use of certain religious utterances.

(1) God is my Creator to whom everything is owed.
and
(2) God is the God of mercy of Whose forgiveness I stand in need.

are paradigms of the above mentioned use of religious discourse; they presumably are fact-stating uses of discourse, though this is not all they are, and they are closely linked with other uses of religious discourse. Such ceremonial and evocative talk as we find in Christianity could hardly exist if it were not for such uses of language as exhibited in (1) and (2). (1) and (2) are not theologians' talk about God but are sample bits of living religious discourse. Yet for believer and nonbeliever alike they are perplexing bits of discourse.

Wittgenstein and others have taught the importance of context. We must not examine religious utterances—especially those which appear to have a statement-making function—in isolation, but we should examine them on location as part of that complex activity we call "religion." To understand a religious utterance properly we must come to understand the topic or topics of our discourse and the purposes for which it is used.

Indeed, in using language we must not forget what Strawson has called the Principle of the Presumption of Knowledge or the Principle of Relevance. Of all speech functions to which this applies, it applies most appositely to the making of statements, which is indeed a central speech function if anything is. That is to say, when "an empirically assertive utterance is made with an informative intention" there is the standing presumption on the part of the speaker that "those who hear him have knowledge of empirical facts relevant to the particular point to be imparted in the utterance." [1] Moreover, statements have topics, they are in that sense about something, and reflect what Strawson calls a "centre of interest." To understand a statement we must understand the topic or center of interest involved in its assertion. We must not forget that we do not characteristically give out information or give voice to utterances in an isolated, unconnected manner; but only as part of some connected discourses. We need a Principle of Relevance to pick out, in terms of the topic in question, the proper kind of answer to what a statement is about. This is integral to our understanding of how to take (understand) the statement in question.

Take the classic example "The King of France is bald." We need a context, an application of the Principles of Relevance and the Presumption of Knowledge, to know how to take it. If our context is the present, and the relevant questions are "What is the king of France like?" or "Is he bald?" then neither "The King of France is bald" nor "The King of France is not bald" would be a correct answer, for the above questions in the above context are not to be answered, but are to be replied to by being rejected. The proper reply—a reply which rejects such questions—is: (De Gaulle notwithstanding) "There is no King of France." But if our topic is historical and, with some specific period in mind, we are asking, "What bald notables are there?"; "The King of France is bald" in such a changed context is an appropriate answer. And here it is a true or false statement.

"God," like "the King of France," is what Strawson calls a referring expression, though this shouldn't be taken to imply that it is *simply* a referring expression. In asserting that they are referring expressions, I am giving you to understand that presumably both expressions make identifying reference. Referring expressions may be names, pronouns, definite descriptions or demonstrative descriptions. In using referring expressions in identifying descriptions to make identifying references, e.g., "The Point Judith Ferry is White" or "Block Island is windy," we do not, Strawson points out, inform the audience of the *existence* of what our referring expressions refer to. Rather the very task of identifying reference can be undertaken "only by a speaker who knows or presumes his audience to be already in possession of such knowledge of existence. . . ."[2]

Similarly, when a religious man utters (1) or (2)—our paradigm religious utterances quoted above—there is the presumption that the speaker understands "God" and knows or believes in the reality of what is being talked about. The acceptance of the truth of (1) and (2) is partially definitive of what it is to be a Jew or Christian. In asserting (1) and (2), the religious man *presupposes* that there is a God and that this God has a certain character. The atheist, on the other hand, does not believe that (1) and (2) are true because he does not accept the presupposition on which they are made, namely that there is a God. He either does not accept such a presupposition because he believes it to be false or because he believes the concept of God to be an incoherent concept. If he believes that the concept of God is incoherent then he must also believe that the presupposition on which (1) and (2) are based could not possibly be true. The agnostic, in turn, does not accept the presupposition on which (1) and (2) are built because he feels that he does not have sufficient grounds for accepting it even on faith, and yet he is not convinced that we have sufficiently good grounds to be justified in dismissing it as false or utterly incoherent.

As I remarked initially, Judaism, Christianity and Islam are not by any means constituted by the making and accepting of certain statements. Rather the making of religious statements like (1) and (2) are the cornerstones on which all the other types of religious utterance in such religions depend; and they in turn presuppose that the statement "There is a God" is true, and that in turn presupposes that "There is a God" is a genuine statement and that the concept of God is a viable concept. The most crucial question we can ask about Judaism, Christianity and Islam is whether these religious presuppositions are justified.

It might be felt that I have already too much ignored context. In live religious discourse, it is sometimes maintained, questions about the existence of God or the coherence of the concept of God do not arise. It is only by ignoring the context of religious talk that I can even make them seem like real questions.

There are multiple confusions involved in this objection. First, believers characteristically have doubts; even the man in "the circle of faith" is threatened with disbelief. Tormenting religious doubts arise in the religious life itself and they are often engendered by some first-order uses of God-talk. "All my life I have lived under an illusion. There is no Divine Reality at all" is first-order God-talk and not talk about talk, e.g., "The word 'God' only has emotive meaning." The above first-order religious utterance has a natural context and topic for a religious man locked in a religious crisis. Most atheists and agnostics were once believers—in our traditions they were once Jews, Christians or Moslems—and they have a participant's understanding of these forms of life. Many of them, like Hägerström, Joyce or Sartre, have been caught up and immersed in such forms of life. They are not like anthropologists who in trying to gain an understanding that approximates a participant's understanding are trying to grasp how the discourses hang together. Moreover —to zero in on the critical objection about context—people who have a participant's grasp of the form of life in which (1) and (2) are embedded know how to use them and can, readily, for certain purposes prescind in reflecting about them from the context in which they are at home; for they know in what sort of linguistic environment they belong and to what sort of topics, centers of interest, they are directed. Reflecting about them in their religious context, we say that they presuppose the intelligibility and truth of "There is a God." Context or not, it is this traditional and central question that we need to face in asking fundamental questions about the Judeo-Christian tradition, though if we do not understand the environment in which the utterances which presuppose it are at home, we will not understand what is involved in such a question.

II

In pursuing this question let us start quite simply but centrally by asking: Why should anyone be an agnostic or an atheist? Why should this question about God be such a biting one? Formerly skeptical philosophers could not bring themselves to accept religious beliefs because they felt the proofs all failed, the problem of evil was intractable and the evidence offered for believing in the existence of God was inadequate. But contemporary philosophical disbelief cuts deeper and poses more fundamental problems, problems which challenge even the fideist who, à la Kierkegaard, would claim that the last thing a genuine knight of faith would want or should have is a proof of God's existence.[3] Ronald Hepburn succinctly states the sort of considerations that are involved in that "deeper ground:"

Where one gives an account of an expression in our language, and where that expression is one that refers to an existent of some kind, one needs to provide not only a set of rules for the use of the expression, but also an indication of how the referring is to be done—through direct pointing, perhaps, or through giving instructions for an indirect method of identifying the entity. Can this be done in the case of God? Pointing, clearly, is inappropriate, God being no finite object in the world. The theologian may suggest a number of options at this point. He may say: God can be identified as that being upon whom the world can be felt as utterly dependent, who is the completion of its incompletenesses, whose presence is faintly adumbrated in experience of the awesome and the numinous. Clear direction-giving has here broken down; the theologian may well admit that his language is less descriptive or argumentative than obliquely evocative. Does this language succeed in establishing that statements about God have a reference? To persons susceptible to religious experience but at the same time logically and critically alert, it may seem just barely to succeed, or it may seem just barely to fail. Some may even oscillate uneasily between these alternatives without finding a definite procedure of decision to help them discriminate once for all.[4]

An agnostic, abreast of contemporary philosophical developments, will indeed oscillate in this fashion. "God" is a referring expression whose referent obviously cannot be indicated by ostension. The agnostic clearly recognizes this and he also recognizes the need to exhibit an adequate nonanthropomorphic extralinguistic referent for "God." In essence his doubt comes to this: is the concept of God sufficiently coherent to make belief possible for a reasonable, nonevasive man? He knows that philosophically sophisticated, reflective Jews and Christians do not deny that the concept of God is a difficult, illusive, paradoxical concept. They stress that it could not be otherwise, but believe that it is not so illusive, not so ill-conceived, as to fail to make an intelligible and yet a religiously appropriate reference. In talking about God, a believer is committed to the belief that we are talking about a mystery, but while God, by common reflective consent, is indeed in large measure incomprehensible, the concept of God is not so utterly incoherent as to vitiate religious belief. This is the minimal commitment of a religious man; he may share much with the agnostic but this much he does believe; he *must* take his stand here.

I shall argue that both the agnostic and the believer are mistaken.

Careful reflection on the use of "God" in the stream of Jewish and Christian life is enough to justify an atheism which asserts that the concept of God is so incoherent that there could not possibly be a referent for the word "God." I take it here that we are speaking of Jews and Christians who have advanced beyond anthropomorphism; Jews and Christians, who as Macquarrie puts it, have revolted decisively "against the idea that the divine can be objectified, so as to manifest itself in sensible phenomena." [5] The Jew, Christian or Moslem who remains an anthropomorphite simply has false, superstitious beliefs. But I am concerned here with the Jew, Christian or Moslem who, consciously at least, is beyond anthropomorphism. I am maintaining against him that his belief in God is so incoherent that it could not possibly be true. If this controversial philosophical thesis is correct, it would have quite concrete normative consequences, for if it is correct, the rational thing to do is to reject belief in the God of the Jews, Christians and Moslems.

III

In arguing that the concept of God is incoherent, I am not claiming that "God" is utterly meaningless. Surely "God" has a use in the language; there are deviant and nondeviant bits of God-talk. If I say "God is a ride in a yellow submarine" or "God brews good coffee" or even "God died," I have not said something that is false; I have not even succeeded in saying something blasphemous; I have rather indicated, if I make such utterances with a serious intent, that I do not understand God-talk. In saying something such as "God is a ride in a yellow submarine" I have said something closer to "Quite grounds calculated carefully" or "Elope sea with trigonometry." In short, my utterances are without a literal meaning. "God is a ride in a yellow submarine" could indeed be a metaphor. In the context of a poem or song, it might be given a meaning, but taken just like that it does not have a meaning. But even out of context—say in the middle of a commencement address —"Pass me a peanut butter sandwich" would be perfectly meaningful, would have a literal meaning, though the point, if any, of uttering it would remain obscure. However, "God brews good coffee," like "Elope sea with trigonometry," are immediately recognized as not even being absurdly false like "Humphrey walked on water" but as being without any literal meaning. "God is a ride in a yellow submarine" or "God brews good coffee" is immediately and unequivocally recognized as deviant by people with a participant's grasp of God-talk, while other bits of God-talk are immediately recognized to be nondeviant and do in fact have a use in the language, e.g., "Oh God be my Sword and my strength" or "God so loved mankind that he gave to the world his only son." Even agnostics and atheists who understand how to use Jewish and Christian religious talk do not balk at such nondeviant utterances. If they are reading a religious novel or sermon, they keep right on going and do not balk at these nondeviant sentences, e.g., "God protect me in my need," as they would at "God lost weight last week." Philosophically perplexed as they are about nondeviant God-talk, they do not balk at it, while they do in a quite ordinary way balk at "Procrastination drinks grief" or "God brews good coffee." There are absurdities and absurdities. Thus it is plainly a mistake to say that God-talk is meaningless.

However, in saying that the concept of God is incoherent, I am saying that where "God" is used nonanthropomorphically, as it is at least officially in developed Jewish and Christian God-talk, there occur sentences such as (1) and (2) which purportedly have a statement-making function, yet no identifiable state of affairs can be characterized which would make such putative religious statements true and no intelligible directions have been given for identifying the supposed referent for the word "God." Religious believers speak of religious truth but "religious truth" is a Holmesless Watson.

God, as Hepburn points out, cannot be pointed to but must be identified intralinguistically through certain descriptions, if He can be identified at all. But the putative descriptions Hepburn mentions will not do. If in trying to identify God we speak of "that being upon whom the world can be felt to be utterly dependent," nothing has been accomplished, for what does it *mean* to speak of "the world (the universe) as being utterly dependent" or even dependent at all? (And if we do not understand this, we do not know what it would be like to *feel* that the world is utterly dependent.) If we are puzzled by "God," we will be equally puzzled by such phrases. We know what it means to say a child, an adult, a nation, a species, a lake is dependent on something. We could even give sense to the earth's being dependent on something, but no sense has been given to the universe's being dependent on anything. What are the sufficient conditions for the universe? What would make it true or false or what would even count for the truth or falsity of the putative statement "The universe is dependent" or "The universe is not dependent"? To answer by speaking of "God," e.g., the universe is dependent because God is its final cause, is to pull oneself up by one's own bootstraps, for talk of the dependency of the universe was appealed to in the first place in order to enable us to identify the alleged referent of "God." And to speak of a *logically* necessary being upon whom the universe depends is to appeal to a self-contradictory conception, for only propositions or statements, not beings, can either be *logically* necessary or fail to be logically necessary. Yet to speak of a "factually necessary being" upon whom the universe depends is again to pull oneself up by one's own bootstraps; for what would count toward establishing the truth or falsity of a statement asserting or denying the existence of such an alleged reality? Nothing has been specified and no directions have been given for identifying "a self-existent being" or "a self-caused being" or "a necessary being" or "a totally independent being." All these expressions purport to be referring expressions, but no rules (implicit or explicit) or regulations have been discovered for identifying their putative referents. With them we are in at least as much trouble as we are with "God," and unlike "God," they do not even have an established use in the language. It is indeed true that Jews and Christians do not think of God as something or someone who might or might not exist. If God exists, He somehow exists necessarily. But given the self-contradictoriness of the concept of a logically necessary being or existent, it cannot be true that there can be anything which must exist simply because its existence is logically possible. Moreover, no sense has been given to the claim that there is something—some given reality—which categorically must exist.

It may well be that when believers use "God" in sentences like (1) and (2) they *feel* à la Otto as if they were in the presence of a reality which is awesome and numinous—an "ultimate reality" whose presence is but faintly adumbrated in experience. Yet if this numinosity is taken to be the God of the developed Judeo-Christian tradition, it is taken to be "transcendent to the world." But, while "transcendent to the world" is at best an obscure phrase, it should still be evident that "a transcendent X" could not be "an X whose presence was given in experience." Something given in experience would *eo ipso* be nontranscendent, for it would automatically be part of the spatio-temporal world. Believers, who in defending the coherence of this belief appeal to their experience of God, are pinned by a Morton's fork: on the one hand, it is not logically possible to encounter a "reality transcendent to the world" and, on the other, if our numinosity is not thought to be transcendent, we are no longer talking of the God of developed Judeo-Christianity.[6]

IV

The central beliefs of Judaism, Christianity and Islam are indeed metaphysical beliefs since their scope purports to transcend the empirical world. If we are to come to grips with Judaism or Christianity there is no avoiding what Hägerström labelled "metaphysical religiosity." Such a metaphysical religiosity remains in even a minimal characterization of the common core of Judaism, Christianity and Islam, for they all affirm the reality of one and only one God who is said to have created the universe out of nothing, and man, regarded as a sinful, creaturely being, is taken to be utterly dependent on this creator in whose purpose man is said to discover his own reason for living. To be a Jew, Christian or Moslem is to believe much more than that but it is to believe that, and it is here that we find, so to say, the basic propositions of faith upon which the whole edifice of western religiosity stands or falls. If in these religions there is to be religious truth, the statements expressing these core religious beliefs must be true, but, it should be objected, their meaning is so indeterminate, so problematical, that it is doubtful whether we have in them anything sufficiently coherent to constitute true or false statements.

To understand what it is to speak of the reality of God essentially involves understanding the phrase "creator of the universe out of nothing." Theologians characteristically do not mean by this that the universe was created at a moment in time. To speak of such a creator is to speak not of an *efficient* cause but of a *final* cause of the universe. It involves making the putative existential claim that there is an eternal, ever present creative source and sustainer of the universe. But do we really understand such talk? We understand what it is for a lake to be a source of a river, for oxygen to be necessary to sustain life, for the winning of the game to be the end for which it is played and for good health to be the reason why we exercise. But "the universe" is not a label for some gigantic thing or process or activity. It is not a name for a determinate reality whose existence can be sustained or not sustained. Moreover, what would we have to discern or fail to discern to discover or to "see" even darkly the end, the purpose or the meaning of the universe? A asserts the universe has a source or a sustainer and B denies it, but no conceivable recognizable turn of events counts for or against either of their claims; we have no idea what would have to obtain for either A's or B's claim to be so or even probably so. Yet both believe they are making assertions which are true or false. Plainly, language has gone on a holiday. We have bits of discourse which purport to be fact-stating but in reality they fail to come off as factual statements; that is to say, they do not function as fact-stating utterances. They purport to be fact-stating but they are not. But with a failure to make sense here, much more talk essential to the Judeo-Christian picture becomes plainly incoherent. Consider such key bits of God-talk as:

(3) God is wholly other than the world He made.
(4) God is the creator of the moral order of the universe.
(5) The universe is absolutely dependent on God.

In reflecting on them, we should not forget that "the world" ("the uni-verse") does not denote a thing, an entity, process or even an aggregate which might be made or brought into existence. Moreover there is the ancient point that "to make something" presupposes that there already is something out of which it is made. If it is replied that I am forgetting my previous remark that God is taken to be the *final* cause and not the efficient cause of the universe and that "make" here means "sustain" or "order," then it should be noted that this still presupposes something to be sustained or ordered; there is no use for "ordering or sustaining out of nothing." Even if we try to give it a use by saying that the universe was chaotic until ordered by God or that unless the universe is a reality ordered by God the universe would be chaotic, we are still lost, for both "the universe is chaotic" and "the universe is not chaotic" are without a coherent use. Since the universe is not an entity or even a totality, there is no sense in talking of its being ordered or not ordered and thus, while we might speak coherently of "the moral order of his life" or "the mo-rality of a culture or ethos," there is no coherent use for "the moral order of the universe," so (4) as well as (3) is nugatory. And again, con-sidering (5), we have seen that no sense has been given to "the universe is dependent" so (5), to put it conservatively, is also conceptually un-happy, i.e., it purports to make a factual statement but we have no idea of what, if anything, could count for or against its truth or falsity.

Some theologians with an antimetaphysical bias would try to avoid treating (3), (4) or (5) as part of the corpus of Judaism or Christianity. If my argument has been correct, this is indeed an inadequate and eva-sive defense against skeptical criticism, but allowing it for the sake of the discussion and returning to (1) and (2), which are surely part of that corpus, with respect to those utterances, we still have overwhelming conceptual difficulties. Consider (2) "God is the God of mercy of Whose forgiveness I stand in need." This statement entails the further statement that God does or can do something, that God acts or can act in a certain way, for it is utterly senseless to speak of being merciful if one could not even in principle act, do or fail to do merciful acts. To recognize and accept this is not to be committed to reductionism or materialism. One might even argue, as Strawson does, that the concept of a person is a primitive notion not fully analyzable in behavioristic terms, but it does not follow from this that there can be "bodiless ac-tion," that we can understand what it would be like for a person to do something without making at least a tacit reference to his body, to a liv-ing, moving being with a spatio-temporal location. But God in devel-oped Judeo-Christianity is supposed to be conceptualized as Pure Spirit; at the very least He cannot be taken to be a reality with a body or as something with a spatio-temporal location. God is not a being existing in space. Some theologians have even wanted to deny that God is *a* being at all. Rather He is Being, but Being or a being, it is certainly evident that God is not conceptualized as a being existing in space. As the above arguments make clear, only something with a body could act, could do something, and thus trivially could act mercifully or fail to act mercifully. But if it is *logically* impossible for X to act or fail to act mercifully then it is also logically impossible for X to be merciful or fail to be merciful. Thus (2), a key bit of God-talk, is also seen to be an incoherent utterance.

To arguments of this sort it has been replied:

Theists . . . are not people who misconceive action in applying it to God; they are simply people who employ this concept of action or agency in contexts where the nontheistic, or nonreligious do not. Which is to say no more than that they believe in God, while others do not. It is certainly not to say that their employment of the concept must be nonsensical.[7]

What is the argument for this? It is pointed out 1) that the language of action is logically distinct from that of bodily movement and that agency is logically distinct from spatio-temporal causation, 2) that there is no sharp distinction between the agent's body and the rest of his physical situation, and 3) that God is an agent without being a person.[8] I think all three of these claims are quite questionable to say the least. But even if we accept them, the argument can still be seen to be defective.

Consider how the argument runs: no matter how detailed our account of bodily movement, alternative descriptions of what an agent did would still always be possible. If my fist bangs against Jones' jaw in the water, this is quite compatible with any of the following three action descriptions (descriptions which in turn are arbitrarily selected from an indefinitely large number of apposite action descriptions of that bodily motion): I was trying to save his life, I was paying him back for an injury, I was trying to kill him. The conclusion which is drawn is that "an account of what is going on in terms of bodily movement, i.e. of spatio-temporal events causally connected, never tells us what the agent is doing." [9] But the acceptance of this argument does nothing at all to show that someone could possibly do anything without making bodily movements or without having a body. But this is what must be shown. A similar thing holds for both the claim that causal talk is not applicable to the language of agency and for the claim that no sharp distinction can be made between the agent and his physical environment. These claims might be accepted and it would still do nothing at all to show that it makes sense to say "action A occurred but nobody or nothing did it." To say "that was a merciful action," implies that some agent acted, but even though agency is hard to isolate from the rest of its physical situation and even if we cannot properly speak of the cause of an action, still an agent is a person and there can be no identifying a person and hence an agent except by reference to their bodies. A necessary condition for understanding the concept of action is the understanding of bodily movement.

However, in trying to resist such a conclusion it has been argued that God is not a person. We indeed, so the argument runs, cannot conceive of a person without a body, but we can, though characteristically we do not, think of agency without some idea of a bodily movement being involved. God, we are told, is to be thought of as an agent without a body; this "bodiless agent" acts without a body; he does merciful things without a body.[10]

I would counter that even when using a term such as "chemical agent"—where we refer to an active force or substance producing an effect—there is still a physically specifiable something which reacts in a determinate physically specifiable way. We have no idea of what it would be like for something to be done, for something to *do* something, for an action to occur, without there being a body in motion. In this connection we need to consider again "God is the God of mercy" ("God is love" would work as well); this means He (it) is conceived of as doing something or being able to do something, but we can only understand the doing of something if there is something identifiable which is said to do it. Moreover, X is only identifiable as an agent, and thus X can only be intelligibly said to be an agent if X has a body. For agency to be logically possible, we must have a discrete something specifiable in spatio-temporal terms. But the transcendent God of Judaism and Christianity is thought to be a wholly independent reality, wholly other than the world which is utterly dependent on this "ultimate reality" and is said to be ultimately unintelligible without reference to this nonphysical *mysterium tremendum et fascinans*. But then it is senseless to speak, as Jews and Christians do, of God as the God of mercy of Whose forgiveness man stands in need. Yet if this is so, it would appear to be the case that Judaism, Christianity and Islam are incoherent *Weltanschauungen*.

V

A standard ploy at this point in the dialectic is to maintain that utterances like "God is all merciful," "God is the Creator of the heavens and the earth" or "God loves all His creation," are symbolic or metaphorical utterances which manifest the Ultimate or Unconditioned

Transcendent but are themselves not literal statements which could be true or false. They hint at an ineffable metaphysical ultimate which is, as Tillich put it, "unconditionally beyond the conceptual sphere." [11] The only thing nonsymbolic we can say about God is:

(6) God is being-itself, the ineffable ultimate.
(7) God is the Unconditioned Transcendent on which everything else is dependent.

On the remarkable assumption that such verbosities are helpful explications, some theologians, addicted to this obscure manner of speaking, have gone on to make remarks like (8) or (9).

(8) Being-itself is not another being but the *transcendens* or *the comprehensive*, the incomparable and wholly other source and unity of all beings.
(9) God is not a being, but Being-itself that wider Being within which all particular beings have their being.

Here "Being"—as well as "Being-itself" in (6)—purportedly functions as a name or referring expression; that is to say, as a word which supposedly denotes or stands for something. But to do this, that is, to function descriptively or designatively, "being" and "being-itself" must have an intelligible opposite. But in the above sentences it has no intelligible opposite. When we use "being," "being-itself," or "being-as-such," in sentences like (6) through (9) we are trying to catch the cognitive import of "God." We are trying to say that there is a realm of being as such over and above the being of individual objects. (The sense of "over and above" remains problematic. It is not a spacial sense, of course, but in what way it is "over and above" remains utterly mysterious.)

Such being is said to be neither a genus nor a property. But then we can scarcely avoid severe philosophical perplexity concerning its character and how, if at all, being is to be identified. To discover this, we would have to discover what it is not; we would have to discover its intelligible opposite; yet the opposite of "being" is "nothing." But "nothing," in ordinary discourse, does not function as a name or referring expression and if we try to regiment discourse and make "nothing" function as a referring expression then we are led to the absurdities that Lewis Carroll satirized in *Through the Looking Glass* when the Red King thought that if Nobody passed the messenger on the road then Nobody would have arrived first. To try to treat "nothing" as a name or referring expression is to get involved in the absurdity of asking what kind of a something, what kind of *a* being or what kind of being is nothing. It involves the incoherent reifying of nothing into a kind of opposed power to being and, at the same time, spoiling its supposed contrast with "being" by treating "nothing" as the name of a mysterious something, which makes it either identical with Being-itself or a being which has its being in Being. In either case we have an absurdity. But unless "Nothing" is treated as a referring expression, "Being," where we try to construe it as a referring expression, has no intelligible opposite and without an intelligible opposite "being" lacks descriptive or designative significance and thus it is not, after all, as the Being-talk-man requires, a referring expression. Superficially it appears to have that role but actually has no such use in the language. For (6), (8) or (9) to come off as intelligible factual assertions, "being" and "being-itself" must be genuine referring expressions with intelligible opposites. Unfortunately, for the theologian committed to such an approach, these expressions do not so function, and thus our sample sentences are not sentences with which we can make factual statements.

Basically the same difficulties apply to the terms in the above sentences which presumably are taken to be elucidations of "being-itself" or "being-as-such" by people who like to talk in this obscure and, I suspect, obscurantist manner. Consider such phrases as "ineffable ultimate," "Unconditioned Transcendent," "*transcendens*," or "the Comprehensive." They are not ordinary language expressions with fixed uses; that is, in order to understand them we must be given some coherent directions concerning their use. But we are hardly given any directions here. Presumably they are putative referring expressions, but how even in principle could we identify their referents? A says "There is really the Comprehensive" and B replies "It's a myth, there is no such reality." C wonders whether there really is an Unconditioned Transcendent, the *transcendens* or an ineffable ultimate and D reassures him that actually there are no such realities. Actually those who are hip on Being-talk never take such a matter-of-fact tone, but even if they did, it is evident that there is not only no way at all of deciding who is right where such matter-of-fact-*sounding* questions are raised, but there is also no way of deciding which putative factual claim is the more probable. Nothing that we could experience now or hereafter, even assuming the intelligibility of "hereafter," helps us out vis-à-vis such "questions." But what then are we talking about if we try to question, affirm or deny that there really is an Unconditioned Transcendent? If, as it certainly seems to be, it is impossible to give an answer, then "being-talk" is only a less familiar and less evocative species of incoherence than God-talk.

At this point we are likely to hear talk about ineffability. To be so analytic, it will be contended, is appropriate to an examination of scientific discourse, but it is not appropriate to religious discourse. Such an analytic approach, it will be proclaimed in certain circles, ignores the existential dimension of man. Suffering from cultural lag, such an analytic approach, still too much in the temper of positivism, fails to take to heart man's existential encounter with Being, when the dread of non-being gives him a sense, scarcely characterizable in words, of his "total existence." Being-talk may indeed be so paradoxical as to be scarcely intelligible, but such concrete human experiences do lead to a confrontation with Being. And being-itself is indeed the Ineffable: that which is beyond all conceptualization. In our despair and estrangement we are led to an ineffable but supremely Holy something which can be experienced in a compelling manner but it can never be more than obliquely and metaphorically hinted at in words, symbols and images. To gain insight here, we need to transcend our pedestrian literalness and acknowledge that there are some things which are literally unsayable or inexpressible but are nonetheless given in those experiences of depth where man must confront his own existence.

What is involved here is the claim that there are "ineffable truths" which cannot be put into words; religious truths—so the argument runs—are species of that genus. Men with the proper experience and attitudes understand them; that is, they in a sense understand the concept of God, but what they know to be true cannot in any way be literally expressed. Our samples of being-talk haltingly and falteringly suggest these truths; they can awake in us the experience of such "ineffable truths" but they do not make true or false statements themselves. Instead they function evocatively to give rise to such experiences or expressively to suggest what cannot be literally stated. Given the proper experience, the reality they obliquely attest to will, while remaining irreducibly mysterious, be humanely speaking undeniable.

Such doctrines of the Ineffable are incoherent and will not enable us to meet or resolve religious quandaries legitimately. To hold such a doctrine is to be committed to the thesis that, though there may be something appropriately called "God," "Being-itself" or "the Unconditioned Transcendent," in reality nothing literal, or at least nothing affirmative, can be said about God. That is to say, no sentences about God or sentences in which "God" occurs literally express a fact or make a true or false assertion. Thus, on such a reading of God-talk, "The world is dependent on God" or any other God-sentence cannot literally make a true or false statement, assert something that is so or is not so, though such sentences are not without sense for they have a metaphorical or symbolic use. But if an utterance P is metaphorical, this entails that it is *logically possible* for there to be some literal statement G which has the same conceptual content. "Metaphorical," or for that matter "symbolic" or "analogical," gets its meaning by being contrastable with "literal." There can be no intelligible metaphorical or symbolic or analogical God-talk if there can be no literal God-talk. Thus the ineffability thesis is internally incoherent.

However, it might be replied that the above argument does not touch the most fundamental core of the ineffability thesis, namely that the man of faith can know what he means by "God" though he cannot, literally or even obliquely, say what he means and what he means cannot in any way be expressed, even if it is given in an ecstatic encounter or confrontation with Being or an Unconditioned Transcendent. The latter part of this is nonsense, for, as I have already pointed out, a reality transcendent to the universe could not be encountered or confronted; only some being in the world could, logically could, be encountered or confronted.

We are, however, still on slightly peripheral ground, for the major claim in the ineffability thesis is that one can know what P means even though P cannot even in principle be expressed or publically exhibited. One can know that there is a God though the concept of God is inexpressible and our talk of God is nonsensical.

What makes this maneuver seem more plausible than it actually is, is its easy confusion with the rather ordinary experience of knowing very well what something is (say a bird one sees) and yet being at that time quite unable to *say* what it is. One looks at the bird and recognizes it but one cannot remember its name. In this context we should also call to mind that we have a whole range of "aha!-experiences." But the ineffability thesis under examination maintains something far more radical than would be encompassed by a theory which took into account, as it indeed should take into account, the above straightforwardly empirical phenomena. The ineffability thesis commits one to the belief that there are things one can know which are *in principle* impossible, that is, logically impossible, to express or to exhibit in any system of notation. In this way "a true religious statement" or "an expressed religious truth" would be self-contradictory.

It is tempting to take the short way with such a thesis and to reject it on the following grounds: 1) If one knows P then P is true, since "I know it but it isn't true" is a contradiction. Thus, since only statements are literally true, there could be no inexpressible knowledge. 2) Reflection on "means" also establishes that there could be no such "ineffable understanding." For something to have a meaning or to have meaning, it must have a use in a language or in some system of notation. This partially specifies what it means for something to have a meaning or have meaning even when we speak of the meaning of a concept, for we use "concept" to signify what is expressed by synonymous expressions in the same or different languages or systems of notation. But only if something has meaning or has a meaning can we understand what it means, so we cannot understand something which is inexpressible *in principle*; there would be nothing to be understood, for there would be nothing that is meaningful.

However, some might think, mistakenly I believe, that some of these premises make unjustified and question-begging assumptions. Rather than extending my argument for them here or entering into complicated questions about so-called "private languages" and the like, I shall see if there are still simpler considerations that can properly be utilized to refute or render implausible the ineffability thesis. (Keep in mind that the job of challenging premises can always go on and on; the most we can hope for in philosophy is to give from the alternatives available the most plausible perspicacious representation of the conceptual area in question.) [12] First, take note of the platitude that if you know something that is literally in principle unsayable, inexpressible, incapable of being shown or in any way exhibited, then there trivially can be no communicating it. You cannot justifiably say it is *God* you experience, know, encounter, love or commit yourself to in utter trust; you, on your own thesis, cannot significantly say that if you do such and such and have such and such experiences, you will come to know God or come to be grasped by God. "What is unsayable is unsayable," is a significant tautology. Only if one could at least obliquely or metaphorically express one's experience of the Divine could one's God-talk have any significance, but on the present *radical* ineffability thesis even the possibility of obliquely expressing one's knowledge or belief is ruled out. So, given such a thesis, there could be no confessional community or circle of faith; in fine, the thesis is reduced to the absurd by making it impossible for those who accept such a thesis to acknowledge the manifest truth that the Judeo-Christian religion is a social reality. On this simple consideration alone, we should surely rule out the ineffability thesis. Thus Dom Illyd Trethowan is wide of the mark when he remarks: "Flew and Nielsen . . . are asking for a description of God. And the believer, again if he knows his business will reply . . . that God cannot be described. God is the Other." [13] If we try to take this claim of Trethowan's literally, then the word "God" is surely not just the vehicle for an incoherent concept, but "God" is *meaningless* for we cannot even say *that* something is if it is indescribable. What is indescribable is also unintelligible.

Three reminders here: 1) In asserting that nonanthropomorphic concepts of God are incoherent and according to some theological construals of "God" even meaningless, I am not merely giving you to understand that skeptics (atheists and agnostics) do not understand God-talk. Rather, I have been contending that, the believer's beliefs *about* his beliefs notwithstanding, the concept of God in developed Judaism and Christianity is an incoherent one and neither believer nor nonbeliever understands what they are talking about when they talk about God or attempt to talk to God. I am not simply urging that the believer make his beliefs meaningful to the skeptic, I am asking that he show how God-talk is a coherent form of language, period.[14] 2) I do not accept either the Wittgensteinian assumption that every form of discourse is all right as it is and that the only thing that could be out of order is the philosophical talk about the talk or the further and related Wittgensteinian claim that philosophy can only relevantly display the forms of life and not relevantly criticize them or assess them. Not only God-talk but also Witch-talk and talk of fairies have their own distinctive uses and even within our culture once constituted a discourse and were embedded in a form of life. But all the same such forms of life were open to criticism and came gradually to be discredited as they were recognized to be incoherent. Indeed in *many cases* first-order discourse and the beliefs embedded in them are beyond philosophical reproach and it is merely the characterization, the second-order discourse, that is troublesome. Thus if someone tells you that you never see tables or chairs and that you do not have a mind, that is a bad joke, but if someone tells you that you do not have a soul, you just think you do, it may very well engender a live dispute or a live worry if you are a traditional Christian. Where God-talk is involved, both the first-order and the second-order discourse are problematical.[15] 3) The acceptance of even a thorough-going fideistic point of view will not protect the believer from my critique. If we understood what it *meant* to assert or deny "And God shall raise the quick and the dead" or "God is the Creator of the Heavens and the earth," we might accept them humbly on faith. We might, out of our desperate need to make sense of our lives, accept them *de fide*. But we can only do that if we have some understanding of what they *mean*. If I ask you to believe in Irglig, you cannot believe in Irglig no matter how deep your need because you do not know *what* to take on faith (on trust). Faith presupposes a *minimal understanding* of what you take on faith, and if my arguments are correct, we do not have that understanding of a nonanthropomorphic concept of God.[16]

VI

It might be contended that I have so far ignored the major and most obvious objection to my procedure. I am, it is natural to say, being a philosophical Neanderthal, for my arguments rest too exclusively on verificationist principles and by now it is well known that the verifiability principle is plainly untenable.[17]

I, of course, agree that it is certainly plainly evident that it is not true that a sentence is meaningful only if it is verifiable. In fact, I would go further and claim that such a claim is itself incoherent. It is sentences, not statements, which are meaningful or meaningless and it is statements, not sentences, which are confirmable or infirmable, true or false. Questions of meaning are logically prior to questions of verification; in order to verify or confirm a statement we must already know what it means. Moreover, many sentences which are plainly meaningful, e.g., "Pass the butter," "Oh, if this agony would only end," "Will the weather change?" do not even purport to make statements, let alone statements of fact which are confirmable or infirmable. It is by now crystal clear that the verifiability principle will never do as a *general* criterion of meaningful discourse.[18]

There are two points, however, that should be made here: 1) it is less evident that some form of the verifiability criterion is not correct as a criterion of *factual* significance and 2) that many of my key arguments do not even depend on or presuppose such a criterion of factual significance. The second point alone is enough to free me from the charge that I am entangled in a thoroughly discredited "logical empiricist metaphysics" but I would like, in what I fear is too brief and too brusk a manner, to defend my first point, for it may seem obscurantist.

Do we have, for the many and varied types of meaningful utterance, a criterion in virtue of which we can decide which of them are fact-stating? I maintain that we do, for a statement has factual content only if it is in principle testable or, to put it differently, for a sentence to function in a discourse as a factual assertion, it must make a statement which it is logically possible to confirm or infirm. If anything can give us "some insight into the ultimate nature of things"—to utter a tantalizing obscurity—it will be factually informative statements, i.e., statements which give us knowledge of what is the case. To have insight into "the ultimate nature of things" would be at least to have some reliable beliefs about what *in fact* the universe is like. That is, we would gain some information about some very fundamental facts. I do not say this is all we would need but we would at least have to have that. But *factually* informative utterances must, in principle, be verifiable. To put the point more exactly, a statement has factual significance only if it is at least logically possible to indicate the conditions or set of conditions under which it could be to some degree confirmed or infirmed, i.e., that it is logically possible to state evidence for or against its truth.[19]

Certainly my claim here is a controversial one—a claim that many analytic philosophers would reject on the grounds that it blurs too many distinctions and relies on too many vague claims. I have already voided some of the usual criticisms through the very specification of its actual scope. Beyond that, all I can do in the space available here is to use Hume's method of challenge and to ask you if you can think of a single unequivocally factual statement—a statement that all parties would agree had factual content—that is not in the sense specified above verifiable (confirmable or infirmable) in principle. If you cannot—and I do not think you can—is it not reasonable to believe that my demarcation line for a statement of fact is justified? [20]

Indeed this gauntlet has been taken up, but the most usual and sophisticated of the alleged counter examples to my claim are of the following two sorts, neither of which seem to me genuine counter examples: 1) "Every human being has some neurotic traits," and 2) "My head aches." As Hempel and Rynin have pointed out, statements of unrestricted generality with mixed quantification are not decisively confirmable or infirmable and we cannot even state a precise probability weight for their confirmation or disconfirmation.[21] But this does not mean that in a weaker and less precise sense we could not give perfectly empirical evidence for or against their truth. Since language is not like a calculus, we should not continue to believe that it will function like one. If we continue to discover neurotic traits in all the people who are so examined and if some independently testable personality theory gives us reason to believe, say, that the very growing up in a family always leads to some neurotic stress, the generalization has some confirmation. On the other hand, if we find a human being who does not, so far as we can determine, behave neurotically at all, the generalization is slightly weakened. The same thing is true for other statements involving mixed quantification which might be plainly thought to have factual content, e.g., "Every substance has some solvent" or "Every planet has some form of life."

"My head aches," or "I have a headache," poses different problems. From the period of *The Blue Book* on, Wittgenstein thought that such utterances do not have a verification. Malcolm points out that in his *Philosophische Bemerkungen* Wittgenstein thought that they could be verified, but after 1932 his recognition that they were avowals rather than statements of fact led to his "turning away from the full-blown verification theory of meaning." [22] However, it is just this conception of avowals that is important for my case. I do not verify, "My head aches," or "I have a headache." After all, in normal circumstances I could not doubt it. I could not inquire into whether my head aches, or check up on whether my head aches or wonder whether my head aches. "My head seems to ache," or "Perhaps my head aches," has no straightforward use. In normal circumstances, I, by my very utterance, simply avow that my head aches. I am not, Wittgenstein argued, trying to state a fact but to give expression to how I feel.

If you reply—and I for one have considerable sympathy with that reply—that this is too extreme, for "head aches," in "My head aches," when uttered by Nielsen, has factual content, note that it has the same factual content as "Nielsen's head aches" and that this statement is perfectly open to confirmation by what I say and do. What makes "Nielsen's head aches" true or false is exactly what makes "My head aches" true or false, where the utterer of this last utterance is Nielsen. So we still have no genuine example of a factual statement which is not verifiable. Either we drop the claim that "My head aches" is true or false in which case no issue arises about its being a factual statement or about how we could come to know that it is so, or we allow it is true or false, in which case we come to know that it is true or false, that it is verified, in the same way that we come to know or verify that "Nielsen's head aches" is true or false. When I utter "My head aches" and Jones utters "Nielsen's head aches," both these claims are, to use a slightly outmoded and pleonastic terminology, intersubjectively verified in the same way, to the extent they are verified or are known to be true or false at all.

There are those who think that behind my talk of "factual significance" and the verifiability principle there lurks a series of false dichotomies such as "factual meaning"/"emotive meaning," "cognitive meaning"/"metaphorical meaning," "literal meaning"/"nonliteral meaning," and the like. I do not think any such "multiplication of meanings beyond need," is involved in what I have argued, but for those who remain unconvinced and suffer from the anxieties described above, I want to stress that what is most essential to my argument about fact-stating discourse can be put in this way: If a sentence is used to make what is thought to be a factual statement and yet the statement made by its use is neither confirmable nor infirmable even in principle, then the statement in question actually fails to come off as a factual statement, i.e., it fails to assert a fact and thus is not a genuine bit of fact-stating discourse. An utterance that comes off as a statement of fact must be verifiable in principle.

To sum up. Judaism and Christianity are thought by Jews and Christians to involve an entry into a relationship with a being transcendent to the world or at least with a creative and gracious "world ground" which is distinct from the world and upon which the world is dependent. Thus we face what for the Jew or Christian is an awkward fact, namely that while being a Jew or Christian consists in much more than believing that certain allegedly factual statements are true, it does, in an utterly irreducible manner, involve the acceptance of what are taken by the faithful to be certain factual beliefs. And these purportedly factual beliefs are often of vast scope; they are not only ordinary empirical beliefs such as Jesus was born in Bethlehem. The expression of such "cosmic factual beliefs" results in the making of religious or, if you will, theological statements, e.g., "There is an infinite, eternal Creator of the world" or "There is an ultimate loving reality in which all men find their being," and these statements are taken by the faithful to be factual statements. Yet they are neither directly nor indirectly confirmable or infirmable even in principle and thus are in reality, as many nonbelievers have suspected, devoid of factual content.[23] They purport to be factual but fail to behave as factual statements. We have no idea of how to establish their truth or probable truth, or their falsity or probable falsity. We have no conception of what it would be like for them to be true (or probably true) or false (or probably false). Yet they are supposedly expressive of factual beliefs. But a statement which is in no way confirmable or infirmable even in principle is not a factual statement. To make sense of such utterances on their own terms, and not just the sense a Santayana or Feuerbach would make of them, believers must believe that these key bits of God-talk are fact-stating, but these utterances fail to come off as bits of fact-stating discourse. So here we have at the very foundation of such faiths a radical incoherence which vitiates such religious claims.[24]

It might be countered that "Every human being is dependent on an infinite 'world ground' transcendent to the universe," is factually intelligible because it is after all weakly confirmable or infirmable in a manner similar to the way "Every human being has some neurotic traits," is confirmable or infirmable. There is weak verification in each case. Feeling dependent and morally insufficient counts weakly for the truth of the putative theological assertion; making sense of one's life and of morality independent of any reference to religion and overcoming feelings of utter dependency counts against its truth. But this is deceiving for atheists can, and *some* do, agree that human beings pervasively have these feelings of dependency and moral insufficiency and still these atheists can make nothing of nonanthropomorphic talk of God or an infinite "world ground" transcendent to the universe. The believer cannot legitimately respond that he is simply talking about such feelings and *nothing more* for then his belief would be indistinguishable from atheism. But it is his alleged "something more" that does not make a verifiable difference even in the weak sense. "God is wholly Other," is, taken by itself, nonsense for it is an incomplete sentence: in order to understand it, we need to know "a wholly other *what*." The alleged answer frequently comes by talk of "Being-in-itself," "Unconditioned Transcendent," "Being transcendent to the world" and the like, but, as we have seen, though they are purportedly referring expressions, no intelligible directions have been given as to how to identify the supposed referents of such referring expressions. The affirmation and denial that there are such "realities" is equally compatible with anything and everything that could conceivably be experienced. Such nonanthropomorphic God-talk does not make verifiable sense.

VII

Such is my argument about God-talk. There are three morals I wish to draw from this, one religious and ideological and the other two about philosophical methodology.

To put the religious or ideological point bluntly: If my central arguments are essentially correct, one should not be a Jew, Christian, Moslem or any kind of theist. To be any of these things involves having beliefs "whose scope transcends the empirical world." More specifically, it involves believing in the reality of God as a creator of the universe. But, if my arguments are near to their mark, such a belief is utterly incoherent. That is to say, with nonanthropomorphic conceptions of God there is nothing intelligible to be believed, so atheism (a reasoned rejection of belief in God) becomes the most reasonable form of life. If beliefs are persisted in where there are no *reasons* for holding them, we should look for the *causes*: look for what makes people believe as they do; belief in God is absurd, but, as Feuerbach, Santayana and Freud have shown, the psychological need for this construct of the human heart is so great that in cultures like ours many people must believe in spite of the manifest absurdity of their belief. They can see and accept this absurdity in the religious beliefs of other tribes and sometimes, as with Hamman and Kierkegaard, they can partially see it and accept it in their own tribe, but the acceptance is not unequivocal and the full absurdity of their own belief remains hidden from them.

It is sometimes objected that no such normative conclusions could follow from purely non-normative premises, and that atheism, as it plainly is for Sartre, ultimately, as John Courtney Murray puts it in his *The Problem of God*, is "a total option made by free decision rather than an intellectual position reached by argument." [25]

There are multiple confusions here. I am philosophically conservative enough to believe, Searle and Black to the contrary notwithstand-

ing, that categorical normative conclusions are not entailed by any set of
purely non-normative premises. But even if I am right about this and
there is such an is/ought divide, it does not at all follow that normative
claims are not supported or justified or at least weakened or strengthened by non-normative claims. After all, entailments are not the only
conceptual connections.[26] And this is all I am maintaining. In other
words, I am only maintaining that, if my arguments about the concept
of God are accepted, it would be unreasonable for those who accept
them to remain Jews, Christians or Moslems. Moreover, in such a circumstance it would be more reasonable to be an atheist than an agnostic. There are in such considerations crucial normative implications
about how to live and die. The clickety-clack of linguistic analysis has
human implications.

I want to turn for a moment to Murray's dichotomy for it is a false
dichotomy. Atheism, like Christianity or any other way of life, does, of
course, involve a normative stance, an option about how to live. But it is
by no means a matter of the godless man of the academy or the market-
place simply willing or opting "to understand the world without God."
Any way of acting which reflects deliberation involves the decision to act
in a certain way; and to act deliberately in a certain way is part of what
it is to live in accordance with norms. That is to say, my remarks here
are conceptual remarks or what Wittgenstein, with a considerable
stretch of "grammatical," called "grammatical remarks." Between men
of God and atheists there is indeed the clash of affirmations. But it is
not *simply* a clash of affirmations or even in *the last analysis* simply a
clash of affirmations. Atheism involves a decision about how to live,
but it also involves an intellectual understanding of what our world is
like; and the decision to reject religious belief would not be made without a certain intellectual understanding of the situation.

My concluding remarks about philosophical methodology are not
unrelated to what I have just maintained. For anyone at all knowledge-
able about philosophical analysis, for anyone touched by the work of
Moore, Wittgenstein, and Austin, it is natural, when faced with my
arguments, to assert that something must have gone wrong somewhere.
Philosophical analysis is normatively and, if you will, ideologically or
metaphysically neutral. It is tempting to maintain that when anyone
claims to have drawn such vast ideological conclusions as I claim to have
drawn from philosophical analysis, you can be quite confident that he is
unwittingly sneaking some nonanalytical element into his philosophical
analysis—that somewhere, somehow some special pleading has occurred
—for philosophical analyses are ideologically neutral.

There is an ambiguity in the phrase "philosophical analysis is neutral" which once exposed will undermine this argument. Philosophical analysis is neutral in the sense that, *independently* of one's normative, ideological, or metaphysical view of the world, it either does or does not follow that to say X ought to do Y presupposes X can do Y, or to say that X knows God is to give one to understand that X loves God, or to say that X believes *in* God presupposes that X believes *that* God exists. These relationships are logical or conceptual, and they either hold or fail to hold, and what in this way holds or fails to hold here is not a factor of one's ideological commitments. In this important sense philosophical analysis is ideologically neutral. If this were not so, philosophical dispute would degenerate into a clash of rival unarguable affirmations. In a very important sense it would cease being *philosophical* and philosophy would itself be impossible.

However, there is another sense in which philosophical analysis is not normatively or ideologically neutral. In carrying out a philosophical analysis, we attempt, through a description of the uses and the unscheduled inferences of philosophically perplexing terms and utterances, to gain a perspicuous representation of the discourse in question. If, after a careful analysis of "can," one concluded that "I can," in moral contexts typically and irreducibly functioned categorically and that these uses of discourse were essential to the understanding of human action, it would be unreasonable to be a soft determinist; if, after a careful analysis of "good," "right," and "ought" in moral contexts, it became apparent that "good" was never equivalent to any term or set of terms standing for purely empirical characteristics or relations, it would be unreasonable to be an ethical naturalist; similarly it would not be reasonable to remain a Jew or a Christian if careful elucidation of "God" and God-talk indicated that, while believers took "God" to be a referring expression, "God" actually functions neither as a name nor as a definite or indefinite description and that there are no directions in the discourse concerning how to identify God so that we could have some idea of what we are talking about when we speak of God.

It is evident in such a situation vis-à-vis soft determinism, ethical naturalism and theism, that certain results of philosophical analysis indicate that a given ideological position is not tenable.[27] In this respect philosophical analysis is not ideologically neutral. But if it were not philosophically neutral in the way I first characterized, analysis itself would be impossible and there could be no philosophically relevant grounds for accepting or rejecting any of these ideological positions.

This leads me to my last point which is a general one about the nature of philosophy. It is tempting to remark that in proceeding as I have in this essay, I have been trying to do something that cannot be done: I have in effect tried to give philosophy a task which cannot be its own; I have implicitly prescribed what activities, what forms of life, are legitimate or rational and what usages, reflecting these forms of life, are coherent, when in actuality philosophy can only legitimately clearly display the actual structure of the discourse embedded in these activities. Again we are back to a very Wittgensteinian point. The claim is that the philosopher's sole legitimate function is to describe our discourse so as to dispel conceptual perplexities engendered by a failure properly to understand the workings of our language.

Certainly such a Wittgensteinian stress is an understandable and justified reaction to the kind of *prescriptivism* which would persuasively redefine "knowledge," "proof," "explanation," "evidence," and the like in such a way that most of the things commonly called such are not *real* knowledge, proof, explanation, evidence and the like. Moore, Wittgenstein and ordinary language philosophers have amply demonstrated the barrenness of such philosophical rationalism. But such a descriptivism can throw out the baby with the bath and utterly lose one of the deepest rationales for doing philosophy, namely that of criticizing received opinions and more generally and uniquely of providing a critical discussion of critical discussions and forms of life.

These are grand old phrases, it might be replied, but they remain empty: what exactly is this critical discussion of critical discussions and what Archimedian point can the philosopher possibly attain which would enable him legitimately to criticize whole forms of life; the very concept of rationality is itself a deeply contested and context-dependent concept.

In considering this, let us start with one of the less contested points first. "Rational" and "rationality" are indeed used eulogistically, but we should beware of concluding that they are just emotive labels or that they are so essentially contested as to be thoroughly subjective. Translation into the concrete should make this evident, though it will not, of course, provide us with an elucidation of the concept of rationality. A man who never listens to others and always shouts others down is not rational; it is also irrational to persist in a practice which gives rise to vast human suffering when this could be avoided by adopting another practice that would achieve much the same thing as the first practice but would cause much less suffering; finally, to point to a specific kind of behavior, to believe in witches or fairies is also irrational if one is a tolerably well-informed Westerner living in the twentieth century. "Rational," whatever its precise analysis, is not so vague that it does not have an established use and evident paradigm cases. Moreover, activities or forms of life are not neatly isolated activities with their own distinctive criteria. There is, for example, no such thing as "religious language," though there are religious discourses carried on in English, Swedish, German, French, etc. And even in these discourses the criteria of relevance, the use of "evidence," "rationality," and the like are not utterly unique to the discourse in question. It is just not so that God-talk is a self-contained form of language or form of life, though it does have its distinctive topics and centers of interest.

The very criticisms I have made of religious beliefs, if they are on the whole correct, constitute a *reductio* of the Wittgensteinian thesis that philosophy can only be descriptive. To this it might be replied that since philosophy can only be descriptive there must be something basically wrong with my arguments about religious belief. Forms of life are immune from anything but piecemeal criticism; there can be no incoherent forms of language or irrational forms of life. But remembering the very different things that philosophy has been throughout its long history, and keeping in mind the immense variety of types of investigation that have gone on under the name of "philosophy," and the precariousness and contested nature of generalizations about the nature of philosophy, is it not—I put it to your reflective consideration—more reasonable to doubt the descriptivist thesis as a completely adequate account of the proper office of philosophy, than to reject my arguments *simply on the grounds that they fail to square with a thesis in the philosophy of philosophy?*

Wittgenstein generalized primarily from reflecting on epistemology, the philosophy of mind, and mathematics. There his descriptivist thesis seems to me thoroughly plausible; but he may, to turn his own phrase against him, have suffered from a one-sided diet. Religion is a form of life that may indeed be given, but it is still not beyond the pale of relevant philosophical criticism.

This essay might have been entitled "A Refutation of Theism" or "A Refutation of Judeo-Christianity." Until and unless specific arguments can be provided to show that my criticisms fail, it is more reasonable to accept them and reject such a form of life than to maintain, on the basis of a general and disputed thesis in the philosophy of philosophy, that such arguments must be mistaken. Even if some—or worse still all—of my criticisms fail, unless criticisms of such *a general type* can be shown to be irrelevant, there is no reason to assume that the descriptivist thesis must be so and that "A Philosophical Refutation of Theism" is a conceptual anomaly.

I admit that the concept of such a type of critical assessment (a "criticism of criticisms" or "a critical discussion of forms of life and of critical discussion") is itself a disputed concept expressive of a controver-

sial thesis in the philosophy of philosophy and that it is in need of a careful elucidation and defense.[28] But *ambulando* what I have done here vis-
à-vis religion and what Ronald Hepburn did in *Christianity and Paradox*
and Antony Flew did in *God and Philosophy* are examples of what I
have in mind. We have learned from Moore and Ryle that we can typically do with words what we may not in fact be able on demand to
characterize adequately.

It is also well known that "What is philosophy?" is itself a deeply
contested philosophical problem and many men—past and present—
who considered themselves philosophers and who are generally considered philosophers have thought they could provide disciplined, rational
criticism of ways-of-life. Moreover, they thought they were doing this in
the course of philosophizing **and** not as an activity that was ancillary to
their philosophizing.[29] I have tried to do just that for a family of ways-
of-life, namely Judaism, Christianity and Islam, by exhibiting the incoherence of absolutely central beliefs they hold in common. Most of
my arguments are fairly specific exercises in philosophical analysis. Unless they and arguments like them fail, we have good grounds for believing that it is not the case that philosophy properly done must always be
purely descriptive. So my exercise gives rise to two important general
claims: it challenges Judeo-Christian belief at its very heart and it also
challenges a fashionable thesis about the nature of philosophy.

One final salvo of I hope not too homiletic a nature. People who
try to apply the techniques of linguistic analysis are still frequently
accused of engaging in trivial endeavors and with what has been called
"an abdication of philosophy." But note this: whatever else may be
wrong with what I have argued here, it remains one example of analytic
philosophy that cannot be so criticized. What the critic must do is to
show that my arguments are mistaken and not complain that they are
trivial because they do not touch fundamental problems of human existence.

NOTES

1. P. F. Strawson, "Identifying Reference and Truth-Values," *Theoria*, Vol.
XXX (1964, Part 2), p. 115.

2. *Ibid.*, p. 101.

3. This view is well expressed by Alasdair MacIntyre in his *Difficulties in
Christian Belief*.

4. Ronald Hepburn, "Agnosticism," Vol. I, *Encyclopedia of Philosophy*,
Paul Edwards, ed. (New York, Macmillan & Co. and The Free Press, 1967), pp. 58–
59.

5. John MacQuarrie, *God-Talk* (New York, Harper & Row, Publishers, Inc., 1967), p. 176.

6. See John Hick, "Christianity," Vol. II, *Encyclopedia of Philosophy*.

7. W. D. Hudson, "Transcendence," *Theology*, Vol. LXIX (March, 1966), p. 104.

8. *Ibid.*, pp. 103–4.

9. *Ibid.*, p. 103.

10. *Ibid.*

11. Paul Tillich, "The Religious Symbol," in *Religious Experience and Truth*, Sidney Hook, ed., p. 303.

12. This conception of philosophy as resting on considerations of plausibility is well expressed by J. J. C. Smart in his *Philosophy and Scientific Realism* (New York, Humanities Press, 1963), pp. 12–13, and in more detail in his "Philosophy and Scientific Plausibility," in Feyerabend, Paul K. and Maxwell, G. E. (eds.) *Mind, Matter, and Method, Essays in Honor of Herbert Feigl* (Minneapolis, Minn., U. of Minn. Press, 1966).

13. Illyd Trethowan, "In Defense of Theism—A Reply to Professor Kai Nielsen," Vol. 2, *Religious Studies*, No. 1 (1966), p. 39.

14. So Trethowan is again wide of the mark when he remarks: "Nielsen will be entitled to say that he can make nothing of it, but (I submit) he will not be entitled to say that there is anything logically the matter with it. He seems to think that a believer is not logically entitled to regard his beliefs as meaningful unless he can make them meaningful to an unbeliever." *Ibid.*, pp. 38–39. Generally, it seems to me, Trethowan's defense of theism and criticisms of my arguments are ineffective.

15. I have stated this rather bruskly and perhaps in a dogmatic sounding way. I have argued for it in some detail in my "Wittgensteinian Fideism," *Philosophy*, Vol. XLII (July, 1967), in "Language and the Concept of God," *Question* 2 (January, 1969), pp. 36–40, in "God and the Forms of Life," *Indian Review of Philosophy*, forthcoming, and in my book *The Quest for God*, forthcoming.

16. I have argued the ins and outs of this in my "Can Faith Validate God-Talk?" *New Theology No. 1*, Martin Marty and Dean Peerman, eds. (New York, Macmillan & Co. and The Free Press, 1964) and in my "Religious Perplexity and Faith," *The Crane Review*, Vol. VIII (Fall, 1965).

17. The application of these considerations to religious discourse have been succinctly stated by Alvin Plantinga, "Analytic Philosophy and Christianity," *Christianity Today* (October 25, 1963), pp. 75–78, and by George I. Mavrodes, "God and Verification," *Canadian Journal of Theology*, Vol. 10 (1964) pp. 187–191. But see my response "God and Verification Again," *Canadian Journal of Theology*, Vol. XI (1965), pp. 135–141.

18. These and other closely related points have been decisively argued by G. J. Warnock, "Verification and the Use of Language," *Revue Internationale de Philosophie*, Vol. 17 (1951); J. L. Evans, "On Meaning and Verification," *Mind*, Vol. LXII (1953) and *The Foundations of Empiricism* (Cardiff, 1965); Paul Marhenke, "The Criterion of Significance," *Proceedings and Addresses of the American Philosophical Association*, 1950; and R. W. Ashby, "Verifiability Principle," Vol. 8, *The Encyclopedia of Philosophy*.

19. Some contemporary philosophers have tried to take up this challenge and show how certain key religious utterances are verifiable. I examine their arguments and attempt to show *that* they fail and *how* they fail in my "Christian Positivism and the Appeal to Religious Experience," *The Journal of Religion*, Vol. XLII (October, 1962); "Eschatological Verification," *Canadian Journal of Theology*, Vol. IX (1962) and "On Fixing the Reference Range of 'God'," *Religious Studies* (October, 1966).

20. I argue for this in detail in my *Quest for God*, forthcoming.

21. Carl Hempel, *Aspects of Scientific Explanation*, Chapter IV (New York, The Free Press, 1965) and David Rynin, "Vindication of L*G*C*L*P*S*T*V*SM,"

Proceedings and Addresses of the American Philosophical Association, 1957.

22. Norman Malcolm, "Wittgenstein's *Philosophische Bemerkungen*," *The Philosophical Review*, Vol. LXXVI (April, 1967), p. 225.

23. This cannot be taken as evidence that we have statements which are plainly factual but still not verifiable, for the examples themselves do not have an undisputed factual status. Many nonbelievers and even some who call themselves believers (Hare, Braithwaite, and Miles) do not regard them as factual statements. Moreover, they do not all make this assumption because they assume the verifiability criterion of factual significance but some do so because they think an examination of the use, the depth grammar, of key religious utterances will show that they have a very different function than do statements of fact.

24. I am not asking that religion become what it plainly is not, i.e., science. There are plenty of fact-stating discourses which are not scientific. Man did not have to wait for the rise of science before he could start stating facts. I am also not ignoring context, for these presuppositions operate in religious contexts. See Crombie's remarks on this in the opening pages of his "The Possibility of Theological Statements," in *Faith and Logic*, Basil Mitchell, ed. (London, Allen & Unwin, 1957), pp. 31–33.

25. John Courtney Murray, *The Problem of God*, p. 84.

26. Stephen Toulmin argues this point very effectively in his *The Uses of Argument* (Cambridge, Cambridge University Press, 1964).

27. It might be objected that this does not hold for ethical naturalism, for ethical naturalism is itself a meta-ethical theory and not a normative ethical theory. That it is a meta-ethical theory is indeed so, and I would further agree that this distinction in ethical theory is an important one. But meta-ethical theories themselves have normative implications. It would be unreasonable for a man not to take the dictates of his own society as normative for his behavior within that society, *if* he believed that "One ought to do Y" *meant* "Y is a dictate of one's society." For a discussion of the normative implications of meta-ethics see my "Problem of Ethics," Vol. 3, *The Encyclopedia of Philosophy*, pp. 119–124.

28. What I have said in the last few pages has been influenced by the views of John Passmore; see his essay "Philosophy" in Vol. 6, *The Encyclopedia of Philosophy*, pp. 216–226. I have tried to say something about philosophy as a criticism of criticisms in my "John Dewey's Conception of Philosophy," *The University of Massachusetts Review*, Vol. II, No. 1 (Autumn, 1960).

29. A powerful case for such ideological considerations being ancillary has been made by Anthony Quinton in "Philosophy and Beliefs," but in line with the point I have been making, note the powerful counter thrusts of Stuart Hampshire and Isaiah Berlin. See A. Quinton, S. Hampshire, S. Murdoch and I. Berlin, "Philosophy and Beliefs," *The Twentieth Century*, Vol. CLVII (1955), pp. 495–521.

PHILOSOPHY OF RELIGION

(A RESPONSE)

John Macquarrie

I'd like to state first of all my very strong agreement with one point that Dr. Nielsen made—namely, that for the Jew, or the Christian, or the Muslim, religion is much more than a metaphysic. It is much more than a belief about the world. It is a whole way of life. And this is surely a point we should bear in mind. If belief in God were simply a remote academic business, if God was just a bit of metaphysical furniture, so to speak, I don't think the question would excite the interest that it does, but it is connected with a whole way of life. Also, I heartily agree with Dr. Nielsen's point that religious language, if we are to talk about it and discuss it, has to be put into context. "Language," Wittgenstein once said, "is a form of life and we've got to put it in its living context." But I rather feel that although Dr. Nielsen paid lip-service to that idea, he very speedily branched off and began to talk about religious language in rather abstract ways.

From the analytical side one gets different kinds of criticism. The most telling criticisms I have come across are those of Ronald Hepburn because I think Ronald Hepburn has discussed language very much in context. He is at least about three-quarters participant in the thing at some times. On the other hand I find a person like Alfred Ayer so far away from what he is discussing that his criticisms have never seemed to me terribly telling. I think Dr. Nielsen somehow swings between these two.

Further, I also want to express agreement with the thought that although Judaism, Christianity, and what not, are ways of life, they do, nevertheless, commit us—and I quote Dr. Nielsen's words—"to an utterly irreducible minimum of belief." In other words, I don't think problems about theism can be solved by saying, Well, let's have a Christianity without God; we would just be deceiving ourselves if we talked in that way and would be much more honest if we followed Dr. Nielsen's advice and put up the shutters.

However, let me go on to a more substantive criticism of what we have here. I feel that Dr. Nielsen begins to sever his connection with the context of religious language when he asks about the referend of the word "God." I think the unconscious assumption in Dr. Nielsen's mind from that point is that just as, let us say the expression, "that lamp" has a referent, so the word "God" is a word for which we have to find something in the world. Let me give you an actual illustration of that. Dr. Nielsen has a certain amount of fun with language like "being" language, for instance, and I don't entirely blame him because I think in this area people are, as it were, groping for the language. I have certainly done this myself when I have spoken about the form of the world and meaning and so on. I have groped for a language but, of course, remembered that from the very beginning philosophers have always had to stretch ordinary language quite a bit. They haven't been able to just use the ordinary, every day language. Language is appropriate for saying something like "there is a cat on the mat," which is a fairly explicable kind of fact but not a terribly important one, but it seems that once you go further you have to develop a more complicated kind of language.

I should like to quote a sentence from Dr. Nielsen's paper in which he says, "here 'being' as well as 'being itself,' a pitch at any actuality, purportedly functions as a name or referring expression, that is to say as a word which supposedly denotes or stands for something." It seems to me that those who use this kind of language take great pains to insist that they don't think that a word like "being" or God stands for something—something meaning some entity, some object in the world. This is precisely what they are not saying. And that is precisely why, of course, we get into these linguistic problems; and yet these words are managing to express something in the kind of language that they use.

Let me go on to show where I think Dr. Nielsen does move away from context and begins to discuss the language of religious faith in an abstract kind of way. He asks, for instance, "What does it mean to say that the world is utterly dependent?" And certainly when a sentence like that is thrown at you, it does make you stop and question. But how do we get around to this kind of language in the first place? I would suggest that this kind of language has a different origin, a different background, a different context from anything that Dr. Nielsen looked at. Similarly, for the notion of necessary being, it is quite rightly pointed out that necessity is a logical notion; we can understand that a proposition may be necessary but how could a "being" be necessary? One could, of course, also say that this kind of language has a philosophical exactness; though I would find this inappropriate. I would suggest that in order to understand what language of this kind is trying to say, we must begin with ourselves. If I were asked, What does it mean to exist or to be; what does being or existence mean?; it seems to me that before I looked around the world and tried to form an idea I would have an immediate *experience* of what it means to be. I am. I do not mean by that the Cartesian argument, *cogito ergo sum*, although that may be one of the strongest arguments in philosophy; I would, rather, be inclined to put it the other way around: *sum, ergo cogito*. Before I started thinking at all I would have had this immediate experience of what it is to be, to exist. And furthermore, having begun to reflect on this I would see that there was a time when I began to exist and there will be a time when I shall cease to exist; I did not bring myself into existence. And so right away, through my experience, I have had some notion of what it means to be a contingent existence, an existence that is not at all necessary. It is in contrast to that that I would begin to develop the notion— if no more than a notion—of a being that is not limited, that is not contingent in this kind of way.

Furthermore, I don't think I ever could form a precise concept of this. And I shall have more to say later about what I think is Dr. Nielsen's unreasonable demand for a kind of literalness in our language or our thinking about God. How could I proceed? I think I could only proceed in a negative kind of way. I could only think, How could there be a being that is different from mine? A being that doesn't just find itself, thrown, as it were, into existence. A being whose existence doesn't begin and terminate and isn't limited in all kinds of ways. And so I don't think I would ever arrive at a full-fledged concept of necessary existence and certainly the Bible does not use this expression. Nevertheless, I think I can see myself pointed towards a kind of being that is quite different from my own, that is wholly other in that sense.

So with many other words that we apply to God. Professor Nielsen didn't mention God's omnipotence but this, I think, is a favorite theme with many philosophers and it is not too hard to show that the concept of omnipotence, if you mean by this an ability to do anything, is a fairly incoherent notion; it breaks down, it becomes self-contradictory. But once again I would say that a precise philosophical concept should not be sought here. What does omnipotent actually mean? It was used once, I believe, in the New Testament, and it translates a Greek word which in turn translates an old Hebrew expression, *Shaddai*. The Hebrews spoke about God as *El Shaddai* and this word *Shaddai* was certainly not anything like a philosophical concept, it was, rather, the notion of a powerful, other, exalted being whom people called God. And even the word omnipotent is not really meant to be an exact concept of that kind. It does not mean an ability to do anything. We talk about omnibuses, but we don't suppose that everybody can climb aboard an omnibus. We might say that man is an omnivorous animal but we don't expect him to have his dinner from—let's say—a slab of cement or anything of that sort. Again, I don't think this notion has to be developed.

We begin with the sense that we ourselves have power, we are able to do certain things and yet we notice that our power is limited in various ways. We can, as it were, reshape the materials of our world, but we cannot create a world. And that leads us to the thought of a power that is not limited in this way; and again I think we could only proceed in a negative kind of way. We could say this would be unlike human power in this or another respect. We could never arrive at a complete concept. Once again, however, we are at least pointing towards something. This kind of God-talk is the language of analogy.

Dr. Nielsen, has, in his paper, written quite a bit about God as a person and God in his relation to the world. Then, of course, he made the point that persons are embodied persons—we would normally think of God as having a body. But again, even the notion of a person can only be used analogously with respect to God. Our language about God does not, as it were, refer to him directly (as when I talk about "that light"; my words refer directly to that light). All our language about God would have to be oblique, that is to say, as if it were to bounce off something else—something that we do have an idea of, something that we can understand and which, is somehow enlightening for this mystery that we call God; and yet remains a mystery that we cannot contain within any other ordinary concepts of thought.

It seems to me that what is most distressing is Dr. Nielsen's literalness. I wonder, for instance, what he would make of poetry; how he would interpret Shelley's address to the Skylark—"hail to thee, blithe Spirit, bird thou never wert." I suspect that Dr. Nielsen might raise an objection there. How can you say that a lark is not a bird? Well, perhaps Shelley was saying something there. Perhaps that's the only way he could say it. I agree, of course, that clarity in language is highly desirable, but I think there are degrees of clarity. We can say some things with almost complete clarity but there are many other things that can be said with but limited clarity.

Dr. Nielson writes that Dom Trethowan, an English Roman Catholic scholar (a Welsh Roman Catholic Scholar, I think) said that Flew and Nielsen are asking for a description of God. The believer, if he knows his business, will reply "God cannot be described." Dr. Nielsen's comment is that Trethowan is wide of the mark. But I would say, on the contrary, that this is precisely where he strikes home. The believer, if he knows his business, will reply, "God cannot be described." The implicit assumption and the demand for this kind of description seems to be that God is another being within the world. God is, for example, like a frog. But the frog could be brought into the lab, pinned down at its four corners and slit up the middle; and you could see and locate its liver, its lungs and all of its other parts. This is quite impossible in the case of God. God is not just another being within the world, if by this word we mean the presupposition and the source of all the beings that are in the world.

I think the real trouble here is that Dr. Nielsen has too narrow a conception of language, experience, and reason. And I would say that although Dr. Nielsen may think of himself as an empiricist, I think there is a strongly anti-empirical element in his whole approach to these matters. He has, as it were, set up a certain apparatus—and let me admit at once that it is a very subtle and powerful apparatus. But nevertheless it is a kind of Procrustean bed and anything that is presented has to find its place within this particular logical apparatus or else it has to be dismissed. Also I can't help noticing that Dr. Nielsen annexes to himself and to his particular way of operating, words like "reason" and "truth" —but we must remember that these are very prestigious words and that, therefore, I think, as the arguments of the religious person are tinged with emotion, the arguments of the atheist are somewhat emotive also.

Sometimes I have the impression that Dr. Nielsen's request that we assign very rigid meanings to our words and apply them only in certain ways, is something like the "newspeak" of which George Orwell talks in 1984. In "newspeak" this is precisely what was to happen. Every word was to have one meaning and one meaning only and all the subsidiary meanings were to be rubbed out. The explanation was given that this would narrow the range of thought, and I think that is precisely what happens. There are, after all, different traditions of empiricism. David Hume was an empiricist; an empiricist, I think, of a very narrow kind. But John Locke was also an empiricist. And he shows us a broader and more flexible kind of empiricism which seems to me to be more truly empirical insofar as it is more open to different kinds of experience.

What I am saying is that we cannot say in advance what is thinkable. Indeed, if man had ever tried to lay down what the term "think" meant, then there would never have been much advance in knowledge at all. There must be a great many things that we know today and a great many ways in which we operate that, not very long ago, would have been deemed inconceivable. If people had simply said "There are all these limits to our thought," they never would have moved into these new areas at all. I don't think we can say in advance what is thinkable; rather, if we find people thinking about certain things and trying to express their thoughts, what we should try to do is to be sympathetic and to enter into their understanding and see what they are talking about.

Dr. Nielsen disclaims that he speaks of God-talk as meaningless. I am not quite certain that his disclaimer can be accepted. He prefers to use the word "incoherent" quite a number of times but I think I also found words like "garbage". This style of argument is really rather old-fashioned. Twenty years ago I used to be kind of upset when someone of positivist leanings would turn around to me and say "I don't know what you're talking about; your remarks have no meaning to me." But I feel much more comforted when I read some of the things that are coming out nowadays. For instance a year or two ago Jonathan Cohen, an Oxford philosopher, brought out a book on the diversity of meaning. And this is precisely one of the points that he makes. Maybe there was a time when it was considered rather devastating to say to your opponent, "what you're saying doesn't have any meaning." But today the correct answer to that is "well, work a little harder on it".

Don't take the above too literally because I know Dr. Nielsen has worked very, very hard on this whole matter of the Philosophy of Religion. But what I'm trying to say is this: I think that is the truly empirical attitude. You find that people do speak in this way; after all God-talk makes sense to an awful lot of people and this is simply an empirical fact that we discover in the world. Now I'm not going to say that all kinds of God-talk add up and make sense. As I said, I'm laboring under great difficulties to find a language. For some time I've been looking around for an alternative to the being-language for talking about God, but I don't quite know where I'm going.

Finally, though, I think, we come back to the point that Dr. Nielsen made last night, that the two of us have different ways of going about the philosophical task. And I don't know whether these are reconcilable (I think this would need to be left to another encounter); but the analyst and the believer are, after all, both human beings and we both have very human interests, and maybe if we started from there we would be able to find some way through some of these difficulties.

KIERKEGAARD'S ARCHIMEDEAN POINT

Winfield E. Nagley

The inner formative forces of Kierkegaard's thought are exemplified in a metaphor involving the Archimedean point which first appeared in the fourth entry of his *Papirer* written on September 11, 1834 and which also played a prominent role in the journal entries of 1834–35 when he was twenty-two and twenty-three years old. The thesis of this paper is that Kierkegaard's encounter with this Archimedean point provided him with the fundamental framework for his life's values and works.

I

Kierkegaard's initial fascination with an Archimedean point was expressed in the contexts of art and science; he enjoyed art, in contrast to the vastness of nature, because in art he found the Archimedean point which clarified every detail and allowed him to see the author's whole individuality—"a sea in which every detail is reflected."

Great geniuses, he observed, were often represented as blind in order to convey the idea that when they sang of the beauties of nature, they paradoxically did not see what they sang of—their song was the revelation of an inner intuition. Apparently with Francois Huber in mind, Kierkegaard wrote that one of the most authoritative writers on bees was blind from childhood and that by a purely mental or spiritual activity he inferred all the visual details which he recounted in his writings—again the paradox of the man who seeing least, sees best.

In Kierkegaard's lengthy letter of 1835 to the scientist Peter Lund, he contrasted scientists who were merely collectors of facts with those who sought and found the Archimedean point as a result of their speculations. Kierkegaard himself considered pursuing scientific studies of a type which would permit him to view details in a comprehensive light, but he decided that what really interested him most was "reason and freedom" and, above all, the elucidation of, and solution to, the riddle of life. Forty years in the wilderness in order to reach the promised land of science, Kierkegaard found too great a price to pay, especially since he believed "that nature can also be understood from a point where an insight into the secrets of science is superfluous." [1]

In the same letter, Kierkegaard made it very clear that neither the "colossus" of Christian theology nor philosophical rationalism was the Archimedean point. He found that systematic, coherent Christian doctrine was a formidable structure, but that though he could agree at certain points, he disagreed at other points and hence left the fundamentals *in dubio*, a foreshadowing of his position that Christianity's truth was an "objective uncertainty." As for philosophical rationalism, taken as a whole it presented "rather a poor figure," Kierkegaard maintained, inasmuch as when rationalism was in agreement with the Scriptures it based its arguments thereon but not otherwise. When rationalism dealt with matters of human concern, it was colored by Christianity and was certainly not what Kierkegaard was in search of.

What he was seeking was initially encountered during his holiday at Gilleleie on July 29, 1835 when he was twenty-three years old. It was then that he climbed to the highest point in the area—itself an interesting intimation of the experience's significance—and faced the sea to the north in which direction the heavens and sea set bounds for each other and were both in opposition to "the busy noise of life." At this moment Kierkegaard found that despite his sense of being out of his body, wafted into the ether with the few dead that were dear to him, he was at one and the same time aware of standing alone and hearing the screech of gulls. As he noted, he did not lose himself in the moment, which he frequently did, but rather saw everything in its entirety but at the same time also differently. He saw the world from the standpoint of another world and yet he was wholly and fully a member of this world— a dialectical and paradoxical mode of reflection which is inherent in the standpoint of the Archimedean point.

Though much of the language in the long passage paraphrased above exhibited uneven rhetoric or a fling at the sermonic, it nevertheless, in a paradoxical and dialectical manner, disclosed "how things really appeared" in a remarkably striking manner:

He has found what the great philosopher—who by this calculation was able to destroy the enemy's engines of war—desired, but did not find: the archimedean point from which he could lift the whole world, the point which for that very reason must lie outside the world, outside the limitations of time and space.[2]

This quotation echoed Plutarch's account of Archimedes's scientific and mechanical genius which was so fully evidenced during the siege of

Syracuse. This genius and its incredible accomplishments, even if we are to discount the accuracy of Plutarch's undoubtedly exaggerated account, were set over against what Kierkegaard considered to be Archimedes's greater desire which was to find the Archimedean point; this search Plutarch described as follows: "If there were another world and he could go to it, he would move this one."

The literal meaning of Plutarch's statement regarding Archimedes's search was turned by Kierkegaard into a metaphorical one—into a root metaphor, a life-permeating frame of reference found in his journals and his books, sometimes by explicit reference and other times by implicit presupposition. The Archimedean point was Kierkegaard's metaphor for the religious life which lay outside the spatio-temporal world, but in such a way that the spatio-temporal man involved could make this Archimedean point his own standpoint from which he could "lift" the world.

Not only was this Archimedean point metaphorical in meaning, it was paradoxical as well in the ordinary sense of being a statement contrary to received opinion or expectation. The complete journal entry, in which the Archimedean point passage was written, set forth one paradoxical expression after another, both preceding and following the section under discussion, which intensified and clarified the Archimedean passage. These many paradoxes were beyond or contrary to usual opinion—they connoted contrariety to what is ordinarily reasonable or possible. The passages indicate that Kierkegaard felt that his consciousness was both within and without his body; everything was seen as a whole instead of, as is more common, having his consciousness lost in the contents of the moment; he felt himself as nothing on the one hand and yet recognized and cared for by the deity on the other. He felt he had united pride and humility in a true "marriage" before the deity; he heard the deep bass of a storm begin its falsetto; he saw the birth and the decline of the world; he was both lord and lowly creature residing in nature; he was both great and small at the same time—all variations on, and exemplifications of, the theme of the Archimedean point.

Not only did the Archimedean point have a metaphorical and a paradoxical meaning; it had a dialectical significance as well. As was the case with Kant's antinomies, it involved two opposite propositions which must be held with equal necessity: man was, and he was not, an existent in the spatio-temporal world. But here there was no solution to this opposition of propositions; the difficulty did not lie in a mistaken use of the category of totality, which was the case in Kant's analysis, or in any other form of conceptual confusion. The conceptualization was imaginative—intuitive and paradoxical, but straightforward and clear in a dialectical sense.

This assertion that Kierkegaard's conception of the Archimedean point was a dialectical one involves one of the most difficult problems in Kierkegaard research, namely the character of Kierkegaard's dialectic. Despite the fact that much has been written on or about Kierkegaard's view of the dialectic (in the process of which didactic dialogue has often been confused with dialectic), Mr. Capel's suggestion that Kierkegaard exploited a "dialectical overlap" in regard to Hegel's conception of the dialectic in the ENCYCLOPEDIA was truly a breakthrough in Kierkegaard scholarship.[3] Just how much in advance of the writing of *Irony*, in 1841, Kierkegaard had begun to exploit this dialectical overlap remains unknown; this exploitation was, however, consistent with the Archimedean point if not presupposed in the formulation of it.

In order to become clear about the way Kierkegaard exploited this dialectical overlap in his concept of the Archimedean point, a brief review of Hegel's three sides or stages of logic is in order: The first stage, Understanding, adhered to the fixity of characteristics and their distinctions; apart from Understanding there was no fixity or accuracy in either theory or practice. In Understanding, thought was acting in its analytic capacity; its canon was identity. The second stage, that of the Dialectic, was the one in which the finite characteristics superseded themselves and passed into their opposites. In the Dialectical stage the one-sidedness and limitations of the predicates of the Understanding were shown to be negations of these predicates. The third stage, that of Speculation, apprehended the unity of terms or propositions in their opposition—it was the stage of Positive Reason because it had a definite content, the result of the negations of specific propositions which were then contained in the final result. This resultant unity was a concrete one, as opposed to a formal one, because it was a unity of distinct propositions.

The possibility of a dialectical overlap was acknowledged by Hegel in discussing the Speculative stage indicated above: "The logic of mere Understanding is involved in Speculative logic, and can at will be elicited from it, by the process of omitting the dialectical and 'reasonable' element." [4] Lee Capel commented on this passage to the effect that the "unity of opposites," in accordance with the logic of Understanding, meant for Kierkegaard "the Protean variability, the vibration between opposites characteristic of romantic irony" and that it was Kierkegaard's "correlation of opposites" which was "fastened together at the top," such as pleasure and pain, which gave the essay a curious fusion and made it in its entirety a "jest," an ironic work on irony.

Kierkegaard's dialectic in the delineation of the Archimedean point was clearly a dialectic of the Understanding, in Hegel's sense, because it omitted the "dialectical and the 'reasonable' element," but it was not a jest in the ordinary sense. Kierkegaard was often serious when he was jesting and jesting when he was serious. What Kierkegaard himself found, and which he offered to his readers in his later writings, was the standpoint of the Archimedean view and it follows that the man who assimilated it can be called the Archimedean man who exists simultaneously both within and without the world of space and time. Kierkegaard's terms were used clearly in the sense of Hegel's Understanding; there was no identity possible for them.

Though Kierkegaard's dialectic was that of the Understanding rather than that of Speculation, it was nevertheless legitimate and traditional dialectic and the Archimedean point was dialectical for him in this traditional sense. Whereas the differentia as determination was contained within the indeterminate category according to Hegel—the negative and the determinate species were reached by the negation of the negation—in Kierkegaard's dialectic the differentia as determination was not contained within the indeterminate category; Kierkegaard here stood with tradition in that the indeterminate genus excluded the differentia. Thus withinness was negated by withoutness and vice versa; each was determined negatively by the other just as in the above passage the sea set boundaries for the sky and the sky for the sea. Each retained its character as an opposite and the "unity of opposites" in Kierkegaard's mind took place in the life of the existing person. The intellectual expression for this "unity" was the paradoxical metaphor in which the participant stood both within and without the spatial and temporal world and was able to "lift" the whole world.

II

Though the encounter with the Archimedean point provided Kierkegaard with a lifelong viewpoint, initially its full significance for him was merely adumbrated as disclosed in the journal entries regarding that first encounter. The Archimedean point, while providing him with an unshakable foundation for his life on the one hand, required on the other hand a long process of clarification. For Kierkegaard it was one thing to discover that one was, metaphysically speaking, an outsider to this world, but it was quite another thing—recognizing that one was also, metaphysically speaking, an insider in a historical sense—to be clear as to what it meant to be an outsider living as a concrete historical person.

In order to achieve clarity regarding this dilemma of what it meant to be an outsider in the space-time world, Kierkegaard became a philosopher—despite his attack on philosophy qua Hegelian rationalism—who was concerned with an analysis of the strengths and weaknesses of the reigning philosophies of Hegelianism and Romanticism. These philosophies were essentially standpoints which had one feature in common, despite their many differences; namely, the viewpoint of the insider. What was clearly shown in the early journal entries of Kierkegaard, both prior to and above all after his encounter with the Archimedean point, was that his standpoint and Hegel's were forever irreconcilable and that his attack on Hegelianism was inevitable. In a letter to Peter Lund, Kierkegaard mentioned that he belonged to a small group which searched for an inner categorical imperative which was then regarded as the "real meaning of the Hegelian dialectic." [5] The already mentioned rejection of philosophical rationalism, as the Archimedean point, seemingly referred to its exponent Hegel rather more pointedly than to any other philosophers in the modern classical period.

The Archimedean point for Kierkegaard expressed a total but not fully developed rejection of Hegelianism as a standpoint. Kierkegaard's dialectic, as already outlined, was that of the Understanding which kept the contrariety of categories—such as external and internal, finite and infinite, withinness and withoutness—as opposites which were not reducible to an identity. This standpoint was that of an outsider, metaphysically speaking, who was yet an insider, historically speaking—these two oppositions were never *aufgehoben*. The standpoint of Hegelian man was that of an insider whose categories in finite and infinite were resolved into an identity by positive reason; all categories were within the dialectic of the Absolute. The Archimedean point and the Hegelian standpoint are then fundamentally incommensurate; Kierkegaard spent much of his creative life discovering where and how these incompatibilities occurred and what they signified.

Two aesthetic works of Kierkegaard could be considered as illustrating his criticism of Hegelianism from an insider's standpoint. In *The Concept of Dread*, Hegel's position was depicted as that of a philosophy professor "who *a tout prix* must explain all things" to the advantage of neither logic nor reality; contrary to this viewpoint, Kierkegaard maintained that man, Archimedean man that is, was of eternity and time. His category was that of the temporal, a meeting of eternity and time in the "Instant." Man was thus a synthesis—not the Hegelian *aufgehoben* —of two completely different qualities: the temporal, in the sense of his psychosomatic endowment, and the eternal or spiritual. In *Fear and Trembling*, Kierkegaard transformed the Romantic emphasis upon the rights of the individual conscience into an Archimedean emphasis by his defense of the teleological suspension of the ethical. Against the Hegelian position that the individual conscience cannot be trusted and that therefore one must live by the public morality, the universal law of the state, Kierkegaard argued that after one has submitted to the universal morality, one may stand "higher," i.e., in an absolute relation to the Absolute. Abraham was an outsider, a Knight of Faith, who made the "double movement" of renouncing the world and yet living within it from the Archimedean standpoint which involved practicing resignation from the world yet looking and acting as if he were a tax collector.

Romanticism and Hegelianism were reigning philosophies of the day and Kierkegaard rejected both. Kierkegaard saw Romanticism as an insider viewpoint which he termed "qualitative irony" in which the ironist set himself above the everyday world of persons and events in a quasi-godlike indifference or even hostility. While on the one hand the ironist rejected the world, he remained wholly within it on the other hand, content to point out the foibles of society and content to cultivate himself as a superior person, a genius whose *weltanschauung* was similar to the one depicted in Friedrich Schlegel's *Lucinde*.

In *Either/Or* and in *Stages on Life's Way*, Schlegel's viewpoint was clearly presented; Romanticism was set forth as the standpoint of an insider who inverted the role of deity into that of the demonic Don Juan or into that of the equally demonic Johannes the Seducer. The romantic personality defined himself in a negative way toward the world and yet remained an insider.

Archimedean man and his standpoint was set in contrast to romantic man by the pseudonymous Judge Wilhelm whose ethico-religious position was the Archimedean point from which one could lift the world.[6] This paradoxical and dialectical form, found in Kierkegaard's early exposition of this standpoint, was elucidated in a passage in *Either/Or* in philosophical terms: one was to choose oneself properly, i.e., as just this particular person, who was timeless and yet existed also at a certain time and place in history; who was both free and determined, possible and actual, abstract and concrete. Proper self-choice required that these paradoxical qualities be thought of simultaneously; dialectically, the qualities retained their individual identity and contrariety. What made the self-choice Archimedean was that the self was both an insider and an outsider, a temporal and an eternal self.

The Archimedean viewpoint of Judge Wilhelm illustrates what Kierkegaard meant by Religion A in his *Concluding Unscientific Postscript*. Religion A was an ethico-religious consciousness which put the emphasis upon the temporal facet of the Archimedean point. At its higher reaches, religious consciousness of the A type comprehended the

contradiction between the temporal and the eternal and while emphasizing the ethical it also prevented the individual from remaining within
the confines of immanence.

Beyond Religion A, the territory of Kierkegaard's more fully developed position was laid out which he termed Religion B. This position
was foreshadowed in the sermon in *Either/Or* in which edification was
found in the thought that as against God, man was always in the wrong,
and which was brought out fully in its theoretical detail in the *Postscript*. In Religion B, as it was formulated in the *Postscript*, the kinship
between the temporal and the eternal, which was set forth in Religion
A, was reconceived; now there was a radical break between the temporal
and the eternal because in this higher religious consciousness of Religion
B, the eternal itself had entered time and now constituted the kinship.
The emphasis in Religion B shifted the focus to the eternal facet of the
Archimedean point.

His initial fascination with the Archimedean point gave Kierkegaard a fundamental frame of reference for his life and work and also
the impetus for his attacks, then and later, on Hegelianism and Romanticism. At the age of twenty-three he first saw the Archimedean standpoint but only through the glass darkly—he knew but only in part.
Kierkegaard's life was spent in the task of delineating—never fully to be
sure but increasingly—the meaning of the Archimedean point; this task
only came to an end with his death in 1855.

III

I have discussed the characteristics of Kierkegaard's Archimedean
point which he described in his journal. I have also sketched the manner
in which the Archimedean point became clarified and enlarged upon in
the course of his later writings. Now, I shall assess the significance of his
Archimedean point in terms relevant to the field of philosophy of religion.

In any estimation of the philosophical significance of Kierkegaard's
Archimedean point, it must be understood, on the one hand, that his
exploration of it was not undertaken in the role of a theologian or philosopher as traditionally understood and yet, on the other hand, it must
be realized that he engaged in an intellectual task which can only be
conceived of as being in the realm of that professional work which belongs to a theologian or a philosopher. However, Kierkegaard's delineation of the Archimedean point was not that of a theologian in the respect that he did not provide an apologia for dogma, given through revelation, by employing appeals to the authority of documents, institutions or other historical entities; rather his conception was that of a

theologian in the sense that he provided an apologia for Christianity—in the context of a nominally Christian social order—by reformulating certain Christian beliefs as essays of the imagination in order that his reader could thus be enabled to become what an authentic Christian should become. Regarding his role as philosopher, although Kierkegaard was not one in the sense of having been a speculative rationalist in the manner of modern classical philosophers, yet he was a philosopher in the context under discussion in the sense that he engaged in a multi-faceted analysis and a systematic exposition of the Archimedean point, to say nothing of all else that he philosophically dealt with.

The assessment of Kierkegaard's Archimedean point in this section will focus on two theses: the first that Kierkegaard employed three uses of reason which fused in his conception of the Archimedean point; and the second that this threefold reason is a heuristic adventure in philosophy of religion, particularly with respect to the problem of the limits of religious rationality.

On the thesis that Kierkegaard employed three uses of reason in his conception of the Archimedean point, this paper will follow a lead in Whitehead's discussion of the function of reason in which he set Ulysses, the symbol of practical reason, in contrast to Plato, the symbol of speculative reason, and argued that progress on the human scene has come and will continue to come when these two functions of reason exist side by side and enhance each other. In a review of Whitehead's position concerning the dual function of reason, A. D. Ritchie observed that another function of reason is implicit in Whitehead's thought and he suggested that "Ion" represent this function which is that of intuition.[7]

In this discussion, the Ion function will be extended and applied, along with those functions assigned to Ulysses and Plato, to Kierkegaard's Archimedean point. Thus in addition to the analytic reason symbolized by Ulysses which is practical, analytical, critical, tough-minded if not hard-nosed, and the systematic reason symbolized by Plato which is speculative, synthetic, systematic and normative, there is this Ionic type of rationality which is intuitive, imaginative, Dionysian, and anarchistic. In distinguishing these three functions of reason, it is not maintained that they are opposites in a threefold system. Instead they are characterized, as A. D. Ritchie suggested, more in the manner that contrasting instruments can be singled out in an orchestra performance but only in the context that each is necessary for the full rendering of the music.

This metaphor is also useful in pointing out that Ion, in particular, represents an aesthetically sensitive form of rationality. In the Platonic dialogue, Ion was a rhapsode who looked beautiful, wore fine clothes and spent his time in the company of poets; his was the task of interpreting the mind of the poet to the public. Socrates forced him to admit that he did not have knowledge but Socrates then led Ion on to realize that he was inspired and possessed by divinity.

Keeping these multifaceted and interrelated functions of reason in mind, this discussion will now examine in turn the manner in which Ulysses, Plato and Ion are found in Kierkegaard's presentation of the Archimedean point. Kierkegaard employed the Ulyssean function of reason in his initial writing regarding the Archimedean point and in his later exposition of it. The practical, analytic function of reason seen in the initial journal entries pertains to his finding the Archimedean point; Kierkegaard was clearly aware of the screech of gulls and the absence of any sail on the sea in his analysis of what happened on that important day.

Kierkegaard analytic powers were so many-faceted and disparate that a clear picture of them is not easy to arrive at and this has misled critics into withholding the term "philosopher" from him or begrudgingly bestowing it with qualifications. The question, regarding whether Kierkegaard was a philosopher or not, turns in part on the meaning of the term "analysis," and in this discussion it is maintained that there are at least three ways in which Kierkegaard engaged in philosophical analysis in his explication of the significance of the Archimedean point. First, in addition to the obvious linguistic and historical talents displayed in his analysis of texts, his manner of examining texts is interpreted as philosophical in the sense that he noted shifts of meaning, ambiguity in key arguments, omissions which the author ought not to have made, contradictions within the argument under examination, and so forth. He sought to make explicit, presuppositions that are implicit; e.g., in reply to Hegel's assertion that his was a system without presuppositions, Kierkegaard pointed out that Hegel himself presupposed the existence of Christianity as historical; hence not only was Hegel wrong in his assertion that his system was without presuppositions, but by presupposing Christianity to be historical, Hegel misrepresented it as well—a Ulyssean double entendre in that the Christian religion because of its Archimedean character is both historical and yet nonhistorical according to Kierkegaard whose many talents often got in the way of each other so that a logical point was often made in the satirical or humorous manner of Ion which leaves the reader amused but perhaps unaware of the actual weight of the criticism and the power of his Ulyssean aspect.

Second, Kierkegaard offers to the reader philosophical analyses of several systematic views of life, *weltanschauungen*. In *Irony* he set forth alternatives to the Archimedean point—namely Hegelianism and Romanticism. In *Either/Or* he engaged not only in presenting various aesthetic, ethical, and religious standpoints but also in analyzing the essential features of each—their archetypal patterns—in terms of the logic of their positions illustrated in his studies of Don Juan, Johannes the Seducer, and Judge Wilhelm.

Third, Kierkegaard's writing offers philosophical analyses of many aspects of self-consciousness to the perceptive reader, particularly those analyses pertaining to the relation of the total person to his own cognitive content. Kierkegaard took very seriously the Socratic directive "know thyself" as the essential task of every man, and, following his own bent for the darker side of life, explored such experiences as despair, dread, and so forth. These analyses are psychological and philosophical after the manner of the Danish philosophical tradition which Kierkegaard reaffirmed in his revolt against Hegelianism; they also reflect the singular power of his own strange and complex genius. His analytic focus is on conceptual frameworks—as much shrouded in obscurity as they are revealed in experience—expressed in terms such as "despair" and "dread." The power of these analyses in good part undoubtedly explains Wittgenstein's breathtaking observation that Kierkegaard was the greatest philosopher of the nineteenth century. It also attests to the strong empirical strain, though it is focused on self-knowledge rather than object knowledge, which was characteristic of Danish philosophy. This then is Kierkegaard's Ulyssean aspect.

But Kierkegaard also employed the systematic reason of Plato although not so extensively nor so clearly as he used the Ulyssean type of reason. This Platonic reason was expressed in an incipient manner in Kierkegaard's initial encounter with the Archimedean point. Instead of losing himself in the moment—a moment in which his mind was flooded with sensations both realistic and fantastic—he saw everything as a whole, and, from this total perspective, he also saw everything differently.

The stated purpose of his authorship, to lead nominal Christians to authentic Christianity, is of course a facet of Platonic reason in the sense that he strove to consistently express that purpose in a great number of his writings. The fact that at one and the same time he practised self-analysis—endeavoring to explain himself to Regina, attacking the editor of the Corsair, and so forth—and also assumed that there was a much clearer explication of the themes in his individual works and a tighter developmental relationship among his works than his readers were able to discern, does not in itself constitute a refutation of the thesis that he valued and seriously employed Platonic reason.

Specifically, Platonic reason is found in certain systematic charac-

teristics of Kierkegaard's work. Though he intensely disliked the speculative system of Hegel, he learned much from it and one of his acquisitions from Hegel was a respect for the value of a consistent use of categories. At times he fell far short of his goal yet often he enriched the
meanings of his categories and applied them to many areas of human
concern with results that are piquant and valuable.

Another expression of his Platonic, systematic bent of mind is that
he deliberately proposed a possible point of view, a possible choice between alternatives which he employed frequently. It is as if he were saying to his reader, "Let us assume," after which he proceeded to put together a "project of thought"—to use a chapter title from the *Frag-
ments*. Having briefly sketched the topic of his disquisition, he then
traced its many sides, examined its meaning (Ulyssean reason here joins
with Platonic), explored its consequences for the purpose of edification,
and juxtaposed it against differing positions. At times these very systematic and extensive examinations lead the reader into increasing exas-
peration at the lengthy and tortuous passages which he must wade
through without becoming lost, e.g., the more than twenty pages of discussion regarding whether a person can be consistent if he believes that
a man can do nothing of himself and yet, after this line of thought, then
that person proceeds to go on an outing in Deer Park.

The above observation that, in Kierkegaard's explorations of various
points of view, Ulysses joins Plato, points to the fact that analysis and
systematic exposition are more often than not almost inevitably con-
joined in a creative work, and in Kierkegaard's conception of the
Archimedean point, both initially and throughout the explication of its
significance, this is most certainly evident.

In contrast to the reason of Ulysses and Plato, Ion possesses an intuitive reason which expresses itself primarily in the form of poetry,
mythology, irony, humor, love, art, or morality, and of course in religious experience; Ionic reason plays a distinctly subordinate role in
mathematics and science which are domains of Ulysses and Plato. Ion
forever encounters the distrust of both Ulysses and Plato, and with good
cause for he is indeed often wayward, Dionysian, anarchistic, and destructive of establishments both social and intellectual. Ion leaps over
the conventional walls which men build in an attempt to make their
world safe.

Just as Ulysses needs Plato to put the facts together, and Plato
needs Ulysses to keep him intellectually clear and relevant to the facts
of experience, so both Ulysses and Plato need Ion to forever remind
them that their clear, light-filled intellectual cities are surrounded by a
jungle that, on the one hand, is a constant threat, and yet, on the other

hand, that that jungle surrounding their intellectual cities is the locus of ultimate meaning—to echo Pitcher's most apt analogy in his account of Wittgenstein's *Tractatus.*

Ion needs Ulysses in order to ascertain whether or not he is making sense to his listeners and readers, and Ion needs Plato in order to ascertain whether or not his flashing, piecemeal insights are relevant to the issues, problems and predicaments of men's intellectual and social systems.

The intuitive reason of Ion provides the framework with which one gets to the core of Kierkegaard's account of the Archimedean point. In his initial encounter with it, the highly symbolic expression for the Ionic reason is the fantasy language of the journal's passage in which Kierkegaard felt that he rested in the embrace of a few dear dead—they then seemed as though they had not died and he felt as if he were out of his body and wafted into the ether. It is important to note that his Ionic mentality is interlaced with Ulyssean since he was at one and the same time aware of the screech of gulls and his aloneness on the cliff; and furthermore that the Platonic mentality is represented in his having seen everything as a whole.

The language used in this initial encounter with the Archimedean point is not only the language of fantasy but also the language of a Plato and a Ulysses, formulated, however, in such a way so as to require the paradoxical conception of being within and without the world of space and time, which is philosophically scandalous from the viewpoints of Ulysses and Plato which seek to resolve paralogisms and to solve antinomies.

Though the paradox in this may be attributed to an Ionic influence, and though it cannot be reformulated into a nonparadoxical position, this epistemological position is fundamental to religious experience both in the East and West and hence provides a heuristic exercise which is respectable for both Ulysses and Plato to engage in. To say that a person is both within and without the world of space and time is also to say that the space-time world is both a conceptual scheme of the world within which man is to be placed, and a conceptual scheme such that man is outside the scheme at least in the sense that he is its conceiver.

IV

In the last section of this paper the following propositions are asserted: First, that the Archimedean point is inherently dualistic in epistemological terms, after the manner of Kant; Second, this dualistic epistemology of the Archimedean point is the only position which can account for religious experience both in the East and the West; Third, this dualistic epistemology is a basis upon which oppositional if not contradictory religio-philosophical systems are fashioned, superstructures which are thinkable but not demonstrable; Fourth, these superstructures, which are essentially the work of Ulysses and Plato, are fundamentally regulatory, indicating the preconditions and post-conditions of the Archimedean point; Five, the incentive to build a religio-philosophical superstructure is provided by Ion whose encounter with the Archimedean point is paradoxically both effable and ineffable.

In regard to the first proposition, which is that the epistemological position is Kantian in character and belongs to the realm of Ulysses and Plato: In the "I think" of Kant, the self has consciousness of itself as existing, its existence is given; however, again after Kant, the determination of this self is not given but to be made in conformity with the forms of sensibility in the world of space and time. The self thus is both within and without the *mundus sensibilis*. The self-consciousness of the Archimedean point is not consciousness of how I appear to myself or what I am in myself but rather, it is a consciousness of being in the *mundus intelligibilis*.

To discover oneself in the *mundus intelligibilis*, from the standpoint of the dualistic epistemology of the Archimedean point, is to find that one is both within and without the *mundus sensibilis*. As with Kant, Kierkegaard was adamant that one has no knowledge of a supersensible world and hence one is in the ironic position of knowing that the world we know is—in a metaphysical sense—unknowable. Logical systems, in the sense of systems descriptive of phenomena, are indeed possible; however, an existential system, that is a systematic account of the *mundus intelligibilis*, cannot be formulated.

There is of course no contradiction in maintaining that a supersensible world can exist, even though the determinations pertaining to its existence remain problematical—what Kierkegaard called "an objective uncertainty." He found the conditions for the discovery of the *mundus intelligibilis* in the ethical reality of the self, the only reality to which one has a more than cognitive relationship.

In regard to the elaboration of the second proposition, that the paradoxical epistemology of the Archimedean point—in which the finding of the *mundus intelligibilis* is identified as the discovery of the self both within and without the *mundus sensibilis*—is inherent in religious experience either as a starting point or as an ultimate affirmation both in the West and Asia: in some religious traditions, it is retained through the religious life of the self whereas in others the distinction between the knower and what is known is transcended. Kierkegaard, who spoke primarily for Augustinian-Lutheran Christianity, held this dualism to be inviolate: A system of existence is an impossibility because any system excludes the existing conceiver. In Advaita Vedanta philosophy the dualism between the empirical self and the world is the point of departure which is to be overcome by the philosophical task of discovering the metaphysical Self which is identical with Brahman—the empirical self and the world hence lack full reality. Thus the dualism between the knower and what is known reduces to a metaphysical monism which, however, permits a vestige of the original dualism to remain as a kind of magic show. For the Vedantin who achieves *moksha* there is only one reality, Brahman, yet at the level of appearance the distinction between knower and known is insisted upon. In the Ch'an-Zen tradition, the dualistic framework of the Archimedean point is obliterated; there is neither knower nor that which is known—only Śūnyatā (no-thing-ness, a void which is nothing and everything). Though the mutual conditioning of opposites, frequently found in the queries of monks to masters, disappears from consciousness, it must not be forgotten that this dualism is a point of departure in this Buddhist tradition; consciousness of the self and the world are necessary to each other. It is difficult to conceive of a position in philosophy of religion which does not, at least as a point of departure, presuppose epistemological dualism. And so it is with the Archimedean point which is inconsistent with epistemological monism.

On the third proposition, that this dualistic epistemology is a basis upon which opposing if not contradictory religio-philosophical systems are constructed: these systems are thinkable and regulative for conduct but they are not demonstrable; in Kierkegaard's case, the epistemology of the Archimedean point was used to construct his distinctively Christian world view.

In Kierkegaard's description of his early encounter with the Archimedean point, the language is that of a philosophical theism with affinities to the religious philosophy of Kant and Fichte who were both mentioned by Kierkegaard in the general discussion preceding and following the initial entries on the Archimedean point. To put it another way, Kierkegaard's language appears to be that of an incipient Judge Wilhelm; it is not only that the self is both within and without the world of space and time—the epistemological sense of the Archimedean point—but also that this same self is before the Deity. It is the conception of the divine and human encounter that provides the distinctly Christian meaning of the Archimedean point. In that encounter man is lord of nature and yet he feels that he must bow down before that "something higher" than himself.

Regarding the fourth proposition that these superstructures are regulatory in that they describe and prescribe the preconditions and post-conditions of the Archimedean point: these superstructures, whether they are classified as natural or revealed theology, are the work of Ulysses and Plato and are essentially regulatory in the thought and life of the person who seeks to gain his religious *summum bonum*. Against an objection that there is no justification for a regulatory system unless its propositions are true, the Platonic reply might well be that the most important task a philosopher performs is to produce ideas regarding which he suspends judgment on their truth. From the point of view of this paper, there is an unintended, oracular sense in Bertrand Russell's remark that the reason philosophers do not find the truth is because they are not looking for it. However, some philosophers are on a legitimate search for that which is beyond merely the truth of particular propositions; they are looking for visions or that Socratic virtue, wisdom, although it is granted that tough-minded philosophers only cite wisdom to freshman students or on ceremonial occasions. But they forget at whose behest Ulysses and Plato labor in the vineyard of metaphysics.

On the fifth proposition that the incentive to build a religio-philosophical structure is provided by Ion whose encounter with the Archimedean point is paradoxically both effable and ineffable: Ion is a religious poet in the broad sense of one who has great powers of imagination, intuition and expression. He partakes of the quality of a jinni—he is a supernatural being who assumes the form of a human; his influence upon human beings can be either sublime or diabolical, but in the realm of metaphysics it is seminal.

The generative power of Ion produces ambivalent responses from Ulysses and Plato. On the one hand, they are fascinated and hypnotized by what he tells them about themselves and the world in which they live; he reminds and challenges them to recognize that their reason has another component, little used perhaps since childhood, the use of which is essential to their metaphysical fulfillment. On the other hand, Ulysses and Plato, while fascinated by Ion's words, are at the same time fearful and trembling in response to the other's inspirited discourse, and so they adopt a defensive posture in their requirement that what Ion says must be measured against their criteria of meaning, consistency, utility and truthfulness and when thus measured they find his utterances unacceptable.

The Archimedean point for Ion is both expressible and inexpressible. It is expressible in that what he says about it makes use of what he has learned from Ulysses and Plato but in such a way that the use he makes of their analytic and systematic work is poetic in the sense of

Nietzsche's creator of new values. Ion creates new values within the traditional frameworks provided by Ulysses and Plato.

This ineffable side of Ion's paradoxical encounter with the Archimedean point can be seen in Christian metaphysics as the divine encounter with the human—what Brunner calls the *Anknupfungspunkt,* about which nothing can be said; it is neither authentic nor inauthentic, neither rational nor irrational, neither good nor evil, and so forth. It is not a matter of being unable to find the proper words, perhaps due to a momentary lapse of command in language ability which can be overcome, but rather that there are no words at all which are available and there are no thoughts either.

It is in the reason of Ion that the limits of the reasonable and the expressible are properly to be found. Can the paradoxes that abound here be avoided by a different formulation of the Archimedean point? Perhaps. If these limits are to be drawn differently, Ulysses and Plato must ceaselessly heed the promptings and the proclamations of Ion but forever distrust them. Ion will not be docile; he will find that whatever Ulysses and Plato have to say is problematic, pedestrian and devoid of inspiration. Their labors, from Ion's point of view, are similar to Kierkegaard's example of the gander who informed the geese that they could fly but then he and the geese continued to do nothing but waddle.

In Kierkegaard's own case, Ion leads Ulysses and Plato on a wild, tortuous chase exploring what his Archimedean experience means. Ion's moral and religious instruction offers unusual observations, frequently through analogy and metaphor, which are expressed in myriads of stories, myths, anecdotes, and humorous sallies as well as in arguments, all to the heuristic end of prodding the reader into finding his own Archimedean point. The reader must choose as he reads Kierkegaard, line by line, possibility by possibility. What is visionary and yet life-enhancing to one reader, may be self-centered and authoritarian to another. But the reader is unable to avoid choosing for himself.

The major weakness in Kierkegaard's Archimedean conception is that Plato and Ulysses do not check and chastise the reason of Ion sufficiently: the flow of passionate dialectic in whole passages which make little sense and the idiosyncrasies of Kierkegaard's style, verbosity in particular, work to weaken the force of his presentation. To this criticism, his reply could well have been that his reader is almost certainly already a follower of Ulysses and Plato, and what he needs, in addition, is the reason of Ion who is inspired and possessed by the gods, and that the task he set himself was to drive his reader out of his bourgeoisie mentality into a life of inspiration by mesmerizing him with words.

Kierkegaard's account of the Archimedean point is analytically

Ulyssean and systematically Platonic but essentially it is an Ionic dance in "the vortex of the infinite." To determine what this Ionic whirlwind consists of is the task of Ulysses and Plato, but they do not dance—that is a privilege and grace reserved for Ion.

NOTES

1. A. Dru, *The Journals of Søren Kierkegaard* (Oxford, Oxford University Press, 1938) page 7.

2. *Ibid.*, p. 13.

3. Søren Kierkegaard, *The Concept of Irony*, tr. by L. M. Capel (New York, Harper & Row, 1965) page 34.

4. William Wallace, *The Logic of Hegel* (Oxford, The Clarendon Press, 1892) pp. 79–82 (sections).

5. Dru, *op. cit.*, 5.

6. F. Schlegel, *Either/Or*, V. II (Garden City, N.J., Doubleday, 1959) p. 270.

7. P. A. Schilpp, *The Philosophy of Alfred North Whitehead* (Evanston, The Library of Living Philosophers, Inc., 1941) p. 335.

THE ARTS

GENRE AND STYLE

Morris Weitz

Genre and style are basic concepts in traditional aesthetics. Particular genre concepts, such as tragedy, have been of philosophical concern at least since Aristotle and are as vigorously discussed today by aestheticians and literary critics as ever they were in the past. Particular style concepts, such as Gothic, High Renaissance, or Baroque, are of relatively recent concern—although there are seminal intimations of them as far back as Vitruvius. Unfortunately they have been of primary interest not to philosophers but to art historians.

Much has been written on the history of genre concepts; the history of style concepts has hardly been started. In twentieth century discussions of the arts, genre is still the central concern of aesthetics and literary criticism. At the same time however, style has become the most important concept of art history.

More striking than this contemporary division is that, historically, style seems to play a minor role in literary criticism, and that genre, except in the special sense of a kind of secular painting, plays an even smaller role in art history. For example, it is a surprising discovery that although there are great critical essays on the characters, plot, philosophy, poetry, symbolism, and imagery of Shakespeare's dramas, there is no comparable work on Shakespeare's style.[1] Obviously, other concepts, which may or may not be equivalent to certain uses of style in literature, have been found to be more efficacious and illuminating than style in the analyses of Shakespeare's dramas. And we can accept, it seems to me, the major corpus of the criticism of those plays, now annotated by ten generations of critics, as a paradigm of literary criticism. If we substitute for Shakespeare's plays the paintings of Leonardo or Raphael, or Rembrandt or Rubens, we can hardly mention a major critical or historical study that does not focus on the style of these artists. In literary criticism, the concept of style seems to be dispensable in a way that it is not in art history. But genre is not dispensable to the literary critic. There is scarcely a book on the tragedies of Shakespeare that does not contain a first or last chapter on the nature of tragedy, a chapter included as an indispensable part of the discussion and judgment. This recurring concern with genre plays no role in art history. There are no first or last chapters on the nature of portraiture, landscape, religious painting, or the nude, when the historian of art tells his particular story. Indeed, when we read Kenneth Clark on *Landscape into Art* or *The Nude*, or Max Friedländer on *Landscape, Portrait, Still-Life*, we realize how ludicrous it would be for these historians to begin, end, or intrude with a definition of these genres, so obvious are they to all.

Whatever the vagaries of the history of genre and style concepts have been, one assumption about these concepts remains invariant: that they are definable in the Aristotelian sense of real definition, i.e., that necessary and sufficient criteria can be stated for their correct use, and that without such definitions, particular genre and style concepts cannot sustain their assigned roles. Many philosophers, literary critics, and art historians concur in this doctrine that there are such definitions and, consequently, they direct much effort to formulating theories of genre in literary criticism, and of style in art history.

In previous writings I have shown that the traditional assumption, shared by aestheticians and literary critics, that all genre concepts are or must be definable in order to render critical discussion and judgment intelligible, is false. For example, the concept of tragedy, examined in its actual role in literary criticism, exhibits itself as an open concept rather than, as it has been traditionally assumed, a closed concept. That the concept of tragedy is open in the precise sense of having no undebatable necessary criteria can be seen in the range of disagreement over the nature of the tragic in general, and over why or whether a particular work is tragic. The tragedy-giving reasons—that is, reasons given as answers to, What is tragedy?, Why is X tragic?, or Is X tragic?—provide the clue to the perennial debatability of the concept and its openness in that sense.

In an early paper, "The Role of Theory in Aesthetics," [2] I argued that a number of genre concepts are open, in contrast to the traditional assumption that they are all closed, i.e., governed by definitive sets of criteria. Thus, I claimed that "novel," "drama," "satire," "tragedy," and "art" itself are open. But considering all these together conflated two very different kinds of concepts, neither of which is governed by sets of necessary and sufficient criteria: those which have no undebatable necessary criteria and those which have some undebatable criteria even though they are neither necessary nor sufficient. "Drama," "novel," and "art"—as their uses reveal—have certain criteria that are neither necessary nor sufficient, yet are undebatable, in a way in which "tragedy" does not. For example, "X is a drama because it has plot" cannot be challenged in the way that "X is a tragedy because it has hamartia" can. "Plot" is neither necessary nor sufficient for something to be a drama, but neither can it be intelligibly challenged, as "hamartia" or any other criterion of "tragedy" can.

Thus I prefer to say that some genre concepts in aesthetics are open in the sense that they have no necessary or sufficient criteria but do have some unchallengeable ones; and that some are open in the sense that they have no necessary or sufficient criteria and no unchallengeable ones. Misled by Waismann's notion of open texture, I erred in thinking, as he did, that the perennial flexibility of a concept entails its perennial debatability. It does not, as the logic of the concept of drama itself shows.

What, now, about style? Are there definitive sets of criteria for the concept of style or for every particular style concept? This is a question I should like to consider here. Instead of beginning with philosophical theories of style, which I find surprisingly unhelpful, I propose to contrast what art historians *say* about style with how they *use* particular style concepts when they write art history. Although some philosophers pay lip service to the need for detailed examination of style concepts, it has not yet been heeded, in spite of the fact that such elucidation is basic in any attempt to determine the nature of style and style concepts.

I shall discuss, in particular, the views of Meyer Schapiro, James Ackerman, Arnold Hauser, and E. H. Gombrich—all art historians—on the nature of style in art history, and then test their claims in relation to the style concept of Mannerism, especially as it has been explored and developed by Walter Friedlaender, Max Dvorak, Craig Smyth, John Shearman, and Sydney Freedberg—all leading art historians of Mannerism and the *maniera*.

I

Meyer Schapiro's "Style" is a deservedly acclaimed classic on the nature of style in art history.[3] Its prime achievement, however, is its compendious and brilliant survey of the major theories of style from Wölfflin to the present day. Schapiro's classification of these theories into cyclical, polar, evolutionary, psychological, and sociological is of singular importance in any philosophical attempt to understand the concept of style in art history. Of special value are his incisive criticisms of the presuppositions and doctrines of Heinrich Wölfflin, Alois Reigl, Paul Frankl, and others. Without making it explicit, he makes us see that theories of style in art history have conflated two distinct problems:

What is a particular or period style in art?, and, How does it arise, mature, and change into a different style? As he abundantly reveals, most theorists are concerned with the second—the causal—question, rather than with the first—the substantive—question; much of Schapiro's critique centers on the deficiencies of the causal theories, especially their implicit determinism, which he rightly attributes to the influence of Hegel.

So far as the substantive question is concerned, Schapiro reminds us of the paucity of explicit definitions of style in art history. Instead of laying down definitive sets of criteria, art historians have applied those criteria that they have found to be "the broadest, most stable, and therefore most reliable" [4] for their purposes of dating and authenticating works of art and narrating a coherent history of art. These criteria—which Schapiro says are insufficient but which he implies are at least necessary in the art historian's use of style concepts—are "form elements or motives, form relationships, and qualities (including an all-over quality which we may call the 'expression')." [5]

Other criteria, advanced by certain theorists, such as technique, subject matter, and material, Schapiro concedes to be important, especially when they are interpreted in formal terms, i.e., as form elements and relations; but he denies that they are necessary features of the concept of style in art history.

Unfortunately, Schapiro does not enlarge upon these formal and expressive criteria, but only because of the encyclopaedic intent of his essay. Nevertheless, the terms are clear enough, both in the tradition of aesthetics and in his own use. For unlike, say, Wölfflin's criterion of *malerisch*, Schapiro's criterion of form element, which he clarifies by means of the example of the pointed as against the round arch, or his criterion of expressive quality which, again, he clarifies by means of the example of the cool or warm tertiary qualities of certain colors, are at least semantically unobjectionable as criteria of style in art.

What is most important and provocative in his essay, I think, and what we must later relate to the practice of art history, is Schapiro's own specific view of the concept of style. "By style [he writes], is meant the constant form—and sometimes the constant elements, qualities, and expression—in the art of an individual or a group." [6] Does his claim about the *constancy* of certain properties as basic to style or a particular style correspond to, for example, the actual use of the concept of Mannerism, as that concept is employed by the art historians of Mannerism? I hope to show that testing this claim brings to light the fundamental weakness of Schapiro's elucidation of the concept of style.

James Ackerman means, by a theory of style, a definition of style and an explanation why style changes.[7] For him both are essential to art history. Style for the art historian is not a discovered concept but one created by abstraction from the ensemble of characteristics of works of art found in a particular span of time and place; this concept he then employs as a tool for dating individual works of art and, more important, as a pattern to provide a structure of stability and flexibility in the history of art.

Works of art have many characteristics; consequently, from among them the art historian must choose those that best satisfy the criteria of stability and flexibility in order to establish an historical order out of the continuum of self-sufficient works of art. On this basis, Ackerman rules out the characteristic of materials (e.g., wood or stone), because it is not sufficiently changeable; he rules out as well the characteristic of unique expressiveness, because it is too ephemeral. These are symptons, not determinants of style. Rather than these characteristics, or even techniques, which are important to style only when they enhance formal or symbolic elements, Ackerman chooses conventions of form and symbolism because they "yield the richest harvest of traits by which to distinguish style." [8] Conventions include "an accepted vocabulary of elements —a scale of color, an architectural Order, an attribute of a God or a saint—and a syntax by which these elements are composed into a still-life, a temple, or a frieze." [9] The assigned meanings of these conventions define the element of symbolism in style.

In explaining why styles change, Ackerman, like Schapiro and others, rejects the traditional determinist theory that style and changes in style follow a preordained pattern of evolution. In place of the notion of stylistic evolution as a succession of steps toward a solution of a given problem, Ackerman argues—and this, I think, is his most original and radical thesis—that we must explain this evolution "as a succession of steps away from one or more original statements of a problem." [10] The history of style is not a series of solutions of problems but "a succession of complex decisions as numerous as the works by which we have defined the style." [11]

This emphasis upon the history of style (and hence, of art) as a series of statements away from an original statement rather than as a sequence of attempted solutions culminating in an ideal statement enables Ackerman to lay down his criteria for the cogency of particular style concepts. Any particular style concept is formed on the assumption that a particular ensemble of conventions and symbolism is sufficiently stable, distinct, and relevant to justify hypothesizing it as a style. Each ensemble represents a class of related solutions to a problem which differs from distinguishable previous or later problems. Because of the limited, restrictive nature of a problem in art, the more modest the extension of a particular style concept, the more rewarding it is for study. There is no such defining problem in the Renaissance or Baroque; hence these are too grand for style analysis. Mannerism, on the other hand, is a limited style, with an ensemble of conventional and symbolic characteristics, embodied in a clearly distinguishable series of statements away from the original statement of a problem.

Ackerman's article raises many issues, all of which merit scrutiny, but I must confine myself to the one issue that relates most immediately to our problem of theory and practice in art history: Is Ackerman's theory of style consonant with the use of the concept of Mannerism by the art historians of that style? Does "Mannerism" serve to mark out, in a challenging, hypothetical way, an ensemble of conventions and symbolism or a series of related solutions to a clearly statable problem? Here, too, as with Schapiro, I shall try to show that Ackerman overstates his case.

Arnold Hauser writes on the nature of style and changes in style in two books, *The Philosophy of Art History* and *Mannerism: The Crisis of the Renaissance and the Origin of Modern Art*.[12] Both are vigorous defenses of the sociological conception of art which, in his modified Marxist version, explains art as an expression, rather than crude reflection, of certain specified economic and social conditions. On his view, Mannerism, for example, is best understood "as an expression of the unrest, anxiety, and bewilderment generated by the process of alienation of the individual from society and the reification of the whole cultural process." [13]

Styles are sociologically conditioned. But to explain them—to do art history—is to understand style itself, without which there can be no history of art. Consequently, much of Hauser's philosophy of art history deals with the substantive question, What is style? In a remarkably eclectic and sometimes penetrating analysis of about 150 pages, in which style is compared to institutions, Gestalts, language, musical themes, and ideal types—and is contrasted with entelechies, organic wholes, predetermined goals, and platonic ideas—Hauser finally settles on his doctrine of style as "a dynamic relational concept with continually varying content, so that it might almost be said to take on a new sense with each new work."

In his book on Mannerism, Hauser so beautifully articulates the meaning and the implications of this doctrine that I cannot forego quoting his full statement:

It can rightly be complained that there is no such thing as a clear and exhaustive definition of mannerism, but the same complaint can be made of
every other style, for there is and can be no such thing. There is always a
centrifugal tendency in the nature of any style, which influences a variety
of not strictly adjustable phenomena. Every style manifests itself in varying
degrees of clarity in different works, few, if any, of which completely fulfil
the stylistic ideal. But the very circumstance that the pattern can be detected
only in varying degrees of approximation in individual works makes stylistic
concepts essential, because without them there would be no associating of
different works with each other, nor should we have any criterion by which
to assess their significance in the history of development, which is by no
means the same thing as their artistic quality. The historical importance
of a work of art lies in its relationship to the stylistic ideal it seems to be
striving to achieve, and that provides the standard by which its original or
derivative, progressive or retrograde, nature can be judged. Style has no
existence other than in the various degrees of approximation towards its
realisation. All that exist in fact are individual works of art, different artistic
phenomena differing in purpose. Style is always a figment, an image, an
ideal type.[15]

As I understand this statement, Hauser's central thesis is that the
concept of style or any particular style concept is and must be governed
by a set of definitive criteria which guarantees its use in the historical
ordering of artistic facts. With this as his fundamental premise, he then
argues that because these criteria—as a complete set—obtain in no one
work of art and yet are essential to art history, they must constitute a
fictional ideal. His theory of style as a necessary ideal fiction rests upon
his presupposition that style concepts, as they are employed in art history, are logically closed. He shares this doctrine with all the traditional
theorists whom he rejects; it is the most vulnerable, I think, when it is
contrasted with the actual procedures of style-giving reasons in art history. Do the historians of Mannerism, for example, talk about its particularity and unity without assuming or needing to assume any set of
definitive criteria, ideal or not? Here, again, the contrast between what
the art historian says about style and how he uses it becomes glaring.

Our fourth example, E. H. Gombrich, has been much concerned
with the many aspects of what he calls "the riddle of style." Among his
writings, the two essays "Norm and Form: the stylistic categories of art
history and their origins in Renaissance ideals" and "Mannerism: the
historiographic background" are most pertinent here.[16]

In "Norm and Form" Gombrich's central theme is the derivation
of all traditional style terms from an acceptance or rejection of the Classic. The origins of the concepts of the Romanesque, Gothic, Manneristic, Baroque, Rococo, and Romantic (all initially terms of abuse) as

well as the origins of the concepts of the Classic, Renaissance, and Neo-classic are normative, not descriptive. From Vasari's castigation of the Gothic or German manner of "Confusion and Disorder" which he bases on Vitruvius' similar denunciation of certain wall decorations of his day, Gombrich contends, traditional concepts of style and particular style concepts in art history blend norm and form, evaluation with description. Every attempt to dissociate these norms from their forms fails, and is bound to fail, because these styles cannot be described without normative criteria. Even Wölfflin's five sets of polarities—linear and painterly, plane and depth, closed and open form, multiplicity and unity, and clarity and obscurity—which Wölfflin claims are descriptive, and which Gombrich reduces to certain principles of composition and representation—function in his art history as normative: i.e., as the classical versus the less than classical.

Traditional style terms are inevitably normative. But, Gombrich suggests, their norms, although historically rooted in the great classic reconciliation of ordered composition and faithful representation, need not be divided neatly into classical and anticlassical. The latter, articulated by the exponents of classicism, tend to be vices or sins to be avoided, and hence function according to "the principle of exclusion." But there are movements or styles in the history of art which do not reject the values they oppose, as anticlassical styles do; rather they recognize the multiplicity of artistic values and choose priorities among them. Such styles, Gombrich says, function according to "the principle of sacrifice." Even though it is difficult to draw a line between these styles, which Gombrich calls "unclassical," and the anticlassical, or between these two and the classical, it can be done by determining which of the two principles is operative. Mannerism has been described as an anti-classical style. But, Gombrich asks, Is it so clear that Mannerism aimed at an avoidance of order and harmony rather than at a shift in priorities?

Gombrich poses this question in his essay on "Mannerism." Here, he argues, as he had in his *Story of Art*, that Mannerism is fundamentally a style of experimentation, of virtuosity, of attempts to outdo one's immediate masters in invention and caprice. It has nothing to do with spiritual or personal crises occasioned, as some historians claim, by social or religious dislocation.

That Mannerism is unclassical, not anticlassical, that it exemplifies a shift in priorities, not a revolt against classic balance and representation: this, Gombrich insists, is a hypothesis, as indeed are all style concepts. Articulated and defended by Vasari, in the form of *bella maniera* (or *maniera moderna* or *terza e perfetta maniera*), and reformulated by

Bellori and later critics who censured it, "Mannerism" as a style concept was created to meet a historiographic need: to secure an artistic ranking for those who emulated and restored the ideal perfection of classical antiquity as against those who merely imitated the great *Cinquecento* masters. Modern historians, such as Dvorak, who praise Mannerism as the sixteenth century style of spiritualism in its perennial struggle against materialism (or even Gombrich himself, who characterizes Mannerism as a distinct style of virtuosity and experimentation) also hypothesize in their efforts to meet their historiographic needs.

I can hardly do justice here to the subtlety of doctrine and argument of these two essays, let alone to the issues they raise. Gombrich's primary achievement, however, must be noted: namely, his insight that no understanding of the concept of style or of particular style concepts is possible without a delineation of the role of these concepts. His brilliant attempt to establish this role in the historical home base of the concepts—in Vasari and Vitruvius—as essentially normative is of great philosophical importance. But is he correct in his central claims that style concepts are hypotheses and that at least the traditional ones are inevitable blends of norm and form? Do the historians of Mannerism, of which he is a distinguished representative, employ the term as a hypothetical norm? It seems to me that Gombrich's interpretation of the concept is more a stipulation as to how we ought to regard it than a correct elucidation of how it is actually used in art history.

Other historians of art theorize about style and its changes. A full account should include at least the theories of Wölfflin, Reigl, Panofsky, Frankl, and even the metaphysical conception of Malraux that style in art is a transformation of the meaning of the universe. Moreover, certain rejections of style as the crucial concept of art history are relevant to our problem. For example, George Kubler has recently pleaded for the replacement of the concept of style by what he calls the idea of "a linked succession of prime works with replications, all being distributed in time as recognizably early and late versions of the same kind of action." [17] Then, too, we must not overlook the fact that great histories of art have been written without the concept of style; it is a refreshing shock, for example, to reread Berenson's *Italian Painters of the Renaissance* and discover, unless I have missed it, that he does not even mention "style." To be sure, he refers to "schools," but the categories by which he analyzes them are the aesthetic ones of form, tactile values, and illustration; obviously, Berenson thought that these aesthetic concepts were sufficient for coherence in his history of art.

Important as all these considerations are, I reluctantly pass them by and, on the assumption that our four examples constitute a fair sample of theory of style in art history, ask instead whether what they say about style corresponds to what art historians do with it when they turn from theory to practice? What can we now learn from the historians of Mannerism about the concept of style?

II

I begin with Walter Friedlaender's "The Anticlassical Style." [18] This essay, a historical gem of iridescent argument and flawless organization, helps lay the foundation of our modern conception of Mannerism. Mannerism, Friedlaender contends, begins in Florence around 1520 as a conscious revolt against the ideals of the High Renaissance, especially as these ideals are embodied in the paintings of Andrea del Sarto and Fra Bartolommeo, and is initiated by two of their pupils, Jacopo da Pontormo and Rosso Fiorentino.

That there is such a break and that it is recognized by their contemporaries, Friedlaender documents from Vasari's condemnation of Pontormo's Certosa frescoes (1522–25). In these frescoes, Vasari narrates, Pontormo repudiates his former beauty and grace to take over the German manner of Dürer lock, stock, and barrel. Vasari, Friedlaender points out, correctly perceives in these frescoes a rejection of the ideals of the High Renaissance—the ideals epitomized in the *terza e perfetta maniera* of Leonardo, Raphael, and Michelangelo.

What are these ideals? According to Friedlaender—and this he feels is basic to understanding the origins of the Anticlassical style—they are certain aesthetic and ethical norms that govern the representation of the human figure in pictorial space. Central in the classical art of the High Renaissance, which for Friedlaender lasts only twenty years and does not include Michelangelo but is best exemplified in the mature work of Raphael, is an objectively idealized harmony of figure and space.

Decisive in Anticlassical Mannerism is the rejection of this normative conception of art. "The canon apparently given by nature and hence generally recognized as law is definitively given up. It is no longer a question of creating a seen object in an artistically new way . . . 'as one ought to see it.' . . . Rather . . . it is to be recreated . . . from purely autonomous motives, [as] one would have it seen." [19] A new conception of the human figure in pictorial space, with its attendant new rhythmic beauty is central in the new style. Figure and space can be distorted. Volume can displace space or create a space that is no longer three-dimensional. Instability rather than harmony becomes the ideal.

Friedlaender sums up Anticlassical Mannerism as a spiritually subjective movement, directed primarily against the canonically objective art of the High Renaissance.

Pontormo is the pioneer of the new style. After a classic and even transitional period, Pontormo, retreating from the plague in Florence, composes five scenes from the Passion in the Certosa of the Valdema near Florence. "As if impelled by the tragedy of the theme toward another and more inward style, Pontormo . . . shed all that was graceful and shining in the Renaissance atmosphere. All that had been established by Andrea del Sarto and his circle, the emphasis on the plastic and the bodily, the material and coloristic, the realized space and the all too blooming flesh tones—everything outwards now disappears. In its place are a formal and psychological simplification, a rhythm, a subdued but still beautiful coloring . . . and above all an expression rising from the depth of the soul and hitherto unknown in this age and style." [20] The figures, Gothically thin or bodiless, swaying or elongated; the space, unnatural or unreal; the discordant motifs; and the intense religiosity— in part derived from Dürer, some anticipated in Pontormo's early work, but now transmuted—all these establish Pontormo as the first great artist of Mannerism.

Pontormo's translation of the artistically observed object into subjectively spiritual terms is paralleled by the work of Rosso Fiorentino. After his own period of classicism, followed by one of vacillation, Rosso "takes the decisive step away from the balanced and classical towards the spiritual and subjective" [21] in his *Deposition from the Cross*, in Volterra (1521). Intertwinings of vertical ladders and elongated, swaying figures, unreal space, sharp light and color, even cubistic surfaces and angularity, together with emotional intensity contribute "to a new spirituality, an astonishing soulful expressiveness, which even Rosso himself rarely reaches again. . . . Everything is heightened, and everything that would disturb or diminish this heightening—space, perspective, mass, normal proportion—is left out or transformed." [22]

Rosso's *Moses Defending the Daughters of Jethro* (before 1523) goes further in the quest for pure abstraction. Psychic depth is supplanted by an aesthetics of form, color, ornamental overlapping, and spatial layers, which produce an unstable tension between picture surface and spatial depth. In construction and color, Friedlaender says, "this painting . . . is the strangest, wildest picture created in the whole period, and stands quite apart from every canonical normative feeling." [23]

The third of the founders of Anticlassical Mannerism is the non-Florentine, Francesco Parmigianino. In Parma, under Corregio's tutelage, he inclines toward the bizarre and unnatural. But it is in Rome (1523–27), where he probably encounters Rosso, and after the sack of the city (1527) when he leaves Rome, that his mannerist style emerges. His famous verticalism, so pronounced in his *Vision of St. Jerome* (before 1527) and especially in his *Madonna of the Long Neck* (1535–40), where it becomes elegantly elongated, is probably influenced by Rosso and is certainly anticlassical. The *Madonna of the Long Neck*, not only in its elongations of figure and column but in its astonishing and ambiguous asymmetrical relations and its over-all expressive quality of exquisite grace, becomes another of the paradigms of the early Mannerist style of Italian art.

The new style, thus, rests on Pontormo, Rosso, and Parmigianino. It is fully formed between 1520 and 1523. From Florence it proceeds to Rome where, after the sack and the consequent scattering of artists from Rome, it spreads, mainly through Rosso and his follower Primaticcio to the court at Fontainebleau and then to northern Europe. Through Parmigianino it enters the Venetian art of Bassano and Tintoretto, and through Tintoretto influences the greatest of the Mannerists, El Greco. In Florence Pontormo's pupil, Bronzino, carries on the style that then evolves into the *maniera*—or second generation of Mannerism—which Friedlaender in a later essay, "The Anti-Mannerist Style," characterizes as a degeneration of "the noble, pure, idealistic, and abstract style" [24] of Anticlassical Mannerism.

Friedlaender draws two important conclusions from his account: that Michelangelo is not the founder of Mannerism, and that Mannerism is not a weak imitation of Michelangelo. While it is true that Michelangelo is anticlassical almost from the beginnings of his work, that there are strong mannerist elements in his treatment of space as far back as 1511 in the spandrels of the Sistine Ceiling, and that his *Last Judgment* (1541) is the "overwhelming paradigm of Mannerism," his characteristic elongations and distortions—so typical of Mannerism—turn up after 1520. Indeed, Friedlaender argues, Michelangelo is a Mannerist only from 1525 to 1530, when he returns to Florence to create the Medici *Madonna* and the *Victor*; and he is manneristic only in some of his works since this is the period of his great non-Mannerist *Times of Day* of the Medici Chapel.

Friedlaender's brilliant revolutionary essay has been much praised and criticized. Few if any question what is undoubtedly his greatest achievement: that of bringing us to look at the work of three neglected great artists in a new, historically grounded, and enhancing light. Many, however, object to his chronology, his specific attributions and explanations of influence, his particular examples or criteria of Mannerism, and his interpretation of the work of Pontormo, Rosso, and Parmigianino in relation to that of the *maniera* proper.

What has not been done and needs doing if we wish to understand the concept of style in art history is to elucidate the role Friedlaender assigns to his basic style term, "Anticlassical Mannerism."

What Friedlaender does is to employ a style term which he borrows from the seventeenth century detractors of the *maniera*, and which he extends to cover the sources of the *maniera* in Pontormo, Rosso, and Parmigianino, in order to distinguish, characterize, relate, and revaluate a whole group of artists and their work. As he employs the term to cover the first generation of painters he is concerned with in his Inaugural Lecture, "Anticlassical Mannerism" functions under certain criteria, but these criteria add up to no definitive set and correspond to no essential set of properties shared by all anticlassical mannerist works. Friedlaender offers no definition—hence, in one sense of theory, no theory of Mannerism—no statement of its essence. Nor does he state or imply that without such a definition he can give no cogent reasons for particular works being manneristic. All Friedlaender suggests is a "decisive" criterion: a new artistic relation to the observed object that, more particularly, is a spiritual or subjective (in a nonoptical sense) conception of figure and space in their asymmetrical relations. It is this criterion that he falls back on both to characterize Mannerism and to contrast that style with the normative, balanced, unambiguous, and stable ideal governing the relations between figure and space of the High Renaissance.

That Friedlaender has no definitive set of criteria for his style term, and hence no real definition of "Anticlassical Mannerism" can be best seen if we look at the various reasons he gives for particular works being manneristic. They comprise a large group. A particular painting, he says, is manneristic because it has crowding of figures, a narrow layer of space, half-figures seen from the back, bodiless figures, elongated figures, swaying figures, spilling of figures or, pictorial elements over the frame, impetuous or harsh color, preciosity, cubistic surfaces, rejection of perspective, overlapping of spatial layers, compression of space, elegant grace, violence, turmoil, the bizarre, or a particular kind of spirituality. And there are others.

As diverse as these reasons are, they function as "mannerist reasons" for Friedlaender, I submit, only because they derive from or center on the decisive criterion of the subjective relation between figure and space. This criterion, I have already suggested, is not necessary and sufficient—definitive—for Friedlaender. But is it either necessary or sufficient, as he uses it? It seems to me absolutely clear that this criterion is not sufficient since he rejects certain works, such as Michelangelo's late frescoes, *Conversion of St. Paul* and *Crucifixion of St. Peter* and his Rondanini *Pieta*, as manneristic even though they satisfy this criterion. We must acknowledge, however, that the criterion is necessary for him because there is no example in his essay of a work that is in the Mannerist style that does not satisfy this criterion.

And now we must ask, Is this criterion clear? If we spell it out, as Friedlaender so beautifully does, as an asymmetrical, uncanonical relation between figure and space with its consequent artistically subjective, spiritual, expressive quality or, even more fully, in terms of all the "mannerist reasons" he presents throughout his essay, we do have a criterion or rather a related cluster of criteria regarding unnatural space and figure, asymmetry, violence, elongation, elegance, and the like, that are as empirically grounded as they can be. They have their empirical counterparts in the world outside of art. If, for example, "elongation" is vague, its vagueness rests on its ordinary use, not on its use in talking about style. So too, it seems to me, for all the criteria surrounding Friedlaender's one decisive criterion. The possible exception is spirituality. But here again, I think, Friedlaender provides clear, empirically grounded criteria: painting an observed object as you would want it seen as against how it ought to be seen according to an objective canon.

I do not wish to suggest that all of Friedlaender's criteria or reasons, even if they are clear in the sense of being empirically grounded, are descriptive of properties in works of art in the same way. It may well be, as I think it is, that "spiritual," unlike, say, "violent," or "elegant," is more interpretive or explanatory than descriptive. I shall return to this problem later. All that needs saying here is that Friedlaender's criteria are not vague in the way other criteria of style concepts, such as Wölfflin's "*malerisch*" or even Dvorak's own use of "spiritual," are. The vagueness is not in Friedlaender's decisive criterion or cluster of criteria for "Mannerism" but in the concept itself. This vagueness is the clue to the logic of style concepts, which is not to be found in Friedlaender or any other art historian considered in isolation, and which hence has been overlooked by all the art historians writing *about* style concepts. It can be discovered only in the disagreements among the art historians over the criteria—clear or vague—for their style concepts as they employ these concepts in their separate histories.

"El Greco and Mannerism," by Max Dvorak, is another classic in the modern conception of Mannerism.[25] Starting with the climax rather than the beginnings of sixteenth century Mannerism, Dvorak

finds in the Spanish work of El Greco the culmination of three tendencies: the late antinatural form of Michelangelo, the antinatural color
and composition of Tintoretto, and the new spirituality of St. Theresa
and the Spanish mystics. All three influence El Greco, all three are embodied in his work, and all three, with minor variations on the new spirituality, characterize the whole of sixteenth century European Mannerism and show it to be an expression of the perennial conflict between
spiritualism and materialism in European culture.

There are great methodological differences between Dvorak and
Friedlaender regarding the explanation of the origins of Mannerism.
Dvorak concentrates on cultural, Friedlaender, on artistic factors in the
development of the new style, but there is little disagreement on the
distinguishing features of Mannerism itself as a post High Renaissance
style. Dvorak emphasizes a particular range of light and color perhaps
more than Friedlaender, but both stress antinatural figure and space.
And both center on the new spirituality. Their great difference is over
the content of spirituality. For Friedlaender, we remember, it is purely
formal, having to do with an autonomous, subjective mode of observing
artistic objects. For Dvorak, it is not formal but iconographical, having
to do with artistic embodiments of the doctrine that our knowledge of
God and of the Christian mysteries consists in their immediate emotional certainty: "to know what you do not know." This rejection of rationality for mysticism, already present in the late works of Michelangelo and his disillusionment with the ideals of the Renaissance, and
dominant in the visionary style of Tintoretto as well as in the French
artists, Dubois and Bellange, culminates in the works of El Greco in
Toledo.

"What I see," said St. Theresa, "is a white and red that cannot be
found anywhere in nature, which give forth a brighter and more radiant
light than anything man can see, and pictures such as no painter has yet
painted, whose models are nowhere to be found, yet are nature herself
and life itself and the most glorious beauty man can conceive." [26]

El Greco, Dvorak says, "sought to paint the kind of things the saint
beheld in her ecstasy." [27] In the *Burial of Count Orgaz* (1586–88),
Christ in the Garden of Gethsemane (1608–14), the *Opening of the
Fifth Seal* (1610–14), *Resurrection* (1597–1604), and *Toledo in a
Storm* (1595–1600), to mention only those Dvorak does, El Greco
fuses the formal qualities of antinatural color, figure, and space with the
iconographic quality of the vision of the supernatural. These paintings
do not represent the supernatural: they reveal it.

Sixteenth century Mannerism, then, as Dvorak characterizes it, is
primarily spiritual in its pictorial manifestation of the mystical knowl-

edge of God and the world. Whether Dvorak regards this spirituality, with or without the formal qualities of antinatural color, space, and figure, as a real definition of "Mannerism," I do not know; that he so regards it is certainly not so obvious as some of his commentators and critics claim. What is obvious—and important to the elucidation of the concept of Mannerism—is that he differs from Friedlaender not over the definition or criteria of "Mannerism" but primarily over the meaning and criteria of "spirituality." Dvorak's use of "spirituality," unlike Friedlaender's, is, I think, vague precisely because it is obscure: how can immediate, emotional knowledge of the supernatural, whatever that is, become part of a painting? If Friedlaender's "spiritual" is interpretive in an explanatory sense, Dvorak's is at best interpretive in a purely invitational sense. That is, Dvorak's is not a hypothesis that helps to explain a picture: it is a recommendation to see it in a certain way.

I want now to turn to some recent discussions of Mannerism that are radically different from Friedlaender's or Dvorak's. But before I do, I must say something, even if in the baldest way, about one other philosophically important variant on the use of "Mannerism." In *From Leonardo to El Greco*,[28] Lionello Venturi writes on Mannerism as one aspect of European painting in the sixteenth century. On the whole, his account is based on Friedlaender's (and others') with a stress on anti-classicism, which Venturi traces to the neo-platonism of Ficino, and the pure formalism of the movement. The great reconciliation of the ideal with the real of classical art is rejected by Mannerism; nature is repudiated and the ideal is transformed into a cultivation of abstract forms for their own sake, in which imitation of the High Renaissance masters (especially in figures and motifs) and inventions that are purely imaginative supplant imitation of nature. Eventually this imitation and invention lead to mere repetition of forms (in the second generation of Mannerism) with the consequent debilitation of the movement.

Venturi insists that either in its Italian development or as a European International Style, Mannerism is too varied and complex to yield a definition. Rather than an essence or common denominator, Venturi offers "salient characteristics." Hence, what makes his account philosophically significant is that the reasons he gives for particular works or artists being manneristic rest on a family of characteristics, with none of them seemingly necessary or sufficient. Pontormo and Rosso, for example, are Mannerists because of their antinatural treatment of figure and space; but Domenico Beccafumi's "sensitive handling of light [e.g., in his *Birth of the Virgin*, 1543] and his *sfumato* implemented by a dexterous use of lights and darks qualify him to rank as a mannerist." [29]

Venturi's most provocative claim, however, has to do with some of the major works of Tintoretto, which most art historians today would assign among the paradigms of Mannerism. To the contrary, Venturi argues that Tintoretto briefly flirts with Mannerism, then, like Titian and other Venetians, rejects it; consequently, his major works, such as the *Miracle of St. Mark* (1548), the great series in the Scuola di San Rocco (1564–88), or the *Last Supper* (1591–94) in San Giorgio Maggiore are not manneristic. They are unmanneristic, however, not because they fail to meet defining criteria but because their salient characteristics differ from those of Mannerism. These paintings, fundamentally incantatory and religious, stress content, not form. Light and shadow, space and movement, and "one of the richest palettes known to painting" [30] help create a new unity of form and matter, of ideal and real, that transcends Mannerism altogether.

The word Mannerism derives from the Italian *maniera*. Linguists and art historians trace *maniera* to Boccaccio's "manner" of doing or behaving (1353), Cennini's "style" of an individual artist or group of artists (1390), Ghiberti's "style" of an age (1450), Raphael's "three styles" of buildings in ancient Rome (1519), and Vasari's "style," used either with a qualifying term, such as "beautiful" or "German," or used absolutely, in the sense that an artist has style. Vasari's conception of *maniera* is regarded as the most important because of its role in sixteenth century art and criticism. Contemporary art historians debate Vasari's exact meaning of the absolute sense of *maniera* as well as the relation between this use and his other uses. Whatever the resolution of this issue may be, the term takes on the derogatory meaning of "stereotype" for Dolce (1557) and the even more pejorative sense of "fantastic idea" for Bellori (1672). Baldinucci coins *ammanierato*—"mannered"— again as an abusive term (1681). The substantive "mannerist" comes from Fréart de Chambray (1662) and is introduced into English by Dryden in his translation of Du Fresnoy's *De Arte Graphica* (1695). "Mannerism" (*Der Manierismus, Le maniérisme, Il manierismo*) as a style term designating a particular period of Italian art comes into general use only in the nineteenth century.[31]

"Mannerism" derives from *maniera*. In the same way, Mannerist art derives from the art of the *maniera*. The *maniera*, hence Mannerism, is a continuation of High Renaissance ideals; consequently it is not anti-classical in form or content. Such is the major thesis of a number of recent art historians. The first of these I wish to consider is C. H. Smyth. In "Mannerism and *Maniera*," [32] Smyth turns to the sixteenth century conception of *maniera* as it was articulated by Dolce in his dialogue, *The Aretine* (*Dialogo della pittura, intitolato l' Aretino*, 1557) and by

Vasari in his *Lives*, especially the Introduction to Part III (1550; 2nd. ed., 1568), the two basic texts. Central in Dolce's dialogue is his contrast between Michelangelo and Raphael. He praises only Raphael because his paintings have no *maniera*, "namely, bad practice where forms and faces almost always look alike." [33]

This uniformity which Dolce chastises, Smyth claims is the same ideal that Vasari praises: "*La maniera* became *la più bella* from the method of copying frequently the most beautiful things, combining them to make from what was most beautiful (whether hands, heads, bodies, or legs) the best figure possible, *and putting it into use in every work for all the figures.* . . ." [34] It is this ideal that reaches perfection in the sixteenth century.

Although Vasari and Dolce agree that *maniera* idealizes uniformity (the one liking it, the other not), neither, Smyth contends, understands what is behind this uniformity, that which can stand as fundamental in *maniera* painting: namely, "the more or less consistent application of principles that governed form and movement—principles of posing figures at rest or in motion and of delineating, lighting, and grouping them." [35] It is these principles—conventions, habits, formulae—that characterize *maniera* painting and relate to *maniera* as a sixteenth century term.

Here is Smyth's list of these conventions: flattening of figures parallel to the picture plane; twisting of poses in two or three directions; flat light that intensifies the forced flatness of figures; juxtaposition of figures; angularity, especially of the arm across the chest or in the air; transformation of live figures into statues; attention to finish and details; and habitual tipping of the ground of the figures. Of these conventions regarding figure, composition, and space, figure is the most important.

What are the sources of these conventions? Primary is antique relief, especially extant Roman sarcophagi of the second to fourth centuries. *Maniera* painting, unlike painting *all'antica*, elaborates upon and modernizes the flatness of light and figure, the uniformity of poses, and so forth, of its models. Other sources are *Quattrocento* neo-Gothic, Michelangelo's *Battle of Cascina* and the Lazarus he contributes to Sebastiano del Piombo's *Raising of Lazarus*, and even Raphael, in *Parnassus*.

After "the gathering of the *maniera*," it begins in earnest in 1530 in Florence, then Rome, then Fontainebleau. Its best practitioners include Bronzino, Vasari, Salviati, Beccafumi, Polidoro, Perino, and Parmigianino, among others, but not Pontormo in the Certosa frescoes. During its heyday, in spite of its emphasis upon uniformity, it allows for variation and surprise, under another Vasarian rubric of license within the (antique-derived) rules. These variations range from the extremes of emotionless distance to high seriousness. In between, it "is in its element as decorative enrichment, encrusting walls, tapestries, and minor objects." [36] It finally disintegrates when uniformity becomes monotony and invention overelaboration. But in its prime, it creates works of art that can no longer be devalued.

Maniera in theory and practice is essentially an art of pose and gesture, modeled on antique relief. In the art and writings of Vasari, for instance, *maniera* represents no revolt against the High Renaissance, no expression of spiritual crisis. How, then, Smyth asks, can the modern conception of Mannerism as a formally anticlassical and expressively spiritual movement be reconciled with its source, the *maniera*? It cannot; consequently, "Mannerism" should apply only to the *maniera* painters and those who anticipated them. Thus, Pontormo's Visdomini altarpiece (1518) is manneristic but not, for example, his *Christ Before Pilate*, "however sensitive, refined, abstract, private, irrational, or eccentrically expressive." [37] This painting and similar ones (which for Friedlaender are among the paradigms of Mannerism) are best regarded, Smyth suggests, following Gombrich, as post-classic experimentations with High Renaissance forms, not as rejections of them. Rather than a division of painting in the period from about 1515 to 1590 into first and second generation Mannerism, he concludes, it would be better to retain the old term, "Late Renaissance," as a label for the whole period and restrict "Mannerism" to the *maniera* and its immediate antecedents.

John Shearman, in "*Maniera* as an Aesthetic Ideal" and *Mannerism*,[38] goes further than Smyth in the rejection of Mannerism as an anticlassical style and in the identification of Mannerism with the *maniera*. For Shearman, Mannerism has its roots deep in the High Renaissance. "It became something different and individual by taking a part of the High Renaissance and subjecting that part to special development." [39] Among its models are some of Michelangelo's *Ignudi* (1511–12) of the Sistine Ceiling, especially in their elegance, grace, and poise, and the unnatural beauty and harmony of color and form of Raphael's *St. Michael* (1517). Already anticipated by Leonardo, the refined style—which is the clue to the *maniera*, hence to Mannerism—is as much a theme in the full orchestration of the High Renaissance as the proto-Baroque. Mannerism begins and develops easily, as an art of articulate, sophisticated beauty, not out of spiritual crisis and despair. Its pervasive aesthetics of poise and grace rules out completely the tradi-

tionally attributed qualities of strain, brutality, violence, and overt passion. It is neither anticlassical nor a concentration on uniformity of pose
and gesture, modeled on antique relief; both Friedlaender and Smyth,
therefore, are in error in their conception of the Mannerist style.

"Mannerism" must be and can be defined. For without a true definition, Shearman contends, its use remains arbitrary and without controls in the historical account of sixteenth-century art. What is the
proper meaning of "Mannerism"? What are the defining qualities of
mannerist works? What group does the term cover? These are the central questions Shearman sets himself. All three answers lie in the sixteenth-century meaning of "*maniera.*" For when Lanzi first introduces
the term "*manierismo*" (in 1792), which is our direct source of "Mannerism," it applies to painters and the qualities of their work that are
much talked about, appreciated, and criticized in the sixteenth century.

What, then, is *maniera?* Although there is some variation, the evidence garnered from poetry, from the literature of manners, from certain writings of Dolce and Aretino, but most importantly from Vasari's
Lives, points to the overwhelmingly absolute use of the term. *Maniera*
as style which one has or lacks is Vasari's key term. He uses it to distinguish and to rank periods of Italian art; he singles it out as the only term
of his famous five—*regola, ordine, misura, disegno* and *maniera*—that
needs no definition, so well is it understood; and he means by it a certain kind of artistic accomplishment and refinement, with all that these
encompass.

Vasari's and the sixteenth-century absolute sense of "*maniera*" descend from the French courtly literature of manners of the thirteenth to
fifteenth centuries. Central in this tradition is the notion of "*savoir
faire*"—of comporting oneself with civilized sophistication and manner.
To behave with style is to be poised, elegant, refined, and effortless in a
perfected performance. From these positive qualities, certain others,
perennially regarded as negative, follow: To have style is to be unnatural, affected, self-conscious, and ostentatious. Also involved in this artificial code of behavior is the repudiation of revealed passion, evident
effort, and rude naïveté.

Italian literature of manners, especially Castiglione's *Il Cortegiano*
(1528) is basic to Vasari's "*maniera*" as well as to the whole of *maniera*
art and criticism. Elegance, refinement, artificiality, effortless overcoming of difficulties ("sprezzatura"), virtuosity, and grace—all construed as
positive qualities—are the obvious parallels between style in life and
style in art. They are also the defining properties of the *maniera* in
sixteenth-century art.

"Mannerism" has its linguistic and historic roots in the *maniera*. It was and should be once again a term reserved for an art "drenched in *maniera*." [40] The alternative, Shearman says, is the chaos of contemporary arbitrary definitions and the consequent distortion of sixteenth-century art.

Properly understood, Mannerism, in its overriding concern with the perfection of style, is fundamentally the "stylish style." As it develops, it embraces other aesthetic qualities, all compatible with those invested in *maniera*: variety, abundance, complexity, fantasy, obscurity, finish of detail, even the erotic, grotesque, esoteric, and pornographic. Although it is a style in which constituent parts of a work of art become as important as and sometimes more important than its whole, and in which content or subject is subordinate to form, Mannerism is not anticlassical but merely unclassical in its reversal of the normal relation of form and content. Perhaps, Shearman suggests, it is best understood as a super-sophisticated classicism because of its preoccupation with form as style.

Mannerism starts in Rome, not Florence. Its vital years of growth are 1520–27. "There was then in Rome, by chance, a brilliant group of young men, headed by Perino, Polidoro, Rosso, and Parmigianino, and it was in their hands that Mannerism was shaped into a style of universal significance." [41]

Perino del Vaga introduces it to Florence in 1522–23 with his cartoon, the *Martyrdom of the Ten Thousand*, which in spite of its subject exhibits a rarified Olympian ballet of *maniera* qualities to serve as a second great model (the first was Michaelangelo's *Battle of Cascina*) to the young painters. Apparently entered in competition for a commission along with Pontormo's design of the same subject, "full of passion, dynamic sequences of form, and explosive movements," [42] Perino's entry is all refinement and invention. That Perino's manneristic work was chosen instead of the anticlassical contribution of Pontormo constitutes "a turning-point in Florentine art." [43] After his Volterra *Deposition* (1521) and his (newly discovered) *Dead Christ* (1526), done in Rome, Rosso becomes another leader of Mannerism, taking the *maniera* with him to Fontainebleau. The great Florentine period of Mannerism comes in the third through fifth decades of the century, with Bronzino, Vasari, Salviati, Cellini, and Giovanni Bologna. Even Michelangelo at about the same time, in his architecture, sculpture, and drawing, furthers the *maniera* with his inventions, especially his serpentine line.

Mannerism with "its self-conscious stylization [as] its common denominator of all Mannerist works of art" [44] exhibits itself in painting, sculpture, and architecture. It also includes gardens, fountains, and grottoes. Its virtuosity and hedonism accommodate as well the grotesque, the monstrous, and the pornographic—all for the sake of variety and amusement. Its accent on form rather than content, on style for its own 'sake, is also present in music and poetry. Mannerism then, for Shearman, is an International Style of the sixteenth century, covering all the arts.

Shearman raises many issues in his spirited account of Mannerism. Central is his definition of *"maniera"* as a sixteenth-century term for style and as a style term. That Mannerism is not anticlassical in form or expression follows from his definition, as do all the reasons he gives for various works or artists being or not being manneristic. Pontormo is never manneristic, Rosso's *Deposition* is not; nor are El Greco, Tintoretto, Pordenone, or Berruguete, whom he does not mention. Michelangelo is a Mannerist in some of his works—the *Victor*, for example—yet not for Friedlaender's reasons, but because of its "grace, complexity, variety, and difficulty." [45] So, too, with Giulio Romano's Palazzo del Te, whose exterior as well as interior are manneristic not because of their total rejection of classical principles but because of their wonderful assortment of variety and caprice, designed to delight rather than to depress.

As admirable as Shearman's consistency of application of his criteria of "maniera" is, and commendable as his attempt to force a revaluation of the second generation mannerists may be, we must ask: Is his definition of *"maniera"* correct? and, more important, I think, Does his account of Mannerism rest on a true definition of "Mannerism"?

I shall come to these questions presently when we have all the evidence before us. Just here, however, the basic issue between Friedlaender and Shearman can be stated: Is the *maniera*, whatever and whomever it includes a debilitation of the anticlassicism of Pontormo and Rosso or is it an entirely separate movement? Friedlaender rests his case on the *maniera* as an outgrowth of anticlassicism; Shearman, on the *maniera* as one flowering of the High Renaissance.

Can this disagreement be resolved by any true definition of *"maniera"*? Shearman thinks it can and must be. He is positive about *"maniera"* as the refined style. Smyth, we remember, is just as positive that *"maniera"* means ideal uniformity of pose and gesture, modeled on antique relief. Others, even among those who agree that *"maniera"* is predominantly an absolute term of style in the sixteenth century, differ from both Smyth and Shearman that *"maniera"* denotes only "the characteristic and indefinable feature of an artist's expression," [46] thereby functioning in the same way as the later *"je ne sais quoi"* of the French theorists. That the disagreements over the meaning of *"maniera"* can be resolved by a true definition may be as much a delusion as the assumption that a true definition of "Mannerism" can settle the disagreements over that term.

Our final essay is S. J. Freedberg's "Observations on the Painting of the Maniera." [47] As elusive as the *maniera* is, even in its chronology, Freedberg dates it from about 1540 to 1580 and centers it in Florence and Rome. Its pervasive strain is its artificiality of both form and content, which correctly invites its mannered quality as well as its sixteenth-century name.

In its theoretical aspect, *"maniera"* as sophistication and grace is first attributed by Vasari to the masters of the *maniera moderna:* Leonardo, Raphael, and Michelangelo achieve *bella maniera,* which is to function as the subsequent standard for all art. Thus, *maniera* as Vasari conceives it is a special quality which distinguishes the moderns from the *Quattrocento* but which Freedberg claims those masters would not have accepted as their unique and paramount contribution. For the modern style, which we call the High Renaissance, is one that, like all classical styles, is founded on "a synthetic adjustment between aesthetic preference and actuality." [48] Vasari's *"maniera"* or *"bella maniera,"* because of its emphasis upon achieved perfection in art to the neglect of art in relation to nature, is merely classicistic—an imitation of classical models rather than an acceptance of the classical ideal of the reconciliation of the aesthetic with the actual.

That *maniera* is classicistic, and hence both an adherence to and a betrayal of the High Renaissance, Freedberg continues, can be seen in its practice as well as in its theory. In form and content *maniera* painting divorces itself from nature to concentrate upon the aesthetic. Art becomes commentary on appearance instead of description of it. Abstraction and the reworking and transmutation of extant artistic forms replace classical idealization of nature. Plausibility gives way to aesthetic convincingness, achieved by the brilliant technique of hard delineation of line and lucid color, accenting the surfaces of things. Even *maniera's* emphasis upon the plastic, where flesh becomes stone and stone becomes live, is a classicistically borrowed rendition of Michelangelo's sculpture.

In its allegiance to antecedent art as its sole source of inspiration, *maniera* painting is also an art of quotation. Its particular forms and in many cases its particular subjects are taken from High Renaissance or antique models. These quotations, severed from their contexts, become distorted and redirected so that their original meanings change in their new *maniera* settings. Inevitably, ambiguity and multivalence result, Freedberg points out, contributing to the overall elusiveness and artificiality so highly prized by the *maniera*. Even the mask—"the single most pregnant symbol" [49] of the *maniera*—is masked, as in Bronzino's *Allegory,* where it seems to reveal more of life than life's real face.

This penchant for visual quotation often combines with verbal quotation, especially in the *maniera* narrative fresco cycles which, because of their deliberate obscurity of sources or their transformations of them, constitute some of the most difficult rebuses in the history of art. All that remains clear is the ostensible decorative achievement—the reworking of all the materials into an outsize precious ornament, with total disregard for the pre-existing architectural structure surrounding the frescoed wall.

In *maniera* religious art, the apparent contradiction between detached refinement and attached devotion, is resolved by its quality of aesthetic exaltation, which is the *maniera* equivalent of religious devotion, and which is generated by the vibrance of the forms and the tensions of the meanings. This art can be best compared to the traditional icon: "In both, the subject matter is rigidified, translated from history toward symbol; and the form in which it is presented is made crystalline and tends toward the abstract . . . and this form is the object of a precious working and elaboration." [50]

Maniera painting, thus, is an art of disjunction and multivalence. The High Renaissance fuses meanings of form and content. The immediate post-classical painting of some of Raphael's pupils and of Pontormo and Rosso fractures this unity either by emphasizing form or content to the exclusion of the other or by pitting one against the other. But *maniera* makes "an artistic principle of multiplicity and multivalence." [51] What, then, is the relation between the High Renaissance, the post-Raphaelesque Roman school, the expressionism of Pontormo and Rosso, and the *maniera*? How much of the period 1520–80 is Mannerism?

The pupils of Raphael, especially Perino and Polidoro, are classicistic and become, along with the Roman convert Parmigianino, the forerunners of the *maniera*. Pontormo and Rosso—"the fractious Florentines"—are experimental, even to the extreme of being anticlassical, but this is true only from 1520 to 1526, and even then they also strive for the *maniera* qualities of grace, finesse, and ornament. With these two reminders about the limited role of anticlassical revolt and the constant presence of *maniera*, Freedberg returns to the Friedlaender distinction between first generation or Early Mannerism and the *maniera*. Having characterized the various styles between 1540 and 1580, he proposes a proper use of "Mannerism" rather than a definition of it. Basic to his decision is his affirmative answer to the questions: Are the style or styles of Pontormo, Rosso, and others of the so-called first generation of Mannerism "sufficiently close in essential ways to that of the Maniera to be connected with it, rather than distinguished from it by a different name"? and, Are the styles of both Early Mannerism and the *maniera* "sufficiently distinguishable in essential ways from that of the classical High Renaissance"? [52]

Mannerism thus, according to Freedberg, has its linguistic roots in the *maniera* but its artistic roots in the immediate post-classical period of the High Renaissance. The great difference between Early Mannerism and the *maniera* is the restrictive character of the latter. "Its specialized aestheticism is a limit on what we may call the humanity of art." [53] This criterion also serves to relate Tintoretto and El Greco to Mannerism; for both, like Pontormo and Rosso, transcend their *maniera* vocabulary to affirm the "profundity of overt human drama" [54] in art.

III

Other essays, especially some on the architecture of Mannerism and on Mannerism as an International Style, ought to be considered in any complete discussion.[55] Some reputable art historians of the sixteenth century deny that Mannerism is a separate style, preferring to treat its various manifestations as expressions of the late Renaissance under the general rubrics of Early, High, and Late Renaissance art.[56] The arguments advanced by these historians both for the extension and for the elimination of the style term, I believe, add nothing to the logic of the concept of Mannerism since they revolve around the enlargement or rejection of the same sets of criteria employed by those historians whom we have detailed and who do regard Mannerism as a separate style, "with the same kind of reality (and no more) as the other style periods that are commonly acknowledged." [57]

On this assumption that Mannerism is a style in sixteenth-century art, I want now, in our concluding section, to return to our two central questions: How do the historians of Mannerism use the style concept of Mannerism? and, How does their use compare with what art historians say about the concept of style in art history?

Among our six historians, there is much agreement: on the sources, nature, and development of Mannerism and the *maniera* of the sixteenth century, especially in Florence and Rome. But there is as much disagreement over the place and date of the origin of Mannerism, over its specific relation to the High Renaissance, its chronology, its relation to the *maniera*, its paradigms, its range, and its causes.

Fundamental to all these major disagreements, I want to argue, are not the varying purportedly true definitions of "Mannerism," which Shearman claims are the main source of disagreement, but different sets of criteria for the correct use of "Mannerism." If we turn, as we must, from their quarrels about the sources, influences, paradigms, extent, and development of Mannerism to their supporting reasons, we can find the clue to their disagreements as well as to the logic of the concept of Mannerism. Their style-giving reasons are central in the elucidation of the concept of Mannerism. Their answers to What is Mannerism? are to be found in their reasons for particular works or artists being manneristic.

"Mannerism," for each of our six historians, is a style term that functions as a name or label to designate certain sets of characteristics of certain works of art of the sixteenth century whose similarities and differences from previous and later works or from some contemporary works warrant their grouping as an independent unity or style.

Corresponding to these sets of characteristics—"manneristic-making properties"—are certain sets of criteria for the correct use of "Mannerism." Each historian has his own set which differs, sometimes radically, from the others. Only one, Shearman, states that his is a definitive set, and therefore a true definition of Mannerism, although it is possible to attribute such a set to Dvorak and to Smyth as well. However, if my account of Friedlaender is correct, he most certainly has no such set of criteria, only a complex necessary criterion regarding figure in space. And both Venturi and Freedberg disclaim definitions of "Mannerism."

Whatever the claims or disclaimers about definitive sets of criteria or even about necessary criteria for the correct use of Mannerism" as a style term, we must now ask: Is there extant such a set or a necessary criterion? Can there be, if the concept of Mannerism is to retain its assigned role? Need there be, in order to provide a coherent account of Mannerism?

Affirmative answers to these three crucial questions rest on the assumption that Mannerism, indeed that all style terms are logically closed concepts, amenable to true definitions in terms of their necessary and sufficient criteria that correspond to their necessary and sufficient properties.

It is this assumption, I believe, that is false. That it is false can be seen in the actual functioning of the criteria for "Mannerism" as these criteria play their role in the style-giving reasons of the historians of Mannerism. In order to understand the logic of style concepts, we must turn from the debates about the nature of Mannerism to the full range of disagreement over why or whether a particular work or artist is or is not manneristic. There we find that Mannerism is not a closed concept; that it does its assigned job only on the assumption that there is *no* definitive set of criteria, *no* necessary criterion for its correct use. For example, Friedlaender, we recall, says that Michelangelo's *Victor* is manneristic because of the figure's "screw-like upward thrust, his long, stretched-out, athlete's leg, his small Lysippian head, and his regular,

large-scale, somewhat empty features." [58] Shearman agrees that the
work is manneristic but gives reasons which have nothing to do with
anticlassical figure in space: the *Victor* is manneristic because of its
"grace, complexity, variety, and difficulty," [59] achieved mainly through
Michelangelo's serpentine line that expresses completed rather than
restless or disturbed action.

Again, for Friedlaender, Pontormo's *Christ Before Pilate* is a paradigm of Mannerism; for Smyth, it is a paradigm of sixteenth-century expressionism, not manneristic at all because it has no ideal uniformity of
figure or pose.

And so it goes. Without repeating the evidence, I want to insist
that unless it recognizes the indigenous vagueness of the concept, no
reading of the vast array of disagreement among the historians over why
or whether a particular work or artist is or is not an example or even a
paradigm of Mannerism can do justice either to the disagreements or to
Mannerism as an historical phenomenon.

As its use in style-giving reasons reveals, "Mannerism" is not closed,
but vague in the sense that the criteria for its correct use are not complete or completable. To claim that the criteria are complete or could
be—as for example, by stipulation, to render these criteria as a precise
set—is to misunderstand and foreclose on their assigned role in the history of art.

What is this vagueness that I claim is the basic logical feature of
the concept of Mannerism? Consider as an illuminating model an example from C. L. Stevenson: the concept of a cultured person. [60] I say of
someone that he is a cultured person; I am asked why he is or why I say
he is, and I reply: Because he is widely read and acquainted with the
arts. My questioner counters: Nonsense. To be sure, he reads a lot, and
he knows much about the arts, but he has no imaginative sensitivity; so
he's a boor, not a cultured person at all.

In this exchange, both of us are working toward persuasive definitions of "a cultured person," definitions that rest on stressed criteria.
These criteria are vague in two different senses: "Imaginative sensitivity" is unclear and obscure in a way that "widely read" and "acquainted
with the arts" are not. But the latter two are still vague in the sense that
they provide no precise cut-off point or boundary in their application.
Individual criteria, therefore, can be vague in meaning or application.

There is a third kind of vagueness in this example that Stevenson
suggests but does not explore: the inadequacy or incompleteness of the
set of criteria; "cultured" is vague in its extant or professed set of criteria, which differs from the vagueness of the individual criteria. Here
vagueness contrasts with completeness, not with clarity or precision.

"Mannerism" is like "cultured." Its individual criteria may be, although they need not be, vague in their meaning or application. "Spiritual" is obscure in Dvorak's set of criteria. "Elongation" has no exact application in all cases: where, for example, does "elongation" end and "verticality" begin in Friedlaender's set of criteria? Friedlaender's "spiritual," on the other hand, is not obscure; nor is his criterion of "spilling over the frame," which is as exact a criterion and no more vague in application than "pregnant: with child" is.

But "Mannerism," like "cultured," is vague in another sense as well: its set of criteria, whether its individual members are clear or not, exactly instanced or not, is incomplete and incompletable.

As we have amply shown, art historians use "Mannerism" to label, describe, interpret, and evaluate or revaluate certain works of art with certain specified characteristics in a specified region of space and time. It does its assigned job under certain criteria. For one historian (Friedlaender), it functions under a "decisive" criterion, which comprises a number of others, a, b, and c. For a second historian (Dvorak), it functions under similar criteria, a and b, but c has a different interpretation, so let us call it d. For a third historian (Venturi), it functions under a cluster or family of "salient" criteria, a, b, c, e, and f, where no one criterion is necessary, no collection of them is sufficient. For a fourth historian (Smyth), "Mannerism" functions under a general criterion, "*maniera*" (let us call it m), which in turn functions under the criterion of ideal uniformity of pose and gesture, n, and which is regarded as definitive for both "Mannerism" and "*maniera*." For a fifth historian (Shearman), it functions under the same general criterion, "*maniera*," which in turn functions under the criteria of refinement, artificiality, difficulty, and grace, o, p, q, and r, and which are also claimed to be definitive for both "*maniera*" and "Mannerism." Finally, for a sixth historian (Freedberg), it functions under two sets of criteria: "*maniera*," to which he adds the criterion of multiplicity and multivalence of meanings, s; and experimental or anticlassical expressionism, t.

In every case, we can ask whether these criteria are clear and are precisely applicable to the works specified as manneristic by the historians. If they are not clear or are questionable in their application, they are vague. But they are not vague in the way in which the individual sets of criteria—a, b, and c; a, b, and d; "*maniera*" (as n; as o, p, q, and r; as s); or s and t—are vague; or even all these sets together are vague. For the vagueness of the sets, taken individually or collectively, is a vagueness of the incompleteness and incompletability of the set. Therefore the fundamental vagueness of "Mannerism" consists in the perennial possibility of intelligibly enlarging or exchanging the criteria for its correct use. Unless we acknowledge this vagueness of the concept of Mannerism, we cannot make sense of the different moves which our historians have successively made and which future historians may make as they choose different criteria, perhaps even other than formal and iconographical ones, that will enable them to present a new account of Mannerism.

"Mannerism" is not only irreducibly vague; it is also beneficially vague. For the concept, in its incompletability of criteria, which allows for new histories of Mannerism, offers new sources of illumination of the works of art themselves. These new ways of inviting us to look at works of art—explicable only if we assume the possibility of new or enlarged sets of criteria—are as integral a part of art history and the role of style concepts in it as the authentication and dating of works of art. The historian's interpretations of particular works of art or groupings of them are as important as any of his other procedures. Without the vagueness of "Mannerism," these new interpretations, so rich in their aesthetic implications, would cease to come into being. It is consequently simply not true that without a true or real definition of "Mannerism," its history remains chaotic. Indeed, with such a definition—a complete set of necessary and sufficient criteria—there would be no continuing history of Mannerism.

"Mannerism," then, if my argument is correct, has no definition, no set of necessary and sufficient criteria, or even any necessary criterion. It does not need such criteria in order to support its style-giving reasons. It cannot have such criteria if the historical role of "Mannerism" as an irreducibly and beneficially vague concept is to be preserved.

"Mannerism," we have said, functions under certain criteria, none necessary, none sufficient, none definitive. These individual criteria are sometimes clear and clearly instanced but are also often obscure and inexact in their application.

These individual criteria can be classified also as descriptive or interpretive. All are employed by our historians to mark out features of works of art which they label manneristic. But only some of them are descriptive in their use. I suggested in our discussion of Friedlaender that, as he uses the term "spiritually subjective," it functions as an interpretive term to integrate all the manneristic elements of a painting. It purports to explain the work rather than to describe one aspect of it. Because it rests on elements in the work—uncanonical space, antinatural figure, asymmetry, unnatural color—that are related under the category of the nonoptically subjective way of observing objects in space, Friedlaender's "spiritually subjective" is an hypothesis about what is central in a manneristic work. Dvorak's "spirituality" is also in part an interpretation of certain elements in certain works of art, especially the

Toledo paintings of El Greco. But because he invests these works with an element that is not clearly present (namely, emotional certainty of religious beliefs), his criterion serves to invite us to see these paintings as spiritual in his sense rather than as an explanation of the elements to be seen in them.

Many criteria of "Mannerism" are interpretive rather than descriptive in their use. All that are claimed to be central, whether definitively or not, are interpretive, serving as explanatory hypotheses about mannerist works. But there are others, not put forth as central, which are also interpretive: "elusive" as against "violent," "empty features" as against "elongated ones," "menacing" as against "brutal," and so on.

This whole subject of the kinds of criteria or terms and utterances to be found in art history deserves thorough investigation. In *Hamlet and the Philosophy of Literary Criticism,* I have tried to show the fruitfulness of distinguishing among the various kinds of terms and utterances in the clarification of many disputes of literary critics.[61] I have no doubt that similar results could be obtained from a careful consideration of the terms and utterances of art history.

That "Mannerism" is irreducibly vague, it can now be summarily shown, does clarify many of the fundamental disagreements among the historians of Mannerism. Debates about the origins of Mannerism, its place and date of origin, its founders, its paradigms, its range and development, whether or why a particular work or artist or group is or is not manneristic, whether Mannerism is an International Style, encompassing not only painting and sculpture, but architecture, music, and literature as well—all of these, I submit, are not questions that yield true or false answers that ultimately depend upon definitive criteria of "Mannerism." On the contrary, all of them are explicable only in terms of the selected criteria from the inexhaustible, vague set of criteria of "Mannerism." Does Mannerism start in Rome, or in Florence; in 1520, or in 1530; with Pontormo, or with Perino? Is it inspired by Michelangelo, and by his *Battle of Cascina, Ignudi,* or the *Victor?* Does it include Tintoretto? Does it include Pontormo? Is it anticlassical, unclassical, classicistic, or superclassical? Each of the professed answers revolves systematically around criteria that are garnered from an inexhaustible class of criteria.

The attempt to pin down the criteria of "Mannerism" to those of the *maniera* rests, I think, on a double illusion: that the *maniera* is clearly definable and that Mannerism is identical with the *maniera.* As we have seen, there is no agreement on the definition of the *maniera;* what is more devastating, even if there were, it would not follow from such a definition that Mannerism as a style phenomenon descends from the linguistic rather than the artistic roots of the *maniera*. On this issue, Friedlaender and Freedberg exploit one range of possibilities among the criteria of "Mannerism" and Shearman, a different range. Whether Mannerism is to be restricted to its linguistic rather than its artistic origins depends on the historian's decision, not on an historical fact.

That the style concept of Mannerism is irreducibly vague contrasts sharply with the various statements about the concept of style in art history by Schapiro, Ackerman, Hauser, and Gombrich. This contrast, therefore, provides the answer to our second question: namely, How does the use of "Mannerism" compare with art historians' statements about the concept of style in art history? If my account of the role or logical grammar of "Mannerism" is correct, this follows: their doctrines that styles are constancies of form motives, form relations, and expressive qualities; or are stable yet flexible ensembles of characteristics; or are fictional ideals of necessary and sufficient properties; or are hypothetical blends of norms and forms—all these doctrines are inadequate in the same fundamental way. They leave out the irreducible vagueness of at least one style concept, and they do so because they overlook the range and significance of disagreement among art historians in their style-giving reasons.

With the exception of Hauser, whose definition of style as an ideal essence is itself a fiction, invented to satisfy the spurious need for necessary and sufficient criteria as a buttress for style-giving reasons, the various statements about style apply brilliantly to the historians of Mannerism, taken in isolation, independently of their disagreements with one another. Here especially, constancy and ensemble take root in the particular sets of criteria for the correct use of "Mannerism" offered by the individual historians. Both Schapiro and Ackerman give adequate descriptions of our six historians' different uses of "Mannerism." For each of these historians employs criteria that serve to mark out certain constancies of form elements, form relations, and expressive qualities or certain ensembles of convention of form and symbolism on the assumption that these constancies or ensembles are sufficiently stable and flexible to render Mannerism a separate style. Ackerman's additional claim that these ensembles are hypotheses—which Gombrich generalizes as a universal doctrine about style concepts, but which Ackerman restricts to the criteria rather than the style concept—is also sound because the individual sets of criteria for "Mannerism" do function as interpretive hypotheses about what is central, though not necessarily definitive, in mannerist works. It is, therefore, not the emphasis upon the hypothetical character of the criteria that is defective in the art historians' account of style; it is their omission of what is implied by this hypothetical character, namely, the perennial possibility, and thus irreducible vagueness, of competing sets of criteria as integral at least to Mannerism as a style concept. Ackerman's reading of Mannerism or any other legitimate style as a series of related statements away from an original statement of a problem is an especially revealing example of this deficiency. Is there, we must ask, a clearly statable problem of Mannerism? What is to count as an original statement of Mannerism, as the historians of Mannerism make abundantly evident, is itself at stake in the intrinsic debatability of the concept.

Gombrich's contention that all styles are hypothetical blends of norm and form requires special consideration. As it stands, it is ambiguous. If it means in the case of Mannerism that "Mannerism" is used by historians to describe and evaluate, it is certainly true but hardly exciting. If it means that the extant criteria of "Mannerism" comprise both descriptive and evaluative ones, it is true for some historians, e.g., Shearman's "refinement," but not true for others, e.g., Friedlaender's criteria which are descriptive or interpretive. If it means, as I think Gombrich intends it to mean, that *every* criterion for "Mannerism" is both normative and descriptive, then we have a thesis that is as exciting as it is false. For example, are all of Friedlaender's criteria reducible to an implicit preference for "the less than classical" that parallels Gombrich's reduction of Wölfflin's purportedly descriptive polarities to the normative or preferred classical versus "the less than classical"? Does Friedlaender simply exchange one principle of exclusion for another? To be sure, Friedlaender rejects Wölfflin's "sins to be avoided" but he does not offer a new set in their place. It may be argued, as Gombrich does, that this is exactly what Dvorak attempts with his criterion of "spirituality." But as we have seen, Friedlaender's "spiritually subjective" functions as an interpretive, not as an evaluative or even descriptive, criterion. Once it is introduced, he also employs it as a basis for a revaluation of Mannerism. Its introduction, however, blends description of artistic elements with an interpretation of them. Friedlaender offers an hypothesis about form—i. e., antinatural figure in unnatural space—in order to dissociate this form from a traditionally invested norm. This procedure is not to blend norm and form, any more than cleansing our eyes is to exchange one pair of glasses for another. Gombrich, it seems to me, confuses blending norm and form with neutralizing traditional blends in order to procure a new evaluation of form. To neutralize is not necessarily to evaluate or revaluate, although it may be motivated or succeeded by them.

In this paper I have tried mainly to show that at least one style concept is irreducibly vague; that this vagueness is the fundamental logical feature of the role of this concept, to be discerned best in the range of disagreements among the historians in their style-giving reasons; and consequently that it is false that all style concepts or the concept of style in art history are logically closed in the sense that they do have, must have, or require sets of necessary, sufficient, or definitive critera and their corresponding properties in order to provide a coherent history of art. Whether other style concepts, such as High Renaissance or Baroque or Gothic, are also irreducibly vague, although I believe that they are, I leave open. Whether all style concepts, including Impressionism, Cubism or Abstract Expressionism are irreducibly vague, although I think they are not, I also leave open. Furthermore, there are other issues—for example, the causal use of style—about which I have said little or nothing, even though they may be as important as the substantive use of style. But it seems to me that the latter problem is central in the clarification of the other issues of art history, and that is why I have concentrated on it.

One question remains: What is the relation between the openness of at least some genre concepts and the irreducible vagueness of at least one style concept? Is "Mannerism" like "tragedy," which is open in the sense of having no necessary or sufficient criteria and no undebatable criteria, or like "drama" or "novel," which are open in the sense of having no necessary or sufficient criteria but at least some undebatable ones, such as "plot" or "character"? "Mannerism," I have argued, has no necessary or sufficient criteria and no unchallengeable criteria, and thus is more like "tragedy" than like "drama" or "novel." But it differs from these genre concepts in at least two important respects. First, its assigned role does not require that it accommodate new cases with their new properties: its perennial flexibility does not extend to future works of art in the way that these genre concepts do. Rather its flexibility relates to past works of art that are historically bounded by space and time. Second, the disagreements about the correct use of "Mannerism" converge more on the exchange of sets of criteria than on their enlargement to cover new cases or on the rejection of putatively necessary criteria.

Because of these two differences, I am inclined to regard "Mannerism" as distinct from genre concepts and perhaps akin to the explanatory concept of centrality in the criticism of works of art. For the debates and disagreements over what is central or most important in a particular work of art seem to have the same vast array of irreducible vagueness about what is to count as Mannerism.[62] On this interpretation of "Mannerism," we have a striking vindication of Gombrich's hypothesis that style concepts function as hypotheses in art history because they attempt to formulate what is central or most important and distinctive in certain groupings of works of art.

Whether these two differences between "Mannerism" and genre concepts entail a radical distinction between openness and irreducible vagueness, I do not know. But I am confident that all efforts to render open concepts closed and vague concepts complete at once misunderstand those concepts entirely and foreclose on their historically assigned roles altogether.

NOTES

1. See, e.g., M. C. Bradbrook, "Fifty Years of the Criticism of Shakespeare's Style: a Retrospect," *Shakespeare Survey*, VII (1954): "There is no question relating to Shakespeare as a writer that does not involve his style . . . . Yet on this central problem comparatively little has been written" (p. 1).

2. First published in *Journal of Aesthetics and Art Criticism*, XV (1956).

3. Meyer Schapiro, "Style," first published in A. L. Kroeber, ed., *Anthropology Today* (Chicago, University of Chicago Press, 1953); reprinted in M. Philipson, ed., *Aesthetics Today* (New York, Meridian, World Publishing Co., 1961). All references are to this reprint.

4. Shapiro, p. 83.

5. *Ibid.*

6. *Ibid.*, p. 81.

7. James S. Ackerman, "A Theory of Style," *Journal of Aesthetics and Art Criticism*, XXI (1962). Reprinted in M. C. Beardsley and H. M. Schueller, eds., *Aesthetic Inquiry* (Belmont, California, Dickenson Publishing Co., 1967). All references are to this reprint.

8. Ackerman, p. 56.

9. *Ibid.*

10. *Ibid.*, p. 59.

11. *Ibid.*, p. 60.

12. Arnold Hauser, *The Philosophy of Art History* (New York, Alfred A. Knopf, 1963) and *Mannerism*, 2 vols. (London, Routledge, Kegan Paul, 1965).

13. Hauser, *Mannerism*, I, 111.

14. Hauser, *Phil. of Art Hist.*, p. 209.

15. Hauser, *Mannerism*, I, 18–19.

16. Both essays are collected in E. H. Gombrich, *Norm and Form: studies in the art of the Renaissance* (London, Phaidon, 1966).

17. George Kubler, *The Shape of Time* (New Haven, Yale University Press, 1962), p. 130.

18. Inaugural Lecture, 1914. Published in translation in 1925, under the full title "The Rise of the Anticlassical Style in Italian Painting in 1520." Reprinted in Walter Friedlaender, *Mannerism and Anti-Mannerism in Italian Painting* (New York, Schoken Books, Inc., 1965). All references are to this reprint.

19. Friedlaender, p. 6.

20. *Ibid.*, pp. 23–24.
21. *Ibid.*, p. 29.
22. *Ibid.*, p. 31.
23. *Ibid.*, p. 34.
24. The full title of the translated essay is "The Anti-Mannerist Style around 1590 and its Relation to the Transcendental" (1930). Reprinted in Friedlaender. I quote from p. 48.
25. First delivered as a lecture in 1920 and published in Max Dvorak, *Kunstgeschichte als Geistesgeschichte*, 1953. Translated in *Magazine of Art*, XLVI (1953). All references are to this translation.
26. Dvorak, p. 21.
27. *Ibid.*
28. Lionello Venturi, *From Leonardo to El Greco* (New York, World Publishing Co., 1956).
29. *Ibid.*, p. 234.
30. *Ibid.*, p. 216.
31. On the history of *"maniera,"* see esp. Marco Treves, *"Maniera,* the history of a Word," *Marsyas*, I (1941); Sir Anthony Blunt, *Artistic Theory in Italy, 1450–1600* (London, 1940), ch. 7; and R. Klein and H. Zerner, eds., *Italian Art, 1500–1600* ("Sources and Documents in the History of Art Series," Englewood Cliffs, Prentice-Hall, Inc., 1966), esp. pp. 53–91.
32. C. H. Smyth, "Mannerism and *Maniera*" in M. Meiss, ed., *The Renaissance and Mannerism (Studies in Western Art: Acts of the Twentieth International Congress of the History of Art*, Princeton, Princeton University Press, 1963), II, 174–199.
33. Quoted by Smyth, *op. cit.*, p. 177.
34. Quoted by Smyth, *ibid.*
35. Smyth, *op. cit.*, p. 181.
36. *Ibid.*, p. 194.
37. *Ibid.*, p. 198.
38. John Shearman, *"Maniera* as an Aesthetic Ideal" in Meiss, *The Renaissance and Mannerism*; and Shearman, *Mannerism* (Baltimore, Penguin Books, 1967).
39. Shearman, *"Maniera* as an Aesthetic Ideal," p. 213.
40. Shearman, *Mannerism*, p. 23.
41. Shearman, *"Maniera* as an Aesthetic Ideal," *op. cit.*, p. 215.
42. *Ibid.*, p. 217.
43. *Ibid.*
44. Shearman, *Mannerism*, p. 35.
45. *Ibid.*, p. 84.
46. Giuliano Briganti, *Italian Mannerism*, tr. M. Kunzle (Leipzig, Volkseiger Betrieb, 1962), p. 6 *Cf.* Blunt, ch. 7.
47. Sydney J. Freedberg, "Observations on the Painting of the Maniera," *The Art Bulletin*, XLVII (1965). Freedberg discusses Mannerism also in *Parmigianino* (Cambridge, Harvard University Press, 1950) and in *Painting of the High Renaissance in Rome and Florence*, 2 vols. (Cambridge, Harvard University Press, 1961).
48. Freedberg, "Observations," *op. cit.*, p. 188.
49. *Ibid.*, p. 187.
50. *Ibid.*, p. 194.
51. *Ibid.*
52. *Ibid.*, p. 195.
53. *Ibid.*
54. *Ibid.*, p. 196.
55. On Mannerist architecture, a concise study is Nikolaus Pevsner, *An Outline of European Architecture* (Baltimore, Penguin Books, 1951), ch. 5; on

Mannerism as an International Style, see F. Würtenberger, *Mannerism: the European Style of the Sixteenth Century*, trans. by M. Heron (New York, Holt, Rinehart, and Winston, 1963). Both contain good bibliographies on their subjects.

56. See, e.g., M. Salmi, "Tardo Rinascimento e primo Barocco, Manierismo, Barocco, Rococò: Concetti e termini," *Convegno int.*, Rome 1960 (Rome, Academia Nazionale dei Lincei, 1962), pp. 305–17.

57. John Shearman, *Mannerism*, p. 15.

58. Walter Friedlaender, p. 13.

59. Shearman, *Mannerism*, p. 84.

60. C. L. Stevenson, "Persuasive Definitions," *Mind*, 47 (1938).

61. See esp. Part II.

62. On centrality as an explanatory concept, see my *Hamlet and the Philosophy of Literary Criticism*, ch. xv.

THE AESTHETIC POINT OF VIEW

Monroe C. Beardsley

There has been a persistent effort to discover the uniquely aesthetic component, aspect, or ingredient in whatever is or is experienced. Unlike some other philosophical quarries, the object of this chase has not proved as elusive as the snark, the Holy Grail, or Judge Crater—the hunters have returned not empty-handed, but overburdened. For they have found a rich array of candidates for the basically and essentially aesthetic:

aesthetic experience	aesthetic objects
aesthetic value	aesthetic concepts
aesthetic enjoyment	aesthetic situations.
aesthetic satisfaction	

Confronted with such trophies, we cannot easily doubt that there *is* something peculiarly aesthetic to be found in our world or our experience; yet its exact location and its categorial status remain in question. This is my justification for conducting yet another raid on the ineffable, with the help of a different concept, one in the contemporary philosophical style.

I

When the conservationist and the attorney for Con Edison argue their conflicting cases before a state commission that is deciding whether a nuclear power plant shall be built beside the Hudson River, we can say they do not merely disagree; they regard that power plant from different points of view. When the head of the Histadrut Publishing House refused to publish the novel *Exodus* in Israel, he said: "If it is to be read as history, it is inaccurate. If it is to be read as literature, it is vulgar." [1] And Maxim Gorky reports a remark that Lenin once made to him:

'I know nothing that is greater than [Beethoven's] *Appassionata*. I would like to listen to it every day. A marvelous, superhuman music. I always say with pride—a naive pride perhaps: What miracles human beings can perform!' Then screwing his eyes [Lenin] added, smiling sadly, 'But I can't listen to music too often; it affects your nerves. One wants to say stupid nice things and stroke on the head the people who can create such beauty while living in this vile hell. And now you must not stroke anyone on the head: you'll have your hands beaten off. You have to hit them on the head without mercy, though our ideal is not to use violence against anyone. Hmm, hmm,—an infernally cruel job we have.' [2]

In each of these examples, it seems plausible to say that one of the conflicting points of view is a peculiarly aesthetic one: that of the conservationist troubled by threats to the Hudson's scenic beauty; that of the publisher who refers to reading *Exodus* "as literature"; that of Lenin, who appears to hold that we ought to adopt the political (rather than the aesthetic) point of view toward Beethoven's sonata, because of the unfortunate political consequences of adopting the aesthetic point of view.

If the notion of the aesthetic point of view can be made clear, it should be useful from the philosophical point of view. The first philosophical use is in mediating certain kinds of dispute. To understand a particular point of view, we must envision its alternatives. Unless there can be more than one point of view toward something the concept breaks down. Consider, for example, the case of architecture. The classic criteria of Vitruvius were stated tersely by Sir Henry Wotton in these words: "Well-building hath three conditions: Commodity, Firmness, and Delight." Commodity is function: that it makes a good church or house or school. Firmness is construction: that the building holds itself up. Suppose we were comparing a number of buildings to see how well built they are, according to these "conditions." We would find some that are functionally effective, structurally sound, and visually attractive. We would find others—old worn-out buildings or new suburban shacks —that are pretty poor in each of these departments. But also we would find that the characteristics vary independently over a wide range; that some extremely solid old bank buildings have Firmness (they are knocked down at great cost) without much Commodity or Delight, that some highly delightful buildings are functionally hopeless, that some convenient bridges collapse.

Now suppose we are faced with one of these mixed structures, and invited to say whether it is a good building, or how good it is. Someone might say the bank is very well built, because it is strong; another might reply that nevertheless its ugliness and inconvenience make it a very poor building. Someone might say that the bridge couldn't have been much good if it collapsed; but another might reply that it was a most excellent bridge, while it lasted—that encomium cannot be taken from it merely because it did not last long.

Such disputes may well make us wonder—as Geoffrey Scott wonders in his book on *The Architecture of Humanism* [3]—whether these "conditions" belong in the same discussion. Scott says that to lump them together is confusing: it is to "force on architecture an unreal unity of aim," since they are "incommensurable virtues." For clarity in architectural discussion, then, we might separate the three criteria, and say that they arise in connection with three different points of view— the practical, the engineering, and the aesthetic. In this way, the notion of a point of view is introduced to break up a dispute into segments that seem likely to be more manageable. Instead of asking one question— whether this is a good building—we divide it into three. Considering the building from the aesthetic point of view, we ask whether it is a good work of architecture; from the engineering point of view, whether it is a good structure; and from the practical point of view, whether it is a good machine for living.

Thus one way of clarifying the notion of a point of view would be in terms of the notion of being *good of a kind*.[4] We might say that to adopt the aesthetic point of view toward a building is to classify it as belonging to a species of aesthetic objects—namely, works of architecture—and then to take an interest in whether or not it is a *good* work of architecture. Of course, when an object belongs to one obvious and notable kind, and we judge it in relation to that kind, the "point of view" terminology is unnecessary. We wouldn't ordinarily speak of considering music from a musical point of view, because it wouldn't occur to us that someone might regard it from a political point of view. In the same way, it would be natural to speak of considering whiskey from a medical point of view but not of considering penicillin from a medical point of view. This shows that the "point of view" terminology is implicitly rejective: it is a device for setting aside considerations advanced by others (such as that the bridge will fall) in order to focus attention on the set of considerations that *we* wish to emphasize (such as that the sweep and soar of the bridge are a joy to behold).

The "point of view" terminology, however, is more elastic than the "good of its kind" terminology. To consider a bridge or music or sculpture as an aesthetic object is to consider it from the aesthetic point of

view. But what about a mountain, a sea shell, or a tiger? These are neither musical compositions, paintings, poems, nor sculptures. A sea shell
cannot be *good* sculpture if it is not sculpture at all. But evidently we
can adopt the aesthetic point of view toward these things. In fact, some
aesthetic athletes (or athletic aesthetes) have claimed the ability to
adopt the aesthetic point of view toward anything at all—toward *The
Story of O* (this is what Elliot Fremont-Smith has called "beyond
pornography"), toward a garbage dump, toward the murders of three
civil-rights workers in Philadelphia, Mississippi. (This claim has been
put to a severe test by some of our more far-out sculptors.) Perhaps even
more remarkable is the feat recently performed by those who viewed the
solemn installation of an "invisible sculpture" behind the Metropolitan
Museum of Art. The installation consisted in digging a grave-size hole
and filling it in again. "It is really an underground sculpture," said its
conceiver, Claes Oldenburg, "I think of it as the dirt being loosened
from the sides in a certain section of Central Park." [5] The city's architectural consultant, Sam Green, commented on the proceedings:

This is a conceptual work of art and is as much valid as something you
can actually see. Everything is art if it is chosen by the artist to be art. You
can say it is good art or bad art, but you can't say it isn't art. Just because
you can't see a statue doesn't mean that it isn't there.

This, of course, is but one of countless examples of the current tendency
to stretch the boundaries of the concept of "art."
    The second philosophical use of the notion of the aesthetic point of
view is to provide a broad concept of art that might be helpful for certain purposes. We might say:

A work of art (in the broad sense) is any perceptual or intentional object
that is deliberately regarded from the aesthetic point of view.[6]

Here, "regarding" would have to include looking, listening, reading, and
similar acts of attention, and also what I call "exhibiting"—picking up
an object and placing it where it readily permits such attention, or presenting the object to persons acting as spectators.

II

What, then, is the aesthetic point of view? I propose the following:

To adopt the aesthetic point of view with regard to X is to take
an interest in whatever aesthetic value X may possess.

I ask myself what I am doing in adopting a particular point of view, and acting toward an object in a way that is appropriate to that point of view; and, so far as I can see, it consists in searching out a corresponding value in the object, to discover whether any of it is present. Sometimes it is to go farther: to cash in on that value, to realize it, to avail myself of it. All this searching, seeking and, if possible, realizing, I subsume under the general phrase "taking an interest in." To listen to Beethoven's *Appassionata* with pleasure and a sense that it is "marvelous, superhuman music," is to seek—and find—aesthetic value in it. To read the novel *Exodus* "as literature," and be repelled because it is "vulgar," is (I take it) to seek aesthetic value in it, but not find very much of it. And when Geoffrey Scott makes his distinction between different ways of regarding a building, and between that "constructive integrity in fact" which belongs under Firmness, and that "constructive vividness in appearance" which is a source of architectural Delight, he adds that "their value in the building is of a wholly disparate kind" [7]; in short, the two points of view, the engineering and the aesthetic, involve two kinds of value.

This proposed definition of "aesthetic point of view" will not, as it stands, fit all of the ordinary uses of this phrase. There is a further complication. I am thinking of a remark by John Hightower, Executive Director of the New York State Council on the Arts, about the Council's aim to "encourage some sort of aesthetic standards." He said, "There are lots of laws that unconsciously inhibit the arts. Architecture is the most dramatic example. Nobody has looked at the laws from an aesthetic point of view." [8] And I am thinking of a statement in the *Yale Alumni Magazine* [9] that the Yale City Planning Department was undertaking "a pioneering two-year research project to study highway environment from an aesthetic point of view." I suppose the attention in these cases was not on the supposed aesthetic value of the laws or of the present "highway environment," but rather in the aesthetic value that might be achieved by changes in these things. Perhaps that is why these examples speak of "*an* aesthetic point of view," rather than "*the* aesthetic point of view." And we could, if we wish, make use of this verbal distinction in our broadened definition:

To adopt *an* aesthetic point of view with regard to X is to take an interest in whatever aesthetic value that X may possess *or that is obtainable by means of X*.

I have allowed the phrase "adopting the aesthetic point of view" to cover a variety of activities. One of them is judging:

> To judge X from the aesthetic point of view is to estimate the aesthetic value of X.

Those who are familiar with Paul Taylor's treatment of points of view in his book *Normative Discourse* will note how the order I find in these concepts differs from the one he finds. His account applies only to judging, which makes it too narrow to suit me. It also has, I think, another flaw. He holds that:

Taking a certain point of view is nothing but adopting certain canons of reasoning as the framework within which value judgments are to be justified; the canons of reasoning define the point of view. . . . We have already said that a value judgment is a moral judgment if it is made from the moral point of view.[10]

Thus we could ask of Taylor, What is an aesthetic value judgment? He would reply, It is one made from the aesthetic point of view. And which are those? They are the ones justified by appeal to certain "canons of reasoning," and more particularly the "rules of relevance." But which are the aesthetic rules of relevance? These are the rules "implicitly or explicitly followed by people" in using the aesthetic value-language— that is, in making judgments of aesthetic value. Perhaps I have misunderstood Taylor's line of thought here, but the path it seems to trace is circular. I hope to escape this trap by breaking into the chain at a different point.

I define "aesthetic point of view" in terms of "aesthetic value." And while I think this step is by no means a trivial one, it is not very enlightening unless it is accompanied by some account of aesthetic value. I don't propose to present a detailed theory on this occasion, but I shall extend my chain of definitions to a few more links, and provide some defense against suspected weaknesses. What, then, is aesthetic value?

> The aesthetic value of an object is the value it possesses in virtue of its capacity to provide aesthetic gratification.

There are three points about this definition that require some attention.

First, it will be noted that this is not a definition of "value." It purports to distinguish *aesthetic* value from other kinds of value in terms of a particular capacity. It says that in judging the total value of an object we must include that part of its value which is due to its capacity to provide aesthetic gratification.

The second point concerns "aesthetic gratification." My earliest version of this capacity-definition of "aesthetic value" employed the concept of aesthetic experience.[11] I am still not persuaded that this concept must be abandoned as hopeless, but it needs further elaboration in the face of the criticism coming from George Dickie, whose relentless attack on unnecessarily multiplied entities in aesthetics has led him to skepticism about whether there is such a thing as aesthetic experience.[12] I have tried working with the concept of aesthetic enjoyment instead,[13] and that may be on the right track. For the present occasion, I have chosen a term that I think is somewhat broader in scope, and perhaps therefore slightly less misleading.

Again, however, the term "aesthetic gratification" is not self-explanatory. It seems clear that one kind of gratification can be distinguished from another only in terms of its intentional object: that is, of the properties that the pleasure is taken *in*, or the enjoyment is enjoyment *of*. To discriminate aesthetic gratification—and consequently aesthetic value and the aesthetic point of view—we must specify what it is obtained from. I offer the following:

> Gratification is aesthetic when it is obtained primarily from attention to the formal unity and/or the regional qualities of a complex whole, and when its magnitude is a function of the degree of formal unity and/or the intensity of regional quality.

The defense of such a proposal would have to answer two questions. First, is there such a type of gratification? I think there is, and I think that it can be distinguished from other types of gratification, though it is often commingled with them. Second, what is the justification for calling this type of gratification "aesthetic"? The answer to this question would be more complicated. Essentially, I would argue that there are certain clear-cut exemplary cases of works of art—that is, poems, plays, musical compositions, etc.—that must be counted as works of art if anything is. There is a type of gratification characteristically and preeminently provided by such works, and this type of gratification is the type I have distinguished above. Finally, this type of gratification (once distinguished) has a paramount claim to be denominated "aesthetic"—even though there are many other things that works of art can do to you, such as inspire you, startle you, or give you a headache.

If this line of argument can be made convincing, we find ourselves with what might be called primary *marks* of the aesthetic: It is the presence in the object of some notable degree of unity and/or the presence of some notable intensity of regional quality that indicates that the en-

joyments or satisfactions it affords are aesthetic—insofar as those enjoyments or satisfactions are afforded by these properties. I shall return to
these marks a little later, and show the sort of use I think can be made
of them.

III

But before we come to that, we must consider the third point
about the capacity-definition of "aesthetic value"—and this is the most
troublesome of them all.

The term "capacity" has been chosen with care. My view is that
the aesthetic value of an object is not a function of the actual degree of
gratification obtained from it. It is not an average, or the mean degree of
gratification obtained from it by various perceivers. It is not a sum, or
the total gratification obtained from it in the course of its existence. All
these depend in part on external considerations, including the qualifications of those who happen to resort to libraries, museums, and concerts,
and the circumstances of their visits. I am thinking in terms of particular exposures to the work—a particular experience of the music, of the
poem, of the painting—and of the degree of aesthetic gratification obtained on each occasion. Aesthetic value depends on the highest degree
obtainable under optimal circumstances. Thus my last definition should
be supplemented by another one:

> The amount of aesthetic value possessed by an object is a func-
> tion of the degree of aesthetic gratification it is capable of pro-
> viding in a particular experience of it.

My reason for holding this view is that I want to say that a critical
evaluation is a judgment of aesthetic value, and it seems clear to me that
estimating capacities is both the least and the most we can ask of the
critical evaluator. I take it that when a literary critic, for example, judges
the goodness of a poem (from the aesthetic point of view), and is prepared to back up his judgment with reasons, he must be saying something about the relationship of the poem to the experiences of actual or
potential readers. The question is, What is this relationship? When a
critic says that a poem is good, he is hardly ever in a position to predict
the gratification that particular readers or groups of readers will receive
from it. Moreover, he is usually not in a position to generalize about
tendencies, to say, for instance, that readers of such-and-such propensities, preferences, or preparations will probably be delighted by the
poem. If the critic has at his disposal the information required to support such statements, he is of course at liberty to say such things as:

"This would have appealed to President Kennedy," or "This is an ideal Christmas gift for your friends who love mountain climbing." But when he simply says, "This is a good poem," we must interpret him as saying something weaker (though still significant) about the capacity of the work to provide a notable degree of aesthetic gratification. For *that* is a judgment he should be able to support, if he understands the poem.

The question, however, is whether the capacity-definition of "aesthetic value" is too weak, as a report of what actually happens in art criticism. I can think of three difficulties that have been or could be raised. They might be called (1) the unrecognized masterpiece problem, (2) the LSD problem, and (3) the Edgar Rice Burroughs problem. Or, to give them more abstract names, they are (1) the problem of falsification, (2) the problem of illusion, and (3) the problem of devaluation.

(1) Some people are troubled by one consequence of the capacity-definition—that objects can possess aesthetic value that never has been and never will be realized, such as the "gems of purest ray serene the dark unfathomed caves of ocean bear." This ought not to trouble us, I think. It is no real paradox that many objects worth looking at can never be looked at. But there is another kind of aesthetic inaccessibility in the highly complicated and obscure work that no critic can find substantial value in, though it may still be there. In Balzac's short story, "Le Chef-d'oeuvre inconnu," the master painter works in solitude for years, striving for the perfection of his greatest work; but in his dedication and delusion he overlays the canvas with so many brush strokes that the work is ruined. When his fellow artists finally see the painting, they are appalled by it. But how can they be sure that the painting doesn't have aesthetic value, merely because they have not found any? The capacity to provide aesthetic gratification of a high order may still be there, though they are not sharp or sensitive enough to take advantage of it.

If my proposed definition entailed that negative judgments of aesthetic value cannot even in principle be justified, then we would naturally mistrust it. But of course this consequence is not necessary. What does follow is that there is a certain asymmetry between negative and affirmative judgments, with respect to their degree of confirmation; but this is so between negative and affirmative existential statements in general. The experienced critic may have good reason in many cases not only for confessing that he finds little value in a painting, but for adding that very probably no one ever will find great value in it.

(2) If aesthetic value involves a capacity, then its presence can no doubt be sufficiently attested by a single realization. What a work *does* provide, it clearly *can* provide. And if my definition simply refers to the capacity, without qualification, then it makes no difference under what

conditions that realization occurs. Now take any object you like, no matter how plain or ugly—say a heap of street sweepings awaiting the return of the street cleaner. Certainly we want to say that it is lacking in aesthetic value. But suppose someone whose consciousness is rapidly expanding under the influence of LSD or some other hallucinogenic drug happens to look at this heap and it gives him exquisite aesthetic gratification. Then it has the capacity to do so, and so it has high aesthetic value. But then perhaps every visual object has high aesthetic value, and all to about the same degree—if the reports may be trusted.

I cannot speak authoritatively of the LSD experience, but I gather that when a trip is successful, the object, however humble, may glow with unwonted intensity of color and its shapes assume an unexpected order and harmony. In short, the experience is illusory. This is certainly suggested by the most recent report I have run across.[14] Dr. Lloyd A. Grumbles, a Philadelphia psychiatrist,

said that while listening to Beethoven's *Eroica*, particularly the third movement, he felt simultaneously 'insatiable longing and total gratification' . . . Dr. Grumbles said he also looked at prints of Picasso and Renoir paintings and realized, for the first time, 'they were striving for the same goal.'

Now you *know* he was under the influence of LSD.

This example suggests a modification of the definition given earlier:

The aesthetic value of X is the value that X possesses in virtue of its capacity to provide aesthetic gratification when *correctly experienced*.

(3) The problem of devaluation can perhaps be regarded as a generalization of the LSD problem.[15] When I was young I was for a time an avid reader of the Martian novels of Edgar Rice Burroughs. Recently when I bought the Dover paperback edition and looked at them again, I found that I could hardly read them. Their style alone is enough to repel you, if you really pay attention to it.

The problem is this: if on Monday I enjoy a novel very much, and thus know that it has the capacity to provide gratification, then how can I ever reverse that judgment and say the novel lacks that capacity? If the judgment that the novel is a good one is a capacity-judgment, it would seem that downward reevaluations (that is, devaluations) are always false—assuming that the original higher judgment was based on direct experience. There is no problem about upward reevaluations: when I say on Tuesday that the novel is better than I thought on Monday, this means that I have discovered the novel to have a greater capacity than I had realized. But how can we explain the lowering of an aesthetic evaluation and still maintain that these evaluations are capacity-judgments?

Some cases of devaluation can no doubt be taken care of without modifying the definition of "aesthetic value." The devaluation may be due to a shift in our value grades caused by enlargement of our range of experience. I might think that *Gone with the Wind* is a great novel, because it is the best I have read, but later I might take away that encomium and give it to *War and Peace*. Or the devaluation may be due to the belated recognition that my previous satisfaction in the work was a response to extra-aesthetic features. I now realize that my earlier enjoyment of detective stories was probably caused only in small part by their literary qualities, and was much more of a game-type pleasure.

But setting these cases aside, there remain cases where on perfectly sound and legitimate grounds I decide that the work, though it has provided a certain level of aesthetic gratification, is in fact not really that good. I have over-estimated it. Evidently the definition of "aesthetic value" must be modified again. One thing we might do is insert a stipulation that the work be a reliable or dependable source of gratification: flukes don't count. We need not change the judgment into a straight tendency-statement. But we might insist that the enjoyment of the novel must at least be a repeatable experience. Something like this notion seems to underlie the frequent claim that our first reactions to a new work of art are not wholly to be trusted, that we should wait awhile and try it again; that we should see whether we can find at least one other person to corroborate our judgment; or that only posterity will be in a position to know whether the work is great.

I grant that all these precautions are helpful—indeed, they enable us to avoid the two sources of error mentioned a moment ago: having an inadequately formulated set of grading terms, and confusing aesthetic with nonaesthetic gratification. But I think it ought to be possible for a person, after a single experience of a work, to have excellent grounds for thinking it good and for commending it to others. And I think he would be justified in pointing out that he has found a potential source of aesthetic gratification that lies ready to be taken advantage of—even though he does not yet know how readily, how easily, how conveniently, or how frequently recourse may be had to it. Thus my escape from the difficulty is to revise the definition of "aesthetic value" again so as to stipulate that it is the value of the whole work that is in question:

> The aesthetic value of X is the value that X possesses in virtue of its capacity to provide aesthetic gratification *when correctly and completely experienced.*

The youth who was carried away by the adventures of Thuvia and the green men of Mars and the other denizens of that strange planet may well have gotten greater aesthetic gratification than the elderly person who returned to them after so many years. For the youth was fairly oblivious to the faults of style, and he filled in the flat characterizations with his own imagination, giving himself up unselfconsciously to the dramatic events and exotic scenery. But, though he was lucky in a way, his judgment of the *whole* work was not to be trusted.

IV

We saw earlier that the notion of a point of view plays a particular role in focusing or forwarding certain disputes by limiting the range of relevant considerations. We invoke the aesthetic point of view when we want to set aside certain considerations that others have advanced—as that a poem is pornographic, or that a painting is a forgery—or that (as Jacques Maritain remarks) "A splendid house without a door is not a good work of architecture." [16] But the person whose considerations are thus rejected may feel that the decision is arbitrary, and enter an appeal, in the hope that a higher philosophical tribunal will rule that the lower court erred in its exclusions. How do we know whether being pornographic, or being a forgery, or lacking a door, is irrelevant from the aesthetic point of view? I propose this answer:

> A consideration about an object is relevant to the aesthetic point of view if and only if it is a fact about the object that affects the degree to which the marks of aesthetic gratification (formal unity and intensity of regional quality) are present in the object.

Thus: Is the fact that a painting is a forgery relevant to a judgment of it from the aesthetic point of view? No; because it has no bearing on its form or quality. Is the fact that a painting is a seascape relevant? Sometimes. It is when the subject contributes to, or detracts from, its degree of unity or its qualitative intensity. Is the biography of the composer relevant? According to a writer in *The Music Review:*

It is a well-known fact that knowledge of the circumstances surrounding the composition of a work enhances the audience's appreciation. . . . It is

because of this that programme notes, radio comments, and music appreciation courses are in such demand. To secure such knowledge is one of the
important tasks of musical research.[17]

Now, I'm not sure that this "well-known fact" is really a fact, but let us
assume that it is. Does it follow that information about the circumstances of composition is relevant to consideration of the work from an
aesthetic point of view? We can imagine this sort of thing:

It was a cold rainy day in Vienna, and Schubert was down to his last
crust of bread. As he looked about his dingy garret, listening to the
rain that beat down, he reflected that he could not even afford to
feed his mice. He recalled a sad poem by Goethe, and suddenly a
melody sprang into his head. He seized an old piece of paper, and
began to write feverishly. Thus was "Death and the Maiden" born.

Now even if everyone, or *nearly* everyone, who reads this program note
finds that it increases his appreciation of the song, a condition of appreciation is not necessarily a condition of value. From this information—
say, that it was raining—nothing can be inferred about the specifically
aesthetic characters of the song. (It is relevant, of course, that the words
and music match each other in certain ways; however, we know that not
by biographical investigation but by listening to the song itself.)

Here is one more example. In a very interesting article "On the
Aesthetic Attitude in Romanesque Art," Meyer Schapiro has argued
that:

Contrary to the general belief that in the Middle Ages the work of art was
considered mainly as a vehicle of religious teaching or as a piece of crafts-
manship serving a useful end, and that beauty of form and color was no
object of contemplation in itself, these texts abound in aesthetic judgments
and in statements about the qualities and structure of the work. They speak
of the fascination of the image, its marvelous likeness to physical reality,
and the artist's wonderful skill, often in complete abstraction from the content of the object of art.[18]

Schapiro is inquiring whether medieval people were capable of taking
the aesthetic point of view in some independence of the religious and
technological points of view. He studies various texts in which aesthetic
objects are described and praised, to elicit the grounds on which this ad-
miration is based, and to discover whether these grounds are relevant to
the aesthetic point of view. Form and color, for example, are clearly

relevant, and so to praise a work for its form or color is to adopt the aesthetic point of view. And I should think the same can be said for "the fascination of the image"—by which Schapiro refers to the extraordinary interest in the grotesque figures freely carved by the stonecutters in Romanesque buildings. These centaurs, chimeras, two-headed animals, creatures with feet and the tail of a serpent, etc., are the images deplored by St. Bernard with an ambivalence like that in Lenin's remark about Beethoven:

In the cloister, under the eyes of the brethren who read there, what profit is there in those ridiculous monsters, in that marvelous and deformed beauty, in that beautiful deformity? [19]

But what of Schapiro's other points—the image's "marvelous likeness to physical reality, and the artist's wonderful skill"?

If a person admires skill in depiction, he is certainly not taking a religious point of view—but is he taking the aesthetic point of view? I should think not. No doubt when he notices the accuracy of depiction, reflects on the skill required to achieve it, and thus admires the artist, he may be placed in a more favorable psychological posture toward the work itself. But this contributes to the conditions of the experience; it does not enter into the experience directly, as does the perception of form and color, or the recognition of the represented objects as saints or serpents. So I would say that the fact that the medieval writer admired the skill in depiction is *not* evidence that he took the aesthetic point of view, though it is evidence that he took *an* aesthetic point of view, since skill was involved in the production of the work.

V

There is one final problem that may be worth raising and commenting upon briefly—although it is not at all clear to me how the problem should even be formulated. It concerns the justification of adopting the aesthetic point of view, and its potential conflicts with other points of view. On one hand, it is interesting to note that much effort has been spent (especially during recent decades) in getting people to adopt the aesthetic point of view much more firmly and continuously than has been common in our country. The conservationists are trying to arouse us to concern for the preservation of natural beauties, instead of automatically assuming that they have a lower priority than any other interest that happens to come up—such as installing power lines, or slaughtering deer, or advertising beer. And those who are concerned with "education of the eye," or "visual education," are always developing new methods of teaching the theory and practice of good design; the aim being to produce people who are aware of the growing hideousness of our cities and towns, and who are troubled enough to work for changes.

But the effort to broaden the adoption of the aesthetic point of view sometimes takes another form. According to its leading theoretician, the "Camp sensibility" is characterized by the great range of material to which it can respond: "Camp is the consistently aesthetic experience of the world," writes Susan Sontag. "It incarnates a victory of style over content, of aesthetics over morality, of irony over tragedy." [20]

Here is an extreme consequence of trying to increase the amount of aesthetic value of which we can take advantage. But it also gives rise to an interesting problem, which might be called "the dilemma of aesthetic education." The problem is pointed up by a cartoon I saw not long ago (by David Gerard), showing the proprietor of a junkyard named "Sam's Salvage" standing by a huge pile of junked cars, and saying to two other men: "Whattya mean it's an ugly eyesore? If I'd paid Picasso to pile it up, you'd call it a work of art."

The central task of aesthetic education, as traditionally conceived, is the improvement of taste, involving the development of two dispositions: (1) the capacity to obtain aesthetic gratification from increasingly subtle and complex aesthetic objects that are characterized by various forms of unity—in short, the response to beauty in one main sense; and (2) an increasing dependence on objects beautiful in this way (having harmony, order, balance, proportion) as sources of aesthetic satisfaction. It is this impulse that is behind the usual concept of "beautification"— shielding the highways from junkyards and billboards, and providing more trees and flowers and grass. As long as the individual's aesthetic development in this sense is accompanied by increasing access to beautiful sights and sounds, it is all to the good. His taste improves; his aesthetic pleasures are keener; and when he encounters unavoidable ugliness, he may be moved to eliminate it by labor or by law. On the other hand, suppose he finds that his environment grows uglier, as the economy progresses, and that the ugliness becomes harder to escape. Second, suppose he comes to enjoy another kind of aesthetic value, one that derives from intensity of regional quality more than formal fitness. And third, suppose he comes to realize that his aesthetic gratification is affected by the demands he makes upon an object—especially because the intensity of its regional qualities partly depends on its symbolic import. For example, the plain ordinary object may be seen as a kind of symbol, and become expressive (i.e., assume a noteworthy quality) if the individual attends to it in a way that invites these features to emerge. Suddenly, a whole new field of aesthetic gratification opens up. Trivial objects, the accidental, the neglected, the meretricious and vulgar, all take on new excitement. The automobile graveyard and the weed-filled garden are seen to have their own wild and grotesque expressiveness as well as symbolic import. The kewpie doll, the Christmas card, the Tiffany lampshade, can be enjoyed aesthetically, not for their beauty but for their bizarre qualities and their implicit reflection of social attitudes. This is a way of transfiguring reality, and though not everything can be transfigured, perhaps, it turns out that much can.

What I mean by the dilemma of aesthetic education is this: that we are torn between conflicting ways of redirecting taste. One is the way of love of beauty, which is limited in its range of enjoyment, but is reformist by implication, since it seeks a world that conforms to its ideal. The other is the way of aestheticizing everything—of taking the aesthetic point of view wherever possible—and this widens enjoyment, but is defeatist, since instead of eliminating the junkyard and the slum it tries to see them as expressive and symbolic. The conflict here is analogous to that between the social gospel and personal salvation in some of our churches—though no doubt its consequences are not equally momentous. I don't suppose this dilemma is ultimately unresolvable, though I cannot consider it further at the moment. I point it out as one of the implications of the tendency (which I have been briefly exploring) to extend the aesthetic point of view as widely as possible.

But there is another weighty tradition opposed to this expansion. Lenin and St. Bernard stand witness to the possibility that there may be situations in which it is morally objectionable to adopt the aesthetic point of view. A man who had escaped from Auschwitz commented on Rolf Hochmuth's play: *"The Deputy* should not be considered as a historical work or even as a work of art, but as a moral lesson." [21] Perhaps he only meant that looking for historical truth or artistic merit in *The Deputy* is a waste of time. But he may also have meant that there is something blameworthy about anyone who is capable of contemplating those terrible events from a purely historical or purely aesthetic point of view. Renata Adler, reporting in *The New Yorker* [22] on the New Politics Convention that took place in Chicago on Labor Day weekend, 1967, listed various types of self-styled "revolutionaries" who attended, including "the aesthetic-analogy revolutionaries, who discussed riots as though they were folk songs or pieces of local theatre, subject to appraisal in literary terms ('authentic,' 'beautiful')." That is carrying the aesthetic point of view pretty far.

This possibility has not gone unnoticed by imaginative writers—notably Henry James and Henrik Ibsen.[23] The tragedy of Mrs. Gereth, in *The Spoils of Poynton,* is that of a woman who could not escape the aesthetic point of view. She had a "passion for the exquisite" that made her prone "to be rendered unhappy by the presence of the dreadful [and] she was condemned to wince wherever she turned." In fact, the things that troubled her most—and she encountered them everywhere, but nowhere in more abundance than the country house known as Waterbath—were just the campy items featured by Miss Sontag: "trumpery ornament and scrapbook art, with strange excrescences and bunchy draperies, with gimcracks that might have been keepsakes for maid-servants [and even] a souvenir from some centennial or other Exhibition." The tragedy of the sculptor, Professor Rubek, in *When We Dead Awaken,* is that he so utterly aestheticized the woman who loved him and who was his model that she was not a person to him. As she says, "The work of art first—then the human being." It may even be—and I say this with the utmost hesitation, since I have no wish to sink in these muddy waters—that this is the theme of Antonioni's film, *Blow-Up:* the emptiness that comes from utter absorption in an aesthetic point of view of a photographer to whom every person and every event seems to represent only the possibility of a new photographic image. In that respect, Antonioni's photographer is certainly worse than Professor Rubek.

The mere confrontation of these two vague and general social philosophies of art will not, of course, take us very far in understanding the possibilities and the limitations of the aesthetic point of view. I leave matters unresolved, with questions hanging in the air. Whatever resolution we ultimately find, however, will surely incorporate two observations that may serve as a pair of conclusions.

First, there are occasions on which it would be wrong to adopt the aesthetic point of view, because there is a conflict of values and the values that are in peril are, in that particular case, clearly higher. Once in a while you see a striking photograph or film sequence in which someone is (for example) lying in the street after an accident, in need of immediate attention. And it is a shock to think suddenly that the photographer must have been on hand. I don't want to argue ethics of news photography, but if someone, out of the highest aesthetic motives, withheld first-aid to a bleeding accident victim in order to record the scene, with careful attention to lighting and camera speed, then it is doubtful that that picture could be so splendid a work of art as to justify neglecting so stringent a moral obligation.

The second conclusion is that there is nothing—no object or event—

that is *per se* wrong to consider from the aesthetic point of view. This, I think, is part of the truth in the art-for-art's-sake doctrine. To adopt the aesthetic point of view is simply to seek out a source of value. And it can never be a moral error to realize value—barring conflict with other values. Some people seem to fear that a serious and persistent aesthetic interest will become an enervating hyperaestheticism, a paralysis of will like that reported in advanced cases of psychedelic dependence. But the objects of aesthetic interest—such as harmonious design, good proportions, intense expressiveness—are not drugs, but part of the breath of life. Their cumulative effect is increased sensitization, fuller awareness, a closer touch with the environment and concern for what it is and might be. It seems to me very doubtful that we could have too much of these good things, or that they have inherent defects that prevent them from being an integral part of a good life.

NOTES

1. *New Republic* (January 16, 1961), p. 23. *Cf.* Brendan Gill, in *The New Yorker* (March 5, 1966): "It is a lot easier to recommend attendance at 'The Gospel According to St. Matthew' as an act of penitential piety during the Lenten season than it is to praise the movie as a movie. Whether or not the life and death of Our Lord is the greatest story ever told, it is so far from being merely a story that we cannot deal with it in literary terms (if we could, I think we would have to begin by saying that in respect to construction and motivation it leaves much to be desired); our difficulty is enormously increased when we try to pass judgment on the story itself once it has been turned into a screenplay."

2. From Gorky's essay on Lenin, *Collected Works*, XVII (Moscow, 1950), pp. 39–40. My colleague Professor Olga Lang called my attention to this passage and translated it for me. *Cf. Days with Lenin* (New York, International Publishers, 1932), p. 52. *Time* (April 30, 1965, p. 50) reported that the Chinese Communists had forbidden the performance of Beethoven's works because they "paralyze one's revolutionary fighting will." A Chinese bacteriologist, in a letter to a Peking newspaper, wrote after listening to Beethoven, "I began to have strange illusions about a world filled with friendly love."

3. (New York, Doubleday Anchor Books, 1954), p. 15, where he quotes Wotton.

4. In this discussion, I have been stimulated by an unpublished paper by J. O. Urmson on "Good of a Kind and Good from a Point of View," which I saw in manuscript in 1961. I should also like to thank him for comments on an earlier version of this paper. (*Cf.* his note added to "What Makes a Situation Aesthetic?" in Joseph Margolis, ed., *Philosophy Looks at the Arts* (New York, Charles Scribner's Sons, 1962), p. 26. I also note that John Hospers has some interesting remarks on the aesthetic point of view in "The Ideal Aesthetic Observer," *British Journal of Aesthetics*, II (1962): 99–111.

5. *The New York Times*, Oct. 2, 1967, p. 55.

6. *Cf.* my "Comments" on Stanley Cavell's paper, in W. H. Capitan and

D. D. Merrill, eds., *Art, Mind, and Religion* (Pittsburgh, University of Pittsburgh Press, 1967), esp. pp. 107–109.

7. *Op. cit.*, p. 89; cf. pp. 90–91, 95. In case it may be thought that architects who have the highest respect for their materials might repudiate my distinction, I quote Pier Luigi Nervi (in his Charles Eliot Norton lectures): "There does not exist, either in the past or in the present, a work of architecture which is accepted and recognized as excellent from the aesthetic point of view which is not also excellent from a technical point of view." From *Aesthetics and Technology in Building* (Cambridge, Harvard University Press, 1965), p. 2. Though arguing that one kind of value is a necessary (but not a sufficient) condition of the other, Nervi clearly assumes that there is a distinguishable aesthetic point of view.

8. *The New York Times*, April 2, 1967, p. 94.

9. December 1966, p. 20.

10. Paul Taylor, *Normative Discourse* (Englewood Cliffs, N.J., Prentice-Hall, Inc., 1961), p. 109.

11. See *Aesthetics: Problems in the Philosophy of Criticism* (New York, Harcourt, Brace & World, Inc., 1958), Ch. 11.

12. See "Beardsley's Phantom Aesthetic Experience," *Journal of Philosophy* LXII (1965): 129–136, and my "Aesthetic Experience Regained," forthcoming in the *Journal of Aesthetics and Art Criticism*.

13. "The Discrimination of Aesthetic Enjoyment," *British Journal of Aesthetics*, III (1963): 291–300.

14. In the *Delaware County Daily Times* (Chester, Pa.), February 10, 1967.

15. It was discussed briefly in my *Aesthetics* (New York, Harcourt, Brace, & World, 1958), pp. 534–535, but has since been called to my attention more sharply and forcefully by Professor Thomas Regan.

16. *L'Intuition Créatrice dans l'Art et dans la Poésie* (Paris, Desclée de Brouwer, 1966), p. 53.

17. Hans Tischler, "The Aesthetic Experience," *Music Review*, XVII (1956): 200.

18. In K. Bharatha Iyer, ed., *Art and Thought* (London, Luzac, 1947), p. 138. I thank my colleague John Williams for calling my attention to this essay.

19. *Ibid.*, p. 133.

20. Susan Sontag, "Notes on Camp," *Partisan Review*, XXXI (Fall 1964): 526.

21. *The New York Times*, May 4, 1966.

22. September 23, 1967.

23. I set aside the somewhat indelicate verse by W. H. Auden, called "The Aesthetic Point of View."

CREATIVE ACTS

W. E. Kennick

In James Joyce's *Portrait of the Artist as a Young Man* [1] Stephen Daedalus tells his friend Lynch that he has a book at home in which he writes down questions and that in finding answers to them he has found "the theory of the esthetic" which he is trying to explain to Lynch. Among these is the question: "If a man hacking in fury at a block of wood make there an image of a cow, is that image a work of art? If not, why not?" ("That's a lovely one—said Lynch, laughing again.—That has the true scholastic stink.") The scholastic stink not withstanding, I propose to begin my inquiry into some features of the concept of creativity in art with Stephen's question.

Just what is the puzzle expressed by this question? As I see it, there are two points from which doubt might stem. The first concerns the image: Can an image of a cow be a work of art? This question can easily be answered in the affirmative: There is no reason why an image of a cow *cannot* be a work of art, any more than there is a reason why an image of Moses or of the Virgin Mary cannot be a work of art. That something is an image of a cow does not entail that it is a work of art, but that it is a work of art does not entail that it is not an image of a cow. The second point from which doubt might arise has to do not with the image but with the manner of its production, with the man's making it by or as a result of hacking in fury at a block of wood. To obviate the first difficulty and to dramatize the second, let us change Stephen's question to read: If a man (Donatello) hacking in fury at a block of marble make there an image of a prophet, [2] is that image a work of art? If not, why not? Now what is the problem? I do not suggest that Donatello actually produced his famous *Zuccone* by hacking in fury at a block of marble; so the issue is not the empirical issue of whether he produced it in this way or not. I leave that to the art historians to decide. My question is purely supposititious: *had* Donatello produced his statue in the manner described, *would* that affect its status as a work of art?

The interest of aestheticians in the problem of creativity, by which I mean in part the problem of *how* works of art are produced, what might be called their mode of genesis, has hardly any parallels in other areas of philosophy. The literature of aesthetics is replete with speculations about the nature of the creative process, as it is usually called, about what "goes on" when an artist carves a statue, writes a poem, or paints a picture. And these speculations are most often of a psychological (or apparently psychological) nature, leading some philosophers to expect, I think, that advances in the psychology of artistic creation would somehow contribute to the solution of certain philosophical problems of aesthetics.[3] We do not find moral philosophers exhibiting quite the same interest in, say, the psychology of murder or of obligation (feeling obliged), nor epistemologists in cognitive psychology or the psychology of perception; or at least we do not find many philosophers who suppose that problems in ethics or epistemology will be *solved* by the empirical investigations of psychologists. The problem at issue here, of course, is the nature of a philosophical question. If a philosophical question is (as it is now widely supposed that it is) a question that may appear to be a request for information about some non-conceptual (or even non-linguistic) matter of fact when it is really a request for the analysis, partial or complete, of a concept (or for information about what certain expressions mean),[4] then it is indeed difficult to see just how psychological, or other scientific, information *could* be relevant to the solution of a philosophical problem.[5] Yet even on this view of philosophy, and hence of philosophical aesthetics, the question remains: Does a proposition of the form, "X is a work of art," or, "X is a creative work of art," entail a proposition—referring, perhaps, to the psychology of the artist—about X's mode of genesis? If it does, then we have a reason other than scientific curiosity for the aesthetician's interest in what "goes on" when a work of art is produced.

Let us consider first whether a statement to the effect that something is a work of art entails any statement about its mode of genesis. (We will postpone the question of whether a statement to the effect that something is a *creative* work of art entails a statement about its mode of genesis.) Some aestheticians, if I understand them aright, have claimed that to identify something as a work of (fine) art logically commits one to the view that it was produced in a certain way. Jacques Maritain, for example,[6] holds that a work of art (useful *or* fine) is essentially a product of the intellect, specifically of the practical intellect, and still more specifically of that activity of the practical intellect which has to do with "works to be made" as against "actions to be done." The proposition, therefore, that the *Zuccone* is a work of art entails the proposition that it was produced by an agent exercising the specified sort of intellect or intelligence. Professor Stolnitz, as I understand him, agrees with Maritain. Although he warns us against committing the genetic fallacy ("the genesis of *x* is one thing, *x* itself is something else. Once *x* has been brought into being, it has, so to speak, a life of its own"),[7] nevertheless he holds—and not inconsistently—that "art-objects of any sort are set off from non-artistic objects such as rocks, trees, and yawns because of the way in which they are created. Hence, any definition of 'art' as an *object* must make reference to its origins." [8]

On the other side of the fence from Maritain and Stolnitz, however, we find those philosophers who hold that art objects are not set off from nonartistic objects by their mode of genesis. Thus Professor Beardsley writes:

What difference does it make to our relationship with the arts that we understand the creative process in one way or another? And here my answer is brief and unequivocal. It makes no difference at all. I think it is interesting in itself to know, if we can, how the artist's mind works, but I do not see that this has any bearing upon the value of what he produces. For that value is independent of the manner of production, even whether the work was produced by an animal or by a computer or by a volcano or by a falling slop bucket.[9]

Taking the last sentence to read "For the value of a *work of art* is independent of the manner of production, even whether the *work of art* was produced by an animal or by a computer etc.," we get an implied denial of Maritain's or Stolnitz's thesis. For that last sentence, so read, implies that a work of art *can* be produced by a volcano, and this is precisely what Maritain and Stolnitz deny. But Professor Weitz seems to agree with Professor Beardsley. "Mostly, when we describe something as a work of art [he writes [10]] we do so under the conditions of there being some sort of artifact, made by human skill, ingenuity, and imagination . . . [But] 'X is a work of art and . . . was made by no one,' or . . . 'was made when he spilled the paint on the canvas,' . . . are sensible and capable of being true in certain circumstances." That something must be a product of human creation is neither a necessary nor a sufficient condition of its being a work of art. "Consider: 'This piece of driftwood is a lovely piece of sculpture.' "

If wind and water acting on a piece of stone make there an image of a man, is that image a work of art? As I understand it, Maritain and Stolnitz would say, "No, it is not a work of art, and if anybody took it for a work of art he would be making a mistake"; whereas Beardsley and Weitz would say at least that it *could* be a work of art, that in identifying or describing it as a work of art a man *need* not be making a mistake. Here we have an interesting opposition. How is it to be resolved?

If the question is simply which of these views more nearly describes our actual employment of the concept of art, my own sense of the matter is that Maritain and Stolnitz are closer to the truth than are Beardsley and Weitz. In the words of Miss Meager:

> If we know for a fact that an object was the result of erosion and not of Barbara Hepworth, or of a chimpanzee and not Joan Miro, this would disqualify it altogether from the work-of-art stakes, though not . . . from the beauty stakes nor from the aesthetic object stakes.[11]

Whatever its aesthetic merits may be, the Great Stone Face, unlike the sculptures on Mt. Rushmore, simply is not a work of art—not even a bad work of art. "This piece of driftwood is a lovely piece of sculpture," said in a situation in which we are speaking about what is simply a piece of driftwood—and not, say, about a piece of driftwood that has been incorporated into a piece of sculpture or about a piece of sculpture that represents a piece of driftwood—is as paradoxical or as *literally* senseless as "This dog is a very efficient automobile."

Doubtless the concept of art is what Professor Hampshire calls an "essentially disputed" concept or what Professor Weitz calls an "open" concept,[12] and borderline cases are not difficult to conceive. But however vaguely it may be marked, there is a border. The concept of art, like other descriptive concepts, is not *wide* open. The appeal to "family resemblances" among objects to justify our classification of otherwise disparate and heterogeneous things under the same genus or our extension of the concept to cover novel and unanticipated cases, is a game that, as things stand now—and have stood for some time—cannot even begin until the area of play has been circumscribed so as to include only products of human fabrication. Surely an ear not dulled to all nuances of linguistic usage still recognizes a live metaphor in such phrases as "the art of chimpanzees." What we *would* say, were chimpanzees to commence turning out objects on an aesthetic par with the sculptures of Donatello or the paintings of Titian, has no bearing on the present point. J. L. Austin has remarked somewhere that we can easily imagine situations in which we would not know *what* to say, but this does not mean that we do not know what to say as things stand now. One might guess, or even predict, that were chimpanzees (or the processes of erosion, etc.) to begin behaving in the way indicated we would call their "works" works of art, but that would be to guess at, or predict, a linguistic or conceptual *innovation*.

The invention of the computer, of course, has brought us closer to the borderline of the concept of art, as it has brought us closer to the borderline of a host of other concepts, the most important of which is the concept of thought. Can computers write poems or compose symphonies? The question is essentially a conceptual one, concerned not with what words *will* mean, or *can* mean, but with what they now *do* mean; and my own sense of the present situation is reflected in Douglas Morgan's remark that it is "possible that a piece of electronically composed music could fool me into thinking that a musical man, and not a musical machine, had done the work. . . . [But] if I were to hear some machine-made music which I esteemed highly, I would tend to attribute its 'creativity' to the man who coded the machine, rather than to the machine itself." [13]

The point I have been trying to make can be put schematically as follows: A proposition of the form "x is a work of art," entails a proposition of the form "$(\exists y)$ y is a person and y created x." This tells us that a logically *necessary* condition of something's being a work of art is that it has been created by a person.[14] (I here ignore the question of sufficient conditions, where, perhaps, we must appeal to something like Wittgenstein's "family resemblances" among created objects.) The question that concerns me has to do with the meaning of the word "created" in this formula: Does the word "created," as Maritain and Stolnitz appear to hold, designate some specific psychological process or mental act or happening such that if that process or act or happening does not occur the object in question is not a work of art?

To begin with, we must distinguish between creative acts and creative processes. Most writers on creativity speak of "the creative process," meaning, usually, what happens or "goes on" in the artist's mind when he creates a work of art. But processes are not acts: although such processes as that of the refining of aluminum from bauxite may involve, or even consist of, a series of acts. Words naming or describing processes (e.g., growth, gestation, digestion, fermentation) tell us what happens in or to something rather than what is being, or has been, done.[15] But "to create," used with a personal subject and taking as direct object a name, description, or demonstrative that designates a work of art, is generically what Anthony Kenny calls "a verb of action," i.e., "a verb which may occur as the main verb in answer to a question of the form 'What did A do?'"[16] Specifically, it is what Kenny calls a "performance-verb" (one that signifies a performance), as opposed to a "static-verb" (one that signifies a state) or an "activity-verb" (one that signifies an activity). Two of the distinctive features of performance-verbs are: (1) that they have continuous tenses—which separates them from static-verbs, and (2) that where ϕ stands for a performance-verb "A is ϕing" implies "A has not ϕd"—which separates them from activity-verbs, which are such that "A is ϕing" implies "A has ϕd." [17]

"To create," however, is only the most general performance verb that can be used in this connection with works of art—and, as I shall try to show below, it or some similar performance verb is required; but its direct use is not very frequent. More often we use such performance verbs as "write a poem," "paint a picture," "carve a statue," "design a building," and so on. Writing poems, painting pictures, composing music, and the like, are, of course, not inherently artistic acts or performances; by which I mean that "A wrote (painted) x" does not entail "x is a work of art," or, variously, "A wrote a poem (painted a picture)" does not entail "A created a work of art." But these acts or performances *are* such that in doing one or more of them a man *may* be creating a work of art; and I propose to call them *creative acts* if they are such that in performing (having performed) one or more of them a man is creating (has created) a work of art.

If someone is painting it may not be clear or certain that he is performing a creative act, until he has finished (or ceased), i.e., until as a result of his painting he has brought a work of art (even an "unfinished" work of art, like Schubert's famous Unfinished Symphony) into existence. But then again it might be clear from the context of his performance, or he might truly describe his act in such a way, that we could say (truly) that the intended object of his act is a work of art, and that hence his act is a creative act.[18] It is not requisite for an act to be a creative act that a work of art be the actual result of it, i.e., that a work of art be brought into existence by it: An artist might destroy his work before it is, or could be, clear from the *work* that it is a work of art. But neither is it requisite for an act to be a creative act that the intended object of the act be a work of art. Something can be a work of art and also an idol, and it can be an idol and not be a work of art. But from the fact that the intended object of a man's carving is an idol, together with the fact that the idol he is carving is (or will be) also a work of art, it does not follow that the intended object of his act is a work of art. In this way, works of art can be created unintentionally or incidentally. It is at least doubtful that the sculptors of those great Egyptian statues of gods intended to produce works of art as well as idols; but that they did intend to produce idols is hardly a matter of doubt, and that they did produce works of art is certain.[19]

To return to Stephen Daedalus's question, or our emended version of it: If a man hacking in fury at a block of marble make there an image of a prophet, is that image a work of art? That the man has made (created) an image of a prophet, is granted *ex hypothesi*; and that something may be an image of a prophet and also a work of art is certain. The puzzle, therefore, would seem to be concerned with whether a man can make (create), in the way described, what is at least, other things being equal, a possible work of art. Well, suppose that the purpose or objective of the man's hacking—which is an activity, by the way, and not a performance—is not to create a work of art, or even to produce an image of a prophet, but is rather to work off a burden of anger or rage, can he not also be creating a work of art? As far as I can see, he can. He can be purposively or intentionally doing one thing (working off his rage) and incidentally doing another (creating a work of art).[20] And the converse is also true: he can be purposively or intentionally creating a work of art and incidentally working off his rage or satisfying some repressed wish (Freud).

Parenthetically, another interpretation is possible of the sentence "Hacking in fury at a block of marble, he made there an image of a prophet." The "hacking in fury . . ." clause may be seen as having adverbial force, as describing the *manner* of the making. Read in this way "hacking in fury at a block of marble" would contrast with something like "chipping calmly away at the block of marble." This reading, I think, raises no difficulties at all.

"There is not necessarily one, and only one, correct description of a given act," says Eric D'Arcy.[21] To put the point another way: A man can be doing two or more things—even doing them purposively or intentionally—at the same time; not in the way that I may deliver a lecture, write on the blackboard, and jingle my keys at the same time, but in the way that I may write my name, sign a check, pay a bill, and discharge a financial obligation at the same time. It was his realization of this phenomenon as it operates in the area of speech that led J. L. Austin to draw his now well known distinction between locutionary, illocutionary, and perlocutionary acts; and perhaps a parallel set of distinctions will be of some use in aesthetics. To perform a locutionary act is to say something, and such an act is normally what is reported when we quote directly what someone said. The performance of a locutionary act is thus the performance of an act *of* saying something. To perform a locutionary act, however, is usually also to perform an illocutionary act, i.e., to do something *in* saying something (e.g., to ask a question, issue an order, announce a verdict, make an appointment, etc.); and one may use the same locution (perform the same locutionary act) in performing different illocutionary acts. But in performing a locutionary act, and at the same time performing some illocutionary act, we may also be performing an act of yet another kind: "Saying something will often, or even normally, produce certain consequential effects upon the feelings, thoughts, or actions of the audience, of the speaker, or of other persons: and it may be done with the design, intention, or purpose of producing them." To do this is to perform a perlocutionary act, i.e., to do something *by* saying something; and by performing the same illocutionary act one may perform different perlocutionary acts.[22]

Now there is at least a partial analogy between, on the one hand, painting pictures, composing music, or carving statues, and, on the other hand, speaking; indeed, so-called "semiotic" theories of the nature of art would have it that there is at least a partial identity. Painting a picture, to put it loosely, resembles uttering a sentence, performing a locutionary act. But *in* painting a picture a man may be creating a work of art, and thereby doing something analogous to performing an illocutionary act. And just as to perform the same locutionary act may be to perform different illocutionary acts, so also in painting a picture a man may be doing something as well as or in addition to creating a work of art: e.g., making a likeness of someone (Valasquez's portrait of Pope Innocent X), celebrating or commenting on an event (Goya's *The Third of May, 1808*), or illustrating a religious text (*Christ Washing the Feet of Peter* from the Gospel Book of Otto III). I say "doing something as well as or in addition to creating a work of art" for the reason that one may create a work of art without doing any of the things mentioned—or anything else of the same kind—and he may do any of the things mentioned without creating a work of art; so that where any of the things mentioned is being done, in painting a picture a man is doing *two* things: creating a work of art and illustrating a text, or whatever.[23] In writing my name I may be signing a check *and* paying a bill *and* overdrawing my account. Doing the one is not the same as doing the others, though all may be done at the same time, i.e., *in* doing one and the same thing, namely, writing my name; and it is possible that I am consciously or purposively doing one of them while being unaware that I am also doing the others. Further, painting a picture or writing a sonnet "will often, or even normally, produce certain consequential effects upon the feelings, thoughts, or actions" of the painter or writer or of others; "and it may be done with the design, intention or purpose of producing them." Hence, *by* painting a picture or writing verse a man may be doing something analogous to performing a perlocutionary act: vicariously satisfying some unfulfilled repressed wish of his own, calling our attention to certain evils of the social system, reminding us of our mortality, amusing us, instructing us, shocking us, or, as Plato complained of Homer and the tragedians in *Republic* II and X, leading us astray theologically and corrupting us morally.

I have defined creative acts as acts or performances that are such, that *in* doing (having done) one or more of them a man is creating (has created) a work of art. This means that creating a work of art is an act analogous to an illocutionary, not a perlocutionary, act. There are theories of art—for example, Tolstoy's and Freud's—that "define" art by reference to the performance of a perlocutionary-like act.[24] As interesting and important as such theories may be, they cannot, I think, be taken as adequate definitions of art: given any perlocutionary-like act, a, it is in principle possible for someone to create a work of art without doing a. Which is to say that the connection between creating a work of art and producing effects of some kind is not necessary or logical, but contingent. But the connection between creating a work of art and performing some locutionary-like act is necessary or logical, not contingent; in that if a man created a work of art he must have painted or drawn or composed or written or. . . . I know of no way of circumscribing or delimiting this list of potentially creative acts, i.e., acts that are such that in doing one or more of them a man may be creating a work of art. The number of things men can do, the number of locutionary-like acts they can perform—fastening together the detached seat and handlebar of a bicycle (Picasso's *Head of a Bull*), pasting bits of paper together, programming a computer, arranging stones, and what not—that may result in a work of art is indefinitely large; all we can say with certainty is that a work of art must be the result of *some* such act(s) or performance(s).

Nor can we, I think, *identify* creative acts with some one independently specifiable illocutionary-like act. R. G. Collingwood uses the notion of expressing an emotion as a performance-concept [25] and as one applicable to illocutionary-like acts: In painting a picture or carving a statue a man need not be creating a work of art, for he may be working magic or attempting to amuse someone, but he is creating a work of art if and only if in painting a picture or carving a statue he is expressing an emotion. To express an emotion and to create a work of art are, thus, to do the same thing. Yet the fact remains that the notions of expressing an emotion and creating a work of art are not *logically* related in the way Collingwood says they are, for no paradox or logical incoherence obtains from asserting that a man has created a work of art and denying that he has expressed an emotion (in Collingwood's sense). Hence, even if it were true that whenever a man creates a work of art he expresses an emotion, and conversely, it would not follow that creating a work of art and expressing an emotion are one and the same act. The connection between them, again, would be contingent and not necessary. And this argument, as far as I can see, applies *mutatis mutandis* to any other independently identifiable illocutionary-like act (e.g., "imitating" or representing some object or action, presentationally symbolizing forms of feeling, or portraying the "contradictions" of social life of a given historical epoch—assuming that we know what it would be to do any of these things).

To return briefly to "the creative process": The same simple argument that I have used against attempts to "define" art in terms of the performance of some perlocutionary-like act as well as against efforts to identify "the" creative act with some independently specifiable illocutionary-like act can, I think, be used to counteract the tendency—not always easy to detect amid the vagaries of speculation about what happens in the artist's mind when he creates a work of art—to define works of art as products of some specifiable *process*. To put it schematically: There is no psychological process, p, conscious or unconscious, such that "X is a work of art" entails that p has occurred. Or, as F. E. Sparshott puts it:

Even if it were to be found to be true that some describable process did always occur in the production of works of art, the discovery would be of marginal interest to aesthetics; for the concept of a work of art is not a psychological concept, and it would remain possible that a work of art should appear without the process. What possible reason, then, can we have for postulating such a process? [26]

We can go even further than Professor Sparshott, in asserting that "to create"—unlike "to think," "to deliberate," "to dream," "to imagine," and the like—is not the name of a mental act, activity, or process, any more than "to drive a car" or "to program a computer" is. That only persons can create works of art and that whatever is a person has a mind does not imply that "to create" is a psychological verb, as philosophical idealists such as Croce have apparently supposed.

I turn now to the justification of my use of the verb "to create"—as opposed to, say, "to make" or "to produce"—in the formula: "X is a work of art" entails that there is at least one y such that y is a person and y created x. We need some such distinction as that between making and creating because we have committed ourselves, in talking about some kinds of art, to such distinctions as those between copy and original, design and execution.

Many works of art exist in replica; some exist only in replica. For example, the work of Wu Tao-tzu, whom Sherman Lee describes as "certainly the greatest name of the Tang Dynasty, if not the greatest name in Chinese painting [is] known to us only from copies." [27] Let us suppose that these copies are faithful replicas of their originals: Are they works of art separate from and additional to the works of Wu that are now lost? The correct answer, I think, is given by Miss Meager: "[W]e treat copies, when not mechanically produced, as also works of art, but not additional works of art." [28] What we possess in possessing a faithful copy of a painting by Wu is not a new work of art but simply a painting by Wu—in replica. The *creator* of the work of art in question was Wu, although the person who executed, produced or made the object that we have was not Wu. But how is a faithful copy or replica to be distinguished from its (the) original? Two criteria immediately suggest themselves: *c* is an exact copy of *o* (1) if *c* is qualitatively indistinguishable from *o* and (2) if *c* was produced later in time than *o*. But these criteria will not do. This point is dramatized by Miss Meager's ingenious supposititious case:

Imagine Joyce Cary's Mister Johnson when young, pupil at a native school in Darkest Africa, whose English Literature syllabus had consisted entirely of the Bible and Basic English, and who had had no other contact with the tongue of Shakespeare; whose girl friend's name was Pippa, and who one year for his school magazine threw off 'Pippa Passes,' word for word the replica of Browning's poem.[29]

The question raised for me by this imaginary case is not the same as that raised for Miss Meager, viz., whether *if* two men independently produced qualitatively indistinguishable works, their products would be two poems or one. My question is whether Mr. Johnson's "Pippa Passes" would be a *copy* of Browning's; and I assume that it would not be, despite the fact that *ex hypothesi* it is qualitatively indistinguishable from Browning's poem and was produced at a later date. If this is correct, then the criteria given will not serve to distinguish copy from original, or creative artist from copyist. What is needed is some reference to what Miss Meager calls "original activity":

We may take 'original activity' here to mean an activity not wholly determined in detail by its being mere obedience to specifications already laid down; and by 'mere obedience to specifications' we can mean the execution of specifications without reflective choice between possible ways of carrying them out resulting in different possible manifestations.[30]

This definition of "original activity" (which I would prefer to call an original act or performance) is, for our purposes, a reasonably adequate, though negative, analysis of the notion of *creating*, and it will serve to remove the taint of circularity from my original definition of "creative acts." Creative acts are acts such that in performing (having performed) one or more of them a man is performing (has performed) an *original* act of producing a work of art. And if we understand creative acts in this way, then Browning's act of writing "Pippa Passes" and Mr. Johnson's act of writing "Pippa Passes" are both creative acts, even if we choose to say that Mr. Johnson implausibly—or miraculously—produced the *same* work of art as Robert Browning. (We allow that two men can independently make the same discovery or invent the same thing. Is there anything in the concept of creation or in that of art that disallows the possibility of two men independently creating the same work of art?)

A work of art has necessarily at least one creator, but it does not follow from this that whoever created it necessarily created it.[31] "Regarded as a sentence about the Mona Lisa, [says Anthony Kenny] 'Leonardo painted the Mona Lisa' seems to be a necessary proposition, since the Mona Lisa is essentially a painting by Leonardo; regarded as a sentence about Leonardo, 'Leonardo painted the Mona Lisa' is contingent, since Leonardo, while remaining Leonardo, might never have painted anything." [32] But this is surely wrong. For if this were the case, it would be logically impossible for the *Mona Lisa* to turn out to have been painted by anyone other than Leonardo; but that the Mona Lisa *might* have been painted by someone other than Leonardo is at least a possible art-historical hypothesis. Furthermore, if it is argued that what we *mean* by the *Mona Lisa* is a painting by Leonardo having such and such characteristics, by parity of reasoning it can be argued that what we mean by "Leonardo" is the man who, among other things, painted the *Mona Lisa*—in which case, regarded as a sentence about Leonardo, "Leonardo painted the *Mona Lisa*" would express a necessary proposition. In point of fact, the name "Leonardo" and the expression "the *Mona Lisa*" are not used in such a way that there is a necessary or logical connection between them.

Products of original acts, and *a fortiori* of creative acts, need not be original in the sense that they are qualitatively unlike the products of unoriginal acts or of other original acts. Consider speech acts, i.e., locutionary acts: It is possible for me to repeat or copy what someone else has said (Repeat after me: I, John, take thee, Mary. . . ; I, John, take thee, Mary. . . .); but it is also possible for me to say, on my own, the same thing as someone else. In this case the former speech act and my, latter speech act are both original acts, although not necessarily creative acts as in the hypothetical case of Browning and Mr. Johnson. The sentences we produce are tokens of the same type, differing from one another *solo numero*.[33] And if what I say on my own is said later than what the other speaker says on his own, what I say is nothing new or novel in the sense that it is unlike something already said. Should we both say the same thing at the same time, what each of us says, i.e., what both of us say, might be new or novel in that it is quite unlike anything anyone has already said. Speech (locutionary) acts are among the most familiar and conspicuous examples of original acts, many, if not most, of the products of which are original. Surely, much of what every one of us says in the course of his life is in *some* way unlike anything anyone else has said, i.e., not exactly what someone else has said. The same is true in art.

To determine whether an act is an original act, it is not enough to consider the product of that act, i.e., to discover whether it is a token of the same type as the token product of another act. One must consider how the act is performed, whether it is an act of repeating or copying something already said or done. But since it is a matter of empirical or contingent fact that different *creative* acts (A's act as opposed to B's) never, or rarely, issue in the same product (tokens of the same type), if we know that something (a work of art) is the token product of a creative act, we can be reasonably confident that it is something new or original, that it differs qualitatively in some way, however insignificantly or unimportantly, from any other work of art yet produced. This judgment, however, that it does differ qualitatively from any work of art yet produced, does not depend on our knowing that it is the product of a creative act but upon a comparison of products of acts, creative or uncreative. But the fact that products of creative acts are usually, or even always, qualitatively new or original has apparently led some theorists of art to propound what might be called a paradox of creativity. Professor Janson puts it this way:

The making of a work of art has little in common with what we ordinarily mean by 'making.' It is a strange and risky business in which the maker never quite knows what he is making until he has actually made it; or, to put it another way, it is a game of find-and-seek in which the seeker is not sure what he is looking for until he has found it.[34]

And Professor Tomas puts it this way:

To create is to originate. And it follows from this that prior to creation the creator does not foresee what will result from it.[35]

This is an interesting claim about which we might ask, where did Janson and Tomas get this information? To which the answer is, I gather, not from an empirical study of the lives of artists, but from reflection on the meaning of the operative verb, "to make, or to create, a work of art." In other words, it is true of Milton that (A) at some time he had not yet written or composed (created) *Il Penseroso*, although he was writing or composing *Il Penseroso*; but (B) until he had written or composed *Il Penseroso*, he did not know what he was writing or composing, did not foresee what would result from his act of writing or composing. How we know whether (A) is true of Milton is unproblematic; the question is, how we know whether (B) is true. And the claim in question, I take it, is that if (A) is true, then (B) is true; in short, (A) implies (B). In which case the claim is actually stronger than it is stated: It is not that a man *does* not know or foresee what will result from his own creative acts, but that he *cannot* know or foresee this. For if (A) entails or logically implies (B), then it is *impossible* for (A) to be true and (B) to be false.

Clearly, the claim that prior to creation the creator cannot know or foresee what will result from his creative act cannot be accepted in its present unrestricted form. For surely, assuming that it is possible for a man *ever* to know what he is going to do (something that some philosophers would deny), a man can know that he is going to paint a picture, say, and not write a poem or compose a symphony; can know that he is going to paint a seascape, say, and not a portrait or a still-life; can know that he is going to paint a seascape of Honfleur, say, and not of Antibes or Monhegan Island, before he has actually painted it. But, it may be replied, although he can know *in general* what he is going to do (create) before he has actually done (created) it, he cannot quite know, fully know, or know exactly what he is making until he has actually made it.

If we separate inner or mental acts from overt or physical acts, one may, of course, allow that a man can fully know in advance what he is overtly going to do (create) because he has already thought out and decided just what to do (create); in which case the creative act would probably be said to have been performed in the mind of the creator—which is where some philosophers would urge that it is always and necessarily performed. I do not wish to deny that creative acts can be performed in the mind, for clearly a man can compose a symphony or a poem "in his head." The question is whether creative acts must be performed in the mind (and not merely by using one's mind), i.e., whether overt creative acts must be preceded by inward or mental creative acts, and whether a man can be said to know in advance just what he is overtly going to do only if this is so.

Knowing what one is going to do overtly is not to have already done it inwardly. A: What were you about to say before you were interrupted? B: I was about to say. . . . To know what he was about to say, must B already have said inwardly what he was about to say? Suppose I ask myself, What was I about to say? Oh, yes. . . . To know what I was about to say, must I be recalling something I have already rehearsed inwardly? The answer to these questions, I take it, is No.[36] But speech acts, as we have noted, are among the more conspicuous of original acts, and their results—what is said, or the sentences produced—are among the more conspicuous of original products. But if a man can know just what he is going to say without already having said it inwardly (inwardly rehearsed it, worked it out in his head), and when what he says is something new, novel, or original in that it differs in some way from anything that has already been said, then I do not see what logical obstacle stands in the way of someone's knowing just what he is going to create without having already done it inwardly (e.g., having worked it out in detail in his head), when what he is going to create is an original work of art. If a poet or a painter were to tell us that before he had finished his poem or his picture he knew just what he was going to do, i.e., just what he was going to write or to paint, although he had not already composed the poem or worked out the picture in detail in his head, would his statement be paradoxical, senseless, logically incoherent? As far as I can see, it would not be. And if it would not be, then although to create is to originate, this does *not* imply that prior to creation the creator cannot know or foresee what will result from his creative act—a point perhaps supported by the logical coherence or intelligibility of the old theological doctrine that God knew from eternity just what He would create when He came to create the world. It may be the case, as I presume that it is the case in some kinds of creative performances, e.g., automatic writing and action painting, that the artist does not know just what he is doing until he has done it, where what he is doing is described *after the fact* by a statement to the effect that he was creating this picture or that poem; but I do not see that there is anything in the concept of creation that necessitates this.

That one can know in advance what he is going to create does not imply, however, that one can know in advance (1) that what he is going to create is something original or (2) just how original it will be or wherein its originality will lie, i.e., in just what respects it will be original, even where what he is going to create *is* something original. And this may be the point of the paradox of creativity that we have been considering. Those who say that the artist does not, or cannot, know or foresee what he is creating until he has created it may have it in mind that he does not, or cannot, know in advance (1) that his work will be original or (2) just wherein its originality will lie. Clearly, one may know what he is doing without knowing all there is to know about what he is doing; and that one may be doing something original, or doing something original in a particular way, may be one of those things that one does not, or cannot, know about what he is doing until he has done it.

Consider first the knowledge *that* one's work will be original. I have already pointed out that it is a matter of empirical fact that different creative acts never issue in qualitatively identical products. There was nothing surprising in Ludwig Richter's discovery that if you set four men to paint the same landscape, "all four firmly resolved not to deviate from nature by a hair's breadth [the result will be] four totally different pictures, as different from each other as the personalities of the four painters." [37] Given any creative act, it is highly probable—even inductively certain—that the product of that act will be something original, something that differs qualitatively in some way from the products of all other creative acts. Cases like our imaginary case of Browning and Mister Johnson just do not arise—a fact that is no more mysterious or surprising than the fact that no two finger prints are the same. Given this fact one can know in advance that what he will create will be something original.

Consider now the knowledge of how original one's work will be or wherein its originality will lie. Here, it seems to me, we can reasonably say that a man cannot know in advance how original his work will be or just wherein its originality will lie. Just as one can know in advance that the product of his creative act will in *some* way be unlike the products of all other creative acts, so he might know in advance, assuming that he does know what he is going to create, whether what he is going to create will be similar to something already created and wherein it will be similar; namely, by finding the relevantly similar work. Had Mr. Johnson known what he was going to write before he wrote it—and without having worked it out in his head in advance—and chanced upon Browning's poem as he was about to write, he could have seen at once that what he was about to write was the same as what Browning had already written. (Compare speech acts again: I was just about to say the same thing myself.) But just how original a man's work will be or wherein its originality will lie is something that he cannot similarly foresee. The class of works of art, like the class of utterances, and unlike the class of words on this page, is indefinitely large; we have no criterion for knowing when we have completed the enumeration of the class. Hence we can easily tell whether, and how, a given work of art, even a projected work of art, is similar to a work already produced; namely, by finding the relevant work. But we cannot similarly tell how or to what degree a given work of art will be *unlike* any work of art yet produced, for, as Stuart Hampshire put it, "the power and quality of the work [and here he is talking about its originality] is only known and understood in retrospect, often after many years." [38] An artist may know in advance what he wants to do or what he is going to do, but just how and to what degree what he is going to do will be original or creative awaits the doing of it and the comparison of what he has done with what has been done already. The determination of the originality or creativity of the *work*, as opposed to that of the *act*, comes only after the completion of the creative act.

Closely associated with this point is another, namely, that if it is the case that "voluntary action is action which can be commanded; one can ϕ voluntarily only if one can ϕ when one is told to." [39] Accordingly doing something original, especially something distinctively or markedly original, and a fortiori creating a distinctively original work of art, is, qua doing something *original* involuntary—even though there is an inductive certainty that if one performs a creative act the product of that act will be something that is somehow original. One can sensibly be commanded to paint a landscape, write a novel, or compose a sonata, but not to paint a masterpiece, write The Great American Novel, or be the Mozart of our time. One can be commanded, in other words, to perform an original act, but not to produce as a result of that act something distinctively original. One can, of course, *try* to do something original, creative, inventive, imaginative, and to enjoin this attempt is the point of such injunctions as, Be original, Use your imagination; but *success* depends upon the outcome of what has been done. The difference between performing an original, and a fortiori a creative, act and producing as a result of that act something original, is like the difference between looking for something and finding it. As Aristotle might put it, the creation of an original work of art may be an object of *boulesis* (wish) but not of *proairesis* (choice). One can choose to paint or not to paint, and he can choose what to paint, but he can only wish or hope that what he chooses to paint will turn out to be something distinctively, and not just trivially, original. (Compare the commands: Say something. Now say something original, something unlike anything that has ever been said before. Except in special circumstances, I do not *try* to obey the first command; but I can only try to obey the second and hope that I will succeed.)

So far, I have, for the most part, been using the word "original," as applied to works of art, in a somewhat technical sense to mean different in some qualitative way from any other work of art. If we now restrict our attention to original products of creative acts, in this sense of "original," we find that we have a fairly rich vocabulary for describing the nature or character of the originality in any given case: novel, odd, experimental, new, fresh, eccentric, unique, bizarre, outlandish, avant-garde, creative, imaginative, inventive, inspired, and so on; terms that in various ways contrast with or complement such terms as, uninspired, imitative, unimaginative, mere hack-work, old hat, traditional, academic, and the like. But of the terms used to mark kinds of originality, aestheticians have concentrated on creative, imaginative, and inspired, terms applicable both to artists and to their works. Whether we wish to say that such terms are honorific or evaluative (they strike me as being similar to kind, generous, intelligent, and so on, as applied to a man or to his acts or deeds, which are not always honorific or evaluative as opposed to merely descriptive) the fact remains that "creative," in this sense, is different from "creative" in the phrase "creative act," or "creative process." "Creative" in "creative act" is simply an adjective formed from the verb "to create." It is like "creative" in the phrase "creative writing course": in a creative writing course, a work might be produced, i.e., created, which is not creative; indeed, I presume that most work produced in creative writing courses is not (very) creative. The product of an original act which is also a creative act, in short, must be created but need not be creative. To merit the judgment that it is creative (imaginative, inspired) a work of art must not only be different from other works of art but, as Professor Tomas puts it, "different in an interesting, important, fruitful, or other valuable way." [40] This means that the assessment of the creativity of a work of art requires aesthetic judgment; requires, in other words, an exercise of taste, of aesthetic sensibility or discrimination. Anyone can tell at a glance whether two paintings or two poems are different, but not just anyone can tell at a glance which of two paintings or poems is the more creative. To tell this, one must be acquainted with properly comparable works of art and be able to appreciate the aesthetic significance of any artistic innovation, see how it enlarges the range of viable artistic alternatives and thereby "places" what has already been done by putting it, so to speak, in a new light.[41] If Cézanne was a creative artist, and not merely a creator of works of art, it was because he painted portraits, landscapes, still lifes that were markedly and distinctively different, in perceivable and specifiable ways, from any hitherto painted and such that they were artistically or aesthetically successful.

It would appear that one reason why some aesthetic theorists have been interested in the so-called creative process is that they believe (1) that in judging a work of art to be creative we are implicitly or by implication saying something about the psychology of the creator, and/or (2) that we can explain the difference between creative and noncreative art only by reference to the psychology of the creator.

(1) It has been said—by Professor Tomas, for example (*loc. cit.*) —that "what we have in mind when we speak of creative art" is something about the way it came into being; in particular, we "have in mind" that it was inspired (where "being inspired" is taken as the name of a psychological event) and that in the production of it the artist exercised critical control. But as far as I can see, we have nothing of the sort in mind. We determine whether a work of art is creative by looking at the work and by comparing it with previously produced works of art in the same or in the nearest comparable medium or genre. If the concept

of a work of art is not a psychological concept, and therefore implies no reference to any specifiable process or mental happening, neither is the concept of creativity as applied to works of art a psychological concept. That a work of art is creative, implies nothing about the psychology of the artist. To be sure, if a work of art is creative, then its artist is creative. But this is an empty or uninformative tautology. If Jones' swimming is graceful, then Jones is a graceful swimmer. Antecedent and consequent say the same thing.

(2) The same difficulty bedevils any philosophical attempt to *explain* why certain works of art are creative while others are not. Coleridge tells us that his famous distinction between the Fancy and the Secondary Imagination or Esemplastic Power came to him as a result of his discovery of Wordsworth's poetry.[42] The question he sought to answer was, To what is Wordsworth's superiority as a poet due? His answer, To an exercise of Imagination as opposed to Fancy. And the same will explain Milton's superiority to Cowley: "Milton had a highly *imaginative*, Cowley a very *fanciful*, mind." What Coleridge attempted to do with the notion of Imagination, others before him and since have tried to do with such notions as those of inspiration or divine possession (Plato) and creative intuition (Maritain). The trouble with all such attempts, however, is that they are otiose: like the old explanation of the phenomena of heat and combustion by reference to the presence of caloric substance, they give us bogus explanations, statements that have the mere appearance of an explanation. For no test or criterion of the exercise of esemplastic power or of creative intuition or of the occurrence of divine possession is provided, independent of the imaginativeness, creativity, or inspired quality of the works of art in question. To say that a certain piece of wood will burn because it contains caloric is merely to say that it will burn because it will burn; for the criterion of its containing caloric is that it will burn. Similarly, to say that Milton was superior to Cowley as a poet because Milton had the esemplastic power that Cowley lacked is to say no more than that Milton's *poetry* is imaginative whereas Cowley's is merely fanciful; for the sole criterion of Milton's possession of the esemplastic power is the imaginativeness of his verse. There is here no contingent connection between the imaginative or inspired quality of the work and the artist's exercise of some psychological power or faculty, his performance of some independently specifiable mental act; there is merely a logical connection between two statements, one of which only appears to be a psychological statement, a report of a mental act. "Milton's *Paradise Lost* is an imaginative poem" *entails* that Milton was an imaginative poet. To tell whether someone is an artist, or has created a work of art, we must look to him as well as to

what he has produced; to tell whether a work of art is creative, imaginative, or inspired, we must look to the work of art as it compares with other works of art; and to tell whether someone is a creative artist, we must do both—the first to determine whether he is an artist, the second to determine whether he is creative. "A produced at least one work of art, w, and w is creative" is logically equivalent to "A is a creative artist."

In Plato's *Euthyphro* (10) Socrates points out that it is not because something is seen that someone sees it, but because someone sees it that it is seen; not because something is led that someone leads it, but because someone leads it that it is led; and so on. To be sure, "x is seen" entails that someone or something sees x, and conversely. The two propositions are equivalent. Still, we say that the first is true *because* the second is true, and not that the second is true because the first is true. Similarly, although "A is a creative artist" entails that A's work is creative, and conversely, we say that the first is true *because* the second is true, and not that the second is true because the first is true. The artist may be the "cause" of his work, but it is because of the nature of his work that he is a creative artist.

I do not wish to deny that it is possible to establish genuine explanatory correlations between independently specifiable psychological characteristics, processes, or events on the one hand and the creation of imaginative or inspired works of art on the other. My claim is simply that we can know whether a work of art is creative, imaginative, or inspired while knowing nothing about the psychology of creation generally or about the psychology of a given creative artist specifically. Indeed, if we could not ascertain the originality or creativity of artistic work independently of our knowing anything about the psychology of creation, a psychology of creation would be impossible. Which is to say again what I have, in a way, been arguing throughout this paper: The concept of creativity is not a psychological concept.

NOTES

1. (New York, The Modern Library, 1928).
2. I have in mind the so-called "Zuccone" from the Campanile of the cathedral of Florence.
3. For a general repudiation of the view that psychological information (or scientific information in general) is relevant to the solution of problems in aesthet-

ics, see George Dickie, "Is Psychology Relevant to Aesthetics?" *The Philosophical Review*, LXXI (1962), pp. 285–302. Dickie does not discuss the question of artistic creation.

4. When a question is put in the ontological or "material" mode, as opposed to the conceptual, linguistic, logical, or "formal" mode, it may easily appear to be a request for information about something in the world other than our concepts or expressions. "What is (the nature of) art?," for example, may be a way of asking "What does 'art' mean?" or "What other propositions does a proposition of the form 'x is a work of art' entail; or with what propositions is it logically compatible?"; or it may be a way of asking "What features or properties, if any, do all and only works of art share, as a matter of empirical or contingent fact?" On the view of philosophy given, only the first of these questions is a philosophical question.

5. This does not mean that empirical discoveries in the sciences can in no way *affect* the answers that philosophers will give to their questions.

6. See Jacques Maritain, *Creative Intuition in Art and Poetry* (New York, Pantheon, 1953), Ch. II.

7. Jerome Stolnitz, *Aesthetics and Philosophy of Criticism* (Boston, Houghton Mifflin Co., 1960), p. 88.

8. *Ibid.*, p. 93. By an "art-object" Stolnitz means any object produced by art, i.e., by "the skilled, deliberate manipulation of a medium for the achievement of some purpose." I cannot see that there is much, if any, difference between this conception of art and Maritain's conception of art as "a virtue of the practical intellect."

9. Monroe C. Beardsley, "On the Creation of Art," *Journal of Aesthetics and Art Criticism*, XXIII (1965), p. 301. There are several issues that need to be sorted out here, but I am concerned with only one of them, and one that is probably tangential to Beardsley's main line of thought. My interpretation of Beardsley's statement, however, is reinforced by other things he says in the same place: "What I want to say is that the true locus of creativity is not the genetic process prior to the work but the work itself as it lives in the experience of the beholder. . . . Artistic creation is nothing more than the production of a self-creative object."

10. Morris Weitz, "The Role of Theory in Aesthetics," *Problems in Aesthetics: An Introductory Book of Readings*, by Morris Weitz, ed. (New York, Macmillan & Co., 1959), pp. 153–154.

11. Ruby Meager, "The Uniqueness of a Work of Art," *Collected Papers on Aesthetics*, Cyril Barrett, ed. (New York, Barnes & Noble, 1965), pp. 32–33.

12. Stuart Hampshire, *Thought and Action* (New York, Viking, 1959), pp. 230–231: Weitz, *op. cit.*, p. 151. "A concept is open if its conditions of application are emendable and corrigible; i.e. if a situation or case can be imagined or secured which would call for some sort of *decision* on our part to extend the use of the concept to cover this, or to close the concept and invent a new one to deal with the new case and its new property." Weitz is correct in saying that under this definition of an open concept all empirical or descriptive concepts are open. But it does not follow from this definition, as Weitz appears to think that it does, that there are or can be no necessary or sufficient conditions for the application of an open concept. The concept 'bachelor' is an empirical-descriptive concept, but a necessary condition for its application is that the person to whom it is applied be unmarried. And it is a sufficient condition for a person's being married that he have a valid license to be married from the Commonwealth of Massachusetts and that he has been joined in wedlock to a member of the opposite sex by a clergyman licensed by the Commonwealth of Massachusetts.

13. Douglas N. Morgan, "Creativity Today," *Journal of Aesthetics and Art Criticism*, XII (1952), pp. 8–9. One's high esteem for the music and its 'creativity' have nothing significant to do with the issue with which I am here concerned.

14. Below I try to justify the use of the word "created" as opposed to "made" or "produced."

15. *Cf.* F.E. Sparshott, *The Structure of Aesthetics* (Toronto, University of Toronto Press, 1963), p. 227: "To speak of 'the creative process' implies that the production of art is involuntary and unconscious—something that happens to one, not something one does." The production of art may at times be involuntary and unconscious, but it is still something one does and not something that happens to one.

16. Anthony Kenny, *Action, Emotion and Will* (New York, Humanities Press Inc., 1963), p. 154. A is obviously a variable a significant value of which must be a proper name, a description, or a pronoun that designates a person. Actually, the verb "to create" is not merely the name of an action but of an act: "As a general rule an action is called an act only when it can be described in a proposition with a personal subject; the actions of signing a check or killing a rival are acts, for one can say, 'I signed the check,' or 'He killed his rival;' but the beating of the heart and the working of the liver [the heart's action, the liver's action] are not acts: one cannot say, 'I beat my heart,' or 'I worked my liver'. . . . Every act, then (whether voluntary or involuntary), is an action; but not every action is an act." Eric D'Arcy, *Human Acts* (Oxford, Oxford University Press, 1963), pp. 6–7.

17. Kenny, *op. cit.*, pp. 171 ff. Not all performance verbs take a direct object, e.g., "to grow up"; but when they do the accusative may be read as part of the verb, e.g., "to paint a picture" as against "to paint." "To paint," "to write," etc. have a use as activity-verbs in addition to their use as performance-verbs: "Monet was painting all day in the fields" (activity-verb); "Valasquez painted the portrait of Pope Innocent X" (performance-verb). This is true also of the general verb "to create": compare "He's been creating a nuisance all morning" with "Mozart created the symphony in one day." "I was (still) writing the sonnet when you came in" (performance-verb) implies "I had not (yet) written the sonnet when you came in."

As Kenny points out (p. 173, n. 2) his performances correspond to Aristotle's *Kineseis* as opposed to his *Energeiai*: specifically, Kenny's distinction between "performance" and "activity" corresponds to Aristotle's distinction between two kinds of Kinesis: *Poesis* and *Praxis*. This latter distinction is probably the source of Maritain's distinction between "works to be made" and "actions to be done."

18. By the object of an act such as writing I mean that which is written (e.g., the sonnet); of painting, that which is painted (e.g., the portrait); and, in general, of creating, that which is created, the work of art. An intended object is not the same as an intentional object. If I set out to write a sonnet, the sonnet is the intended object of my writing; but if I fear that I shall never write a good sonnet, that I shall never write a good sonnet is the intentional object of my fear. *Cf.* Kenny, *op. cit.*, Ch. IX.

19. See Monroe C. Beardsley, *Aesthetics from Classical Greece to the Present* (New York & London, Macmillan & Co., 1966), pp. 22–23.

20. Related questions: Can a man create a work of art (write a poem, paint a picture) in his sleep, under hypnosis, under the influence of drugs, or, in general, in situations in which he might be said not to know what he is doing, i.e. not to know that he is writing a poem, painting a picture? I do not see how an affirmative answer is logically ruled out by the rules governing the concepts in question. "He wrote a sonnet and his sonnet is a work of art, but at the time he wrote it he did not know what he was doing" makes sense; it is not paradoxical, self-contradictory, or incoherent. Whether such a statement is ever true is another matter.

Professor Stolnitz tells us (*op. cit.*, p. 95) that his definition of art "implies that the artist is in conscious control of the process" of creation. In defense of this against artists who claim that creation is involuntary or unconscious—like gestation—he says: "And yet we must remember that neither 'involuntariness' nor 'gestation' is reported in *all* instances of creation. They are widespread, but not universal. Hence they cannot be used to define the activity of 'art.' " (p. 97) But by parity of reasoning, neither can deliberation or conscious control be so used; not *all* artists report this.

Cf. Vincent Tomas, "Creativity in Art," *The Philosophical Review*, LXVII (1958), p. 3: "Creative activity in art . . . is activity subject to critical control by the artist. . . ." For my assessment of this claim, see ART AND PHILOSOPHY, ed. by W. E. Kennick (New York, St. Martin's Press, Inc., 1964), pp. 377–78.

21. *Op. cit.*, p. 10.

22. See J. L. Austin, *How to do Things With Words* (Cambridge, Mass., Harvard University Press, 1962), pp. 94 ff. Report of locutionary act: "He said to me, 'You shouldn't do that.' " Report of illocutionary act: "He protested against (disapproved of) my doing that." Report of perlocutionary act: "He checked me (prevented my doing that, stopped me before it was too late, brought me to my senses, annoyed me, embarrassed me)." These are all ways of *saying what he did*.

23. For this reason portraits, illustrations, etc. are not species of art in the way that cats, dogs, etc. are species of animal. "C is a cat" entails "C is an animal," but "P is a portrait" does not entail "P is a work of art."

24. Even Clive Bell's theory does this at times: "*Paddington Station* is not a work of art; it is an interesting and amusing document. In it line and color are used to recount anecdotes, suggest ideas, and indicate the manners and customs of an age [all illocutionary-like acts]: they are not used to provoke aesthetic emotion [a perlocutionary-like act]." *Art* (London, H. Grevel & Co., 1913), p. 18. The suggestion is that only if a painter uses line and color to provoke aesthetic emotion is his painting a work of art.

25. For Collingwood "to express an emotion" is a performance-verb. It has continuous tenses and "A is expressing an emotion" implies "A has not (yet) expressed that emotion." See *The Principles of Art* (Oxford, The Cleverdon Press, 1938), *passim*, but esp. Ch. VI.

26. Sparshott, *op. cit.*, pp. 227–28.

27. Sherman E. Lee, *A History of Far Eastern Art* (Englewood Cliffs, N.J. & New York, Prentice-Hall, Inc. and Harry N. Abrams, Inc., 1964), p. 265.

28. Ruby Meager, *op. cit.*, p. 26. I deal only with exact or faithful copies or replicas here; so-called "creative" copies (e.g. Dürer's drawing *Battle of the Sea Gods* after Mantegna's engraving) raise issues of another sort that are touched on in the last paragraphs of this paper.

29. *Ibid.*, pp. 31–32. The poem, I take it, is not the whole of "Pippa Passes" but "Pippa's Song": "The year's at the spring / And day's at the morn. . . . God's in his heaven— / All's right with the world."

30. *Ibid.*, p. 31. The term "manifestation" is used in a technical sense: "Let us call the spatio-temporal phenomena [e.g., two or more bronze castings of the same statue, two or more performances of the same symphony] so related to a work of art that when a person sees or hears them he is seeing or hearing the work, *manifestations* of the work." (*Ibid.*, pp. 25–26.)

Cf. Vincent Tomas, *op. cit.*, pp. 1–2: "When we congratulate an artist for being creative . . . it was not because he was able to obey rules that were known before he painted his picture or wrote his novel or poem, so that thereby he succeeded in doing what had been done before. We congratulate him because he embodied in colors or in language something the like of which did not exist before, and because he was the originator of the rules he implicitly followed while he was painting or writing. Afterwards, others may *explicitly* follow the same rules and thereby achieve similar successes." For my criticism of this way of putting the point, see *Art and Philosophy*, p. 377.

On my understanding of Miss Meager's definition of "original activity" it does not follow that an original act entails an exercise of "reflective choice." Briefly, if an act is an original act (O), then it is not an act of mere obedience to specifications already laid down (not-M); if it is an act of mere obedience to specifications already laid down (M), then it is not an act involving reflective choice (not-R). But "(O → not-M) & (M → not-R)" does not imply "(O → R)."

31. That is, "N(x is a work of art → there is someone, y, who created x)" does not imply "N(y created x)."

32. *Op. cit.*, p. 168.

33. Note again that the locutionary acts may be the same, though the illocutionary and perlocutionary acts differ; and the illocutionary or perlocutionary acts may be the same, though the locutionary acts differ.

34. H. W. Janson, *History of Art* (Englewood Cliffs, N.J. & New York, Prentice-Hall, Inc. and Harry N. Abrams, Inc. 1962), p. 11.

35. *Op. cit.*, p. 4. *Cf.* also Stuart Hampshire, *op. cit.*, pp. 246–47.

36. *Cf.* Ludwig Wittgenstein, *Zettel* (Oxford, Basil Blackwell, 1967), 1, 2, 38, 44, 45, 57, 137.

37. Heinrich Wölfflin, *Principles of Art History*, tr. by M. D. Hottinger (New York, Dover Publications, Inc., n.d.), p. 1.

38. *Op. cit.*, p. 247.

39. Anthony Kenny, *op. cit.*, p. 183.

40. *Op. cit.*, p. 286. *Cf.* Poincaré on mathematical creativity: "What is mathematical creation? It does not consist in making new combinations with mathematical entities already known. Anyone could do that, but the combinations so made would be infinite in number and most of them absolutely without interest. To create consists precisely in not making useless combinations and in making those which are useful. . . ." Quoted by D. N. Morgan, *op. cit.*, p. 8, n. 18.

41. *Cf.* Douglas Morgan, *op. cit.*, p. 19: "In rough, over-simplified terms . . . a painting . . . counts as 'creative' if it gives us a new way of seeing, as a Picasso or a Turner does. . . ." But seeing what? Other paintings, I take it. Every creative innovation in an art, e.g., Surrealism, gives as a new way of seeing at least some other products of that art, e.g., the paintings of Jerome Bosch, and thereby provides us with the basis for a (possible) reassessment of the artistic or aesthetic significance of those other works. Whether, as Morgan suggests, this is a conceptual truth, having to do with the meaning of "creative," or an empirical truth is difficult to determine, but I am inclined to agree with Morgan that it is a conceptual truth; that we would withhold the predicate "creative" from work that did not have this tendency. A judgment of creativity is in this way retrospective: it directs our attention not only to the work so judged, but to *previous* comparable works. "Inventive," on the other hand, seems to have prospective force: an artist is inventive, but not necessarily creative, if he devises new ways of doing things that affect the practice of artists who come after him. Cézanne was both a creative and an inventive painter.

42. Samuel Taylor Coleridge, *Biographia Literaria*, Chs. IV, XIII; and see Basil Willey, *Nineteenth Century Studies* (New York, Columbia University Press, 1949), Ch. I, esp. sec. III.

ON CREATING

(A RESPONSE)

Jack Glickman

"Create" is not a psychological verb, and creating is not the name of a mental act, activity, or process; on this I agree wholeheartedly with Professor Kennick. I will, however, suggest an analysis of the verb "create" that is somewhat different from his.

Consider first, *creating* and *making*: there are crucial differences between these two concepts. Consider the following sentences. The seamstress made a new dress; The fashion designer created a new dress; The chef made a new soup today; The chef created a new soup today. Although the same noun occurs as direct object in both sentences of each pair, with "make" the noun designates a particular thing, but with "create" the noun is generic. The seamstress made a particular, individual dress; but the fashion designer did not create a particular, individual dress, he created a new kind of dress, a new style. If the chef created a new soup, he created a new kind of soup, a new recipe; he may not have made the soup. But if we say, He made a new soup today, "soup" refers to some particular pot(s) of soup he prepared. Particulars are made, types created.

Suppose a potter makes a vase and creates a new design on the surface. It may seem that the design is a particular thing, but what was created is a particular design only in that it is a particular *type* of design. If he created a new design, what he created is not the one specific configuration of lines located on the surface of the vase. Suppose I make a thousand copies of that vase; I could then show the potter any of the copies and ask, Did you create the design on *this* vase? The answer in all cases would be, Yes. The answer would be No, if I asked, Did you make the design on *this* vase? With "make," "design" refers to an individual; with "create," "design" refers to a type. Someone might, in the same process, both make something and create something, but not the same

262

something. A potter, for example, might, in the same process, both make a design (individual) and create a design (type). "Work of art," often the object of "create," refers to what is a type in the required sense. This is more obvious with works of literature and music than with paintings, but even with paintings we have a case analogous to the vase example above, for one could see in an exact reproduction what the artist had created.

It might be objected that "create" and "make" do not always indicate a different sort of object. We do not distinguish the kind of "product" (individual or type) when, for example, we say, He created a disturbance, rather than, He made a disturbance; but I am concerned only with creating that is *creative*. One can create all sorts of things: before lighting a fire in the fireplace, one heats the chimney to create a draft; one can create a disturbance, or create a nuisance; one can create difficulties, create an impression, create opinion. If someone creates a certain impression, it is no reason to call him creative; he may create the impression of himself that he is uncreative. If someone creates a menace, or creates difficulties, it is no reason to call him creative. But if a chef creates a new dish, a businessman creates a new way of merchandising, or a painter creates a work of art, these are reasons to call that person creative. My remarks about the verb "create" apply only to cases in which if we say that A has created something, his having created it would count as a reason for saying that A is creative; in such cases the direct object of "create" refers to a type rather than to an individual.

One reason, then, why it would be wrong to characterize creating as a kind of making, is that what is created (a type) is not what is made (an individual); on this I think Kennick and I agree. Consider Kennick's example of Wu Tao-tzu, the Tang Dynasty's greatest painter, who is known only through copies of his work. If the copies are faithful replicas of their originals, then we do have the works that Wu created, for what he created were types which we have through the copies, although we do not have the individual works he "made."

Also, because what is created is a type rather than an individual, it is possible (though unlikely) that two persons might independently create the same work of art. Suppose that A and B each write a poem, and it turns out that their poems are about the same subject and are word-for-word the same. One might want to say, They cannot be the same because *this* (pointing to mss. *a*) is A's poem, created by A. And *this* (pointing to mss. *b*) is B's poem, created by B. They have different properties—one created by A, the other by B—and so are not the same. This would not hold as an argument that two persons cannot create the same poem, for as such it would beg the question at issue; moreover, if my argument, that what is created is a type, is correct, then what one should say in such a case is, *This* poem (pointing to mss. *a*) was created by *both A and B*, and *this* poem (pointing to mss. *b*) was created by *both A and B*. Both created the same type, although each produced different tokens. (Concerning Miss Meager's example, though, I do not think that Browning's "Pippa Passes" and Mister Johnson's "Pippa Passes" are the same poem, for Mister Johnson's poem is about Mister Johnson's girl-friend Pippa, and Browning's poem is not about Mister Johnson's girl-friend Pippa.)

Now to the main issue: why creating is not an activity or process. Someone might create in a number of ways—by composing music, for example, by painting, by writing poetry. We might say of someone that he was not only painting but creating, or that he was not only writing but creating, and in such a case, Kennick says, there is a sense in which one would be doing two things at the same time—not in the way that one might lecture, write on the blackboard, and jingle his keys at the same time, but in the way one might write his name, sign a check, and pay a bill at the same time. But notice that one can lecture, write on the blackboard, or jingle his keys, do any one of these things, without doing any of the others. And the same with writing his name, signing a check, and paying a bill: one can write his name without signing a check or paying a bill, and can pay a bill without signing a check or writing his name. The crucial point about creating is that if one were not only writing or painting but also creating, one could not be creating *without* also writing or painting. Creating is not an isolable activity; someone cannot *just* create, he must be doing something we could describe as writing, painting, composing, or whatever. One does not always create when one paints, writes, or composes, but rather these are means by which one might create. A number of activities sometimes qualify as creating.

Kennick claims that "create" is a performance verb, but it seems to me that "create" does not satisfy the two conditions for performance verbs: (1) they have continuous tenses, and (2) where $\emptyset$ stands for a performance-verb, A is $\emptyset$ing implies A has not $\emptyset$d. It is unusual to say, I am creating; "create" is seldom used in the continuous present tense. A painter, say, *might* after a bit of especially satisfying work, exclaim, I am creating!, but the creating is not something he is doing at the moment, it is something he has done. If we ask, How do you know you're creating?, he might answer, Just look at what I've painted. To know whether someone has created, we have to see the results of his work, and also the creator himself knows he has created only by seeing what he has done. Hence it makes sense to ask, How do you know you're creating?, whereas it would be silly to ask, How do you know you're painting?. Similarly, one might be surprised that he has created, but not surprised that he has painted. We say an activity such as painting, writing or composing is creating if it achieves new and valuable results, but no isolable activity, *creating*, corresponds to the verb "create" as painting, for example, corresponds to the verb "paint."

"Create," I suggest, is one of a class of verbs Gilbert Ryle has labeled "achievement verbs." The verb "win," for example, signifies not an activity but an achievement. Winning a race requires some sort of activity, such as running, but winning is itself not an activity.

One big difference between the logical force of a task verb and that of a corresponding achievement verb is that in applying an achievement verb we are asserting that some state of affairs obtains over and above that which consists in the performance, if any, of the subservient task activity. For a runner to win, not only must he run but also his rivals must be at the tape later than he; for a doctor to effect a cure, his patient must both be treated and be well again. . . . An autobiographical account of the agent's exertions and feelings does not by itself tell whether he has brought off what he was trying to bring off.[1]

For a painter, musician, or writer to create, not only must he paint, compose, or write, he must also produce something that is new and valuable. Whether we call the activity "creating" depends on the product. Certainly the agent, in order to create, must do something, but nothing specific; the criteria for using the verb "create" apply to the product, not to the activity that produced it.

If creating were a process or activity we would expect that one could decide to create or could create at will. Given the technical knowledge, one can decide or choose to write, paint, or compose, but not to create. In this regard it should be noted that creating, which Kennick calls an "illocutionary-like" act, is in important respects *unlike* illocutionary acts. It is unlike illocutionary acts in that it cannot be done at will. Creating is unlike illocutionary acts in that it is not a specifiable act. And creating is unlike illocutionary acts in that it is not liable to error.

If creating were a process or activity we would expect the possibility of error. It is easy, for example, to *make* something *wrong*. But one cannot create something wrong; one either creates or one does not. But just as winning is not an infallible kind of running, creating is not an infallible kind of making; it is an achievement.

NOTES

1. Gilbert Ryle, *The Concept of Mind*, (New York, Barnes & Noble, 1950), p. 150.

THE ARTISTIC AND THE AESTHETIC

Jerome Stolnitz

Against the received understanding of the appreciation of art, recent aesthetics has encouraged doubt and has suggested alternatives. I want to work out a series of arguments that will define and support the newer way of thinking. I have two objectives: to provide a pattern of understanding for the reaction against received thought by showing that it arises from the interaction between the concepts of art and the aesthetic; and to give reasons why the newer way of thinking ought to prevail.

In traditional aesthetic theory, the process of art—skilled production, in answer to an envisioned goal and at the last realizing it—is decisive in determining what the subsequent experience of the audience will consist in. For the properties of the thing that the audience apprehends, and the structure of those properties, are just those which were purposefully devised by the artist. He brought into being an object where nothing or only something inchoate existed before. *He made the thing to be what it is.* He singled out one among numberless possible manifolds of elements, singled out that one for its unique suitability to the purpose that governed his entire activity. Then the audience must needs perceive both the surface properties, open to seeing and hearing, selected by the artist, and those less overt significances of theme, mood, and the unspoken allusions of elements to one another, for which the surface properties were the chosen vehicles. Irrespective of any communicative intent, the relation between the creative process and the audience's experience is, accordingly, that of communicating and sharing.

This way of thinking runs throughout aesthetics and criticism as far back as the *Ion*, whose figure of the magnet which unites the creative artist, the interpretive artist, and the audience, in a "long chain," may be taken as a prototype. Philosophers and critics who have shared this view have divided in identifying the artist's goal, thereby differing over the aptitudes requisite to creativity. Yet whatever the theoretical candidates for these places, they confidently assume the further work of explaining the content of the spectator's experience and also its goodness. Because this way of thinking has been ubiquitous, but even more, because it has not seemed less correct for being taken for granted, it should be brought up, I think, from the level of quiet certitude to explicit statement and assigned a habitation and a name. I propose the name, "the Identity Thesis." Pending the several formulations of the Thesis in the body of the paper, let us understand by it now either that the structure of overt properties and thematic and expressive significances apprehended by the audience is identical with that knowingly created by the artist or else, that it ought to be.

Whether descriptive or normative, the Identity Thesis is a thesis about the aesthetic experiencing of art. We can say, to sum up what has just been said, that the Identity Thesis has the artistic legislate over the aesthetic. But this is something of a solecism, since the word and, considerably more important, the concept of the aesthetic are, as these things are measured, relatively new. The fact of appreciation was handled in the manner of the Identity Thesis before ever the aesthetic arose as a self-aware and articulate idea.[1] It emerged when inquiry turned upon the fact of appreciation to make out its indigenous characteristics. The concept of the aesthetic enables the distinction between the aesthetic and nonaesthetic nature of art and that between art, which is pre-eminently valuable in aesthetic experience ("fine art"), and nonartistic objects. But because the concept has made a place for itself in inquiry, the aesthetic experiencing of art can no longer be a mere corollary of the creative process. It must be studied in its own right. This is the point of interaction between the older and the newer concepts. Does aesthetic experience proceed along the lines marked out by creation or, if not, ought it to do so?

The first step in answering this question is to realize that, on the usual analyses of the aesthetic, the concepts of art and the aesthetic turn out to be, in salient respects, opposites to each other. Whereas art is a kind of doing, an effort of shaping or hewing out a thing, "aesthetic" is taken to refer, as it does etymologically, to a kind of perceiving. It is an awareness and relishing of something found, that confronts the beholder. He is much closer to the theoretical knower than to the doer. Then since the artistic process begins with what is rudimentary or amorphous, it employs means. These are trials, possibly rejected, toward the envisioned goal. They may also suggest that the goal be made more specific and more practicable. Aesthetic perceiving, free of the intent and the onus of doing, is markedly noninstrumental, so much so that this commends itself to many thinkers as an important defining property of the aesthetic. The elements of the object are not for the spectator, as once for the artist, matter for trial and error. To the spectator, they are terminal, not problematic and exploratory.

These points of opposition effectively challenge that version of the Identity Thesis which has the percipient retracing just the steps taken by the artist during the creative act. Understood in anything like a literal sense, this kind of theory is unacceptable as a description of the appreciative experience or as an attainable ideal for such experience. "Re-creationism" is not, however, the most frequent version of the Identity Thesis. The creative process, in light of which the work of art and the audience's experience are to be understood, does not include false starts and trial and error. The false starts were not incorporated in the end-product. All of the elements that finally make up the work of art, realize, in the artist's judgment, his envisioned goal. The work of art is and should be appreciated as the success of the creative process.

Yet there is a further respect, more consequential than those just cited, in which the concepts of art and the aesthetic are opposed to each other. "Aesthetic" has commonly been taken to connote an exclusive concern for the intrinsic nature of an object. The observer's attention, devoted to the thing present to him and sustained by it, ignores what lies outside it. He therefore ignores relations to other things in which the object may figure. But among these relations are its origins. They are part of the history of the object but divagations from its presence. Viewing the object as a term in these relations, the job of the biographer or the anthropologist, would attenuate or subvert appreciation. On this understanding of the concept, the aesthetic excludes just what is integral to the meaning of "art," when it refers to a kind of object. Works of art are differentiated from natural objects by the manner of their coming-into-being, i.e., historically or causally. The object is defined by reference to the creative process. The aesthetic significance of the object is, for the Identity Thesis, explicable in the same way.

Here we have the decisive antithesis between "art" and "aesthetic." It is the dialectical pattern that runs through the latter-day debates over the aesthetic experiencing of art.

The critics of the Identity Thesis, stimulated and emboldened by the concept of the aesthetic, call into question the relevant bearing of one or another aspect of artistic creation upon aesthetic appreciation. They lay down exclusionary ordinances against the motive to self-expression and/or the activity of expression, or against artistic intentions in general. Additionally, they proscribe the remoter origins of the object, the social and psychological provenance of the creative act, which had been used to explain the work. Either we do or do not have this causal knowledge. If we do not, it is implausible or false to think that appreciation of the work is therefore debarred to us. If we do, preoccupation with such data will likely sacrifice palpable elements of the work to those tenuously attributed to it as a result of genetic findings. If, however, the inference goes from the properties of the work to biographical or social traits, it adds nothing for aesthetic purposes.

The Identity Thesis has survived this battery of criticisms. Though belief in the Thesis has probably never been less stable and assured, it remains a live option at this time. I am going to try to explain why this is so. The Identity Thesis has survived not only theoretical objection but also factual evidence which seems to tell against it, though such evidence is conspicuous and readily available. Whereas the dialectical challenge has come from the concept of the aesthetic, with its impulse toward the intrinsic, toward presence, the empirical challenge has come from the development of professional art criticism and consequently of a large, public literature of art criticism. This literature exhibits a plurality of detailed and sensitive readings of a single work of art, arrayed alongside of each other. It has therefore cast doubt on the notion of a single-track communication between artist and audience. Not for the first time, however, the inherited mode of thinking has led its adherents to ignore or to minimize the negative evidence. My paper therefore undertakes at various points the philosophical work of "assembling reminders for a particular purpose."

I

It will be instructive to begin with a paper by Roman Ingarden. For this is an aesthetician who has, as clearly as any, driven a wedge between the artistic and the aesthetic. Ingarden sees appreciation, so far from being subject to the artist's control, often proceeding counter to his control, and not as a matter of ignorance or error. Therefore, when Ingarden later runs together the artistic and aesthetic, it is not out of doctrinal allegiance, like a defender of the Identity Thesis. His doing so is, rather, an inadvertency, a blurring of the distinction that elsewhere he marks so carefully.

Freedom in appreciating the work of art is necessitated by the nature of the work. The work of art is, characteristically, what Ingarden calls "indeterminate," "schematic," "potential." [2] For aesthetic appreciation, the work must be articulated and fleshed out. The indeterminate suggestions of form and theme that it makes must be particularized.

Only in this way can the work take on the body and unity that are grasped in aesthetic experience. This is the task of the observer. What he apprehends is, then, the "joint product" of his agency and the artist's.

Ingarden says, echoing the customary view, that "The work of art . . . is the product of the intentional activities of an artist." [3] But Ingarden also has it that it is *this* thing which is significantly unrealized and therefore opaque. Not that such things are bad works of art; all works of art are of this sort. So it would have to follow from Ingarden's statements that creation terminates in these objects. But what Ingarden calls the "true object" of creation is surely not an object *manqué*. The artist does not propose and approve such an object.

This consequence of Ingarden's position, which can itself be set right, brings out interestingly his relation to the Identity Thesis. It is a mirror-image of the Thesis. The Thesis takes the object, complete with the significances and values that were achieved and accepted by the artist, to be just the object apprehended by the percipient. At the point at which Ingarden starts—confrontation of the created object by the audience, rather than the creative process—he finds the object wanting in concreteness. This is how it appears to the percipient. Then this object becomes, inferentially, the "true object" of creation. We must, I want to show, keep firmly in view those features of the confrontation with art that Ingarden has underscored. This does not, however, cost us gratuitous misrepresentation of the creative act. We need not slip over from the aesthetic to the artistic—Ingarden's error is peculiarly of recent vintage—any more than in the other direction.

What we need here is the venerable device of drawing distinctions. Assume that the artist undertakes to create an object that will be delightful or otherwise absorbing to aesthetic perception. Depending on the specification of the meaning of "aesthetic," this will pretty surely be dubious or false for a certain number of those generally accredited as artists, and it will not unlikely be so on any unsurprising meaning of the term. I take this, however, merely as a monitory reminder of the difference between the two activities. Making the assumption, we describe creation as proceeding toward and therefore as under the aegis of the envisioned object. This object is, or becomes at the last, determinate in the required sense. It possesses the concreteness and form which endow it with aesthetic value. The composer creates music with a specific tempo, pulse, accent, and expressive quality that commend it to him. But the artist also produces a second object which is not determinate in the same way, though it has specific, identifiable properties. The composer creates music and he also writes a score, which is not auditory.

The score fixes the music that he has created. The tempo, accents, etc., indicated in the score are not the same as, though they are as close as he can get to the tempo, accents, etc., of the music that he has picked out on the piano or perhaps heard only with the mind's ear. Yet by reading or playing the score, the composer can hear the music that he has created. Music is, in obvious ways, exceptional. The distinction between the two created objects is most conspicuous there. The second object is only a "notation" of the first; the second, unlike the first, is seen and read; and the notation is, at best, approximate. But if we go to the visual arts, where notation does not occur, neither is the canvas or sculpture the sole created object. The artist saw these shapes setting up certain movements toward their neighbors—chose them, indeed, because they did so—and as the bearers of certain ideational overtones. These determinate formal and conceptual significances make up the aesthetically valuable object that he brought into being. The shapes are visible on the canvas; the formal networks and the conceptual overtones are not. Yet the latter elements are, to the artist, immanent in the canvas, which therefore fixes the aesthetic object that is original with him.

Let us call the canvas, the sculpture, or, though with some verbal strain, the printed poem, or, with considerable verbal strain, the score, *the art object*. And let us call the aesthetic object, such as the heard music, which is, to the artist's satisfaction, immanent within or realizable by means of the art object, *the work of art*. Thus "work of art," as I will be using this term, denotes a particular aesthetic object, that brought into being and finally approved by the creative artist.

Then what I will call *the first form of the Identity Thesis* may be defined: the object, with determinate properties of form, theme, and expression, which is apprehended when one attends aesthetically to the canvas or to the reading or sounding of the printed poem or score, is in fact identical with the work of art (descriptive). If it is not, appreciation has failed to grasp its object, because of ignorance or some other shortcoming in the percipient. In the optimal experience of the art object, the aesthetic object is identical with the work of art (normative).

An implication of this Thesis points to the first reason for doubting the Thesis. We have to accept that the art object does or should function in just the same way for any aesthetic percipient as it did for the artist. But their respective purposes are not the same. The primary purpose of creation is to bring into being a specific aesthetic object—the work of art. The art object functions to fix the work of art. The artist considers the art object, in the course of creation, in the light of the work of art. Most notably in the plastic arts, the shaping of the art object may suggest additions or emendations in the work of art. But the sculptor must approve the aesthetic object thus revised and, for that reason, retains the features of the art object that gave the new lead. This judgment governs the creative process up to and at its close. The artist would have thought his telic activity a failure were he unable to produce a score or canvas within which the work of art could be discerned. The same demand is not inherent in aesthetic appreciation. There are certain conditions that must be met by the percipient. If they are not, we may doubt that his experience is genuinely aesthetic. The percipient must bend devotedly to the art object; he must discriminate the elements that make it up and the connections between them; he must be alert to what is singular about this object. The object which possesses a determinate form and theme and expressive quality must be apprehended with no purpose other than just attending to or dwelling upon it. For the percipient, the art object functions to constitute an aesthetic object, *some* aesthetic object.

There is at least the possibility that this object will differ from the work of art, i.e., the aesthetic object known to the artist. Neither the descriptive nor the normative Thesis is necessitated on the grounds on which the experience is accounted aesthetic. On the other hand, neither Thesis is as yet excluded on those grounds. The possibility that the aesthetic object is or ought to be identical with the work of art remains open.

The descriptive Thesis is vulnerable to factual refutation. That a single art object gives rise to a number, even an indefinitely large number of aesthetic objects, not all of them, presumably, identical with the work of art, would seem to be demonstrated by evidence of criticism and performance that is everywhere to hand. Yet the thrust of these facts has been resisted by and blunted against received ways of thinking, notably a line of thought to this effect: What I am calling the art object is, like the work of art, brought into being through knowing, deliberate activity. It suits the artist's purpose. It was probably blue-pencilled and revised in the light of that purpose. An object so scrupulously and finely shaped during its creation must surely be through-and-through defined. Then this object must be rigorous and lucid in enforcing its being upon the beholder. Its character is explicable by its origin in singleness of purpose. Unless the artist's purpose was blurred or he was guilty of technical ineptitude, the art object speaks to us aesthetically with greater authority than any other kind of object.

I submit that the line of thinking here stated overtly has been a confident though unvoiced assumption of much aesthetic theory and art criticism. It is not peculiar to any one, partisan conception of the creative process and the art object. If I am right in this, it is worth setting out the assumption and making it tractable to criticism.

Once again, the criticism proceeds by coming down heavily on the distinctness of the context of creation from that of appreciation. Though they are distinct, they have in common the art object. This object has properties that are recognizably present in both contexts. The point at issue is whether the relation which the art object bore to the work of art at the close of creation is preserved following creation, whether it is, so to speak, locked in. In the ideal case that we are supposing, the artist's purpose is wholly precise, at least at the end, and he judges correctly that the art object suits his purpose. This means that he can discern in the art object with these properties, but not in any other, the work of art. This object, and no other, suits his purpose. From which it does not follow that this object can suit no other (aesthetic), purpose.

A condition of believing that the art object is tied to the work of art is believing that the elements which make up the art object are such that they *can* sustain an exclusive relation to that aesthetic object known to the artist. The overt properties are alone what is, for certain, present to the object's audiences. If they cannot sustain the tie to the work of art uniquely, then it is no good saying what the art object "must" be like in view of its genesis. Singleness of artistic purpose cannot guarantee singleness of aesthetic import if the materials upon which the purpose is exercised lack any single import. The Identity Thesis has perpetuated an image of the art object as defined, firm, chiselled, durably self-identical in the significances that it discloses to aesthetic experience. The image may be doubted and so, therefore, the Thesis. But they have effectively obscured what seem to be clear truths about art objects.

Directives, such as the tempo or dynamic markings in a score, chosen by the artist because of their peculiar suitability to the work of art, insure, if they are respected, against aesthetic realizations that are flagrantly different from the work of art. Yet within the limits set by the markings, the conductor must select one and only one tempo, one and only one particular volume. Maverick readings are now excluded. We must not say, however, that the differences among those which remain are fairly inconsequential. We might want to say that the aesthetic objects constituted by these readings are substantially like or very close to the work of art. There is a *prima facie* plausibility to this but the remark is greatly misleading. The work of art, like any aesthetic object, enjoyed its own distinctive character. It achieved a balancing of the energies within it and an affective tang peculiar to itself. It was this individuality of the work of art which commended it to the artist; the effort of the conductor is to define such an individuality and of the audience to dwell upon and savor it. In our nonaesthetic dealings, any one of substantially similar things will often do. But it is the exception rather than the rule that we will take one reading of a musical score as well as another. Each may have merits, yet given any appreciable capacity of discrimination, we do not think of them as interchangeable. The music hitherto serene puts on a different face in new performances. It is grave or, beyond that, its gravity is edged with poignancy. A change in tempo or volume which is slight as measured by clock time or decibel count is radical in its aesthetic import. This is so certain that in comparing two performances, we might well find one more similar in felt quality to a performance of a different score than to a second performance of the same score. Our choice of formal and expressive predicates would evidence our finding. That there is this much latitude in rendering the score aesthetically determinate is perfectly consistent with the fact that just this score, perhaps arrived at by prolonged and laborious trial and error, fixed for the composer the determinate work of art—the particular music that he heard.

Directives, like a score marking or a stage direction, assist in organizing a pattern of emphasis, caesura, and denouement. But this task is not generally performed by detached comments on the notes or words. The pattern is constituted out of the elements themselves. They must bear covertly marks of their place in the unfolding of a structure. We must be able to make out what Lord Shaftesbury called the "interior numbers," the unseen pattern, like a meter, that runs through and animates the aesthetic object. But the "weight" of a color is not like its hue; the impulse toward another area of the picture that is set up by a line is not like its straightness. To see the color as weighted, with a specific weight that is played off against the other color areas, to sense the impulse across the picture that is generated by the line—this requires some supplementation of what is open to normal eyesight. The hue and other intrinsic components of the color set limits to the color-weight, the shape of the line to the line of force. So far as there are limits, the activity of kinesthetic and imaginative supplementation is not random; within those limits, it is not bound. The weight of the color, the propulsiveness of the line, are not fixed into the art object in a way that uniquely constrains the content and direction of viewing. And, as in the case of *andante* or *forte*, the differences among the qualities which remain within the limits, slim and conceptually elusive as they may be, are not to be burked in thinking about aesthetic experience, which lives upon such qualities. The specification of quality made by the viewer of the painting does not seem to him, as it might, possibly, to the conductor, a matter of decision-making. This is how he "takes" or "feels" the painting, feeling it irresistibly so. That it is a choice all the same, he often proves to himself in later transactions with the painting. There is now another pattern of stress and hiatus in the little drama that the canvas plays out. There are now, consequently, other values in his experience. That the painting, determinate, firm, enforces its structure and meaning upon us, is an accurate account of how the painting appears to us *after* selecting, from among those that it makes possible, a particular constellation of properties that make up an object for aesthetic experience.

The score markings and colors just discussed are only instances of what we find in art objects. Yet it will be granted that they are representative instances. Their indeterminateness measures the distance between the art object and the aesthetic object. It jars the image of the art object as a wholly defined and articulated entity. Further, it helps to explain a phenomenon that I will dub "the transforming suggestion."

Specifying a tempo or the directional forces in a painting qualifies significantly the global character of the aesthetic object. Our orthodoxies concerning the distinctive part-whole relationship in beautiful things endorse this assertion. What is interesting, even remarkable to see, is the readiness with which the object can take on a markedly different character from that which it had worn before, as the result of a comment upon it which says nothing about such properties as tempo or color-weight. The suggestion is of the expressive atmosphere in which the aesthetic object moves. The suggestion may have been hitherto undreamed of. It might appear at first wildly misdirected. And yet colors and like properties can be assimilated to it and, still within the limits set by the art object, can be made to converge upon and support this expressive character.

One viewing the painting of "The Night Café" sees the chairs and tables round the periphery, the small bar at the rear, the billiard table off-center. Several people, the patrons, are seated at the tables; the proprietor stands alongside the billiard table. The viewer sees all of this. He sees everything that anyone at all could see. He attends diligently to the painting and enjoys doing so. The painting has for him a character much like Dutch *genre* paintings. It is a detailed rendering of quotidian existence which, by choosing this subject and detailing it, endows quotidian existence with importance. "The Night Café" is more or more obviously intense and focused than most of Dutch *genre*. Like those paintings, however, it renders the intimacy and richness of a mundane setting. Integral to this feeling is the warmth of the reds and greens that are conspicuous in the canvas. Then our viewer hears it said about the painting that it "expresses the terrible passions of humanity." He is surprised, possibly abashed, because this is so far from what he himself would have said. But his further viewing of the painting now being di-

rected by this suggestion, the felt quality of the aesthetic object is transformed or, better, one aesthetic object gives way to another. The intimacy of the café becomes claustrophobic, its warmth a burden. The
several elements of the painting are commensurately transformed. The
reds and greens become febrile; space congests, then, at the rear of the
painting, whirls away; the human beings are stricken. These are record-
ings of our viewer's felt experience. They show that he still attends diligently to the painting's local detail, only now as it is unified by the expressive significance suggested by the comment. It might be noted, additionally, that nothing idiosyncratic, such as a clearly personal association
or recollection, has intruded into either the first or the later viewing.
Both have decent claim to be accounted veritably aesthetic.

This well-known remark about the painting happens to come from
the artist. It reads: "I have tried to express the terrible passions of humanity by means of red and green." [4] The quotation, including the
larger passage in which it occurs, is interesting on several counts. It is a
prose statement about the determinate work of art, which steers the
viewer's experience closer to the work of art. The relative vagueness of
the prose makes it difficult to speak with confidence of identity. Still an
approach to identity becomes, in measure, attainable. But there was
nothing like identity in the first viewing, when the painter's statement
was as yet unknown. How could the two experiences be so unlike and
why was it only after the statement became known to the viewer that he
could find in the canvas something like the work of art? The answer to
both questions is in the statement itself, viz., the relating together, in the
form of a means-end relation, of "the terrible passions of humanity" and
the colors, red and green. Elsewhere the artist describes his colors more
specifically. And though he speaks, in the passage in question, exclusively of color, obviously a good deal else was involved in the visual in-
carnation of "the terrible passions." These qualifications mitigate, they
do not overcome the oddness of the relation announced by the painter.
It is not as though he had spoken of a means-end relation between
green and the depiction or evocation of nature. The idea or the expressive quality of "the terrible passions" is so much more remote from the
color that the significances which the color bore, we need not doubt, in
the work of art, could hardly be insured by it in later aesthetic experience. Our friend, who was not oblivious to the greens and reds on first
viewing, found them warm and exuberant. They were therefore all of a
piece with the global quality of the painting—the richness even of a prosaic human environment. Our viewer found the colors anything but
"terrible" or daemonic. Their felt quality is transformed when the
painting is transformed. That they can be transformed and in the direction of the work of art, shows why the object that was deliberately and

successfully designed to fix the work of art, may *need* to be turned toward it, e.g., by the remarks of artists and critics, but also why the art object is subject to yet other transformations, these *not* in the direction of the work of art.

The fact of diverse specifications of the same art object is omnipresent in criticism and performance. The fact is not little-sized or, in some sense of the term that would encourage the Identity Thesis, contingent. It is rooted in the elements, such as the directives and colors, which make up the art object. They do not sustain because they cannot sustain an exclusive relation to the work of art. It is because of their plasticity that the object of which they are parts is open to the transforming suggestion.

Appreciation demands that the art object yield up an object to be dwelled upon and savored: *some* aesthetic object. The aesthetic object may not in fact be the same as the work of art. The normative Identity Thesis is not thereby invalidated. Rather, at just this point it enters the discussion: of the several experiences of the art object, the most fitting or optimal is that in which the aesthetic object is identical with the work of art. To the extent that aesthetic experience falls away from this norm, it is not appropriate to the art object.[5]

We can helpfully approach this Thesis through the notion of interpretation. On the normative Thesis, the overt elements of the art object can be related to each other in various ways—one of which is privileged—to make up an aesthetic object, not itself overt until this activity is completed, which determinately possesses such properties as form, thematic meaning, and expressive quality. "Interpretation" is the usual designation of this activity, whether the interpretation is enacted, as in the performing arts, or set out discursively, as in criticism of all of the arts, including the visual arts. The issue raised by the normative Thesis may therefore be put as determining the conditions under which some interpretations are to be accredited as sound interpretations of the art object and, among these, which interpretation, if any, is privileged. I take no appreciable time to defend my choice of "sound" as the operative adjective or to canvass alternatives. (There are many.[6]) Any word will do that: 1) has a clear connotation of what is valid and therefore authoritative, and of the distinction from the opposite of these, in a sense of validity appropriate in speaking of interpretations; 2) demands or encourages reason-giving in support of the claim to validity; 3) does not restrict validity to one and only one attainable instance of it but rather has the opposite connotation. It may be that the term "interpretation" itself satisfies 3). If it does, that meaning can be annulled by certain adjectives, e.g., "the right interpretation," whereas "the sound interpretation" is odd. Finally, though "sound" is recognizably normative, it is, perhaps, as words of this sort go, relatively bland. It suggests a rather modest, not very importunate normative claim ("he is a perfectly sound historian"). In this respect, too, my choice of the word intimates the conclusions I now want to argue for.

I do so by examining the two conditions of sound interpretation which, more than any other, recur in the recent literature. They are called by some, though not all of these authors, "correspondence" and "coherence." [7]

Though it varies, of course, from writer to writer, the meaning of "correspondence" may be stated substantially as "inclusion within the interpretation of the elements demonstrably present in the art object, without misreading or representing inaccurately any of them, and leaving out none of them." The latter requirement is not simply that binding upon interpretation in general that relevant data must not be ignored. It has an application peculiar to aesthetic interpretation. Interpretation in the service of the aesthetic must, when enacted, consitute a concrete presence out of what it interprets. The same is not true of interpretation of the art object as a cultural or biographical document. Such interpretation issues in a cognitive statement. It is bound only to so much of the object as is thought to be historically revealing. It can, for its purposes, ignore elements of the art object which would be ignored in aesthetic experience because of a lapse of attention. Aesthetic interpretation must be tangent with the full, concrete detail that aesthetic perception will later dwell upon. It is bound to the individual notes and words which, when they are rendered determinate, make up the aesthetic object. By pointing out manifest properties of the art object which have been omitted from some interpretation, it can be shown that and how the interpretation has not been faithful to the object. The interpretation is not of *that* object.

The burden of correspondence falls chiefly, however, on the requirement that the object's elements be represented accurately. The danger of going wrong in this respect is larger and more serious. There are numerous possibilities, among them imputing to the poem imagery inconsistent with the established semantic meanings of its words; the "stock response," triggered by a symbol or image, which forces other elements of the art object into the preconception at the expense of their overt sensory or representational character; [8] simple ignorance or confusion about the directives in a score. But though there are many ways to go wrong, it is, clearly, not also the case that there is just one way to go right. "Correspondence"—a term taken over from another field of philosophy, where it serves a different purpose—has to mean here that specification, e.g., of the duration and loudness of a chord, must be within the limits stipulated in the score. (What kind of specification is required will, of course, vary with each of the arts.) In all cases, however, the limits must be set by elements that are manifestly, unarguably in the object. That they are is not itself subject to interpretation. Otherwise correspondence could not be used to adjudicate among competing interpretations. The limits set to interpretation are, however, typically expansive rather than the reverse. The various soundings of the notated chord have properties the differences among which are, as I suggested previously, anything but trivial, aesthetically. Conventional semantic meanings are consistent with a broad range of images and overtones which they do not, however, enjoin. Any of these "readings" of the word or chord satisfies the joint requirements of correspondence.

The condition of correspondence is not empty. The condition can be met only if the art object is interpreted carefully and knowingly. Correspondence equips us with reasons for rejecting certain interpretations. Even so, it is a tolerant and permissive condition. It has to be, given the peculiar character of the object which requires interpretation.

Correspondence is with the terms of the relations which satisfy coherence. The second condition is imposed by those who advocate it to insure a unity in the interpretation which is more than the additive sum of correspondences with the several manifest elements. We can justly demand of interpretation that it should bring out cross-connections between the elements, show how they nuance each other, and how the anticipatory references set up in some areas are fulfilled in others. Any interpretation which fails to do this job is only a very partially sound interpretation. On this ground—sound interpretation—coherence is an appropriate, even indispensable condition.

It may be imposed, however, on quite another ground. Coherence may be required in order that our aesthetic experience should be as good as possible. The interpretation will thereby meet the demand of aesthetic experience for the fluid but compact unification of its object. The term "coherence" itself shows that the condition lends itself to this use. "Coherence," unlike the axiologically neutral term "correspondence," has been widely used to designate an important kind of aesthetic value.

But we cannot justly employ the condition of coherence as a demand that the object delineated by interpretation be unified. This cannot be a condition of sound interpretation. Some art is bad and some bad art is so because it is incoherent. Where internal connections are promised but not fulfilled, any interpretation which satisfied this condition would not be faithful to the art object. Even if we make room, as I think we should, for the possibility that one and the same art object proves, taken one way, aesthetically coherent, taken another way, aesthetically incoherent, the latter interpretation is not, for that reason, unsound.

Because the two are persistently run together, it needs to be stressed that the desire that our aesthetic experience should be of the greatest possible value, worthy as it is, has nothing, logically, to do with soundness of interpretation. If it were the test of soundness, the interpreter would be entitled to ignore or change about the elements of the art object. Our craving for aesthetic value is, indeed, so insistent that we are often willing to accept, say, deliberate omission of parts of the object, particularly when it is constructed on a large scale. Art objects can be improved upon. But this fact underscores, it does not obliterate the distinction between aesthetic goodness and interpretation that is faithful to the given object. Alternatively, goodness might be taken as a joint condition along with correspondence in this way: of two interpretations which equally satisfy the condition of correspondence, the one is most sound which, when enacted, yields an experience of greater value. This is to grant, however, that the rejected interpretation has also taken exhaustive and accurate account of the manifest elements of the art object. The proposal therefore looks much more like a set of conditions for a rewarding than for a sound interpretation. Finally, the relation between goodness and sound interpretation might be loosened up, as I think it should be, goodness being dropped as a condition. It might still be held that, as a matter of fact, all sound interpretations yield aesthetic objects roughly equal in value and of greater value than those yielded by less sound interpretations. But this is false.

Once we give up its axiological use, coherence is, as I remarked previously, an appropriate demand upon interpretation. In marking the relations within the object (or their absence), it is, like correspondence, required for a comprehensive detailing of the object. But I now want to suggest that coherence can be assimilated even more closely to correspondence.

The familiar instances of unity—thematic meaning, expressive quality, an equipoise of forces—are more often intimated than overt. Only the terms of these unifying relations, the individual episodes or areas, can be said to be given. It is the task of the interpreter to make palpable the "interior numbers" which run between them. How little palpable they are in the art object is evidenced by Mahler's otherwise startling dictum, "What is most important is not in the notes." The imaginativeness of the interpreter must therefore be called upon. If there is latitude in rendering the printed chord or word determinate, there is greater latitude still in elaborating the coherences between them. Indeed, it is the latter decisions which most often raise the nice, probably unanswerable question, whether the interpreter is finding or creating.

If coherence is to recognize and thereby avert interpretive license, it must appeal to properties manifestly and therefore unarguably in the art object. The condition is binding on all interpretations whatever only if there are properties to which all interpretations are responsible, not properties which can just as plausibly be said to be constituted as observed by some particular interpretation. Sometimes we find directives governing large sections or the entirety of the work, e.g., expressive markings, "a comedy." Sometimes the repetition of an element is obvious. Where the overall structure, theme, or mood, are not comparably indicated, they must still rest on visible *points d'appui*. In all of these cases, the interpretation must represent, accurately and exhaustively, the elements of the art object. But this is just the requirement of correspondence. Whether he is fixing the duration of a chord or the meaning of a word, or establishing their bearing on their neighbors, the interpreter has to make a choice within the limits countenanced by the printed chord or word. Indeed, the two choices will generally influence each other. It may be, then, that coherence can be absorbed into the condition of correspondence, distinguishing within it the relational properties of the elements.

I have not urged that correspondence is a tolerant condition and that coherence may be expendable, in order to pave the way for other, more restrictive limitations on interpretation. We are not, presumably, establishing conditions with the purpose of discouraging or, alternatively, of legitimizing a profusion of interpretations. We are, presumably, seeking conditions whose tolerance is approximately congruent with the openness of the art object to interpretation. I urge that permissive conditions are just what we ought to settle for in our theory, not grudgingly, or even gladly, because it will encourage novel aesthetic delights, but just because an art object is not typically the sort of thing that invites a fairly narrow range of readings. The notes, colors, directives, which make each object what it is and identify it as the same object throughout its aesthetic transformations—these elements, concrete and particular as they are, are, in their aesthetic import, broadly indeterminate.

The nature of the interpreted object helps to explain certain notable features of aesthetic interpretation. There are options to be exercised by the interpreter but it is difficult in the extreme to find a point at which these options can be said to be used up. Criticism and performance continue to turn up new interpretations which could not have been even remotely predicted on the strength of thorough familiarity with the art object. They may startle us at first. Yet to say that the interpreter has "found something new" in the art object, though itself a dubious locution, is considerably more often defensible than the charge that he has misrepresented it. Indeed, at the level of recognizably professional performance, interpretation that must be judged clearly unsound is fairly rare. Not that there is any dearth of accusations that some critic or actor or conductor has gotten it all wrong. The fervor of these accusations is, however, no index of their justifiability. I suspect that they often come to little more than the report that the interpretation in question has been found less valuable in aesthetic experience than some familiar alternative. But this fact, I have tried to show, does not support a judgment of "wrong interpretation."

Still, even if we sometimes find a plurality of interpretations, is not my emphasis on this fact misplaced? It has often been said to be the hallmark of the greatest art that it is inexhaustible. Let it be granted that the values of such art cannot be arrayed in a single interpretation. Lesser art, which is to say most art, yields up its significance quite readily. The object wears just one face. On this objection, I would first offer the obvious comment that, if it is true, then it is precisely the art that interests us most which is conceded. How far is the objection true? It would be very difficult to pass on this. There appears to be no paucity of interpretations of art objects commonly placed below the first rank. But my rejoinder is this question, put rhetorically: When can we confidently say that an art object is no longer, in principle or as a relatively assured likelihood, subject to reinterpretation? This is, pretty clearly, the decisive theoretical question, not whether a given object has, in fact, been reinterpreted.

To return, now, to the normative Identity Thesis. Once a multiplicity of admissible interpretations is recognized, the notion of the art object as so precisely and tightly wrought that only the relation to the work of art is locked in, has been given up. On what grounds could that relation be considered privileged? If it is shown that some interpretation diverges from the work of art and overlooks or misrepresents some manifest elements of the art object, then it is for the latter reason, not the former, that it is culpable. If the normative Thesis moves from the truths that the art object would not have been brought into being nor have the properties which it does have, save for its adequacy to the work of art, to the prescription that this genetic fact must be honored in interpretation, then the Thesis seems to reduce to, The most faithful and therefore the privileged interpretation of the art object as it was understood by the artist is the interpretation most faithful to the artist's understanding of the art object. Again, Identity-theorists sometimes make explicit [9] a view more often taken for granted, but which is, in either event, a powerful motive to their belief, viz., that among competing interpretations, one closest to the work of art yields the maximally valuable aesthetic experience. Yet there is no logical connection between these two concepts and that the connection does not always hold even in fact the artist himself sometimes testifies.[10]

So far there seems to me no persuasive reason entitling the interpretation that is tied to the artistic to privilege in the class of sound interpretations. Such a reason must take the form of showing that if we do not consider the art object as product of the creative act, we necessarily miss certain of its crucial properties and so far fail to satisfy correspondence. Were this shown, it would have to be agreed that any such interpretation is unsound and any experience instructed by such interpretation falls short of grasping its object.

The properties now in question, which have not yet been mentioned, are those of the technical skill and of the artist's personality which are the mark of the workman upon his work. Such properties cannot be found in natural objects. They therefore mark the salient distinction in the aesthetic properties of the two classes of objects, which otherwise have in common sensory, formal and affective qualities. The manner of its coming-into-being, which defines "art," is important beyond theory. It makes a difference within our felt aesthetic experience. In the appreciation of art, the percipient enjoys the distinctive sense of personal communion with the artist.

There can be no doubt that this view is widely attested. It results from our feeling that we are "coerced" by the art object, as we are not by a scene or event in nature. Objects of the latter sort can be aesthetically gratifying. Yet they do not enlist and hold perception like art objects. In the confrontation with art, our attention seems to be directed scrupulously along fixed lines; we trace out the energies of form and theme immanent in the object; we follow the lead that is given us. Perception is not now restless, as in much of ordinary experience, nor does it have the freedom afforded it by natural objects. But this shows *that* the object is artistic. We are coerced by the art object because we are coerced by the artist. His purposes have shaped the object toward just this end. These last assertions are not inferential or mediate. A pervasive and dominating feature of the experience is that we feel ourselves caught up in the exercise of the artist's powers. We respond, as our *post facto* judgments show, to his technical resourcefulness and/or the traits of his personality.

Our current question is not whether this experience is widely shared and recorded. Nor is it whether this fact has encouraged those who hold that failure to discern the artist's skill and personality is a failure to take account of crucial features of the art object. The question is how far this fact justifies the normative demand which they proceed to impose on aesthetic interpretation and perception.

The first difficulty is, to put it neatly, that the sense of personal communion with the artist does not entail personal communion with the artist. The feeling may be had where there is no such communion. The feeling may even be, itself, indubitable. Yet given the radical diversity of interpretations, we cannot believe that all of them bring the artist before us. It was not all of these aesthetic objects but only one, the work of art, which he envisioned and approved. So it cannot be the sense of personal communion itself that renders some experience "fitting" or "optimal," for the Identity-theorist. It must be the authentic encounter with the artist and his artistry that does so.

Whether it be the artist's skill or the traits of his character that is in question, what it is taken to be depends upon and varies with interpretation of the art object. Whether the artist was skilful and in what way necessarily involves the ends for which skill was exercised and the problems that it had to meet. Whether the artist possessed largeness of sympathy turns on the predicament of the protagonists and the attitude that is implicitly taken toward them. Differences in ascribing these attributes to the artist, even extending to the ascription of their opposites —instead of skill, ineptitude, instead of sympathy, callousness toward the protagonists—will be as extensive as the differences in specifying form and theme. Some (it may be all) of these ascriptions will be false. The artist did not exercise that skill or display that trait of character, because he did not envision the aesthetic object defined by the interpreters. This does not keep the technical virtuosity or human sympathy from seeming ingredient in the aesthetic object and therefore coercing the observer. But we must say that the interpretations which define these objects are just mistaken. They find what is not there. It is in dealing with the values of artist and artistry that the connection between optimal interpretation and the work of art becomes most clear and inescapable.

The strength of this argument on behalf of the Identity Thesis is not lessened by the practical difficulty of ascertaining what the work of art was like. It was doubtless their ignorance on this score that has encouraged critics and other percipients in their confident ascription of the artistic values.[11] The falsifying evidence has not always, perhaps even usually, been available. The coerciveness of the experience has then been the sole and, though unwarrantedly, the decisive evidence. Still, the normative Thesis is not therefore vitiated. Since the relevant evidence is in principle attainable, when attained we can know which reading of the art object is most authoritative.

At this point, I think it has to be granted, the normative Thesis is markedly cogent. The artistic values can be known only if the work of art is known. Only in this way can these values be correctly ascribed and appreciated. Unless the attributes of virtuosity and personal character are those which actually came into play during the creative process, we are dealing in falsehoods. Or else we are speaking *als ob*, as when we speak of the artistry exhibited by a scene or object in nature. The force of the Identity Thesis at the present juncture is due precisely to the difference between the artistic values and those, e.g., formal structure or expressiveness, mentioned earlier. The latter values are made out by sound interpretation of the art object. They do not involve, logically, any reference to the artist. The expressiveness of the aesthetic object is readily distinguishable from creative self-expression.

I can therefore see no way to avoid the conclusion that if artistic values must be included in interpretation, then any interpretation which does not do so, fails for just the reason given in the normative Identity Thesis. Nor can we doubt that the artistic values have been a major preoccupation of the aesthetic experience of art and of talk about such experience. I see only one way to contest the Thesis here, viz., to deny that any interpretation which does not take account of artistic values is necessarily unsound. Granted that the percipient is often or generally on the lookout for virtuosity. This does not keep us from holding that experience devoid of any such concern is no less authentically aesthetic. And any interpretation which instructs such experience does not misread or ignore and is therefore no less responsible to the manifest elements of the art object.

As good an example as one could find of artistic dexterity is in the transitions from one area or section of the object to another. The Identity-theorist will say, as critical discourse says, that the artist has "managed" these transitions expertly. What will he point to, to justify his praise of the artist? He will point to a shape that is of focal interest in the sculpture, which urges toward and eases into another area, this one different in shape and tactile quality, with no dead spots in between. Or a secondary theme which, though it runs its own course, at the end makes covert harmonic approximations to the main theme, so that the return to the tonic is more a fulfillment than an orthodoxy. Now an attentive percipient has already seen this for himself. He was sensitive to the movement from one area of the wood to another (in one way of viewing the sculpture), the intimations of the tonic. It was not, for this percipient, a case of one thing and then, later, another. His perception has been vigilant and unifying. What he has *not* been aware of, however, is that these transitions were "managed," skilfully or any other way. He does not take the object present to him as an object purposefully created by an artist. This is possible, even if it is unlikely. It is also possible he does not know that the object is an art object. Yet all of the properties to which the Identity-theorist would point, the sensory givens and the suggestions, whether more obvious or more covert, of the formal bonds between them, our percipient has grasped. There has been no lapse in attention, no grossness in discrimination.

Concern for artistic values is another option for authentically aesthetic experience. The manifest properties must again be apprehended, only now in light of the creative process which antedated the present object. At the least, the percipient must bear in mind that the artist faced alternatives and that he selected among them. This invites the familiar though not inconsequential dangers that the object will recede from the center of attention or that it will be used as a springboard for some kind of historical inquiry. If these dangers are averted, however, the properties of the object can be seen as the execution of the artist's choices. The wood might have been shaped otherwise, he might have made the music traverse a series of ponderous and obvious moves to get back to the first subject. His virtuosity can therefore be felt and esteemed.

This kind of viewing brings to bear a special concern with the art object and with a special, restricted class of values. It seems, however, only a loose or an invidious manner of speaking to say that such viewing is "more" discriminating than that described previously. No new detail of the art object has been unearthed, no formal transition has been made out that the other percipient missed. Only now the transitions are perceived and described differently, as "managed." The concern with artist and artistry is a special concern and a legitimate one. It is not, so far as I can see, in any way privileged among the various modes of responsible aesthetic transaction with the art object.

I therefore urge the view, counter-intuitive as I suppose it is, that when an art object is an object of aesthetic perception or interpretation, it is an art object only *per accidens*. There may be certain elements of art objects that have no counterpart in nature, e.g., the scale. Then the workings of these elements within the art object must be understood if the art object is to be understood. By contrast, that the object was the product of telic activity need not be understood, though it *can* be so taken.

Nor will it do for the Identity-theorist to say, yet again, that because the object was the product of telic activity, it must, for that reason, be taken as such. Granted that the object is, precisely, an *art* object. It was so and remains so. That is its defining characteristic. Yet as I have tried to show in several ways now, this does not and cannot legislate for the aesthetic experiencing of the object. Whether a thing is an art object is settled by the manner of its coming-into-being; whether that thing becomes an aesthetic object and, if so, what its significance is found to be, are not settled in the same manner. Indeed, hardly any concept in the whole range of philosophy could show more clearly than "art" how definition is inadequate to explain the existential history of a thing. But it is just this concept which the Identity Thesis has employed to explain what does or what ought to occur during the aesthetic career of the art object.

II

The arguments of sect. I progressively remove the aesthetic from the artistic until the relation between them becomes accidental. In response to the demands of the aesthetic, the creative process recedes in favor of its product, here and now present to appreciation. This object permits of a plurality, apparently open-ended, of sound interpretations.

Even so, there is a large theoretical possibility still to consider, viz., that each of the sound interpretations is partial and complementary to the others. Then the optimum aesthetic experience is that which brings together all these interpretations. Reference to the work of art now drops out. Yet this view is significantly cognate with the normative Identity Thesis just discussed. Both espouse the norm of a single, optimum aesthetic object for every art object. I will therefore speak of *the second form of the Identity Thesis*. (I want to show later that the second form is an outgrowth of ways of thinking that have inspired the more pristine version of the Thesis.)

It is noteworthy that this position commends itself to such a theorist as Professor Stephen Pepper, who has done pioneer work in developing the distinction between the artistic and the aesthetic. The first form of the Thesis is not to be found in Pepper's recent writings. He notes that the artist is not always in full conscious control of the creative process; Pepper shows that the art object is not taken in all at once and that frequent returns to it are generally required; he urges that the object is amenable to different readings.[12] These points effectively impugn the simplistic conception of the aesthetic experience of art as a single-track communication between artist and audience. But though Pepper cites the diversity of experiences had in the face of the art object, he thinks that these ultimately "converge" upon a single "aesthetic work of art." [13] Thus the relation between art object and aesthetic object is one-one.

There is a powerful motive to believe this which has nothing to do with aesthetic theory. We would like to find that different interpretations, which yield different enjoyments of the one object, do not preclude each other. If they can be incorporated, that would be clear gain. It would afford us the "richer" and "fuller" appreciation that is always being talked about. We want, if we can get them, such cumulative interpretations. The question is whether this norm, of theory and practice, is attainable.

We can take better hold of the question if we first deal with different cases from that which it puts. To begin with, the case in which we do not attempt to bring together two interpretations but rather supplement a single interpretation. Some detail in the art object has gone unnoticed; or it has not gone unnoticed, but it has not been made to fit into the interpretation, so that it has remained something of a blind spot; or it has been assigned a meaning within the interpretation but the kinship of that meaning to some other in a distant area of the object has not been brought out. Then the detail is remarked, say, the recurrence of "nothing" at widely separated points in *King Lear*. The text of the play—the art object—does not constrain the interpreter to make much or anything out of this repetition. But correspondence permits him to make of the repetition a formal or thematic connection. And if he holds to a so-called "pessimistic" interpretation of *Lear*, he will welcome remarking the detail and he will point it up in criticism or in staging. Such an interpretation can absorb the finding successfully. The interpretation is recognizably the same, only now it is strengthened. The interpretation is not shattered by the change. Instead, the usual talk about a "richer" or "fuller" experience is here in order.

Next comes the case of uniting two different interpretations. Clear examples do not flock into view, a fact which has a bearing on our question. Happily, Roger Fry has analyzed some examples.[14] These are of the union of interpretations after his fashion, with others that revolve around the representational subject matter of the painting. The viewer's attention can sometimes embrace both the plastic and representational elements, so that they are not distinct for him as they are analytically. The pattern of emphasis and transition set up by the form coincides with that of narrative or dramatic significance. Therefore the same direction of the viewer's attention is traced by both interpretations. The affective qualities of the two sets of elements are closely congruous and therefore support each other. The observer does not oscillate between appreciation of a spatial and a psychological construction. Uniting the two interpretations is appropriately said to give him a greater comprehension of the painting and, again, his experience is "richer" for it. So there is a significant affinity between this case and that of the newly remarked detail, though here two interpretations, each specifying the global quality of the aesthetic object, are in question.

We have it, then, on very considerable authority, that the union of two interpretations or two kinds of interpretation sometimes occurs. Fry also thought, however, that this does not occur universally and that it is, in fact, rather rare.[15] Attention to subject matter almost always obstructs appreciation of form. We should also note that both the formalist and "literary" interpretations of which Fry speaks are, in a clear respect, one-sided. The first studiously ignores, as a matter of theoretical principle, the representational elements which certainly belong to the art object. The polar interpretation ignores the plastic elements. The two interpretations bring together more of the manifest properties of the art object than does either. We can speak, as in the preceding case, almost in additive terms.

Beyond these cases, however, such terms are generally inept. Fry's opinion of the likelihood of uniting interpretations, generalized to all of the arts, turns out to be the truth of the matter.

An interpretation does not normally fail to correspond with any of the elements demonstrably present in the art object. But it seizes upon one of the aesthetic significances that an element might bear and enforces this significance by apposite decisions across the art object. Each element is specifically shaded and each assumes a certain size. A second interpretation will also distribute the stresses and pauses. If we thought to unite the two, we would generally find that the organization constituted by the first reading is not altered but disrupted. The most obvious instance is not uncommon in criticism and performance, viz., when the second interpretation installs climaxes in areas formerly recessive. Not that one can, as we say, "build" climaxes at any point whatever. But there are passages which can be used merely to swell the dramatic progress or else as its culmination. The passage or scene in the art object may be taken in both these ways but not within the aesthetic object. The first decision excludes the second and conversely; so too the entire balance of forces of either interpretation. Yet both interpretations are sound. Neither can be charged with simply missing a feature of the art object. Neither has dropped out the passage, as is sometimes done. The formal and thematic weight of the passage is not, however, overt, like the representation of a doctor at a bedside.

To say of a passage that it is at once dominant and recessive is very like a self-contradiction. The same is not true of the piece of music mentioned earlier which sounds, in various performances, now serene, now grave, now poignant. These predicates are not logically exclusive. In the vocabulary of emotional terms, they are within hailing distance of each other. Yet here too the interpretations resist incorporation for logical reasons. If these qualities are not exclusive, the properties in the sounding of the music on which they depend, are so. The chord is held just this long, the orchestral voices are balanced in just these proportions, to achieve the serenity. A change, slight enough as measured by clock time, puts a new face on the music. With the portentous prolongation of the chord and the accentuation of the darker-hued instruments, the music loses its placidity. There can be no question of adding together these readings. The one determinate sounding of the music precludes the others.

But suppose now that the predicates which describe the formal emphases or any other attributes of the several aesthetic objects are not logically exclusive. Even then, I suggest, the interpretation of an art object usually resists incorporation. Interpretation defines the character of the aesthetic object. It describes or, when enacted, shows us this individuality being shaped and modulated across the unfolding object. All the elements of the object are biased, by interpretive decision, toward the constituting of this character. Its expressive timbre and imagery are peculiar to this object. Verbal labelling and paraphrase do not replace them. Nor would we readily give up one object because there are others whose qualities and meanings are accurately described by similar terms or even the same terms, e.g., "serene." To superimpose a second interpretation, this one, too, detailing an aesthetic individuality, will, much more likely than not, blunt both interpretations. Neither will remain unimpaired. The case is not that of the formalist and narrative interpretations reinforcing each other. Nor is it like two distinct meanings standing alongside of each other, as when we unpack an ambiguous sentence. It is more like two atmospheres being brought together and in consequence warping each other. What results might just possibly be a coherent object for contemplation and it might be rewarding to contemplate. But we cannot then correctly say that we are enjoying the values realized by the first interpretation and those of the second as well. It is not out of lack of imagination or ignorance of the alternatives that the staging of a play renders it either a psychological study or a social commentary. The text often admits of both. Yet dramatic instinct apparently tends to reject one of the alternatives. Otherwise the impact of the chosen interpretation would be dissipated. On our present supposition, it is true that the alternatives are not logically exclusive but it is not, aesthetically, to the point.

Could we not have an interpretation which gives prominence to one pattern of meanings and qualities, say the psychological, while the social meanings hover over the edges of the play? Clearly we can. There are interpretations which exploit this interplay. There are art objects that invite such readings. Yet to note these truths is to recognize their limitations. It is only one kind of interpretation that encourages penumbral significances in the aesthetic object. Other interpretations define objects that are straightforward and sharp-edged, to which the secondary significances would be alien, a discordance of tone and a blurring of outline. To introduce the social commentary, even in a subordinate position, would not be an enrichment of such an interpretation, but the opposite. This does not mean, needless to remark, that there is just one way to mark out a sharp-edged interpretation of the art object. But then that is another reason why the notion of somehow reconciling all legitimate readings is illusory.

To understand why it is illusory, even when the exclusion is not logical, we must consider the aesthetic percipient. An interpretation—this can be shown most clearly where the percipient is already familiar with it—demands of him that he organize his energies of perception, imagination, and feeling into a certain set. He must dwell upon selected features and areas of the object and, in proportion, slight others; he must discern internal connections, both when they are prefigured and when they materialize; he must dispose himself to a certain tone or mood. Another interpretation, not logically inconsistent with the first, makes corresponding though different demands. Attention can be intensified, recall can be expanded, but within the limits of human capacity. An attempt to follow the lead of both interpretations, in all of their intricacy, will shortly approach those limits. Moreover, the pace at which the aesthetic object should unfold will be slowed by its burden of conceptual and formal detail. These details need to get caught up in the movement of the experience; it is not enough to know them discursively. What was wrong with the linguistic exfoliation carried on by the New Critics was not their ingenuity, but their disregard for the difference between critical exegesis and aesthetic perception. Such perception sets conditions which must be honored by any one interpretation and which become the more exigent where an effort is made to incorporate two or more interpretations.

For the above reasons, a conclusion that would, I think, be commonly accepted, simply on the evidence of criticism and performance, were it not that the persisting authority of the Identity Thesis interposes itself against the evidence: the usual relation between an art object and the aesthetic objects elaborated upon it by sound interpretation is, irreducibly, a one-many relation. The second form of the Identity Thesis is untenable because the norm that it holds up is impracticable.

Professor Pepper asserts the second form of the Thesis descriptively, as matter of historical fact, as well as normatively. This position is of less theoretical interest, but it is no less dubious. On which interpretation of the four major tragedies have Shakespearean criticism and performance converged? On which interpretation do they show signs of converging? Given what we know of the history of criticism and performance, is it plausible to expect that they will converge in future? Then, if the empirical assertion is false, we need not have recourse, like Pepper,[16] to the putative biological and cultural similarity of observers, in order to explain why it is true. Rather, we will expect, as the normal state of affairs in art, the appearance of interpretations which cannot be absorbed into extant readings.

Whether descriptive or normative, the second form of the Thesis is clearly distinct from the first. The creative process falls away from Pepper's account and with it the aesthetic object envisaged by the artist. Pepper focuses on the art object. As has been noted, he does not believe that this object is always the product of knowing control. And yet, I want to suggest, Pepper treats the art object as if it were the product of such activity. His conception of the art object is significantly like that of earlier Identity-theorists. For Pepper as well, the aesthetic import of the art object is self-consistent and unitary. Whence his confidence that diversities of interpretation can and will be overcome in a single "aesthetic work of art." Moreover, Pepper remarks that artistic objects, unlike natural objects, have predictable aesthetic effects.[17] So Pepper endows the object with the character that it would have if, as earlier theorists believed, singleness of creative purpose had fixed its aesthetic significance once for all.

I have tried to show that this image of the art object is greatly misleading. Let artistry be as knowing and single-minded as may be. That does not insure that its product will wear just one face. Neither is the usual image of the art object justified, though it has surely been perpetuated, by the fact that our aesthetic experience is often of an object that seems to us defined, articulate, enforcing its own meaning and tone, proudly resistant to alteration. Art objects are malleable. They can be transformed aesthetically.

At this point, let me call your attention to "a paradox, a most ingenious paradox" in the dialectic with the Identity Thesis that we have pursued. I have been arguing the claims of the aesthetic against the artistic. Appreciation is necessarily directed toward the art object, not necessarily toward the creative process or what I have called the work of art. The usual slogans for this line of thinking in recent years have been "the work of art itself" or "the poem as a poem." These slogans were reactions against the vagaries of genetic criticism—intentionalist, biographical, social, etc. So far from preserving the unitary character of the art object, such criticism permitted in practice the intrusion of all manner of irrelevancies. The work of art (in the usual acceptation) was subjected to psychological or historical romanticizing. The work splintered into numerous, often dissimilar objects as a result. The buoyant hope and expectation expressed in the slogans was that the integrity of the work could be restored, once criticism addressed itself to the intrinsic structure of the work. We must now, I think, judge that the hope is unjustified. "The work of art itself," apt though it was as a polemical device, promises too much. The work is *not* self-identical in that mode of its being—the aesthetic—to which the slogans referred. The creative shaping of the art object cannot decide its aesthetic character once for all. But no more can the approach to "the poem itself."

Once we draw the distinction between the work of art, the art object, and the plurality of aesthetic objects elaborated responsibly upon the art object, we can make provision in theory for the liberality and richness of the aesthetic experience of art. We can rid ourselves of the gratuitous constraints upon such experience imposed by both forms of the Identity Thesis. The Thesis is venerable; it is plausible; it therefore runs very deep in educated consciousness. But ideas have historical as well as logical being and though the longevity of an idea may, indeed, generally does exceed its logical right to survive, it must finally give up its hold on the mind. When, but only when the Identity Thesis has done so, we will, as I think, arrive at a view of the aesthetic life at once more realistic and more tolerant.

NOTES

1. *Cf.* Jerome Stolnitz, "On the Origins of 'Aesthetic Disinterestedness,'" *Journal of Aesthetics and Art Criticism*, XX (1961), 131–143.
2. Roman Ingarden, "Artistic and Aesthetic Values," *British Journal of Aesthetics*, Vol. 4, No. 3 (1964), 199.
3. *Ibid.*
4. *The Complete Letters of Vincent van Gogh* (Greenwich, Conn., n.d.), III, 28.
5. *Cf.* R. S. Crane, *The Languages of Criticism and the Structure of Poetry* (Toronto, University of Toronto Press, 1953), pp. 33–34; Leonard B. Meyer, *Emotion and Meaning in Music* (Chicago, Ill., University of Chicago Press, 1956), p. 41; E. H. Gombrich, *Meditations on a Hobby Horse* (London, 1963), pp. 31 ff., 62 ff., 84.
6. *Cf.* Stuart Hampshire, "Types of Interpretation," in *Art and Philosophy*, ed. Sidney Hook (New York, N.Y., New York University Press, 1966), p. 108.
7. Abraham Kaplan and Ernst Kris, "Esthetic Ambiguity," *Philosophy and*

Phenomenological Research, VIII (1948), 415–435; Isabel Hungerland, "The Interpretation of Poetry," *Journal of Aesthetics and Art Criticism*, XIII (1955), 351–359; Stephen Pepper, *The Work of Art* (Bloomington, Ind., Indiana University Press, 1955), pp. 36–40, 56, 72–73.

8. *Cf.* I. A. Richards, *Practical Criticism* (New York, Harcourt, Brace, 1952), pp. 15–16, 240 ff.

9. *Cf.* F. Cioffi, "Intention and Interpretation in Criticism," in *Collected Papers on Aesthetics*, ed. Cyril Barrett (New York, Barnes and Noble, 1966), pp. 164–165. Cioffi holds that this is "usually" the case.

10. *Cf.* Charles Munch, *I Am A Conductor*, trans. Leonard Burkat (New York, Oxford University Press, 1955), p. 52.

11. I take this phrase from Roman Ingarden, *loc. cit.*

12. Stephen C. Pepper, *The Basis of Criticism in the Arts* (Cambridge, Mass., Harvard University Press, 1946), *Supplementary Essay*, pp. 142–171; *The Work of Art*, chaps. I, IV.

13. *The Basis of Criticism in the Arts*, p. 167; *The Work of Art*, pp. 132–133. *Cf.*, however, *The Basis of Criticism*, p. 157, and *The Work of Art*, pp. 59, 104, where Pepper acknowledges incompatible interpretations.

14. Roger Fry, *Vision and Design* (New York, Brentano's, n.d.), pp. 35, 166–168, 268; Roger Fry, *Transformations* (Garden City, N.Y., Doubleday Inc., 1956), pp. 30–31.

15. *Vision and Design*, pp. 300–301; *Transformations*, pp. 13–30.

16. *Cf. The Basis of Criticism in the Arts*, pp. 167–169; *The Work of Art*, pp. 92 ff.

17. *The Work of Art*, pp. 62–65; *cf.*, however, pp. 119–121.

THE ART HISTORIAN'S COMMENTS

H. W. Janson

There are art critics (Sir Herbert Read comes to mind as a distinguished example) who may be said to practice "applied aesthetics"; they judge individual works of art in the light of a comprehensive theory of art (or, if you will, a system of aesthetics). Certain modern artists, too, I suspect, have been influenced by aesthetics; and to the extent that such influence is found in their work they are practitioners of aesthetics. But I think I speak for the overwhelming majority of my professional colleagues in asserting that art historians do not think of themselves as practitioners of aesthetics. We think of ourselves as historians who happen to specialize in the history of the visual arts as others specialize in the history of economics, music, political institutions, or what have you. Our aims, then—or at least our conscious aims—are those of our fellow students of man's past. If some of our methods are unique to our discipline, this merely reflects the particular character of our material; historians of music, or economics, also have certain methods without exact parallel in other fields of historical study.

Still, in one respect art historians *are* concerned with aesthetics: to the extent that art theories have influenced artists and critics, they have influenced the history of art and are thus of interest to art historians. The theoretical writings of Leone Battista Alberti—to cite a specific example—undoubtedly help us to understand some aspects of some works of art created in Early Renaissance Italy, although we often find that the theories are ex post facto, tailored to fit a body of already existing works of art rather than giving rise to these works by inspiring artists to put the theories into practice. I expect that art historians of the future looking back at the 20th century will try to relate the aesthetics of our time to our artistic practice in much the same way. In fact, the outlines of such a relationship can already be perceived. The near unanimity, for instance, with which modern aestheticians proclaim the irrelevance of subject matter—indeed, of representation *tout court*—in painting and sculpture, must be in some way linked to the decay of traditional subjects in these fields since the end of the 18th century and to the artist's growing preoccupation with the "how" at the expense of the "what" of his work. But art historians interested in post-Kantian aesthetics because of its relationship to the art of its time do not accept this aesthetics as valid for themselves. How indeed could we, in the light of 20,000 years of artistic practice, believe with Sir Herbert Read that the development of all art before the 20th century had been constricted by what he terms "the representational fallacy"? We ask ourselves, rather, where he got this strange notion, and we end up with a chapter in the history of ideas that might be titled, "from *ut pictura poesis* to *ut pictura musica*," and which tells us since when it has been possible to believe that all art aspires to the condition of music.

Modern aesthetics, then, does have some practical implications; it has influenced the vocabulary of critics, and these in turn have influenced both artists and art patrons. How significant this influence has been, and how far aestheticians in turn have been influenced by artistic and critical practice, is a legitimate subject of historical inquiry, and one that art historians are better equipped to tackle than anybody else. At this point, I find myself in a somewhat paradoxical position: it is the aestheticians who are the practitioners, who actually formulate theories of art; in relation to what they are doing, I am the theoretician, since I take their formulations and try to understand them in the context of a historic process that embraces both artistic theory and practice. To the extent that I generalize about the relationship of the two (if, for instance, I maintain that art theory always follows changes in artistic practice rather than the other way around), I use the theories of aesthetics as raw materials for a theory of my own, this being, however, a historical rather than a philosophic theory.

There remains one further possibility so far as the art historian's relation to aesthetics is concerned. Somewhat earlier, I said that the *conscious* aim of the art historian is the same as that of all other historians. It is conceivable that he might be influenced by aesthetics without being aware of such influences. And I do not now mean to dismiss this possibility completely. Art historians, after all, constantly have to make judgments of value; we say this picture is better, or more interesting, or more important, than that one. Without such judgments, we should be quite unable to decide what subjects to do research on (and we do have an almost limitless choice) or to come to any conclusions once we had started work on a given project. Why, for instance, has Mannerism been so fashionable a topic among art historians for the past half-century? Such questions are far from easy to answer, for most art historians are not self-conscious enough about their own work to be able to tell us how they happened to choose one line of inquiry rather than another. Moreover, as a scholarly discipline the history of art is too young to have produced much of a historical perspective on itself; inquiries into the history of the history of art are few and far between. Nonetheless we can discern some long-range changes in the "style" of art historians over the past hundred years or so.

In the mid-19th century, art historians tended to be either diggers in archives like Milanesi (whose annotated edition of Vasari's *Lives* remains indispensable) or cultural historians like Burckhardt. Then came the "age of the great connoisseurs" (whose last representative was Bernard Berenson), of scholars with a new sensitivity for individual artists' styles which enabled them to rectify uncounted thousands of traditional mistaken attributions, but with little interest in broader historic questions. Toward 1900, problems of evolution came to the fore, or, more specifically, "problems of form." How to explain the succession of historic styles? Was there an internal dynamic that "inevitably" led from Gothic to Renaissance, from Renaissance to Baroque, and so forth? If the answer is yes, as Wölfflin, Riegl, and others maintained, the history of art was really a history of style, independent of what happened in other fields of human endeavor and *almost* independent of the work of individual artists. "Art history without names," an art history of broad impersonal movements, was much in vogue, and this led to the rediscovery and reevaluation of periods where artists' names were either unavailable or insignificant, such as Byzantine art or the art of the earlier Middle Ages. This preoccupation with form was soon followed by a new concern with subject matter, or iconography. For Aby Warburg and those who followed his lead, the content of a work of art was indispensable for an understanding of its style. In their work, the history of art appeared once again as part of general cultural history, but as an autonomous entity within a larger field rather than as a mere reflection of it. Another attempt to reach the same goal was centered in Vienna: Whereas Warburg traced the link between art and civilization in painstaking historic detail, Dvořák painted the history of art with broad Hegelian strokes as part of a general *Geistesgeschichte*.

These changes of goal and emphasis, and the different values they imply, can be accounted for in part by the evolution (or, if you will, the internal dynamics) of the history of art as a scholarly discipline; in part, they also reflect the changing artistic movements of the time. Thus Wölfflin, for example, might be viewed as a kind of Cézanne among art

historians, and the new importance of subject matter in the iconographic studies of the 1920's and 1930's coincides with the rise of Surrealism. Dvořák and other *Geistesgeschichte* art historians seem related
to Expressionism. Sometimes this correlation works out in surprising detail: it surely is no coincidence that Vermeer was rediscovered by Thoré-
Bürger, an early defender of Manet. In other words, to some extent art
historians restructure the past in the light of present-day events. There is
nothing surprising in this—all historians do it—nor does it invalidate
their findings. Let me add a small instance from personal experience:
Some ten years ago I became interested—I still am—in the exploitation
of chance effects in the art of the past; I found that this was a very old
tradition going back at least as far as Hellenistic Greece. What started
me on this line of research was, generally speaking, the obvious importance of aleatory factors in certain kinds of modern art, such as the
paintings of Jackson Pollock; and, more specifically, a young chimpanzee
named Betsy in the Baltimore Zoo who had been supplied with paints
and canvas and was turning out "pictures" which the layman, and many
critics, could not readily distinguish from the works of Abstract Expres-
sionist painters. I tried to resolve this dilemma by gaining some historic
perspective on aleatory effects in art: were they thought legitimate, and
if so, under what circumstances; were they a matter of theory, of artistic
practice, or both? When I was ready to publish my first paper on the
subject some ten years ago, I discovered that at least two art historians
in Europe had quite independently hit on the same topic, and our
papers came out almost simultaneously. I venture to guess that these
colleagues of mine were acting in response to the same stimulus that
had impelled me toward "chance in art."

I could cite many more instances of the same kind. My point here
is that the values of art historians may be molded by contemporary artistic production but not, so far as I am aware, by aesthetics. Perhaps we
need to allow for a partial exception in the case of the German-Austrian
"formalist" school (Wölfflin, Riegl) and of the *Geistesgeschichte* art
historians, who seem indebted to Hegel, directly or indirectly. But their
Hegelianism derives, I suspect, from Hegel's philosophy in general,
rather than from his aesthetics. It is also conceivable that an art historian will profess to accept this or that brand of aesthetics; if he does, this
conviction is likely to remain without practical consequences. For, as I
have tried to suggest above, any theory of art, no matter how universal
its claimed validity, is likely to be tailored to fit the artistic conditions of
its time and thus to become a strait jacket when projected into the
past.

This dilemma is actually of quite recent origin. Until about two hundred years ago, historians and theorists both viewed the art of the past in the light of present-day aims, so they had no cause for quarrel. Moreover, the very concept of "art" had not yet been invented. There were *the arts*, the mechanical and liberal, but not "art" as a category embracing painting, sculpture, architecture, music, poetry, the dance, etc.; consequently, nobody had any theories about "art" as such; they were always theories about a particular art. Vasari's *Artists' Lives* were not issued under that title, they were the *Lives of the Most Eminent Painters, Sculptors, and Architects,* since the author had no collective term for them at his disposal. Nor was there the term "aesthetics" to denote "theory of art." Unless I am badly mistaken, "art" and "aesthetics" as we use them today were born together toward the end of the eighteenth century. Indeed, aesthetics since Kant rests entirely, it seems to me, on "art" as shorthand for all those countless activities concerned with the creation of beauty, beauty being what painting, sculpture, architecture, poetry, music, the dance, etc., have in common. How far "art" in this technical aesthetic sense has become common parlance is difficult to say. "Art" is also shorthand for painting, sculpture, and architecture (as in "art historian"), and for painting and sculpture alone (as "the art and architecture of India," this being the pattern followed in the titles of the multi-volume *Pelican History of Art*). If aesthetics were confined to "art" in this more limited sense, art historians might find it more meaningful than they do. Unfortunately, it is not. In fact, it is not even about "art" in the broad, all-embracing sense; it is about "beauty," the creation and experiencing thereof, and more particularly the experiencing. The aesthetician's assumption, then, is that painters, sculptors, architects, musicians, poets, etc., all have a common aim: to create something beautiful. And beauty, being the essence of any work of art, can be experienced by the beholder only if that beholder adopts an "aesthetic attitude" (or, to speak with Professor Beardsley, "the aesthetic point of view"), refusing to be distracted by all "non-aesthetic" factors such as subject appeal, symbolic meaning, etc. This ideal, disinterested aesthetic beholder has been with us ever since Kant —but, I suspect, only in the minds of aestheticians. Let us look at some of the examples Professor Beardsley cites in his attempt to make clear that "there *is* something peculiarly aesthetic to be found in the world of our experience." There is, first of all, the conservationist who argues against a power plant beside the Hudson River because of his "aesthetic point of view" toward the Hudson's scenic beauty. Has Professor Beardsley really listened to the conservationist's pleas against that power plant? If so, he has skipped an awful lot of arguments that can hardly be termed "aesthetic": What will the plant do to wild life? Will it pollute the water? How will it affect the recreation areas nearby? Will it attract industry to the site? And so forth and so on. The conservationist's values, it seems to me, are not formal, aesthetic values (such as "the plant will spoil the line of the hills around it") but human values. He argues that people draw spiritual sustenance from unspoiled nature, that we must conserve the wilderness in order to keep urban man from deteriorating still further. He is *not* saying, "this is an ugly power plant," or "it spoils the line of the hills," for Con Edison might then have the plant redesigned so that it *wouldn't* spoil the line of the hills, and the conservationist wouldn't like it a whit better. He objects to any power plant in that spot, not because the spot, or the entire Hudson valley, is uniquely beautiful but because of the social and ethical values he associates with the preservation of wilderness areas near large cities. Nevertheless, we all know there are people who will look at a landscape and exclaim, "how beautiful!" I suspect, in fact, that such a confrontation of man and nature was the original model for "the aesthetic attitude," since it was new and fashionable in the late 18th century to be awed by the Sublime. But when we take a closer look at the places that were regarded as particularly beautiful then, or are now, the beauty of the landscape never turns out to be simply a matter of such "aesthetic properties" as form and color. It is the associations the view evokes which make it beautiful—associations with history, religious sentiment, literature, even painting (as implied by the term "picturesque"). Under some cultural circumstances, mountains are thought beautiful, under others not. It depends not on the shape of the mountains but on the associations they evoke. Thus the ability to find the Alps beautiful is not a matter of aesthetic sensibility but of cultural conditioning. And I rather suspect that the ability to find a painting or a piece of music beautiful is similarly determined by cultural and historic factors. Maybe, then, we are mistaken if we impute to all artists the desire to create "a thing of beauty." Certainly nobody ever said so before the 19th century. Instead, artists were making Madonnas, setting words to music, telling stories; the beauty of these things was a predicate, not something to be extracted by disregarding the subject, or the words, or the story. What I mean by this is that a Madonna was judged beautiful by comparison with other Madonnas, a narrative poem by comparison with other narrative poems, etc.; whereas the aestheticians demand of us that we say, "this Madonna is beautiful *quite apart* from the fact that she is a Madonna" (or, according to Sir Herbert Read, "*despite* the fact that she is a Madonna"). This, I submit, is contrary to human experience. Apparently the nonempirical character of aesthetics does not disturb the aestheticians. It does mean, however, that they can talk only to each other, thus minimizing the practical implications of their theories.

Let me return for a moment to Professor Beardsley's conservationist. The choice of the Hudson River as an example of something toward which it is possible to adopt the aesthetic point of view leads him to the conclusion that the Hudson River is a work of art. He states that "a work of art (in the broad sense) is any perceptual or intentional object that is deliberately regarded from the aesthestic point of view." Since we cannot imagine anything that cannot be so regarded (i.e., that cannot conceivably be pronounced beautiful by somebody under some circumstances), any sense experience is a work of art. Which means that there is no such category as "work of art." I do hope Professor Beardsley will demonstrate that I have misinterpreted him by citing at least one object that is not a work of art. If he sticks to his definition, I do not think he can. I must admit, though, that his conclusion follows logically once we accept "the aesthetic point of view" as something found in our world of experience.

Another of Professor Beardsley's examples, that of Lenin rejecting the aesthetic point of view toward Beethoven's *Appassionata*, again fails to show what he says it does. Lenin objects to the *Appassionata* not because it is beautiful but because it puts him in a benevolent frame of mind at a time when he feels he must "hit people over the head without mercy." This seems to me clearly a *moral* judgment—he might have objected to taking tranquillizers on the same ground. If I were Professor Beardsley, I would have to say that Lenin had adopted the moral point of view toward the *Appassionata*. Yet Lenin, it seems to me, has done nothing of the sort: he responds to the *Appassionata* the way everybody (except perhaps aestheticians) responds to a work of art that genuinely impresses him—with his entire being. It stirs him so profoundly that he feels it commands him to change his entire outlook on humanity, and it is with real regret that he resists this command. He responds, in other words, as Rilke responded to a Greek Archaic head in the Louvre, in a famous poem whose final line is, "You must change your life." To try to disentangle the "aesthetic" from the "nonaesthetic" components in Lenin's response seems to me a task as hopeless as it is unrewarding. We could, however, inquire how it happened that Lenin responded so strongly to this particular piece of music. Aestheticians of a more formalist and normative disposition than Professor Beardsley would try to find the answer in the special qualities of the *Appassionata*; psychologists would probe Lenin's psyche instead. The art historian, on the other hand, would start out by trying to determine how individual Lenin's response really was; and he would find, I think, that a lot of others, especially in 19th century Russia, had responded to the *Appassionata* as Lenin did. Lenin's response, in other words, would probably turn out to be quite a conventional one, determined not by his childhood experiences or similar factors that molded his psyche, but by the traditional pattern of "*Appassionata* appreciation." Which would lead us to the broader question of why it was this particular Beethoven sonata, rather than another, that achieved this special status in the 19th century. Such a question, I think, could be answered, within limits, and it would give us an insight into the history of the Romantic movement as well as into the cultural life of the educated classes in 19th century Russia. But from the aesthetician's point of view, all of this would be irrelevant—I would be "misusing" a work of art as the subject of "mere" historical inquiry.

Professor Kennick, unlike Professor Beardsley, retains the distinction between works of art and "non-works" of art. His argument is with those of his colleagues, such as Maritain and Stolnitz, who maintain that "art-objects are set off from nonartistic objects because of the way in which they were created." He concludes that "we can know whether a work of art is creative, imaginative, or inspired while knowing nothing about the psychology of creation generally or about the psychology of a given creative artist specifically." Hence "the concept of creativity is not a psychological concept." I quite agree. But Professor Kennick's is a Pyrrhic victory, it seems to me. What kind of a concept *is* "creativity"? I can find no clear answer to this question in Professor Kennick's paper, and I suspect it is not a question to which a nonempirical answer is possible. Empirically, I should say "creativity" is a mythic concept that claims an analogy between God, the paradigm of the true creator, and the artist, even though God, by definition, creates *ex nihilo* while the artist does no such thing. The concept was first applied in the 16th century, to and by artists who accepted this quasi-divine status, such as Michelangelo and Dürer. Since then, it has been so cheapened by overuse (we hear not only of new lipsticks "created" by cosmetics experts but of the "creativity" evidenced by children's drawings and even by those of chimpanzees) that the only thing to do is to leave it alone. If we don't, we get into the kind of trouble Professor Kennick makes for himself when he says "we can know whether a work of art is creative, imaginative, or inspired." He thereby implies the existence of noncreative, unimaginative, and uninspired works of art, and in the body of his paper considerable attention is paid to this distinction. "Making," Professor Kennick says, must be distinguished from "creating," with the latter term reserved for "creative works of art." And he cites copies or replicas of works of art as instances of noncreative works of art. For his definition of "creating" he adopts what Miss Meager calls "original activity," which is defined as "an activity not wholly determined by its being mere obedience to specifications already laid down." By "mere obedience" is meant "the execution of specifications without reflective choice between possible ways of carrying them out." At this point, it seems to me, Professor Kennick's devil, having been thrown out the front door, reenters through a basement window. For, if we have to inquire whether or not there was reflective choice between possible ways of carrying out specifications, are we not once again defining a creative work of art by the way it was produced—in other words, psychologically? I submit that it is quite impossible to know whether or not there was "reflective choice" in any given instance, and that it would make no difference if it *were* possible to know. Must we not concede that a copyist (and all artists are to some extent copyists) may be fully determined to produce nothing but a faithful replica while in actual fact he produces something that is clearly distinct from his model? Standards for what constitutes a faithful copy vary greatly through the ages; in medieval times the presence of a few key features was enough, as attested by the countless "copies" of the Holy Sepulchre. We might, in fact, go a step further and maintain that there can be no such thing as a perfectly faithful copy, for if there were we couldn't tell it from the original. But both Professor Kennick and Miss Meager are careful not to test their definition empirically. One instance citied concerns the Chinese painter Wu Tao-tzu, whose work is known to us only from copies. Professor Kennick, faithful to his nonempirical stance, does not ask how the experts in early Chinese painting assess these copies and their relation to the lost originals. Instead, he asks, "suppose that these copies are faithful replicas . . . are they works of art separate from and additional to the [lost] works of Wu?" And he answers, "they are also works of art, but not additional works of art." My own answer would be that any copy is an additional work of art, since no copy can be completely faithful, but that most copies are works of art of a rather low order. It is a matter of degree rather than of "yes" and "no"; such an answer, however, lacks the neatness necessary for philosophical discourse. Professor Kennick's other illustration is adopted from Miss Meager: Suppose that somebody who had no possible way of knowing Browning's poem, "Pippa Passes," happened to independently compose another poem that agrees word for word with Browning's? He concludes that the second poem would not be a copy of the first, since both resulted from creative acts. My own conclusion is that this hypothetical case teaches us nothing since it is outside our realm of experience, like the famous story of the chimpanzees pounding typewriters at random and ultimately producing all the books in the British Museum. I should like to see Professor Kennick and Miss Meager cope with the philosophical implications of that one.

Let us now return for a moment to Professor Kennick's and Miss Meager's "original activity" or "creative act." Since the only "unoriginal activity" they acknowledge is that of making a perfect copy and nothing but a copy of a given original; and since perfect copies do not exist, it would seem to follow that even the copyist is performing an original act and that hence all human activity results in creative works of art. But if everything is creative, then "creative" as a distinguishable category ceases to exist. Still, Professor Kennick's definition of a work of art is more restrictive than Professor Beardsley's: it must be the result of human activity, he claims, and he drives home this point by declaring that the statement, "[t]his piece of driftwood is a lovely piece of sculpture," is as senseless as "[t]his dog is a very efficient automobile." He might have chosen a more persuasive example; a dog, after all, may be viewed as an internal combustion engine whose chief purpose is locomotion on the ground, and thus a possible model for an automobile with legs rather than wheels. The sentence seems to me no more senseless than saying, "this bird is a very efficient aeroplane." As for the statement about the piece of driftwood, the fact is that for thousands of years natural objects of certain distinctive shapes *have* been collected as works of art. Here, I am afraid, Professor Kennick is as dogmatic as Sir Herbert Read with his "representational fallacy." Apparently he conceives of the process of "making" or "creating," at least in the visual arts, as a physical shaping of materials.

That indeed is what is usually involved, but not always. The Japanese who finds an odd-shaped rock that resembles a miniature mountain landscape and displays it in his home; Marcel Duchamp's "readymades" (such as the urinal he exhibited with the title *fontaine*); Picasso combining a bicycle seat and handlebars into a bull's head; all these are instances of the creative act as a process of discovery or selection, with physical manipulation reduced to a minumum. I think Professor Kennick will concede that at least Picasso's *Bull's Head*, of the examples cited, is a work of art; yet Picasso made neither the bicycle seat nor the handlebars; all he did was to put one on top of the other, an act so simple that he might have directed a child to do it for him. Yet it was clearly Picasso and no one else who created the *Bull's Head*.

In deducing from Professor Kennick's paper that in his view all human activity except the making of a perfect replica is an "original activity" and hence results in a work of art, I may have done him an injustice. There is a tacit assumption in his discourse that we all know what works of art are; he excludes the products of nonhuman agents, but, so far as human activities are concerned, he differentiates only between "works of art" and "creative works of art," not between "works of art" and "non-works of art." Certainly his concept of originality as the hallmark of "creative works of art" does not help us to distinguish art from non-art, since it is of a very low order. "Painting a picture," he says, "resembles uttering a sentence" (or, as he prefers to call it, "performing a locutionary act")—*ut pictura prosa* rather than *ut pictura poesis*. We further learn that speech acts are among the most familiar examples of original acts: "much of what each of us says in the course of his life is in some way unlike anything anyone else has said." If, as the context suggests, Professor Kennick is here referring to the everyday speech of the average man, he is in my view wildly optimistic. Nothing seems to me more stereotyped than everyday speech. But suppose Professor Kennick were right: would this mean that "much of what each of us says in the course of his life" must be classed as poetry? A strange and flattering notion! The simile does show, however, that Professor Kennick's criteria of originality are not very demanding. A product of a human act is "original," hence "creative," so long as it does not wholly resemble another and earlier such product. Apparently Professor Kennick puts no limits on the standards by which we determine resemblance; we can choose to make them as exacting as we please. It would be an easy matter to refine them to a point where we can pick two nails out of a barrel and demonstrate that one is not a perfect replica of the other. Have we thereby shown that they must be the products of original acts, that is, works of art? I am sure Professor Kennick would deny this. But he does not help us resolve our dilemma, especially since he explicitly admits the possibility of works of art being created unintentionally or incidentally, which would surely be true of our two nails.

The idea that works of art can be created unintentionally or incidentally is a very old one, its paradigm being the Greek painter Protogenes, who in a rage hurled a dirty sponge at his picture and thereby achieved a pictorial effect he had been trying in vain to produce by conscious effort. Professor Kennick's way of illustrating the concept is rather less persuasive, however. "It is at least doubtful," he says, "that the sculptors of those great Egyptian statues of gods intended to produce works of art as well as idols." I think Professor Kennick's doubts can be set at rest; we *know* that the Egyptian sculptors could not possibly have intended to produce works of art, because the Egyptian language lacked a term for "works of art" in Professor Kennick's sense. If we could ask them, they would undoubtedly reply that they intended to make the image of a god, and hopefully a good one, otherwise the god would refuse to dwell in it. The possibility of producing an idol that is not a work of art would have struck them as incomprehensible. And I must confess it strikes me the same way. But I trust Professor Kennick will be able to show us at least one idol that is *not* a work of art, since he clearly shares Sir Herbert Read's faith in the "representational fallacy."

This dismembering of works of art by conceptual surgery is more successfully practiced in Professor Stolnitz's paper. Not only does he enjoin us to be concerned only with the intrinsic nature of the work of art, ignoring its relations to other things, such as its history, lest our attitude not be truly aesthetic; we are especially warned against the danger of making the work of art a springboard for some kind of historical inquiry. There is nothing unexpected about this doctrine of "Ask not for whom the bell tolls; concentrate on the music." But Professor Stolnitz splits up the work of art in yet another way. It is really two objects: the canvas, sculpture, printed poem, musical score, he proposes to call "the art object"; and that which is antecedent to them in the artist's mind, and which is immanent within or realizable by means of the "art object," he terms "the work or art." Finally, there is a third object, the "aesthetic object," which is what the art object constitutes for the beholder. I must confess that I find this novel use of the term "work of art," in a sense so different from its established meaning, a bit perverse. It makes the reading of Professor Stolnitz's paper inordinately difficult; the terminology becomes a kind of code, where "red" means "blue" and "blue" means "ultraviolet" (an invisible color). Yet I find a kind of symbolic significance in this choice of terms: "work of art" sounds superior to "art object," and so it appears to be in Professor Stolnitz's conception. Though invisible and inaudible, it is the primary phenomenon, accessible to us only more or less imperfectly through the "art object." Its relation to the "art object" would seem to be analogous to that of a Platonic idea to its material (and hence necessarily imperfect) embodiment. Professor Stolnitz's main concern, however, is with the relation between the "art object" and the "aesthetic object." He argues, with great subtlety and logic but on an almost entirely nonempirical plane, against those of his colleagues who hold that this is a one-to-one relation, and he propounds the view that a single "art object" can give rise to an indefinitely large number of "aesthetic objects," all of them arrived at by equally sound interpretation. "Art objects are malleable. They can be transformed aesthetically." Such is his conclusion. And he expresses the hope that it "will help us to arrive at a view of the aesthetic life at once more realistic and more tolerant." By "aesthetic life," I assume, he means the sum total of all acts of "sound interpretation." That his view is more tolerant (within the—to me intolerable—limitations of the "aesthetic attitude") I readily admit. I also concede that it is more logical. But more realistic? The claim strikes me as odd, since Professor Stolnitz's arguments are so very largely theoretical, with only a few passing references to specific "art objects." If, as he asserts, any given "art object" is malleable and capable of giving rise to an unlimited number of competing "aesthetic objects," all with an equal claim to validity, the "art object" itself stands in grave danger of being obscured by its vast progeny of "aesthetic objects," and this, presumably, makes it that much harder to perceive the relationship between the "art object" and its impalpable progenitor, the "work of art." Perhaps a bit of birth control would not be out of place here.

The trouble with Professor Stolnitz's view of what he calls "the aesthetic life" is the imbalance between his need to draw distinctions among "objects"—he has three where I am content with one—and his refusal to draw any distinctions among the *beholders* of works of art. These always figure in his discourse as a single entity, usually termed "the percipient." Who is this percipient? Apparently, he exists independent of time and place, varying only in his individual aesthetic sensibility. Such a percipient, I submit, is like the Man Who Knows Nothing About Art: a myth. Can we really doubt that a given beholder's response to a work of art is significantly affected, not only by the qualities of that work of art and of his individual psyche but by his cultural milieu? As soon as we admit this historical dimension, things become manageable, and we can begin to arrange Professor Stolnitz's undifferentiated mass of "aesthetic objects" (i.e., interpretations of works of art) in some sort of intelligible rank order. We would then think, not of "the percipient" but of many particular audiences, from the artist's own time to the present, audiences whose responses can be analysed in terms of their specific circumstances. But that is exactly what modern aesthetics will not let us do, because it would mean opening the floodgates that have kept empiricism out of the aesthetician's idealistic little domain.

I have placed Professor Weitz's paper last in my sequence of comments, since it deals with a subject that is not only far more specific than those of the other speakers but also of direct relevance to art historians. The title, "Genre and Style," seems to me not entirely apt; the bulk of the paper is devoted to a discussion of the concept of style, and Professor Weitz's opening and closing remarks on the difference between genre and style concepts hardly break new ground. His main question is whether or not art historians practice what they preach regarding style, as demonstrated in their treatment of Mannerism. Professor Weitz very properly distinguishes causal theories, i.e. theories about changes of style, from definitions of style. Only the latter concern him here. But since there is, as he notes, a great paucity of such definitions, he has adopted a method that strikes me as less than perfect: he takes four definitions of style (by Schapiro, Ackerman, Hauser, and Gombrich) and matches them against the performance, not of the authors of these definitions but of various other art historians who have written about Mannerism (Walter Friedlaender, Dvořák, Lionello Venturi, Smyth, Shearman, Freedberg). Inasmuch as the definitions are far from alike, it would have been more instructive to test them against the practice of those who coined them (Hauser and Gombrich have written at length about Mannerism). After all, Friedlaender, Dvořák, Venturi, Smyth, Shearman, and Freedberg might not share any of the four definitions, individually or collectively.

According to Professor Weitz, the definitions of style he cites claim, or at least imply, that style is a logically closed concept, amenable to a true definition in terms of necessary and sufficient criteria, while art historical practice reveals Mannerism to be a logically open concept, "irreducibly vague" as Professor Weitz puts it, since it lacks definitive criteria. Schapiro's, Ackerman's, Hauser's, and Gombrich's definitions of style are all inadequate in the same fundamental way, we learn, because they leave out the irreducible vagueness of at least one style concept, i.e. Mannerism. In his opening remarks, ProfessorWeitz states that one assumption about the concept of style is invariant, namely, that it is definable in the Aristotelian sense and that without such a definition the concept cannot sustain its assigned role. Many art historians, he claims, concur in this doctrine and direct much effort to formulating theories of style. No evidence is cited for this generalization, and a little later Professor Weitz admits to the paucity of definitions of style among art historians (as distinguished from causal theories, which are less rare but are irrelevant to our purpose). The prevalence, in theory if not in practice, of a logically closed concept of style among art historians could hardly be proved from the four definitions cited, even if it were beyond dispute that Schapiro, Ackerman, Hauser, and Gombrich all subscribe to the "closed" concept of style. But do they? Schapiro's definition is the briefest: "By style is meant the constant form—and sometimes the constant elements, qualities, and expression—in the art of an individual or a group." Ackerman's definition can be regarded as a paraphrase of this. (The rest of Ackerman's discussion of style is a causal theory of changes in style and hence does not concern us.) Schapiro's (and Ackerman's) definition of the concept of style might be termed too brief, too vague to tell us how the concept operates in art historical practice. I fail to see, however, that it implies a logically closed concept of style. In saying that "by style is meant . . . the constant elements . . . ," Schapiro surely does not exclude the simultaneous presence of changing elements, nor does he imply that any single form element (such as the pointed arch) or group of elements constitutes definitive criteria for a given style. It is a question of which elements—the constant or the changing ones—seem more important in a body of material. Hauser's definition of style as "a dynamic relational concept with continually varying content" or, elsewhere, as "a figment, an image, an ideal type [which] a work of art . . . seems to be striving to achieve," can be objected to on various grounds, but how does it imply a logically closed concept? In fact, Professor Weitz quotes Hauser as admitting that "there is no such thing as a clear and exhaustive definition of mannerism, but the same complaint can be made of every other style, for there is and can be no such thing." As for Gombrich, he offers no definition of style. Such a definition, he implies, would have to be based on a theory of style, and he denies that there is any such thing at present. "Neither normative criticism nor morphological description alone will ever give us a theory of style," he writes, and adds, "I do not know if such a theory is necessary." Gombrich does, however, generalize about the way art historians use stylistic categories: they have the character of hypotheses, to be tested in observation and to be discarded if they prove unsuitable. He does not claim that this is how *all* art historians actually use these categories; it is, he implies, the sound way to use them, and a good many scholars do this. Others, especially those who have formulated the concept of Mannerism as it stands today, have not followed the prescribed empirical method, and as a consequence have failed to realize that their concept of Mannerism does not fit the facts. Gombrich suggests the need for a radical revision of the present concept so as to make it fit the facts better. According to Professor Weitz, Gombrich also states that all concepts of style are "hypothetical blends of norm and form." This, it seems to me, is an unwarranted inference; Gombrich clearly limits his claim regarding the hidden normative element in stylistic categories to those concepts that began their career as terms of critical abuse (e.g., Gothic, Baroque, Impressionist) or praise (Classical, Renaissance). Many, but by no means all, stylistic categories belong in this class, and Gombrich admits that "up to a point . . . our belief [that we can use them in a purely neutral, descriptive sense] is justified." I can find nothing in Gombrich's discourse to bear out the assumption (which, according to Professor Weitz, Gombrich makes) that definitive criteria can be stated for the correct use of all—or some—style concepts. Indeed, I suspect that Gombrich will be horrified to discover that such a view has been imputed to him. What he actually says, then, may be summed up as follows: *all* style concepts ought to be used by art historians (but not necessarily by others, such as art critics) as hypotheses that must prove their viability by the test of observation. *Some* style concepts are blends of norm and form, at least in theoretical discussions of their limits. Incidentally, these quasi-normative style concepts are a tiny minority among the stylistic categories now in use, even though they have received the bulk of attention by the proponents of causative theories of style. Examples of non-normative style concepts are those named after rulers (Augustan, Hadrianic, Carolingian, Ottonian, Louis Quantorze), places (Byzantine), peoples or tribes (Punic, Iberian, Saxon, Viking—only Gothic is value-charged), and, so far as I can see, all stylistic categories of non-Western art. Non-normative also, with a few exceptions, are the styles of individual artists (e.g., the style of Donatello); it should perhaps be emphasized that the latter, too, are hypotheses, to be verified, adjusted, or discarded empirically (by weeding out fakes and wrong attributions, and admitting correct attributions to the master's oeuvre).

If, then, Schapiro, Ackerman, Hauser, and Gombrich are not "guilty as charged"—and there is, I think, at least a reasonable doubt on that score—whose "invariant assumption" that all style terms are logically closed concepts is Professor Weitz combating? He would, I believe, find few art historians willing to quarrel with his conclusion that of the criteria so far proposed for Mannerism none are necessary, none sufficient, none definitive. But neither are there many art historians who would find this conclusion surprising. That Mannerism is the most problematic among current style concepts has long been a matter of common knowledge. Hence the recent "reductionist" discussions of the style by Smyth and Gombrich. An adequate account of its vicissitudes—Professor Weitz's is a mere sampling of the vast literature—would fill a book. I wonder, therefore, whether Professor Weitz's findings have any implications, practical or otherwise, for art historians. That the concept of Mannerism is irreducibly vague, he claims, "does clarify many of the fundamental disagreements among the historians of Mannerism." It does so, I think, only to the extent that we can now say, "they disagree because the concept is vague," instead of "because they disagree, the concept is vague." How much of a gain this represents I must leave to the aestheticians to decide. Somewhat surprisingly, the vagueness of the concept in no way discourages Professor Weitz from continuing to assume that Mannerism is in fact a style in sixteenth century art. He terms the concept "beneficially vague," because without this vagueness no new interpretations of Mannerism would come into being, which would be a pity, since each is a new way of inviting us to look at works of art. I find this tolerance refreshing, but also dangerous. Does Professor Weitz really welcome *any* new interpretation of *any* style concept, no matter how arbitrary, because it invites us to look at works of art in a new way? He hedges a bit here, it seems to me. Near the end of his paper, he expresses a belief that some other style concepts, such as High Renaissance and Baroque or Gothic, are also irreducibly vague, while others, including Impressionism, Cubism, or Abstract Expressionism, are not. In other words, he would welcome new interpretations of High Renaissance, Baroque, and Gothic, but not of Impressionism, Cubism, or Abstract Expressionism. (I think it a safe bet that he will get them just the same.) Does this mean that Professor Weitz feels the need for two definitions of style, one for the irreducibly vague concepts and another for the rest? Might the views of Schapiro, Ackerman, Hauser, and Gombrich perhaps do for Impressionism, Cubism, and Abstract Expressionism? My own view is that the concept of style employed by art historians is incapable of adequate definition. The reason will, I think, be obvious as soon as we settle down to defining, let us say, Rembrandt's drawing style of the 1640's, this being about as circumscribed and unproblematic a style concept as we can hope to find. We assemble the "safe" drawings, preferably signed and dated ones; scrutinize the formal qualities they have in common; and try to assemble a list of definitive criteria, being very careful to exclude any formal qualities that our group of drawings shares with other drawings by the master, say of the late 1630's and early 1650's; with drawings of the 1640's by Rembrandt pupils; or with later imitations of Rembrandt drawings of the 1640's, including modern facsimile reproductions. By this time, I think, we will have broken out in a cold sweat; the criteria, we realize, are so subtle that we despair of finding words for them. If this example smacks too much of connoisseurship for you, let us take a less individual one, say the Decorated style of English Gothic architecture. How can we set down formal criteria for it that will effectively exclude not only all other styles of Gothic architecture but also any possible Neogothic imitation of the Decorated style? The irreducible obstacle here is always that visual experiences resist translation into concepts. Yet style concepts, while impossible to define, can be demonstrated readily enough by visual comparisons combined with explanatory or evocative verbalization. There is no dearth of issues in art history that need clarification—on this every art historian will agree with Professor Weitz—but the definition of the concept of style is not one of them. Causal theories of style are another matter. They, however, concern the philosopher of history, rather than the aesthetician.

COMMUNICATIONS AND THE ARTS: A PRACTITIONER'S NOTES

Clifton Fadiman

I

In any field of practical endeavor subject to philosophical survey the mere practitioner is low man on the intellectual totem pole. The quotidian nature of his activity tends to cut him off from fruitful meditation upon it. Indeed, it may be perilous even to attempt meditation. He may find himself in the position of the philosophical centipede who remained incapable of movement because he could not decide which leg to move first. (That centipede would have made a fine pet for Zeno the Eleatic.)

I hope you will forgive the sounding of the autobiographical note when I say that my embarrassment in appearing before this learned body is doubled by the circumstance that I am not only a mere practitioner but one as thinly spread as the best margarine. I have mis-spent my life communicating, or at least sending up signals. There are few media into which I have not intruded, from the profession of teaching to what I suppose might be its polar opposite: advising Hollywood on what movies to make. A shameful confession, but the ugly fact remains that I have a more varied superficial acquaintance with the media of communication than have most Americans of my generation. That such acquaintance leads to wisdom is doubtful. One remembers Coleridge likening experience to a lantern attached to the stern of a boat, illuminating only the waters we have passed.

Currently I am a practising encyclopaedist. An encyclopaedist is a communicator who has built his business on a capital foundation consisting largely of impudence. He judges, revises and rearranges in all fields of knowledge the work of those who know more than he does. The consequence is, as another encyclopaedist, Frank Moore Colby, once put it: he is "snubbed by the learned and yet not welcomed by the totally illiterate."

This sketch of my murky, if not sinister, background must have made clear to you that I have been too busy floundering in the ocean of communications to have had any chance to work up a chemical analysis of the water. I am incompetent in general philosophy and, of the particular arts of rhetoric, logic and dialectic, possess but an undergraduate's knowledge. I can offer only some unsystematic notes on the current and probable future condition of communications and the arts, and of the tensions between them. Should one or two of these notes prove interesting to the theoretician, I shall feel that I have not entirely wasted your time.

Anthropologists today are rather skeptical of the vague notion that all past cultures have passed from a predatory to an agricultural economy. But that *some* cultures have done so is probable. Let us then hypostatize a moral philosopher plying his trade during the period just preceding the transition from a hunting to an agricultural culture. Reflecting upon the nature of man, would not our skin-clad philosopher tend to list as dominant and permanent such human traits as a tendency to migration, a tendency to the predatory, a tendency to create basic communities consisting of small family groups, a tendency to live for the day only, and so forth? He would probably *not* tend to conceive of those traits that the succeeding era of agriculture would stimulate: economic foresight, the urge to create large communal units, the urge to accumulate goods, the tendency to attach one's self to the local soil, and so forth.

I am merely restating a cliché when I suggest that at this very moment man is undergoing a cultural transformation far more dramatic and thorough than that associated with the passage from a hunting to an agricultural economy. To employ the usual formula, we are shifting from an industrial to a post-industrial culture. As the biophysicist J. R. Platt has put it: "The present generation is the hinge of history. We may now be in the time of the most rapid change in the whole evolution of the human race, either past or to come." The society of the immediate future—we are already living in its embryo—has been labelled sensate by the late Professor Pitirim Sorokin. It will be technology-oriented, secular, hedonistic and above all efficient. I say, will be; but of course this is a hypothesis. All I am suggesting is that if there is any truth in this hypothesis, that truth might affect your consideration of the nature of communications and the arts—unless one takes the position that these phenomena have essences in no way contingent upon social and psychological changes or mutations.

Let me propose what may seem a simplistic analogy. In a world consisting entirely of blind men, communications and the arts would surely assume forms radically different from those we are familiar with; and consequently, speculation upon these forms would probably be different from the speculation with which our philosophical tradition makes us familiar. A similar situation would result if some techniques were discovered making possible the universal development of extrasensory perception.

The question is, Are the changes now taking place in man's external environment, as well as what Claude Bernard called his internal environment, of an order at all comparable to that suggested by my two melodramatic analogies? Let us look about us. The murderer, they say, tends to return to the scene of the crime. And so, wishing to find out about something, I first turn to the Encylopaedia Britannica, for which I work.

The 1911 edition contains *no* entry for Communication or Communications, in itself a fact of some interest. The 1967 edition, however, contains a rather long article. Reading it, you quickly discover that by communication the writer means *mass* communication. That too is a fact of some interest. The article does not deal with the most mysterious and up to recently the most important form of communication, which is soliloquy, or communication with one's self, or, more simply, thought. That presumably lies within the province of the psychologist and philosopher. The article does not deal with single-person-to-single-person communication, although dialogue is traditionally one of communication's canonical forms. It does not deal with communication within a discrete group, such as the family. Except for a few words on the effect of the mass media on the schools, it does not deal with what we normally consider the most socially creative form of communication—that is, education. Finally, though they are often conceived as the crown of man's communicative endeavors, it does not deal with the arts.

It deals only with the mass media and their effect on certain contemporary institutions. And I would suggest that this apparent constriction of vision is actually a reflection of the fact that communication of all sorts tends increasingly to approach the condition of mass communication or at least to utilize the technology of mass communication. We may put the matter in Darwinian terms: All signals involving the use of technology and having the potential of wholesale diffusion tend to be favored in the struggle for survival. All signals ill-adapted to technology and wholesale diffusion tend to be handicapped in the struggle for survival. The author of the Britannica article is not wearing blinders. He is observing the prospect before him, that of a post-industrial society.

This audience is engaged professionally in an activity once shared by many amateurs. I refer to thinking. Solitary reflection, however elementary, was not unfamiliar to the average sensual man of seventy-five years ago. He introspected, retrospected, meditated, day-dreamed, prayed, kept journals and diaries, wrote long letters to friends and relatives (all these are forms of communication with one's self), not because he was by nature more reflective than his average sensual descendant of today, but because his pre-electronic environment permitted, sometimes even encouraged, such an activity.

Today this is apparently decreasingly the case, and the philosopher of communications may wish to note the fact. It has been asserted that 90 percent of Americans receive 90 percent of their information about the world from TV. In our country 28 percent of all leisure time is spent watching television. As technology forces more leisure time on the unprepared mind, it fills that leisure time with ever-multiplying supplies of mass-signals. Hence we may expect the 28 percent figure to increase. Another 12 percent of our leisure time is spent receiving the signals of all other mass media combined. In a culture so dominated by mass communication, communication with one's self is apt to be handicapped in the struggle for survival.

Accordingly, internally generated reflection tends to become monopolized by mandarin societies. These societies transmit their signals exclusively to an in-group. The thought is isolated within the in-group. There is no osmotic membrane through which the ideas this audience, for example, is concerned with, can pass, and reach the commonalty in any really effective form. For example, in my own small field of literary criticism Virginia Woolf's Common Reader can no longer be served, as he was served only half a century ago. Literary criticism, because its nature hinders adaptation to the mass media, is today as professionalized as symbolic logic, even though its subject matter is theoretically the common thought and feeling of mankind.

Some ideas, of course, do reach the average man. But mass communication has its own patterns of rhetoric, which it cannot help imposing on the original message. One of these patterns involves the paradigmatic signal of our time, which is the text-and-picture advertisement of the TV commercial. All mass-media signals, including political speeches and round-table discussions, tend to approximate the rhetorical form of the commercial, which is why aspirants to political power employ advertising firms. The mass media for example, cannot help taking a system of ideas—say the New Theology—and turning it into a set of phrases that are in essence advertising slogans. As Wendell Willkie once said, "A good catchword can obscure analysis for fifty years." No morality or immorality is here involved: it is merely the nature of the animal—or of the machine.

In thinking about mass communication it is sometimes difficult to determine not *who* is communicating, but *what* the who *is*. Is it an *individual* who is speaking to us or writing at us? Or is he a locus of forces, a resultant rather than a person? The mass-communicator who is an in-basket for the greatest flow of information about what people want to hear, who possesses a plastic talent enabling him to change personae quickly and efficiently, and who can lend himself to the technological requirements of the medium is apt to be successful. In a way the effective mass-communicator, whether he be a standup comic or a Ronald Reagan (perhaps I have chosen insufficiently contrasting examples) is as much a part of the technological process as are Hertzian waves themselves. We can locate the point of origin of a mass-signal; but to determine the essential *character* of that point of origin is more baffling.

We the public are not only resigned to the ambiguity of the situation, we accept it as given. Thus, when we say of Mr. Nixon that he is successfully "changing his image," we are in effect affirming our feeling that a man *is*—and legitimately—a construct or assemblage or series of images. The corollary is that we become accustomed to judging a signal not in terms of its real content but in terms of its dramatic effectiveness, as we judge a lively visual commercial. Thus, and especially for the young, the scenes of real bloodshed and violence, which for the next thirty years or so are bound to dominate the mass media, are absorbed as more or less interesting examples of play-acting. The entire Martin Luther King drama, while a tragedy in essence, was transmitted and received as a national spectacular.

Other things happen to mass-messages. We have noted that, passing through the medium, some are changed, as light is bent passing through a liquid. It may even happen that a signal will arouse a response exactly contrary to that intended: a great many children are asking their fathers for bad breath because they hear it advertised. But many signals arouse no response at all in the receiver simply because of their frequency and omnipresence. The outstanding characteristic of mass communications today is not the technical marvel of its organization, but simply its amount. What technology *can* do, it *will* do. It can create virtually a world plenum of signals; it is on its way to doing so. The novelist Henry Fielding once remarked that if God in his wisdom should for the space of twenty-four hours freeze all phenomena, arrest all movement and change so that *nothing* could happen, nevertheless the very next day the *London Times* would appear in a complete edition.

In the same way radio and television must fill all the available time and reach all the available receivers whether or not the message has content. *Time* magazine must appear fifty-two times a year and be of a certain minimum thickness whether or not anything has happened worth recording.

The frequently noticed consequence of this wholesale manufacture and diffusion of signals is that we are over-informed and consequently, as we say, confused. The over-informed organism responds somewhat liek the over-stimulated laboratory rat. It may retreat into catatonia or violence or dementia. Many shrewd observers are already saying that part of our difficulty in Viet-Nam is the consequence of what has been termed "informational glut."

On the other hand a precisely opposed conclusion is drawn by the television industry itself. I noted recently a full-page ad sponsored by the broadcasters and headed: "All wars are ugly. Why do we bring you closer?" It continued with pride: "All feel the impact of this steady stream of news reports, analysis and in-depth special programs. And, as a result, our society has never been better prepared to make its decisions. Not only about the war but also about race relations, the economy and politics." I leave it to you to determine whether the copiousness of the information with which we are so generously supplied is or is not in direct relation with an increase in our ability to make correct decisions.

Parenthetically I might suggest to philosophers of communication that the news glut we have just mentioned may be merely a special case of a more general condition. Physiologists are now wondering whether certain allergies and other nerve reactions in city-dwellers may not be due to the inaudible low-frequency noises that unintermittently beat upon their ears. Others warn us of the eye degeneration that may be caused by neon signs and other continuously obtrusive visible signals. Are such mundane matters worthy of your attention? Perhaps the moral philosopher might wish to reflect on the value-issues bound up in the proposition: Thou shalt not send each other too many messages. As one who has spent his life communicating, I often recall the words familiar to you from the *Phaedrus*, in which the Egyptian Thamuz scorns the inventor of the alphabet: "This invention of yours will create forgetfulness in the learners' souls because they will not need to use their memories . . . they will appear to be omniscient, and will generally know nothing." Now I think the alphabet, despite the MacLuhanatic energy with which it is being attacked, will continue to be a useful tool; but perhaps there exits an optimum limit to that use.

At the moment the imperative of an accelerating communications technology tells us that to set any limit is not only impossible but subversive. I feel a certain timorousness therefore in submitting a formula that may not go down in history with Parkinson's Law but may nonetheless at least be worth refuting. "Fadiman's Law" runs thus: The integrity of a signal varies inversely with the complexity of the signalling device.

If you will again pardon the intrusion of autobiography, I will illustrate from my own practical experience. I started in the communications business as a teacher. In this simple face-to-face, mind-to-mind situation I enjoyed the maximum freedom consistent with decorum and the necessity of teaching students enough to enable them to pass examinations. When I took the first step downward to radio—*facilis descensus Averno*—my audience increased from thirty to several millions. The factors limiting my freedom of communication also increased. They included: a fixed station, with the mouth a specified distance from the microphone; the necessity for split second timing as well as for continuous sound, or what the communications engineers call noise; constant adaptation to commercials; and many other factors. Descending still further to television involved the imposition of new conditions: movement along guide-lines; limitations on dress and gesture; obedience to a red light; and so forth. Still further limitations arose when I worked before the motion picture camera. The conclusion I drew was this: every increase in the technological sophistication of the medium reduced whatever modest integrity my own personality had possessed when I started teaching.

I recall one television show in which I was interviewed in my home by the voice and image of the late Ed Murrow. To achieve this interview several hundreds of feet of cable were laid around the floors of my home; a forty-foot tower was erected in my backyard; several days of labor were contributed by 103 technicians, of whom 30 worked in my living-room. The net result of the interview was that many people observed that I had an unusually large personal library. They also learned that both Mr. Murrow and I felt well, and that our families felt well. This program was called Person-to-Person.

You may also wish to consider another observation closely connected with the inverse law proposed above. It is this: An original communication of high value may gain rather than lose in effectiveness if forced to encounter resistance. The Sermon on the Mount was originally heard by few. When first transcribed it was read by a minority. It has had to undergo quotation, expounding and interpretation over two millenia. Could it be that this message still retains power in part by reason of these circumstances? Suppose that tomorrow night it were heard *for the first time* over a full network hookup, backed by full orchestra plus electric organ, and bounced off a satellite. Do you suppose it would be remembered for 2,000 more years—even assuming that it was not assisted by Bufferin commercials?

Is it worth asking the question, Is the strength of a given signal not sometimes dissipated by the technological efficiency which destroys all barriers between *in*ception and *re*ception? Is Toynbee's challenge and response theory relevant not only to human societies in general but to the history of the messages the societies create? Can we value what we do not pay for?

Philosophers speculating along such lines may also want to consider the widening gap that has opened between those countries like our own, which are leading the revolution in information systems, and those less developed countries which must for some time remain stuck fast in the Gutenberg troglodyte era. William Knox, formerly a presidential advisor on the horizons opened by computers, has written: "It is conceivable here and now that we will no longer be able to communicate—simply communicate—with people whose technological means are not up to our standards, and who cannot follow the decisive progress being disseminated throughout our industrial structure and which will change its very nature."

The revolution of which Mr. Knox speaks is of course having its impact on education. The subject has been discussed by minds more competent than my own. All I wish to do here is invite reflection on the circumstance that in the last five years the point of origin of educational materials and content has undergone a radical shift. The purveyors of educational materials now include names that would have seemed strange only a decade ago: RCA, Raytheon, I.B.M., Xerox, CBS, Readers Digest, General Electric, Burroughs, Philco, Packard-Bell Electronics, Litton Industries. The patterns of decision-making habitual to the remarkable industrialists who run these companies may or may not improve the kind of communication we call education; but all of us will admit that in any case these patterns will somehow change it, just as computerized libraries and the systematic exploitation of games as an educational device will somehow change it. Philosophers may wish to admit into their speculations problems raised by such radical alterations in the origins and channels of instruction.

They may also want to weigh the quantity of truth there may be in MacLuhan's general theory. Nonlearned communication in the past has been largely verbal. Then, about thirty years ago, we began to revert to the communication system of our ancestors and reintroduced the hieroglyphic in the form of the picture. Thus was born one of the most powerful institutions of our time, the picture magazine. About five years ago a third shift became apparent. It has been summarized by the brilliant literary critic, George Steiner: "In the United States, and to a growing extent in Europe, the new literacy is musical rather than verbal." I do not know how true this is; but mere observation reveals that it is truer today than it was five years ago; and that it will be truer still five years from now. The issue is extremely complex—indeed it is not fantastic to suggest that the entire humanistic tradition based on the book may be rejected by large numbers of students during the next fifty years. If so, it may be necessary for trained minds such as yours to set to work on a theory of musical logic, musical rhetoric, and musical dialectic.

Finally, philosophers trying to isolate the is-ness of modern communication must ask themselves whether in its dominant form—mass communication—it has more than an incidental or accidental connection with truth. A theory of modern communication that is not in part a theory of fictions will be incomplete.

You will recall the Houynhnms in *Gulliver's Travels*. Their language had no word to express lying or falsehood. They called it "saying the thing which is not." A Houynhnm visiting us and spending 28 percent of his leisure time listening to television would in short order be removed in a straitjacket.

The mass media in our country rest upon advertising. Virtually all advertising is compelled to say the thing which is not. The compulsion arises from the nature of the medium. The television screen can offer nothing to an advertiser who wishes to state that he has available at a certain price a motorcar that will transport you from A to B—which is the whole truth. No mass medium can offer anything to an advertiser who wishes to state that he will sell you a cigarette that will do you no good and may do you harm—which is the whole truth. Consequently advertising has become a branch of dramaturgy, if not traumaturgy. We, the receivers of the signal, no longer object to this. Buying, one of the major objects of life in modern man, has become simply an exercise of choices among competitive illusions.

Does the thing which is not permeate messages other than those specifically known as advertising? It is an interesting question. We now know that messages from the war front and the political front are frequently lies. But more commonly they fall into the category against which Plato warned us. They approximate that most influential of all signals: the signals of art, especially the popular art of entertainment. They become part of the domain of poetry, fiction, theatre. A television round-table discussion inevitably is transformed into a psychodrama mounted by a producer and realized by actors. And this is true whether or not the participants believe they are being sincere. For the machine changes them. Included in the working parts of the machine is the audience they must play to. Thus all signal-originators, from the announcer of a detergent commercial to the leader of a great country, must be mass-psychologists. They are mass-psychologists first, other things thereafter.

Sometimes an entire country, such as Nazi Germany, may become the signal-originator of that which is not. It may do so in all sincerity—there is no sincerity as pure as the sincerity of those obsessed by a bad idea. In such an event few of the communications can possess any but an accidental or incidental integrity. In our country this extreme condition does not as yet obtain. But we may ask ourselves whether it is not bound to take on greater dominion as we advance toward our goal of a frictionless technological society in which order is acknowledged as the highest good. Truth-telling can make free men. But to make managed men one must use other methods. As for these methods, they have been catalogued in a hundred dystopian novels, notably *1984* and *Brave New World*.

You may therefore in your deliberations wish at least to take into account the possibility that the mass-messages from which most of us derive most of our information about the world will tend to become forms of systematized, mechanized illusion. You may even wish to play with the idea that the current revolt against education—that is, against being taught some rough approximation of reality—is due in part to the fact that much education is still rooted in a pre-technological view of the world. Those pioneering educators who are transforming education into forms of psychodrama, spectacle, multi-sensual impact, and games of simulated experience may very well be in the correct technological groove. They have taken their cue from television and other mass media.

II

As a communications practitioner I have also been requested to comment upon the arts and their relation to the communications system. I shall not touch on the liberal arts, for there I am incompetent. I shall, however, make a few observations on the fine arts with special reference to that art with which I am most familiar: literature. I shall focus on that aspect of the arts most intimately linked with communication. It is apparent to casual observation. We may call it Multiplicity and Diffusion. Here is a simple statement:

> More art objects, of varying degrees of aesthetic value, are today being produced, reproduced and diffused than at any time in recorded history.

This statement, it is submitted, holds true also for the *transmission belts* of art and for the *audience* to whom these transmission belts lead.

Multiplicity and diffusion, then, characterize origins, media, and termini. Multiplicity *and* diffusion—for quantification alone may lack dynamism. The Angkor Vat contains a huge quantity of art. This art will become operative only when the diffusing power of technology converts the Angkor Vat, through reproduction and tourism, into another Chartres, which of course it will do.

It is here argued not only that multiplicity and diffusion set off our era from all other art-producing eras, but also that they comprise a prime differentiator. Their order of energy is *decisively* higher than that suggested by such names as Gutenberg, Mergenthaler, Edison, Niepce, and Daeguerre, who merely hint at the present age. Whether we fasten our attention on the arts, the artists, the transmission belts, or the audience, multiplicity and diffusion would seem to be the order of the day.

Let us look first at the arts themselves.

First, as to *multiplicity*. Though they enjoy varying degrees of health, virtually all the traditional arts survive in our time. There are a few minor exceptions. For example, the Epic appears a corpse. But, as a consequence of the new identity-feelings of emergent nations, it may be pulmotored. Who can say that Nigeria will not produce its Homer? But even certain minor arts, obsolescent or arrested a generation ago, are reviving: for example, stained glass, with Coventry and Marc Chagall. The archaeologizing and preservation passion of modern man is, in the same way, responsible for the retrieving of much classic art: we can today actually read or listen to more Vivaldi than we could in 1920. Certain major arts not only persist in orthodox forms but develop new modes so singular that one may almost list them as additions— electronic music, for example, or mobiles. To these we may add such radical mutations as photography, the animated cartoon, modern musical comedy, and "psychodrama".

Finally, certain modern "destructive" artistic impulses work, by inevitable paradox, toward the creation of new art forms. The revolt against the traditional novel produces the anti-novel of the current French school, a variation completely unexampled in literary history. Destruction must work within highly organized patterns: it can deny only through complex affirmations. Jackson Pollock obeys a stricter esthetic than does Bouguereau or Verestchagin.

As for the future (let us say the next two centuries), it may be incubating a treasury, if not a Pandora's box, of almost inconceivable new arts. For example, we may develop a ballet formulated by computers and based on the movements of illuminated artificial satellites.

In summary: few forms are lost; some rediscovered; many invented.

As to *diffusion*. All these arts, new and old, are diffused centri-fugally by technological transmission belts. Where they cannot be diffused centrifugally, as with a cathedral, they are diffused, so to speak, centripetally. Large-scale tourism, itself the gift of technology, diffuses the impact-power of Coventry. To gauge the quantum-jump of mod-ern diffusion, compare the medieval transmission belt known as the pilgrimage.

Let us now look at the artists.

First, as to *multiplicity*. In proportion to the total population never have there been so many artists on all levels and in all fields, with the possible exception of "serious" musical composition.

Technology is often thought of as the assassin of the artist. This is demonstrably true in certain areas. The advent of technology, for exam-ple, has thinned out the folk artists of Melanesia and Polynesia. It will probably destroy all folk art. On the other hand, the dragon's teeth of technology may propel into being whole new armies of "mass" artists—witness the image-factory of Walt Disney.

The erosion of class lines tends to multiply artists. They now ap-pear on all social levels, whereas they had previously tended to be pro-duced within the confines of a leisured, or at least a "cultured" elite. More British playwrights today emerge from Whitechapel than from Oxford; and as the population of Whitechapel is both denser and (in view of Oxford's reputed habits) more philoprogenitive than that of Oxford, we may expect an intensification of this trend.

The sudden release of emergent peoples into the light of the twen-tieth century generates whole new cadres of artists. How many African novelists and poets existed in 1940? There are several hundred today. Similarly the coalescence into political structures of previously dispersed peoples possessing a powerful intellectual tradition produces an artistic proliferation. Modern Israel is here an exemplary type.

The most potent guarantee, however, of the proliferation of artists (as well as audiences) is of course the universal, and quite recent, acceptance of literacy as a normal component of the human makeup. Artists are spawned by the alphabet—and not only artists of the word. The delighted discovery of tradition creates artists of all kinds, and the spread of tradition rests on the spread of literacy. Or at least this has been the case up to the present time.

As to *diffusion:* Not only is the art object diffused; the artist is also. Modern transmission and communication belts such as foundations, travelling fellowships, and national propaganda agencies stimulate the artist to become traveler and missionary. His physical personality, apart from his productions, is thus widely diffused. The geographically isolated artist familiar in many historical forms (exile, hermit, monk, garret-poet) becomes rarer. The artist who resists being beside other people ends by being beside himself. Gregariousness is the dominant.

Diffusion leads to inclusion. The rebel artist, who could once enjoy the satisfaction of living a life of unremitting defeat at the hands of society, is now driven, by the inexorable forces of modern communication, to the humiliating triumph of incorporation within it. The Establishment is infinitely receptive. The Beats become within five years an accepted part of the scene. Rimbaud agonized, which was what he had in mind. His modern avatar, Henry Miller, is a best-seller and thus an embarrassment to himself. Low lies the water level in Walden Pond.

Let us look at the transmission belts.

First, as to *multiplicity:* To such specialized art-transmission belts as foundation grants, state propaganda mechanisms, travelling fellowships, and loan exhibitions, we must add the all-purpose technological transmission belts: screen, radio, television, camera, high-speed rotary press, and so forth. We may anticipate a startling increase in the mere number of such transmission belts during the next quarter-century. Telstar but faintly foreshadows the future, which may include the disintegration and reconstitution of matter, thus making possible teleportation. It is already feasible to project simple advertising slogans on cloud masses. Why not a sonnet by Shakespeare?

As to *diffusion.* It is the nature of technological transmission belts to universalize themselves, as it was the nature of certain classical transmission belts (medieval illuminated manuscripts, for example) to localize themselves. Clearly the reason is rooted partly in economics: the belt serves an audience conceived less as *appreciators* than as *customers:* and customers are conceived as potentially coextensive with the world population, whereas appreciators are conceived as isolated and self-limiting enclaves.

Let us look at the audience.

The multiplicity and diffusion of the art audience are apparent without demonstration.

Equally apparent are the factors accounting for this multiplicity and diffusion: the population explosion; the potential universalization of literacy; the increase in longevity (the potential art-enjoyer lives today almost twice as long as he did in the eighth century, so that each member of the audience is, so to speak, multiplied by a factor of two); the blurring of traditional class lines; the technological transmission belts, geared to a maximum audience; the advent of leisure, seized upon by a large minority as an opportunity for the enjoyment of art, just as it is seized upon by the vaster majority as an opportunity for the enjoyment of sport; the translation explosion, creating new audiences by circumventing the language barrier; and, perhaps most vital, the quite recent triumph of art as a *mass* prestige symbol, almost comparable in this respect to the motorcar, the individually owned house, and the individually operated, sexually attractive mate. As is often pointed out, among a sensitive (and, I believe, an intellectually disoriented) minority, the prestige symbol of art is etherealized into a quasi-religion.

Multiplication and diffusion in the arts may be viewed as a generalization of the insights expressed in Malraux's *Psychologie de l'Art*. The "Museum Without Walls" applies to the written and spoken word, to architecture, and to music, as well as to the plastic arts. Duplication, reproduction, communication, instantaneous transmission mark the arts in general. We live in the Xerox age.

Or, though with less certainty, we may view multiplication and diffusion in the arts as subject to the same "law" of accelerated invention that operates in the field of technology. It is not only that the acceleration of *mechanical* invention makes possible the permanent storing and universal-jointed diffusion of all art objects now available. Something far eerier may be involved: the *mind* of the artist, for the first time in history, appears to be stripped of its brakes. Aesthetic experiment was formerly undertaken in a pioneering spirit. It is today becoming *natural*, even a reflex. Some sort of spiritual osmosis is taking place through the membrane separating laboratory from studio and writing desk. The artist formerly conceived his vocation as the expression of his personality. He now often conceives it as an opportunity for the generation and metamorphosis of forms. In this sense he has become a technologist and technician, acting in harmony with the "law" of accelerated invention.

In conclusion I shall apply the phenomenon of multiplicity and diffusion—which is the gift of modern communication—to half a dozen specific esthetic and socio-esthetic issues it generates. I shall list these in summary form.

Let us reflect first on the value of a work of literature as perceived by the audience. I have already advanced a theory of creative osmosis. This argues that the total value of a work of literature is perceived more precisely when that work has to pass with a certain difficulty through obstacles of time, place and initial misunderstanding. Multiplicity and diffusion eliminate many of these obstacles in such a way that much of the value of the work of art may be lost (by popularization, modishness, etc.) in the course of immediate, easy transmission.

Second, let us consider the phenomenon of the transmutation of literary forms. The technology of multiplicity and diffusion combines with the operation of the profit motive to stimulate such transmutation. Thus a successful novel may become a film, a play, a musical comedy, a TV drama, a comic strip, or finally, as in the case of *Main Street* or *Babbitt,* a simple cliché.

From the point of view of the audience: What asthetic values are lost (or perhaps gained) when the Shaw who wrote *Pygmalion* becomes in the popular mind the Lerner and Lowe who wrote *My Fair Lady?* At times the original work of art is almost completely lost sight of in the process of multiple metamorphosis.

From the point of view of the creator: the novelist today frequently writes, not for an audience, but for a medium. Thus a novel such as Irving Wallace's *The Prize* is essentially conceived as potential Hollywood material, and is so written. In a case like this the roles may almost be said to be changed: that is, the transmission belt itself becomes, by its seductive power, a kind of creator: it helps to *write* the book. What moral and social values are involved in this curious process? What happens to the mind of the novelist? How many novelists are lost to us through this process? Or is something gained in that a part of the creative energy of the novelist, if only a part, is communicated to a wider audience as a consequence of the transmutation of forms?

Another interesting issue turns on the popularization of ideas. The reference here is to certain well-known agencies of multiplicity and diffusion, such as the *Readers Digest.* What is the effect of such popularization on the original communicator? On the audience? Is one of the effects on the latter the production of a mass of Madame Bovarys, that is a vast population of minds who believe that they have grasped an idea when they have only glimpsed the shadow on the wall of Plato's cave; and whose conduct, like Madame Bovary's, predicates itself on intellectual conceit and callowness?

In this connection, one might consider the whole modern technique of condensation: original communications are more and more frequently encountered in the form of abstracts. The abstract is itself a child of the Multiplicity and Diffusion effect; it could never flourish in an era of imperfect communication. It took five hundred years for someone to think of condensing the *Canterbury Tales;* and almost half as long before Charles and Mary Lamb were hired to condense the plays of Shakespeare for children.

What are the lines of force connecting multiplicity and diffusion, religion and literature? The drama, we are taught, had its origin in religion. The classical epic also had its religious roots. Certain modern theoreticians of literature (Tolstoy) affirm that without a religious base literature is trivial. We are not concerned here to affirm or refute this idea, but we may surely assert that the religious experience has been one of the constituents of many fine works of literary art; and in the case of one supreme work, the *Divine Comedy*, its dominant constituent. If this is true, what will be the effect of an era of multiplicity and diffusion? What is today diffused in all the verbal arts is, with rare exceptions, a secular view of life. It is this view of life that surrounds the beginning artist. How will it affect him? If he resists the onslaught of secular messages, and produces a work religious in spirit, to what audience (for the audience has itself been secularized by multiplicity and diffusion) will he address himself? A sub-issue here has to do with the creation, value and reception, for the first time in history, of a self-consciously and dogmatically atheist literature, which is what we may expect from any and all Marxist countries. Another sub-issue addresses itself to noncontemporary literature: if God is a laughing-stock, how does the beginning reader read, or the teacher teach, the *Divine Comedy*?

Are the comic and tragic sense affected by multiplicity and diffusion? When I state that 7,000,000 Jews were exterminated by the Germans, you find it difficult today to react appropriately. That is not because of hardness of heart, but because the fact has been diffused so often and in so many different forms that your sense of tragedy has become blunted. We have heard too often that Aristides is just. If I am to interest you in the statement, I would have to put it differently, adding some new detail that you may be unfamiliar with. Thus, if I say, 7,000,000 Jews were murdered by the men, women and *children* of Germany; and that nine-year-old boys were systematically supplied with revolvers so that they might shoot down the Warsaw Jews as a substitute for hunting rabbits . . . you might find yourself made a little more uncomfortable; your sleeping sense of tragedy would at least stir.

Do multiplicity and diffusion in general blunt the sense of tragedy and also comedy? And if so, what about the effect on great literature, past, present, and to come, which traditionally depends in large part on the possession of these senses by both writer and audience?

Is there any connection between multiplicity and diffusion and present-day poetry? While the workings of multiplicity and diffusion tend to universalize themselves, they have of course in many areas not reached this point. Modern poetry of the more difficult sort is a case in point. What has happened here is the immediate diffusion of this poetry among potential and aspiring poets; so that there are a hundred T. S. Eliots. The diffusion, owing to the difficulty of the poetry, has not extended to many readers. But it has had its effect on the creators: it is difficult to account otherwise for the unexampled multitude of practising poets, many quite good, today. Is this immediate effect good, bad, or indifferent? We may supply an example. Jules Laforgue died in 1887; T. S. Eliot was born in 1888, a remarkable example of almost instantaneous reincarnation. Now, was not there a certain advantage for Eliot in being influenced by Laforgue one generation *later*, rather than during the high point of Laforgue's production? Does not the delay in transmission preclude immediate imitation? Did not the hiatus give Eliot a chance to develop his own personality freely?

And so we could proceed along these lines, multiplying examples of the impact of multiplicity and diffusion, not only on literature, but on all the arts, whether elite or popular. But perhaps you have had more than enough of these random samplings from a practitioner's notebook.

PHILOSOPHY OF COMMUNICATIONS AND THE ARTS

Richard McKeon

An international conference on the uses of philosophy exemplifies the problems which it treats. The problems presented and encountered by philosophies in confrontation with each other are problems of multiple perspectives. Each of the philosophies is used to reorient the perspectives of experience, action, and thought. An international discussion of philosophic problems presents the diversity of philosophies of the world as they have been determined in the long traditions of past speculations by the new circumstances of present problems, while the uses of philosophies of the world are oriented to the future. New problems will be formed and presented by peoples philosophizing about common problems conceived and analyzed by use of divergent philosophic concepts. The perspectives of cultural space, in which the many philosophic traditions of mankind are lines of direction and orientation, take on a further dynamic dimension in the perspectives of temporal change, in which the problems, the nature, and the parts of philosophies have all undergone alterations.

The uses of philosophy have become its uses for all mankind and for today. What men mean by philosophy, how they use it, and whether or not they think it is useful, however, differ not only from culture to culture and from school to school but from man to man in each culture and in each school. Which philosophies are to be considered for use? How can their advocates make themselves intelligible to each other? Can they be moved to cooperate in understanding and in solving problems somehow recognized to be common in spite of differences of interpretation and specification? What is "philosophy" today; and how is "it" related to the philosophies of the past, and susceptible of adaptation to "uses" in the future?

Philosophers have always pretended to universality of a sort; and they have usually combined the quest for omnicompetence with strictures against the absurdity of assuming universal scope in the determinations of human knowledge or the applications of human power. From the beginning of speculation and inquiry, thinkers have justified reason and thought by its uses; and they have usually distinguished the thoughtful achievement of understood objectives and sought goods from unreasoning and unreasonable pursuit of dubious pleasures and questionable utilities. Names have been given to philosophies in past and present communications and controversies among philosophers from the subject-matters or immaterial forms in which they have sought universality and from the arts or unartificial skills by which they have developed uses. The parts of philosophy have been marked off, in like fashions, by names which indicate their uses by determining the subject-matters to which they apply. Traditional names, like "ethics," "aesthetics," and "logic" achieve this purpose by relating character and action, perception and presentation, and thought and speech, aided in the merging of matter and use by ambiguities of etymology and of shifting interpretations; and "metaphysics" could be named to indicate the location of a book in an edition of the works of a philosopher and then be interpreted to signify a subject matter and to indicate the speculative method appropriate to it. The process is clearer in English names constructed to set up new differentiations of parts of philosophy, freed from old ambiguities of designation and use, because the uses of philosophy are indicated by attaching the word "philosophy" with the preposition "of" to a name designating a field. Sometimes the field is another established discipline, as in "philosophy of education," "of religion," "of science," or "of history;" sometimes it is an activity or instrumentality of action, as in "philosophy of practice," "of belief," "of language," or "of mind." These traditional parts and applications of philosophy, ancient and modern, do little to clarify the uses of philosophy and of its parts. The arts developed in discussion of philosophy and its sub-divisions are semantic arts which depend on giving the ambiguous field or activity a fixed definition; and in the practice of these semantic arts any consideration of alternative definitions of the subject-matter, developed by alternative arts, becomes a dispute concerning whether or not the expression "metaphysics," or "epistemology," "philosophy of science," "philosophy of history," or "philosophy of man" has any significance which bears on real problems susceptible of meaningful solutions.

Discussion, in philosophy or in general, depends no less on the richness and suggestibility of the theme explored than on the precision and testability of the consequences traced by different methods of inquiry and proof; the uses of theoretic and practical arts wander from field to field. There can be no discussion without a recognizable common subject-matter or without an identifiable common problem; discussion is likewise impossible when there is complete agreement about what is in question and about the nature and origin of the problem to be considered. It has frequently seemed wise in the past to depart from traditional divisions and applications of philosophy, and to divide and organize philosophy in newly conceived parts. The emergent parts of the philosophy of an age are found in the orientations of actions and interests: they are neither fixed by the nature of an independent subject-matter nor imposed by the inventive art of an arbitrary inquirer. If our interest is in the uses of philosophy in the future, our investigation of them should not be tied down to the classifications of philosophy in the present. Fortunately, in speculating on the evolution of the uses of philosophy, it is not necessary to have the gift of foresight or the art of prediction at each point of the changing uses in order to find indications of possible directions of reorientation. In any age some terms have a prominent place in philosophic discussion and acquire a like place in general discussion of problems of life and action. In both philosophic and common discussions these terms usually take on meanings and are put to applications which are justified by use or mention of devices and conceptions borrowed, by analogy or by heterogeneous substitution, from well-known and widely practiced skills and disciplines. It is possible, therefore, to make a dead-reckoning of the uses of philosophy in the future by mapping directions indicated by current combinations of fashionable ambiguous terms and of esteemed traditional or newly discovered arts.

The subject of a "philosophy of communications and the arts" is indicated and marked off by combining two such terms. "Experience," "existence," "language," and "communication" are familiar ambiguous general terms employed to focus the analysis of philosophical and of practical problems on unambiguous issues and concrete facts. Their meanings are developed by use of distinctions from "arts" and "sciences" transformed to explore concrete problematic circumstances in search of precise determinations for use in further inquiry and action. The arts and their subject-matters have had continuous histories; but arts which are for a time arts of knowing become arts of doing, and are then transformed into arts of making, and then repeat the cycle; the subject-matters of the arts are sought in turn among things, thoughts, action, and language, sometimes on the supposition that thoughts, actions, and discourses take their character from and conform to things, sometimes on the supposition that things are the products and creatures of thoughts, or deeds, or words. The arts and sciences by which we explore experience and existence, language and communication today are arts of discourse and arts of making. The arts of discourse borrow from the long history of the liberal arts, but they have been made arts of language and communication primarily, that is, the liberal arts have been reformulated in terms of grammar and rhetoric; the arts of making borrow from the long history of the fine and the mechanical arts, and transform the arts of knowing and doing into operational devices applied in mathematics, technology, and communications, but they too have been made primarily arts of rhetoric or communication and of grammar or construction. The arts of doing have been transformed into a rhetoric of demonstration, deliberation, and judgment; the arts of knowing have been transformed into a grammar of construction and interpretation of structures. The subject-matter of the arts of communicative discourse and of technological making is existence and experience, and ontological or epistemic principles and consequences are detected in that subject-matter only by statement and operation.

Experience and existence are mutually explanatory. Experience has ceased to be an epistemological grounding in ideas and their combinations for the certainties of knowledge and action, and has become instead a framework of cultural conditions and natural circumstances for the determination and statement of the facts of existence. Existence has ceased to be a metaphysical grounding or sign for the discovery of the principles of being, and has become instead the phenomenal immediacy of encountered nature and experienced art. Logic is freed from ontological commitments and dialectic from mentalistic or spiritualistic forms. In the arts of discourse and making, "demonstration" has been made a manifestation—poetic, practical, or theoretic—rather than an argument; "deliberation" has been made a balance of incitations, in which "decision" is a spontaneous pronouncement, adapted to forming groups in support of policies or opposed to policies, rather than a rational consideration of alternatives, in which decision is a reasoned choice among them; "judgment" has been made individual approval based on self-justification secured by self-representation or image-making rather than the assemblage of particulars in universal combinations and ordering relations.

The unity of philosophy as art and as subject-matter today is as illusive as any of the unities which philosophy has exhibited or professed at any other period of history when new philosophic arts have been devised in renaissances and revolutions to investigate new subject-matters and to treat new problems. There are many modes of communication in which philosophers and philosophically inclined inquirers explore experience and disclose existence; and there are many arts of communication in which the sequences and structures of invention and disclosure are developed and used. The uses of philosophy present a double question as a result of these transformations: (1) What is *philosophy* when it is viewed and practiced as an art of communications? and (2) What are the devices and skills of the particular *arts*—the transformed arts of poetry, of politics, and of rhetoric—when the method of communication is the method of all arts joined and ordered in a philosophy of the arts? The two questions are related to each other reflexively, for the subject-matter of philosophy can be indicated, delimited, and justified only by use of the philosophic arts, and the acquisition and judgment of the arts of philosophy are produced by the practice of the arts on an appropriate and recognized subject-matter. The subject-matter and arts of philosophy today are both fixed by common words of universal generality like "experience," "existence," "language," and "communication": they are synonymous in their scope when they are used to define a single universal subject-matter; they mark off different structures and isolate different elements when they are used to differentiate the devices of operation and statement.

1. *The subject-matter and problems of a philosophy of communications and the arts.*

Like other forms of communication, philosophy is a limited communication of shared words defined in partially shared meanings and attached to partially shared designations. The ambiguity of "communication" affects both the method and the subject-matter of a "philosophy of communications and the arts." The methods of communication range through dialogue, disputation, controversy, and monologue, each of which becomes philosophic by means of devices of "discussion" designed to clarify meanings and determine applications. Discussion and philosophy tend to arise today from controversy concerning meanings dependent on actions (including operations prescribed in languages and in games) rather than from disputation concerning meanings dependent on thoughts or from dialogue concerning meanings dependent on things. This tendency affects the subject-matter of philosophy, for philosophic discussion proceeds by establishing a universal scope within which it delimits proper ranges. It extends the shared meanings of "language" by equating them with "experience," "existence," and "communication," which in the process become comprehensive of all that is and all that is intelligible, and it delimits the specific proper meanings of anything that is experienced, exists, and is communicated in controversial opposition to meaningless statements of unverifiable resolutions of unreal problems. The subject-matter of philosophy was never thought to be unqualified reality or unquestionable things: it has been variously conceived as things certified and warranted in thought, action, and expression. The arts by which such a subject-matter is defined and investigated adapt their devices to all dimensions of their subject-matter by placing primary emphasis on one: they have been at various periods of philosophic discussion arts of essence, of thought, of action, and of discourse adapted to structures of being, sequences of what is, facts of experience, and elements of existence. The subject-matter and problems of philosophical discussion set the requirements of the arts of philosophical discussion; and the arts of being, thought, action, and expression, the arts of dialogue, disputation, controversy, and discussion determine the subject-matter of philosophical inquiry.

The antipathies expressed for subject-matters considered in past discussions of philosophy and for the arts developed to treat those subject-matters provide a key to the shifting subject-matters and altering arts which determine what is the case and what is significant and true about it. We are dubious about the arts of discourse conceived as arts of being based on the nature of things, because metaphysics raises questions about everything, and knowledge of the whole of things is impossible. We are dubious concerning the arts of discourse conceived as arts of thought based on the nature of reason and the passions, on the forms of thought and the association of ideas, because epistemology raises questions about thought and judgment as complexes to be analyzed and about ideas and feelings as simples to be synthesized, and entitizes thoughts, or psychologizes the objects of thought, or separates things thought and things sensed, things willed and things desired into disparate realms. In the place of discredited arts of being and of thought we construct arts of discourse conceived as arts of action in which we test what is presented as that which is or as that which is thought by considering that which is said and that which is done, and by seeking in statement and action the marks and warrants by which to determine and certify being and thought in what is said and done and in consequences discerned in statement and occurrence.

The subject-matter of the arts of being disappears in the use of the arts of communication and construction; but the structure of being is rediscovered in formulating and forming the structure of existence. Uneasiness with metaphysics has arisen periodically from doubts concerning things possessed of fixed essences and natures antecedent to our knowing, doing, or saying them. The arts of being by which they are treated and by which their consequences are explored cannot be applied to the contents of thought, action, or statement as they are in themselves. What is, and what it is, do not provide grounds for distinguishing knowing, doing, or making; the basic distinctions of changeless and changing, of known and perceived, and of natural and artificial have ceased to be necessary, self-evident, or primary, and have come to be probable, dubious, or derived. But metaphysics is not only a science of being qua being; it is also a science of first principles, and the arts of communication and construction must establish and use "principles" which serve a function among the facts of discourse and occurrence not unlike the function of metaphysical principles ordering the structures of actuality and of truth.

Our periodical metaphysical doubts might be resolved once and for all if some clear and indubitable criteria could be found to determine how we know before questions are raised concerning what is and whether it is, concerning how it is qualified and characterized and why. But uneasiness with epistemology has arisen periodically when critical examinations of knowing have uncovered complexities and contradictions reminiscent of the antinomies and paralogisms of metaphysics: it is obviously impossible to conceive elements, modes, or forms of thought ungrounded in reality, unexpressed in language, and inoperative in action. The subject-matter of the arts of knowing disappears, as had the subject-matter of the arts of being, in the arts of communication and construction; but the structure of thought, like the structure of being, is rediscovered in formulating and forming the structure of experience. The subject-matter of the arts of knowing cannot be modes of knowing and their judgmental consequences considered in themselves, unexpressed in language and unembodied in action; and they cannot be applied to the data of experience or the facts of existence objectively segregated from subjective presumptions and associations. The arts of the intelligible, the desirable, and the pleasurable are not arts of thinking or feeling, or laws of theoretical, practical, or productive thought, or manifestations of genius, sagacity, or taste. The sequences and associations of ideas and feelings do not provide methods of distinguishing, determining, or judging the forms or the processes of thought and feeling, or of perception and judgment in themselves, or in knowing, doing, or making; the basic distinctions of knowledge and opinion, intelligibilia and sensibilia, honesta (or the good) and utilia (or the useful) have ceased to be fundamental, sharp, and simple, and have come to be disputable, merged, and complex. But epistemology is not only a science of the elements and forms of human understanding; it is also a critique of methods, and the arts of communication and construction must develop and formulate "methods" of discourse and operation adapted to facts and to the formation and statement of relations among facts.

The subject-matters of the arts of being and the arts of thinking have been abandoned for the subject-matters of the arts of expression and communication and of experimentation and construction, but it has been argued that the change has not been a retrenchment but an aban- donment of old errors concerning what is and what is intelligible, which led, sometimes, to diremptions and dichotomies of a homogeneous world into unrelated parts, like the realms of being and becoming, or of soul and body, or of reality and appearance, and, alternatively, to merg- ings and confusions of processes which are distinct and complementary, like knowledge and belief, or cognitive, emotive, and persuasive uses of language and action, or facts and values, or observed facts and a priori assumptions, or accounts of what is the case and themes of recurrent connections. Such arguments illustrate and demonstrate both the conti- nuity of the philosophic arts and the novelty of the philosophy of com- munications and the arts, for no real subject-matter of inquiry has been lost, and yet more adequate arts of inquiry have turned to other charac- teristics as subjects for inquiry and have wholly changed the subject- matter.

Philosophers are able to continue to use the methods of philosophic hermeneutics by which the arguments of earlier philosophers are inter- preted in meanings and with applications previously unsuspected. They also make use of the methods of philosophic controversy by which the conclusions attributed to other philosophers, earlier or contempo- rary, are shown to express errors and nonsense previously undetected about the nature of things and of knowledge. The subject-matter of the philosophic arts continues to be universal in scope, but the universality of the arts is exercised and exhibited in exploring structures of experi- ence and existence, while the structures of being and of thought have become constructions grounded on inference from concrete facts and encountered data or designed to satisfy deep-seated cravings for general- ity and universality. Whatever is, and what it is, can be brought to light and examined by the arts of communication and construction, of ex- pression and experimentation; and indeed being, and essential proper- ties, can be certified only by such arts since they make possible the repetition of events and experiences in other circumstances and by other people. What is eliminated by the arts of communication and construc- tion cannot be said to be in any respect, for it eludes expression adapted to experience and existence, while "fictive" beings and "eternal" objects, since they are expressed and presented clearly, provide models for seeing and judging other pretenders to being and essence. Whatever is thought and felt can be set forth and examined by the arts of communication and construction, of expression and experimentation; and indeed the only evidence that something has been thought or felt, and the only intimation of what it is, are embodied and conveyed by expression and action. What is eliminated by the arts of communication and construction is not conceivable in any respect, for it slips from experience and existence by eluding expression, like unformulated thoughts and unmanifested emotions; while "imaginary things" and *entia rationis*," since they are apprehended and comprehended clearly, provide models to clarify the subject-matters of direct experience and of empirical knowledge.

The arts of communication and construction are arts of language and action. They provide remedies for false pretensions to universality of knowledge and to universality in determinations of being by seeking objective generality and universality in experience and determining the whole of existence by the scope of experience. They eliminate false divisions and separations by seeking principles of individuation and generalization in occurrences and in law-like formulations of possibilities and consequences in occurring. They serve as bridges between "experience" in the broad sense in which any immediate experience is infinitely rich in aspects on which attention may be fixed and in interpretations by which facts may be specified, and "experiences" in the particular sense in which any fact of experience is fixed and irresistible and is stated unambiguously and precisely in true propositions. They serve as bridges between "existence" in the broad sense in which whatever happens and is perceived exists, including what is thought, said, and done, what is planned, imagined, and desired, and "existences" in the particular sense in which what is thought to exist and what is said to exist are considered not with respect to their existence as actions or statements but with respect to the existences they indicate and signify. They are arts of *inquiry* by which the tangled knots of occurrences and the recurrent themes of connections are undone and arranged in the ordered sequences and consequences of defined events and analyzed statements; and they are the arts of *semantics* by which the divergent accounts of an experience or an existence, worked out by different methods, are set in opposition or in accord, in controversy or disputation, in which the differences are contrarieties or contradictions, or in dialogue or debate, in which they are translatable, one into the other, as verbally different literal statements of the same thing, or as analogous statements of the same thing, or as literal or analogical statements of related things.

The continuity and innovations, the universality and specifications of the philosophic arts and their subject-matter reflect contact between the open, indeterminate problems of inquiry which can be stated and treated only in the closed, precise formulations of a structured semantics. The subject-matter and problems of philosophy change with

changes of semantic schemata. Language and action, existence and experience are not discoveries of the arts of communication, but existence
and experience assume priority in an examination of the concrete and
the factual; and *clarity*, such as is available in a perception or a presentation, is a precondition to the determination of an inquiry or proof or
the testing of its presuppositions or conclusions. The arts of thought
provide a basis for language and action and an account of existence and
experience, but the specification of what is and how it is qualified
assumes priority; and *distinctness*, such as is manifested in an unambiguous account of connections and sequences, provides the test for dubious clarities and dogmatic certainties. The possibility and the structures
of existence and experience and the establishment of principles of being
depend on a critical epistemological investigation of the forms and elements of knowing. The revolution from the arts of thought to the arts
of communication, despite the retention of names like "logic" and "rhetoric" and words like "inference" and "persuasion," and despite controversies between the "old" and the "new," involve a change of subject-
matter and of problems which transform semantic questions of definition and method to ambiguous, substantive questions of inquiry and
invention. The arts of being provide a basis for language, action, and
thought and an account of existence, experience, and knowledge, but
determination of why and principles of being provide the grounds of
method, interpretation, and formulation; and *adequacy* assumes priority
as it did in the search for clear, distinct, and adequate ideas by
seventeenth-century metaphysicians. The principles of all sciences, all
actions, and all productions are principles of being. The subject-matters
change with the changes in the arts, and the arts of language and
action, of expression and communication form different devices for the
treatment of different problems when language and action determine
thought and being than when language and action, together with being,
are conceived as determined by the forms of thought or when language
and action, together with thought, are conceived as determined by the
structure of being. The nature and consequences of the changes in the
subject-matter and problems of philosophy are elucidated best by examining the philosophic arts as arts of communication.

2. *The methods and principles of the arts of communication and
construction.*

The arts by which we come into contact with the facts of existence
and the arts by which we explore the data of experience and uncover the
sequences of changes in what is the case must have universality (that is,
they must apply to whatever is as it is without distortion due to char-

acteristics intruded or neglected or colored by the operation of the arts) and objectivity (that is, they must use methods and devices which indicate and delineate testable factual constructions and not simple fictive fabrications). All arts of communication and construction are universal, that is, apply to everything; and each of them is particular, that is, serves specific purposes and discovers or actualizes specific aspects of its universal subject-matter. There has always been a tendency to controversy among the arts in which the universality of established arts or of arts passing into desuetude is shown to be a dubious universality or a covert particularity, and their objectivity is shown to be subjective or abstract. The arts of being, which deal with matters of communication as aspects of being, are said to have fallen into the rigidities of metaphysicalism and the relativities of skepticism. The arts of thought, which deal with forms of communication as aspects of thought, are said to have fallen into the formalities of epistemologism and the variabilities of psychologism. The arts of communication and construction are arts of conjoining form and matter in the concreteness of experience and the individuality of existence. In the practice of those arts the dangers and errors of the arts of being and of thought are recognized as consequences of separating form and matter. The arts of communication and construction, on the contrary, are arts which move from ambiguity to precision by relating the problems of philosophic inquiry concerning experience and existence, which are infinitely rich in possibilities and aspects, to the problems of philosophic semantics concerning facts and elements, which are determinate in actuality and in formulation.

There are continuities as well as innovations in these transformations of the arts and their subject-matters. A sign of the continuities is in the retention of the names and the vocabulary of the liberal arts in altered meanings and functions. The liberal arts are arts of language and opinion, when philosophy is based on metaphysics as an architectonic science. They provide the techniques of presentation and construction, discussion and debate, refutation and rectification as *instruments* of formal presentation to supplement and complete the methods of inquiry into the nature of things and the processes of change. The liberal arts are arts of language and action, when philosophy is based on epistemology and an architectonic of the sciences as ways of knowing. They provide the laws of thought and expression, induction and deduction, community and communication, paradox and paralogism as *schemata* of material connection to provide criteria and foundations for necessary laws of nature and morals. The question of the priority of the theoretical or the practical and the consequent opposition of basic arts of knowing to basic arts of doing are recognized to be spurious questions

when the arts of communication and construction assume the architectonic functions, previously attributed to metaphysics or epistemology,
for when the basic arts are arts of saying and making, they are arts of the
uses of reason, and the same or comparable devices of rational statement
and construction are found to have theoretical and practical uses. Each
of the traditional arts is broadened to a universal subject-matter, and the
terms of art are adapted to more inclusive functions. They are frequently set in controversial opposition by their imperialistic pretensions
to unique suzerainty in treating all problems, but they exercise different
functions with respect to different aspects of experience and existence;
and recognition of those interrelations provides the possibility of developing a new philosophy of communications and the arts.

Rhetoric is the art of persuasion and debate. When the philosophic
arts are conceived of as arts of being or of thought, rhetoric is not
treated as a philosophic art, although it is used extensively in the controversy and refutation which constitutes communication among philosophies. When the philosophic arts are arts of communication and construction, rhetoric is made into a universal and architectonic art. Cicero
reports the position of rhetoricians who considered it the art of resolving
all questions, general and particular, and did not distinguish rhetoric
from philosophy by limiting rhetoric to particular questions about individual persons and fixed times and places and reserving general questions for philosophy. In the Renaissance rhetoric was used as the
method of the new metaphysics. In the twentieth century rhetoric has
assumed new rhetorical names and descriptions and has moved from the
adjudication of law-court and the administrative committee, the debates
of the legislative assembly, and the harangues of the market place and
crossroads, from the new fine arts of presentation and creative audience
participation, the new arts of scientific discovery, and the renewed arts
of philosophical semantics, to mass communication, advertising, and
technological innovations.

Rhetoric is an art of invention and disposition: it is an art of
communication between a speaker and his audience, and it is therefore
an art of construction of the subject-matter of communication, that is,
of anything whatever that can be an object of attention. What is, is
established by the convictions and agreements of men, and the rich
potentialities of experience and existence are examined and developed
by devices of discrimination and of opposition and adjustment in expression and communication. As an art of invention rhetoric has developed and used "topics" or "commonplaces": they were designed to be
"seats" of invention and "sources" of new arguments; in the history of
their use they have been extended to all fields and their example has

inspired philosophers like Francis Bacon to seek "places" for the discovery not only of words and ideas but of things and of arts, while at the opposite extreme the word "commonplace" has come in its common usage to mean a repeated opinion rather than an instrumentality of novelty and invention.

As an art of communication rhetoric has been designed to make use of all means of persuasion—the character of the speaker, the preconceptions of the audience, and the structure and distortion of argumentation; in the history of their uses the devices of rhetorical argumentation have been extended to all fields, because all subject-matters, whatever else they are presented as, are "objects" of communication and are isolated and formed in a communication and by a communicator who uses data and attitudes previously communicated to him or to his audience to fashion what he presents in further communication. The devices of rhetorical argumentation are devices of "demonstration" in the sense of "manifestation" and "presentation" rather than of deductive "proof" or logical "inquiry." A position or a policy is established by manifestation or assertion of oneself and of what one is saying or doing, of what has been said and done by others, and of what will be said and done; it is not established on the nature of things or by use of the laws of thought, and it is an irrelevance or an impertinence to ask whether the communicator knows what he is talking about or the consequences of what he is doing, because his communication is judged by his success in making or generating the object of his communication—a position or a policy, a habit, skill, or attitude, leading to further statements or actions. The arts of communication and construction are arts of *innovation* and *tradition;* accepted facts and recognized objects are the products not the preconditions of the arts of communication and construction.

The new rhetoric or art of selection is the art of coping with new problems. It is sometimes confused with older or distorted forms of rhetoric in which the business of advancing novel or adapting traditional solutions to new problems is indistinguishable from propaganda, public relations, force, or deception, which employ arts of extending adherence to an opinion already formed, or arts of creating support or disapproval in common opinion for a person or a mode of action attributed to him or to the groups with which he is associated, or arts of lobbying for the passage of a law to enforce a policy or initiate a course of action or change an image. The unknown is the subject-matter of invention and creativity in the transition to the known from the unknown. The unknown is found in experience and in creation, once it can be named and identified after the discovery of the known. The arts and the sciences use what has been done and what has been said, on the frontiers of knowing and making, to explore the new, which at the moment of invention is that which is not yet and nonetheless is the subject-matter of the arts and sciences conceived and developed as arts of communication and construction. The new art of rhetoric is the art of *discovery*. It is not a heuristic *method* or radical *interpretation* but an art of topics or a *selection* of elements which opens the way to the recognition of new facts and to the perception of unnoticed structures and sequences. There is a fundamental rhetoric of all elements which enter into the perspective of everything communicated relative to what has already been done and said, for in the perspective of language and action, taken universally as formative of our worlds, man is the measurer and maker of what is and of what is not. There are also derived rhetorics of pleasing, teaching, and moving: a constitutive-hedonic rhetoric in which communication and construction are rendered effective by pleasing; an epistemic-dispositional rhetoric in which congruous knowledge and emotions are joined to prior knowledge and feelings by teaching; and a pistic-concupiscent-irascible rhetoric in which convictions are changed and perspectives are raised in scales of reality and value by arousing and moving.

Grammar is the art of statement and interpretation. The Greeks used the same word for a letter of the alphabet and an element of physical matter; and we have talked about grammars of language, of science, and of reality, both in the sense of formative rules of construction and in the sense of hermeneutic devices of interpretation. When the philosophic arts are conceived as arts of being or of thought, grammar is not treated as a philosophic art, although it is used extensively to set forth the elements of philosophical formulations and the rules of combination or syntax by which they are formed, and philosophers frequently seek "elements" from which to construct their philosophies in atoms, simple ideas, or undefined terms. Universal or speculative grammars have dealt with modes of being and understanding as well as with modes of signifying.

Grammar is an art of composition and division, or construction and interpretation: it is an art of communication which focuses on the communication itself and on what is communicated, and it is therefore an art of construction in which the nature of language and communicator and the nature of the circumstances and environment of language and man enter, both as matter and as conditioning form of communication. Whereas the object of communication in rhetoric emerges as an invention constructed in communication between communicator and audience, the object of communication in grammar emerges as a construction in discourse as a statement of fact and as an interpretation of the statement. Whatever is, is a nature or a situation; and the nature of communication and communicators is determined and known by consideration of like statements of fact and situation.

As an art of composition, grammar has distinguished and used parts of speech and structures of syntax; in the history of their use they have been extended from the modes of signifying to the modes of being, that is, to factual properties and structures of situations; and they have been extended to the modes of understanding, that is, to ideas and structures of judgment. Statements, situations, and judgments of fact are inseparable from each other and materially identical with each other, that is, they have to do with the same object; but formally they differ, for their composition depends respectively on the nature of things, the nature of thoughts, and the nature of language. "Hypotheses," which are the foundations or suppositions of statement, judgment, and of situation, have undergone the same variabilities between generalization and minimalization as "commonplaces" in rhetoric: they are sometimes used as unifying conceptions in science; they are sometimes avoided as figments of the imagination, unrelated to what is the case or to scientific knowledge. As an art of communication grammar has been designed to decompose any sentence, and therefore any situation or experience, any thought or sentiment, into the elements in which it is grounded, and in turn to compose sentences, situations, and judgments from their elements. The devices of grammatical analysis have been extended to all fields, and the words "elements" or "grammar" have been used in the title of fundamental works in all fields, as in the "elements of geometry" or the "grammar of science." The rules of syntax become, in this broadened analysis, conventional rules which are grounded in and express values: the proposition expresses a judgment of the true or the probable, the good or the useful, the beautiful or the pleasing and signifies a qualified situation. The arts of communication and construction are arts of *facts* and *values*; states of affairs, situations, and facts are recognized and judged relative to their elements and their composition by the arts of communication and construction.

The new grammar or art of interpretation or hermeneutics is the art of interpreting objective evidence, that is, of interpreting what is the case as what is the case. Its subject-matter is all things already known, expressed, and recorded, that is, all communications. Interpretation may focus primarily on statement, thought, or situation, but whatever its focus, each interpretation takes into account statements, judgments, and situations, and from them constructs a possible world and interprets it as one construction among possible worlds. The sciences and the arts are bodies of communications already achieved and recorded, and they provide the materials for the interpretation of facts and values as they have been found to be and present the evidence already available concerning what they are. The new grammar is the art of *recovery*. It is not an art of topics or a *selection* of elements, but an art of hypotheses or an *interpretation* of situations and facts. The subject-matter of the fundamental grammar is all situations and all that is known to be the case. The subject matters of derived grammars emerge when what is the case, situation, judgment, and statement are treated as language and symbol in exegetical grammars of analysis, or as thought and hypotheses in normative grammars of usage, or as things and facts in descriptive grammars of use.

Logic is the art of presentation and analysis, of inquiry and proof. Logical and rational arts, *logoi* and *rationes*, are employed to analyze or resolve problematic situations and to discover or create sequential connections. We find a logic in the flow of statements, of ideas, of occurrence, and of feelings; and we develop and transmit arts and methods for the rational treatment of problems of discourse and discursive sequences, problems of thought and rational illations, problems of experience and factual consequences, and problems of feeling and emotional involvements. When the philosophic arts are conceived as arts of thought, logic provides the structure or essence of philosophy in all its branches, applications, and consequences; and Kant therefore is able to find in transcendental logic an order for the concepts and the problems of theory, practice, and judgment proper to each and relative to each other, and Russell is able to argue that logistic or mathematical logic becomes the "essence of philosophy" by providing a mathematical symbolism for deducing consequences from premises. But logic has a broader sense and scope, and applies to more kinds of discursive sequences of statement, than those of the forms of inference and judgment which fall under Boole's Laws of Thought or even of the forms of reason and judgment which fall under Kant's Aesthetics, Analytics, and Dialectics. There are narrative, descriptive, lyrical, rhetorical, communicative, and expressive as well as inferential and demonstrative consequences; and poetry or politics or rhetoric may become the essence of philosophy as facilely and persuasively as logic or grammar. There are different ways of conveying the same message, account, or proof; and there are different analyses of a single presentation or argument—formal or material, intentional or circumstantial, epistemic, pistic, or constitutive, demonstrative or heuristic.

Logic is an art of connection and conclusion, of inquiry and proof, of question and analysis, of problem and resolution. In Aristotle's logic, the forms of inference and the establishment of principles were treated in two "analytics" (which were sometimes called *"resolutoria"* in Latin), while in the Euclidean tradition principles were established by "analysis" and conclusions were derived by "synthesis." The two movements—from what is sought to what must be assumed, and from what is assumed to what is concluded or what is constructed—may be traced in all the varieties of meaningful connections of discourse, ranging from expressions of ideas and feelings, descriptions of things and situations, creations of artistic wholes through expositions of what is known and inquiries concerning what is not known, to the forms of valid inference and true demonstration. Conclusions are, with a change in the mode of analysis, denouements, consummations, ends, fulfillments, climaxes, or achievements. The rational or logical arts or methods are employed to establish the hypotheses and facts of interpretation and to trace their antecedents and conclusions. The sequences may, moreover, be considered in the forms of community established by communication as well as in the forms of connected statements, thoughts, and things. *Homiletics* reflects *analytics*, for homiletics is communication which forms an assembly or communion (*homilía*) by establishing likenesses or contacts (*homós*) in a crowd (*íle*), and analytics is communication which relates effects to causes.

The object of communication in logic broadly conceived emerges in connections set forth in the "themes" which are traced in their complications and resolutions of actions and their consequences. Themes and structures of connection recur with variations in particular accounts and analyses; and they are transposed from region to region, from science to science, from art to art, and from art to science and back again from science to art. Sequences of events and arguments are particular; formulations of the laws of sequences are universal. The devices of "demonstration" have been broadened in rhetorical argumentation from devices of deduction and proof to include all devices of manifestation, and the devices of "judgment" have been broadened in grammatical argumentation from the devices of forming and interpreting propositions to include all devices of forming and interpreting hypotheses and facts in situations, sentiments, and sentences. The devices of rational or logical argumentation are the devices of "deliberation," broadened from presentation of alternatives in practical actions and choice among them, to include all devices of analysis and decision-making. Homiletics, analytics, and methodologies establish and formulate that which is as it is found in connected subject-matters, in communities associated in common convictions, and in communications about subjects and between associated communicators. The arts of communication and construction are arts of *inquiry* and *presentation*; connections of occurrence, thought, and statement provide the warrant and the framework for what are presented and accepted as the elements of existence and the facts of experience.

The new logic or analytic or art of method is the art of relating, that is, of relating occurrences and reactions in accounts which induce sensitive awareness and consequential judgment. Accounts of sequences and consequences examine and recount recurrent themes in specific or singular variations. An analytic of particular connections uncovers universal relations in individual embodiments of universal laws of connection. It is a method of knowing, doing, and making that which is, by organizing situations and problems, movements and resolutions into a unified, compendent whole or field, and by constituting its particularity in processes and accounts. By uncovering themes it moves from field to field. The new logic is the art of *presentation*. It is not an art of topics or of hypotheses, but an art of themes or a *method* of connections and accounts. The subject-matter of the fundamental logic is all that can be conceived or said to be and all connections which constitute possible worlds, possible laws of thought, and possible modes of statement and expression. The subject-matters of the derived logics emerge when basic connections are established as mapped spaces and loci which reproduce laws of natural occurrences and structures of matter, or as formed inferences and judgments which reproduce laws of thought and definitions of conception, or as expressed implications and variables which reproduce laws of syntax and determinations of vocabulary.

Dialectic is the art of dialogue and insight, of systematization and objectification, of assimilation and division. When the philosophic arts are conceived as arts of being, dialectic is the art of testing first principles, causes, and elements of knowledge, action, and construction. The principles of dialectic ground the compendent sets traced in the connections of things, thoughts, actions, and statements by logical inference or narration. The grounding is provided by establishing coincidences or identities of principles or beginnings of occurrences with principles or beginnings of analytic thought, of reasoned action, or of rational statement; that is, by establishing the compendent sets reflexively on each other in objective systems of identities and differences. Dialectic, as an art of being, makes metaphysics an architectonic science; as an art of thought it seeks connections in spirit or matter, and the architectonic ordering tends to come from practical reason; finally, the arts of communication and construction may transform dialectic and seek architectonic ordering in the dialogue of cultural communication and political construction.

Dialectic is the art of dialogue and insight, of reflexivity and individuation, of principle and encompassing order: it is an art of communication which focuses on the organization and circumstances of communication, and therefore on the cosmos as the model and ground of world order, mutual understanding, and common humanity. It is the system of the arts and sciences, the encyclopaedia of facts and suppositions, the compass of the actualities and potentialities. It is the encompassing dialogue in which "theses" are encountered and enunciated and are tried as principles constitutive of universes or systems of things, of thoughts, of communities, and of communications. In a dialogue which centers on theses and principles, on wholes and parts, self-sufficient parts are constructed into wholes and render them intelligible, and encompassing wholes are distinguished into parts which derive their properties and intelligibility from the wholes in which they function; and systems are transformed by change of principles. The arts of communication and construction are arts of *unification* and *transformation*; perceived or proferred connections are fantastic, subjective, or abstract unless they present evidence of their connection with what is the case and unless their reasons are tied down to the principles and causes of the connections they represent and present.

The new dialectic or systematics or art of principles is the art of structuring action and knowledge, that is, of bringing what we think, and say, and do into relation to what we are and the circumstances in which we find ourselves by forming them into encompassing wholes by reasoned, deliberative, and responsible integration. Principles of knowledge, action, and presentation are theses of being, thought, fact, value, and existence which are accepted and credited after having been tested in the actions which constitute inquiry, proof, discovery, and expression. It is a dialectic of principles and of the transformation of principles operating by an exchange and interpenetration of arts used as architectonic. It is a method of knowing, doing, and making tied to being by postulation of relations among all relevant fields in a system of interdependence. The new dialectic is the art of *action*. It is not an art of topics or of hypotheses or of themes, but an art of theses or *principles* proposed for arts and sciences and their interrelations. The subject-matter of the fundamental dialectic is the total framework of things to be done. The subject-matters of the derived dialectics emerge when it is postulated that metaphysics, or politics, or poetics, or rhetoric are architectonic sciences. The arts of communication and construction may take their ordering principles from models in structures of being or knowing; or the arts of communication and construction may provide the architectonic structures for knowing, doing, making, and saying and for the structures of being that are produced by action in accordance with those structures.

The philosophic arts have always been arts of communication and construction. As arts of forming statements constructed to be true and presenting arguments communicated to convince, they have been designed to achieve objectivity and universality. Yet the frequent changes of philosophic positions and philosophic problems in the history of philosophy have been expressions and manifestations of changes in the philosophic arts, and changes in the arts have brought with them changes in the subject-matter and data of discussion. Subject-matter and arts change from philosophy to philosophy, and communication among philosophers is more frequently ideological controversy concerning methods of determining what is the case than substantive discussion concerning what has been or might be alleged to be the case. Differences in subject-matters are differences concerning what the facts are and whether, once they have been stated clearly, they are indeed facts; they are differences concerning the contexts or universes which facts or occurrences constitute, and by which they are conditioned, and concerning how facts or occurrences are related to, and influence, each other. Differences in the arts are differences of method applied to the problems of knowing, doing, making, and saying, and to the intermingling of those problems which results from changes in subject-matters; they are differences which have been used to separate dialectic, logic, grammar, and rhetoric, to transform and revolutionize them in the history of their development, to delimit or expand the scope of their operation, and to establish the architectonic determination they assume relative to each other. There has been a continuity of structure and purpose in the philosophic arts which may serve as a mark by which to gauge progress in philosophical inquiry in any effort at dead-reckoning the uses of philosophy; but progress in inquiry by use of the philosophical arts has been obscured by semantic changes in the devices of the arts and in the consequent selection of data of existence or interpretation of facts of experience. But inquiry into the problems of existence and experience are inseparable from semantic selection and interpretation of categories and modes of statement, and semantic controversy and refutation has both obscured progress in philosophical inquiry, since an opposed position becomes opaque and meaningless when interpreted according to the assumptions and methods of the opposing philosophy, and has also contributed to the advance of philosophical inquiry, because the diversity of approaches revealed in controversy, once the ardor of debate has cooled, opens up the richness of common problems which are the subject of philosophical inquiry. Common experience and objective existence lie beyond, and exceed, the fixities of judgments in which facts are stated and interpreted and of categories in which terms are selected and defined. The subject-matter and the problems of the philosophic arts find their universal generality in experience and existence, in language and communication, which are the common sources of concrete facts and data, law-like structures and sequences; the assumptions and the devices of the philosophic arts find their neutrality and objectivity by adapting and merging the methods of traditional arts to the concrete specifications of a common subject-matter.

Debate and controversy are functions of the art of rhetoric. Communication among philosophies takes a rhetorical turn in the incidental references which philosophers pause to make to the errors of predecessors or contemporaries. Every philosophy has a place for rhetoric, large or small, positive or pejorative; and judgments about rhetoric, good or bad, as well as rhetorical judgments, prejudiced or judicial, have bases in the principles and methods of philosophy. Statement and interpretation are functions of the art of grammar. Interpretation of philosophical statements in the citations of other philosophers made in the course of philosophic argument uncover a grammar of composition and make use of a grammar of interpretation to disclose meanings, and even in sympathetic interpretations the vocabulary and syntax of the interpreter affects the meaning of the cited words and statements. When the arts of communication and construction assume an architectonic function, the arts of logic and dialectic are practiced by devices borrowed from rhetoric and grammar, and the characteristics of things and thoughts are derived as subject-matter from the concrete data and facts of existence and experience. The fixities and distortions of semantic controversy are rigidified since the refutations and interpretations of rival philosophies are given a putative basis in concrete experience and existence in the statement and construction of each philosophy, but the transition from arbitrary determinations of semantics into structures of closed statements, to ongoing developments of inquiry into opening problems is rendered possible by the broadening and merging of the arts of communications in concrete applications and situations.

The arts of communication and construction give promise of constituting a new philosophy in which the pluralism of arts and philosophies makes use of semantic differences for diversified treatment of the common problems and subject-matters of philosophical inquiry rather than setting the different arts and philosophies in controversial opposition in which semantic differences mark off the rival possibilities of unique statement of truth and determination of values. The new rhetoric may be broadened from persuasion to include all elements of existence and to use commonplaces or topics for discovery of the unknown. The new grammar may be broadened from the composition of statements to include all facts of experience and to use hypotheses of semantics for recovery of the known. The new logic may be broadened from inquiry and proof to include all discursive sequences and all sequential series stated in discourse and to use the themes of the arts for presentation of connections. The new dialectic may be broadened from systems of thought and being to include all ordering principles, elements, and causes and to use the theses of inquiry to unify and transform possible world orders and human orders. The new philosophy can not be a monolithic inclusive shared ideology, but it may oppose the dogmatisms of partial and divisive universalisms to become a philosophy of communications and the arts.

RHETORIC AND COMMUNICATION IN PHILOSOPHY

H. W. Johnstone, Jr.

In his bold and wide-ranging paper, Professor McKeon has sketched the dynamics of a variety of concepts which are both ingredients in the philosophical enterprise and subject to philosophical scrutiny. He has suggested how communication, rhetoric, logic, and grammar interpenetrate, and how, under different historical conditions, they are subject to different interpretations and emphases. In this essay I would like to examine a limited set of the phenomena Professor McKeon has considered. I want to focus on rhetoric and communication, and consider what they are in themselves and how they are involved in philosophical activity. Of course the concepts of rhetoric and communication are not themselves philosophically neutral components of philosophical activity. How one construes the concepts depends upon the overt or covert philosophical position one takes. In investigating the role of rhetoric and communication in philosophy, I cannot help taking a stand on the philosophy *of* rhetoric and communication. To the extent that developing the philosophy *of* anything is an activity in which rhetoric and communication have necessary roles to play, rhetoric and communication are required by the very activity that seeks to define them. I do not believe that the circularity here is vicious: the phenomenon is simply an example of the often noted reflexivity of philosophical activity.

One reason determining the roles of rhetoric and communication in philosophy is a problem is that undue emphasis on one to the exclusion of the other in the pursuit of the philosophical enterprise has usually resulted in a caricature of that enterprise. The belief that the function of philosophy is to communicate and not to persuade is characteristic of at least the extreme forms of positivism. Persuasion is here dismissed as merely a function of emotive language. What positivism has found par excellence communicable, however, has been scientific

351

fact and theory rather than philosophical doctrine. Once the sciences have been identified as the chief locus of communication, there is not much left for philosophy as such to do, except perhaps to formulate the principles of scientific communication. An example of such principles is the Verifiability Criterion, according to which only empirical statements and tautologies can be communicated—everything else is meaningless. But even the ultra-positivist is willing to concede that the principles formulated in his philosophy, including the Verifiability Criterion itself, are neither empirical statements nor tautologies; they are rather conventions. Clearly, conventions are not formulated merely to be ignored. The positivist attaches considerable importance, for example, to a scrupulous observance of the Verifiability Criterion. He insists on this observance as a necessary condition for meaningful discourse. Since such insistence is not grounded in fact or logic, it can only have the status of urgent persuasion. Rhetoric has thus made its uninvited appearance. That the positivist tacitly recognizes its presence is indicated by his vague and apologetic explanation that the Verifiability Criterion has a pragmatic if not a logical or empirical justification. For what has only a pragmatic justification can only be contended for as a means of facilitating action. But a belief that facilitates action is itself an action or a program of action; and it is precisely the function of rhetoric to incite actions and programs.

Philosophies in which rhetoric is given an exaggerated role to play and communication none at all are not likely to have much professional standing, because professionals must communicate; "Publish or perish" is merely a corollary of "If you can't tell us what you're doing, how do we know that you're doing anything at all?" But clearly there are hyper-rhetorical positions, whether or not they are mentioned in academic circles. One symptom of such a position is its use of the idea of Philistinism. The Philistine is the obtuse individual who demands to be told what no one can hope to learn merely by being told. Only by being open to rhetoric can one hope to be sensitized to the doctrine in question, but the Philistine is closed to rhetoric. Implicit in such a hyper-rhetoricism is the principle that one cannot understand a doctrine unless one has been persuaded to believe it. This principle is to rhetoric as the Verifiability Criterion is to communication. As the latter defines the limits of communication without itself being communicated, so the former defines the limits of rhetoric without itself being the object of rhetorical activity. If it were itself the object of rhetorical activity, we would be plunged into an infinite regress, for we would then have to argue that the meta-philistine who cannot understand why to understand is to believe would understand this principle if he believed it. The principle is the inverse of a convention—whatever that is. It is the one principle that the hyperrhetoricist must communicate, and is thus his Achilles heel. Of course, if he saw no one as a philistine, he would have no use for this principle. But it is precisely the beliefs, platitudinous and thoughtless though they are, of those whom the hyperrhetoricist identifies as philistines that define the content and point of his own position. Without philistines to deplore there would be no occasion for exhortations to the faithful. Similarly, without nonsense to attack, the positivist would have nothing philosophical to communicate.

We may note in passing that even though hyperrhetorical positions have little standing in professional circles, the professional philosopher himself may have hyperrhetorical tendencies. Although he can comfortably communicate with his colleagues, he may regard those who are not his colleagues as Philistines. When asked by someone outside the field to describe his concerns, he may find that there is nothing he can communicate which would be of the slightest use, and that all he can say is "If you really want to know, you'd better take my course." To be sure, professional philosophers are by no means alone in this aloofness; professional economists and physicists are inclined to give the same answer, and the aloofness itself can be interpreted as no more than despair over the task of attempting to communicate briefly what can only be communicated at length. Yet there are few professional philosophers who suppose that all they have to convey to their students is information, even of a difficult and involved kind. Most of us have the feeling that the student who merely has the information is still a Philistine, and that some turning, some acquiescence of the will to concerns that must be first accepted if they are to be understood, is required if the student is to be set on the road to becoming a professional philosopher. Since I myself unabashedly share in this feeling, it would be ludicrous of me to condemn it; I cite it only in order to show that hyperrhetoricism is more common than it may at first appear to be.

But the sketches I have drawn of positions in which the roles of communication and rhetoric are exaggerated are themselves exaggerated. Perhaps all that can be safely gleaned from them is just a preliminary understanding of the concepts of communication and rhetoric. Communication, as the positivist embraces it and the hyperrhetoricist rejects it, is a transaction concerned with propositions. A proposition, as I am using the term, must be either true or false, but need not be true. The same proposition, furthermore, can be expressed in a variety of ways. Communication, in the weakest sense of the word, occurs when one person expresses a proposition and, as a result, another person understands the same proposition. If there are no linguistic or intellectual considerations that prevent a recipient of a message from understanding it—if he can read the language in which the message is couched, and the message is not too complex for him to follow—then the Verifiability Criterion can be thought of as an attempt to define what can be communicated in this sense. Nothing meaningless can be communicated; i.e., nothing which is neither a tautology nor empirically testable. It is communication in this weakest sense that the hyperrhetoricist finds ineffectual in reaching the Philistine; for no amount of it will make the philistine understand the doctrine he has, in his oafish good nature, inquired about. A stronger sense of the word is that in which A communicates proposition P to B if and only if as the result of A's efforts B believes P. This is the way in which I will use the word unless I give special notice to the contrary. The strongest sense of "communication" is that in which only true propositions can be communicated; that is, B believes P and P is true. It is in this sense of "communicate" that what one communicates is information.

Rhetoric emerges from our discussion up to this point as concerned with attitudes rather than propositions. To the extent that it is occupied with linguistic forms, it will focus not on propositions as such but upon the sentences that most effectively present them to others. Propositions need not be believed in order to be understood, and communication, in the weakest sense, solicits only the understanding of propositions; but rhetoric solicits belief first in the expectation that understanding will follow. Communication in the strongest sense essentially conveys information, but rhetoric essentially seeks to stimulate action, including the action of adopting a recommended belief. It is thus the art of persuasion. Its success or failure is not to be measured by the truth or falsity of the beliefs it recommends, but by the extent to which others have by its agency been persuaded to accept these beliefs.

I have spoken of the dialectical reversals that await both the ultrapositivist seeking to avoid using rhetoric and the hyperrhetoricist seeking to avoid using communication. What I have just said in the attempt to define communication and rhetoric suggests that even if we do not attempt to erect these concepts into doctrines, as the ultrapositivists and the hyperrhetoricists do, a powerful dialectic is at work that prevents more than a provisional distinction between the concepts themselves. When communication is defined in the intermediate and standard way as getting someone else to believe what one believes, it is obviously difficult to see why such an evocation of belief should not be considered a rhetorical transaction as well as a communicative one. In a perhaps somewhat less obvious way, furthermore, the weakest form of communication is saturated with rhetoric. If I want to get you to understand a proposition that I understand, I may proceed, as the positivist wants me to do, by first making sure that what I have to communicate is actually a proposition; i.e., is empirically testable or logically true. I may then carefully formulate it with your linguistic and intellectual requirements in mind. But surely it is a mistake to suppose that all that I would now have to do is enunciate the proposition as I have now formulated it. What I would also have to do is to get your attention. The art of getting another person's attention, however, clearly falls within the province of rhetoric rather than communication. And there is no genuine act of communication that does require the use of this art. No doubt we can count on having the computer's full attention when we feed it a stack of punched cards, but when we talk of having communicated something to it via these cards we are using "communication" in a borrowed and anthropomorphic way. As the result of having been fed the cards, the computer stores certain values and instructions, but we cannot make sense of the assertion that it has come to understand a proposition. Understanding is an achievement; whatever one understands, one could have failed to understand. But being primed with certain data is no achievement for the machine; it is at best an achievement for its maker or operator. The machine could have stored the wrong values, but we would describe such a situation as a malfunction, not as a failure on the part of the machine to understand what someone had tried to communicate to it.

The concept of rhetoric is similarly not dissociable from that of communication. Having gotten someone to listen to you, you must then proceed to say something. While it is action that rhetoric solicits, it is not action in the service of a proposition. Those whom the hyperrhetoricist recognizes as brothers rather than philistines are united not by conforming behavior but by faith. And if they have come to understand something by just believing it, at least they now understand it—the net effect of the transaction is that they have received a communication.

So far I have schematically described two extremist positions that might be taken toward the roles of communication and rhetoric in philosophy, and from these descriptions I have extracted preliminary definitions of communication and rhetoric themselves. We must now turn to positions that have actually been held, and we must make needed corrections in our notions of communication and of rhetoric. Wittgenstein, in *Tractatus Logico-Philosophicus*, and Heidegger, in *Sein und Zeit*, not only take more or less explicit positions regarding the roles of communication and rhetoric in philosophy but also to some extent practice what they preach. These two books are important, however, not only because of their orientations toward communication and rhetoric but also because these orientations are representative of the broad philosophical camps to which the books belong. In spite of some major differences between Wittgenstein's *Tractatus* and the outlook of many contemporary linguistic analysis, what Wittgenstein says about philosophy in the *Tractatus* sets the tone for much of the Anglo-American linguistic analysis that has ensued upon it. Similarly, the attitude Heidegger takes toward philosophy in *Sein und Zeit* sets the tone of much contemporary Continental European philosophy with respect to the issue of communication and rhetoric in philosophy. Hence reference to these books will enable us to compare two segments of the philosophical world which have often been thought impossible to compare; and possibly we will be able to suggest an area of rapprochement between them.

Wittgenstein declares himself early on the importance of communication. In the second paragraph of the Preface to the *Tractatus*, he writes "What can be said at all can be said clearly, and what we cannot talk about we must pass over in silence." [1] Surely it is communication that Wittgenstein is here emphasizing. The mark of something said clearly is that it is understood; i.e., communicated. His point is that everything sayable must be communicable. One for whom rhetoric had a necessary role could deny this. He would point to the philistine, to whom one can talk until doomsday without communicating anything. The mere fact that one cannot get him to understand one's doctrine by means of any amount of clear talk does not show that one must pass over these doctrines in silence.

The passage I have just quoted, however, is really about communication in every field *except* philosophy. It expresses a systematic limitation on philosophical communication. For philosophy, according to Wittgenstein, has nothing to say. It is "not a body of doctrine but an activity . . . Philosophy does not result in "philosophical propositions", but rather in the clarification of propositions." [2] Wittgenstein seems to be in the position of recommending that we pass over in silence anything that we think we might have to say in the name of philosophy, for it is nothing we can really say at all.

This, however, is far from Wittgenstein's final verdict. In its very concern with the incommunicable, philosophy communicates something: "It will signify what cannot be said, by presenting clearly what can be said." [3] This clear presentation of what can be said is what Wittgenstein has in mind in speaking of philosophy as the activity of clarifying propositions rather than producing propositions itself.

The idea that philosophy is to present clearly what can be said, suggests that it can present clearly what has hitherto been presented obscurely. Wittgenstein attributes much obscurity of this kind to difficulties that philosophers have had with language: "Most of the propositions and questions of philosophers arise from our failure to understand the logic of our language: . . . All philosophy is a 'critique of language.'" [4]

Philosophical activity as Wittgenstein conceives it can be illustrated profusely from his own work as well as from that of many others. Philosophical sentences are exhibited as in fact unsayable by showing that they fail to conform to the logic of our language. Even the language of the *Tractatus* itself must ultimately be left behind, because there is no position beyond our language from which we can *describe* its logic; all that we can hope to do is to simply *show* its logic, by saying as clearly as possible what can be said. Thus at the end of the *Tractatus* Wittgenstein says "My propositions serve as elucidations in the following way: anyone who understands me eventually recognizes them as nonsensical, when he has used them—as steps—to climb up beyond them." [5]

One difference between Wittgenstein's conception of the function of philosophy and that of the ultrapositivists is that the discovery that what the philosopher is inclined to say is unsayable does not undercut the former in the way that the discovery that the Verifiability Criterion is neither empirical nor tautologous undercuts the latter. Having made this shocking discovery, which amounts to the acknowledgment that the Verifiability Criterion cannot be communicated, the ultrapositivist can only make a rhetorical plea for its adoption; but this plea is inconsistent with his basic conviction that the function of philosophy is to communicate and not to persuade. For Wittgenstein, on the other hand, philosophy can elucidate even though it says nothing; and elucidation is clearly a kind of communication. Hence Wittgenstein's view does not have the fundamental incoherence of ultrapositivism.

Anglo-American philosophy has largely adopted Wittgenstein's conception of philosophy as an activity that eliminates problems caused by inattention to the logic of our language. According to this conception, philosophy is clearly communicative; at least when it is done properly. What philosophy has to communicate is not propositions but elucidations. It follows that we must to some extent abandon our preliminary understanding of communication as concerned with propositions. Of course, one could point to the logic that is violated by the problem we seek to elucidate by expressing this logic as a set of propositions in the metalanguage; this approach has often been taken. The fact remains, however, that this is not Wittgenstein's own approach, and his philosophy communicates as much about the sources of our philosophical ills as anyone else's. It communicates because it disseminates as understanding which is not contingent on prior belief. To put the matter in another way, no one stands in relation to Wittgenstein as an intrinsically unreachable philistine; there is always hope that the philosopher can reach his hearers by reformulating his point one more time. If he gives up it is because he is tired, not because they are philistines. Yet notice how the gap between communication and rhetoric has been narrowed. The clarity that the philosopher aims to pass on is as much a reorientation of attitudes as an intellectual reassessment. It is an understanding, but not the kind of understanding that one could put completely in words. It is a release from perplexity, and thus an enhancement of the hearer's well-being. In the last analysis one accepts Wittgenstein's elucidations not because they are true—whatever that could mean—but because one feels better about accepting them. The rhetorical dimension of the transaction resulting in this acceptance is obvious.

An early section of Heidegger's *Sein und Zeit* is entitled "The Lesson of a Destruction of the History of Ontology." [6] It is strange to see a philosopher writing of the *destruction* of anything philosophical; philosophers do not usually suppose that they *destroy* doctrines or the histories of doctrines; they do not imagine that such destruction could even be relevant to the enterprise in which they are engaged. The business in which most philosophers think they are engaged is that of *refuting* rather than destroying. To refute a doctrine is to exhibit it as incoherent and therefore unacceptable. A refuted doctrine can still be *exhibited*; indeed, if it could not, it could not be refuted, for there would be nothing to which we could then ascribe the incoherence that we want to ascribe to the doctrine. To put the matter in another way, the philosopher who regards the refutation of a doctrine as his concern must first make his hearers understand what it is he is attacking. Since the dissemination of understanding falls within the province of communication, refutation is a communicative transaction.

How would the destruction of a doctrine differ from its refutation? If a doctrine were destroyed, it would cease to exist, and therefore could no longer be exhibited, even exhibited as incoherent. If we are too literal-minded, we may find ourselves asking how it is that Heidegger thinks he can write about the history of ontology at all if he has indeed destroyed this history. (We can of course write the history of *things* that have been destroyed, but according to Heidegger's title, it is the very *history* of ontology that is to be destroyed.) Yet we can interpret the destruction of the history of ontology in a more sympathetic way. To destroy this history is to expose it as a bad dream; it is to awaken us from this dream, which has held us in its thrall for two thousand years.

Thus what is destroyed is the power of the history over us. Heidegger can write about this history as one can write about any illusion from which we have been released.

Destruction, then, in Heidegger's terms, is an awakening. To use other words that occur frequently not only in *Sein und Zeit* but throughout Heidegger's works, it is a recall from forgetfulness. Heidegger makes it clear that he regards such an evocation as one of the primary tasks of philosophy, if not its only task. Clearly, then, he conceives of philosophy as fundamentally a rhetorical enterprise. Its function is not only to awaken, but specifically *not* to disseminate understanding. Traditional ontology, for example, is, according to Heidegger, not something that a person could simply understand, prior to deciding whether it is true or false. The person is defined by his ontology, and is held in its grip. He can dissociate himself from it only by being awakened from it; but he can be awakened from it only by becoming a new person. Heidegger's appeal is not merely rhetorical but downright homiletical.

Yet for all his emphasis on the rhetorical nature of the philosophical enterprise, Heidegger is no hyperrhetoricist. For the content and point of his doctrine is not defined simply by contrasting the doctrine with the beliefs of the philistines. In fact, Heidegger's entire position is specifically committed to the task of awakening the philistines from their ontological slumber. Heidegger refers to the philistines as *das Man* —the "they." *Das Man* expects to be told in plain language what he can in fact come to understand only by being awakened. But because Heidegger's entire thrust is *toward* the awakening of *das Man* he cannot reject as a mere philistine the man who fails to understand him. In Heidegger's own terms, he is not successful until he has reached the philistine. Hence in a sense there are no philistines at all for him.

If I am correct in arguing that Heidegger conceives philosophy as basically rhetorical, some revision in our conception of rhetoric is called for. We can no longer think of it as an art of persuasion, except perhaps derivatively; its purpose is not to incite its hearer to action—even the action of adopting some specific belief. Instead, rhetoric totally reorients the hearer; if he listens to it he is in a position to abandon an inauthentic life in favor of an authentic one. Once we see that rhetoric has an at best incidental concern with action, we remove one of the important differences between it and communication. Rhetoric as bound to action is successful or unsuccessful; the question of its validity does not arise. If we have persuaded person A to perform act B or adopt belief C, our rhetoric has been efficacious, and it is gratuitous to ask whether he *ought* to do B or believe C. The validity question more properly arises in connection with communication, especially in the strongest sense in which only the truth can be communicated. Here the test is not only that we have gotten A to believe C but also that C is true. But this test applies to Heidegger's rhetoric too. For it is certainly one of Heidegger's most emphatically expressed doctrines that it is the truth to which a person must be awakened. This doctrine is in fact a corollary of the Heideggerian account of truth as unconcealment.

Just as Wittgenstein's view of philosophy as primarily communicative is echoed by a large segment of Anglo-American philosophy, so Heidegger's rhetorical conception expresses an attitude toward the philosophical enterprise that is widespread on the European continent. It is doubtful that it originated with Heidegger; for the Husserlian phenomenology from which Heidegger took his departure is already fundamentally committed to a rhetorical view of philosophy. While Husserl's talk about essences may suggest that he thought the function of philosophy was to communicate about them; the epoché, or bracketing of ordinary experience that Husserl took to be the starting point of philosophical inquiry is actually an awakening to essence—a laying aside of prosaic concerns and attitudes that permits the person to come to a more authentic form of life. We find the same basic orientation in much post-Heideggerian philosophy on the Continent, as well as in the phenomenological soil from which Heidegger's thought sprang; it is clearly an existentialistic orientation as well as a phenomenological one.

For Wittgenstein, philosophy elucidates, and in so doing engages in nonpropositional communication. For Heidegger, philosophy awakens, and in so doing engages in a nonpersuasive rhetoric. The gap between communication and rhetoric has been narrowed from both sides. Is it possible, indeed, to suppose that there *is* any longer a gap? Wittgenstein and his followers have often spoken of the power of philosophy to remind us of what we already know, as if it were identical with its elucidatory power. To elucidate problems is simply to remind one's hearers of the logic of our language. It is to awaken them from an ontological slumber. To be sure, the slumber with which Wittgenstein is concerned is far different from that with which Heidegger is concerned. It would be a gross distortion to say that Wittgenstein is trying to call his audience to authentic existence, or that Heidegger is trying to call his to an awareness of the logic of our language. The only identity for which I am arguing is the identity of their views of the function of philosophy. Both of them emphasize the call of philosophy. At the same time, both see this call as communicative, as an elucidation or unconcealment.

I want to conclude by formulating the evocative-elucidatory function of philosophy in more general terms. If philosophy has this function in both Anglo-American and Continental European philosophy, it does so because philosophy always has this function, at least when it is not caricaturing itself. Using an odd and somewhat old-fashioned word, I want to say that philosophy is the articulation of morale. Good morale is not associated with a dull or confused person. It belongs only to those who have to some extent broken out from illusion and confusion. They know what they are about, and they have a sense of their own competence. Morale is thus a certain rather explicit self-confidence. It is philosophy, in my view, that renders this self-confidence explicit, and thus distinguishes it from a mere unthinking valor. Of course we cannot point to a prior self-confidence which we then proceed to make explicit; the self-confidence is itself the result of an increasing explicitude in the way we confront the world. Wittgenstein's *Tractatus* is clearly intended to improve the morale of the thinker beset by confusions about the logic of our language. It accomplishes its purpose by making this logic explicit, and thus by giving the thinker an explicit self-confidence with respect to his ability to identify and handle the problems arising from abuses of logic. This ability, however, is more than a technical skill. It is a fundamental stance in the world. The technician, failing to take such a stance, can remain essentially confused about the nature of the problems to which he addresses himself, or even oblivious to their existence; hence the technician can lack morale for all his technical skill. This point is clearly made by Heidegger, who sees technical skill as falling within the competence of *das Man*, the inauthentic one who lacks morale. The "know-how" of *das Man*, his skill, his curiosity, and his preoccupation with jargon, may simply provide him with an excuse for evading the issues to which morale would be relevant.

Not only Wittgenstein and Heidegger, but all important philosophers, have been concerned with man's morale. In different ages they have formulated in different terms the principles upon which an explicit self-confidence can be based. If asked to amplify this remark, I would not hesitate to refer to Professor McKeon's illuminating summary of the historical progress of philosophy. According to Professor McKeon, the fundamental category of ancient philosophy was Being, that of modern philosophy was Thought, and that of contemporary philosophy is Action. The generalization I would base upon this summary is that the ancient philosophers sought to provide man with an explicit self-confidence by exhibiting Man's being as continuous with Being as such; modern philosophers pointed to man's competence as a thinker as a basis for morale; and contemporary philosophers have tried to establish man's morale primarily by making him aware of his role as an agent. If we test the last clause of this generalization by applying it to Wittgenstein and

Heidegger, we see that the fit is not too bad. The action that Wittgenstein is concerned with is the speaking of language; his concern with this action is to render it competent. The action that Heidegger is concerned with is of no specific kind; it is action itself, viewed under the form of time, that occupies Heidegger, and the authenticity of which he seeks to establish.

It remains to be shown what communication and rhetoric have to do with morale. My view is that they are involved in the way in which the philosopher addresses those whose morale he seeks to improve. Such hearers must both find morale desirable and unwittingly lack it. Their lack of morale unbeknownst to themselves can be the result of a relative confusion or dullness. I use the term "relative" because there is a point beyond which a person's dullness or confusion cannot be increased without depriving him of his very desire for morale. To the glassy-eyed person stumbling about in ontological oblivion, there is nothing one can say; any awakening would be a miracle. To the person thoroughly imbued with the courage of his confusions there is likewise nothing one can say, the efficaciousness of which can, to any degree, be counted on. Let us assume, then, that the philosopher's hearers are people under the erroneous impression that their pursuit of morale has been successful. Accordingly the first thing the speaker must do is to point out that those whom he addresses are living in a fool's paradise. Their attempts to formulate an explicit self-confidence have amounted precisely to a denial of the competence they are claiming. This is, for example, the message of the philosophers of Being to those who attempt to articulate man's morale by proclaiming that man is the measure of all things. It is the message of the philosophers of Thought to those who attempt to express morale in terms of man's belonging to the nature of things. It is the message of the philosophers of Action to those who think they have found morale in deductive thought. All such messages are communicative. Their aim is to point out to the hearer something he did not know.

Of course, *any* message is communicative; that is what it means to call it a message. But what philosophers have to say to their hearers are more than messages. They are arguments. Plato did not merely *tell* Protagoras that the morale he had settled for was specious. He also urged him to adopt the higher morale of identification with Being. He could go on to do this only because morale was what Protagoras wanted. Similarly, we will listen to Heidegger's evocations only if his destruction of the history of ontology has created in us the need for a newer morale.

I am obviously now speaking of the rhetorical component of philosophical argumentation. But in suggesting that it can be separated out from the communicative component, I am oversimplifying. The philosopher does not first attack existing formulations of morale and then propose new formulations of it. His very attack introduces his proposal. In Wittgenstein's *Tractatus*, for example, it would be very difficult to distinguish the communicative from the rhetorical. This difficulty has characterized the writings of most important philosophers. Even when a philosophical treatise begins with a polemical section and goes on to propose a positive doctrine, the polemic is likely to be informed with the doctrine that is to be proposed.

Even the very act of proposing a doctrine is far from being a purely rhetorical transaction. Doctrines are proposed in the name of truth; morale has often been thought to reside in the unconcealment of the concealed. It is difficult, on the other hand, to think of any philosophical statement that is purely communicative in intent. It is not the message of the philosopher that catches the attention of his hearers; it is his appeal to them to listen.

In this essay I have made some remarks concerning the nature of philosophy. I hope that these remarks will themselves be construed as philosophical. If they are, of course, they ought to exemplify the very analysis of philosophical expressions which they propound. I am confident that they do. I have not only tried to communicate something about the nature of philosophy, but have also recommended a reformulation of at least one prevailing view toward it. According to this view, Anglo-American philosophy communicates, Continental philosophy exhorts, and ne'er the twain shall meet. This view constitutes a potential morale problem, or perhaps an actual one. How *can* we continue to maintain a formulation of our own competence according to which we have competence but others whom we meet at philosophical congresses are systematically barred from attaining it? Such a view, instead of articulating our morale, ends up by destroying it, because the existence of large numbers of intelligent people with whom we cannot communicate shows that we are incompetent at the very skill by which we attempted to define our competence; namely, communication. We will never really be competent at communication until we are ready to admit that in communicating we are also engaging in rhetoric.

NOTES

1. L. G. Wittgenstein, *Tractatus Logico-Philosophicus*, translated by D. F. Pears and B. F. McGuiness (New York, Humanities Press, 1961). All my Wittgenstein quotations are from this edition.

2. Wittgenstein (4. 112).

3. *Ibid.*

4. *Ibid.*

5. *Ibid.*

6. M. Heidegger, *Sein und Zeit,* 7th ed. (Tübingen, M. Niemeyer, 1953), pp. 19–27.

THE RHETORICAL DIMENSION IN PHILOSOPHY

(A RESPONSE)

George J. Stack

A discussion of the relationship between rhetoric and communication in philosophy raises some fundamental questions about the form of philosophy and the intentions of philosophers. It is said that the basic characteristic of communication is the transmission of information in propositional form. A stronger sense of communication, it is pointed out, entails the communication of *true* propositions which a hearer or reader believes are, in fact, true. It is further argued that, insofar as communication involves the endeavor to have someone else believe what the communicator believes, it can also be construed as a rhetorical transaction. In its weaker sense, it is said, communication solicits only the understanding of propositions—this could be described as the conventional meaning of the term. In the final analysis, according to Johnstone, the gap between communication and rhetoric breaks down.

In the first place, it seems to me that Johnstone has abandoned the original distinction he has made (between communication and rhetoric) too hastily. Merely because communication may employ rhetorical devices (as it invariably does) this does not mean that rhetoric *is* communication or that the concept of rhetoric is not "dissociable" from that of communication. Although it is true that rhetoric does, indeed, communicate, this does not mean that it is indistinguishable from communication. Primarily, rhetoric has the function, it seems to me, of communicating not facts as such, or logical truths, but feelings, attitudes, beliefs, or values. It communicates by means of an evocative use of language, by means of persuasion, by means of what Austin described as performative utterances (or inscriptions). The sentences comprising a predominantly rhetorical argument (or a quasi-rhetorical argument) in philosophy may not be individually true or false, even though it is probable that such arguments would often contain contingent or analytic truths. Rhetoric is primarily the language of values, of feelings, or of the collective sentiments of social groups, sub-cultures, or historical peoples. It communicates by means of contagion of feeling, by means of an appeal to common sentiments and values or, occasionally, an appeal to "reason." One may say that rhetoric is not purely communicative since it is not a mode of transmitting empirical facts or logical truths or some kind of information. An encyclopaedia of the physical sciences, for example, would report or communicate the existing empirical facts which are generally accepted by the scientific community aside from references to theories, hypotheses, or laws. Clearly, the dominant concern of contributors to such works is to communicate information or accepted scientific knowledge. Hence, the rhetorical aspects of such a work would be minimal or nonexistent. The philosopher who freely employs rhetoric, however, desires to communicate (like James Joyce and Kierkegaard) by *indirection*. Philosophical communication, on the other hand, is primarily concerned with the direct transmission of factual information or analytic truths—those already established or explicit as well as those which are shown to be such by virtue of argumentation or discovery. To be sure, the philosopher who is attempting to communicate what he holds to be, or understands to be, or interprets as, factual or analytically true statements may obviously infuse his arguments with rhetoric as a supplementary device intended to reinforce his own position. Gilbert Ryle, for example, shows himself to be a master of polemical rhetoric in *The Concept of Mind*. Insofar as a philosopher who is primarily concerned with communication employs rhetoric or rhetorical devices, I would agree with Johnstone that rhetoric and communication may be said to be often interwoven or interrelated. But I would deny that we are unable to distinguish between the two concepts or that they are not dissociable. If this were truly the case, we could not distinguish between Schopenhauer's assertion that "Life is a pendulum which swings between boredom and pain," and the statement that "Brockport is northwest of New York City."

It would seem to me that just as the primarily rhetorical philosopher appeals to common beliefs, so, too, does the philosopher who is essentially concerned with communication. To be sure, communication, if it is not disguised rhetoric, attempts to transmit what is, generally speaking, intersubjectively verifiable (or confirmable) or, in some sense, indisputable or apparent. However, rhetoric as well as communication also appeals to what we conventionally call "understanding." Both modes of philosophical transaction or activity, contrary to accepted opinion, appeal to the attitudes of the listener or reader. Often, what comes to be accepted as a logically persuasive philosophical argument itself becomes inevitably linked with the sentiments or intellectual orientations of those to whom the arguments are directed. The commonly shared presuppositions and philosophical orientations of the listener or reader provide an analogy with the common sentiments or feelings shared by those to whom a rhetorical argument is directed. This is the case, for example, in Marxist philosophy (and not only there) in which certain basic propositions—e.g., that there is a material dialectical process in nature—are unassailed and not subject to dispute even though they may be construed, from a non-Marxist point of view, as metaphysical beliefs. Although rhetoric has been (and is) usually directed towards the elicitation of action, it has also been employed in order to change the attitudes, feelings, commitments, or values of those to whom it is directed. But merely because there may be a coincidence of effects produced by rhetoric and communication, does not mean that we cannot distinguish the one from the other as Johnstone seems to suggest.

I should now like to turn to a number of specific claims that Johnstone makes in his discussion of the relationship between philosophical communication and rhetoric. At one point it is said that Wittgenstein holds that everything that is "sayable" must be communicable and that this conflicts with the basic intention of the rhetorical philosopher. It would seem to me, that rhetoric also deals with the sayable, with an expressive or emotive rather than a communicative use of language. In a very general sense, it could be said that philosophical language cannot be wholly "purified" of a rhetorical aspect since some of its basic terminology is derived from rhetoric. Thus, such terms as *aitia* (cause) or *kategorein* (literally "to accuse") which have been incorporated into philosophical language emerged out of the forensic rhetoric of the Greeks. At any rate, if it is said that the mark of something said clearly is that it is *understood*, then rhetorical arguments or quasi-rhetorical arguments can also be described as *clear* despite Wittgenstein's strictures upon the proper use of language. Could it possibly be said, for example, that those who listened to Pericles' funeral oration did not understand what he said? Would it make sense to say that such a speech was meaningless or nonsense? In the realm of cultural values or ideals the use of rhetorical language is inevitable since the relevant issues are disputable or dialectical. There are no persuasive deductive arguments which could convince me about what I ought to value. Neither is there any strictly empirical resolution of questions of value. The point is that the attempt to limit knowledge to the propositions of the natural sciences or to tautologies—as the Wittgenstein of the *Tractatus* seemed intent upon doing—is to exclude the realm of personal knowledge, of immediate experience, of social existence, of feeling, of concern, from human understanding. If some form of rhetoric must fill this gap in an account of human knowledge, then I believe that it will be ineluctable in philosophical discourse. For, far more is sayable and comprehensible than is stipulated in Wittgenstein's philosophical analysis.

As a matter of fact, I think it would be legitimate to argue that, insofar as philosophical investigations rely upon fundamental presuppositions they have a rhetorical dimension. Thus, for example, I would take Wittgenstein's elementary presupposition in the *Tractatus*—"language pictures the world"—to be primarily a rhetorical utterance or inscription (e.g., it could be expressed in the following form: "Let us agree that language pictures the world."), one which his own conceptual analysis nullifies since it is neither a tautology, an analytic statement, nor a proposition of the natural sciences. According to Wittgenstein's conception of truth in the *Tractatus*, the statement is simply not true. Generally speaking, then, I would hold that the presuppositions in philosophy, without which philosophy would not be possible, which are, by their very nature, disputable, indicate that there is a rhetorical dimension even in those philosophies which present themselves as primarily concerned with the communication of empirical truths, analytical truths, or the elucidation of the ostensible logic of language. And if we scratch this rhetorical aspect of philosophy, I believe that we will find the existing individual thinker and his values—precisely the individual with which the *soi-disant* "rhetorical" philosophy (existentialism or existential phenomenology) begins. That such a view is not entirely false can be shown by Wittgenstein's remark in the *Philosophical Investigations* that the problems that arise from the misinterpretation of forms of language are "deep disquietudes" which have roots which are "as deep in us as the forms of our language." It is for these reasons that I would disagree with Johnstone's view that Wittgenstein's philosophy communicates because it disseminates an understanding which is not contingent upon prior belief. I think this is questionable for the reasons I have given above. In addition, it might be said that Johnstone's claim is not completely accurate in terms of some of Wittgenstein's fundamental beliefs. For, it is clear that the general claim that there is a logical structure in natural languages (which, incidentally, is treated *as if* it were—as it is not—metaphysically neutral) is not an indisputable truthclaim since it is neither a tautology nor a proposition of the natural sciences. Even in Wittgenstein's own terms he would be hard put to defend such an assertion since he claims, in the *Tractatus*, that it is not humanly possible to gather from it what the language of logic is. If this is the case, it would seem that it would be equally as difficult to gather from it what the logic of language is.

Although I would have to agree with Johnstone that Heidegger's philosophical inquiry has a high rhetorical component (even though his expositional arguments do have a reasonably high degree of internal consistency) insofar as his phenomenological elucidations are often persuasive and appeal to a certain receptivity to existential concerns; I would have to disagree with his claims about the equation of the philistines with those who live in the realm of *das Man* or the inauthentic, anonymous being of *Alltäglichkeit* ("Dailyness"). For, Heidegger is not only addressing himself to the philistine, but to all reflective men— including the philosopher. He explicitly states that inauthenticity does not express any negative evaluation; rather, he claims that *Dasein* or man lives for the most part in a state of "fallenness" in the world of ordinary experience. He maintains that

We would misunderstand the ontological-existential structure of fallenness [or inauthentic being] if we were to ascribe to it the sense of a bad and deplorable factual property of which more advanced stages of human culture might be able to rid themselves. [*Sein und Zeit*, p. 176]

In this sense, his primary concern is with a phenomenological analysis of the various essential modalities of human existence, a fundamental phenomenology. His work is primarily descriptive and not an exhortation even though the rhetorical form of some of his "arguments" is decidedly hortatory, suggesting that he is implicitly saying: It is necessary to change one's life, to strive to transcend the inauthentic mode of being. Nevertheless, he clearly states that his interpretation of the ordinary mode of being of man (*Dasein* or "there-being") is far removed from any moralizing critique of everyday human existence. In this regard, then, I believe that Johnstone has somewhat misrepresented Heidegger's thought even though he is clearly sensitive to the spirit and intention of *Sein und Zeit*.

In regard to Johnstone's assertion that both Heidegger and Wittgenstein are in agreement in their conception of the function of philosophy, I might allow that there may be general agreement in their emphasis upon the "call of philosophy." But this is far too tenuous an agreement. In spirit and intention, in method and philosophical emphasis, they are at opposite poles of the philosophical enterprise. Although I think we may say, as Johnstone does, that both philosophers seek to communicate by means of elucidation (for Heidegger refers to the elucidation of the being of man)—that is, clarification and explanation— Wittgenstein (at least in the *Tractatus*) clearly attempts to limit the scope of the activity of philosophy and attempts to provide restricting boundary conditions of meaning. The ostensibly impersonal anaylsis or critique of language, the showing of the logic of language—these are primarily epistemic concerns. But Heidegger, on the other hand, seems to believe (at least in *Sein und Zeit*) that truth is revealed to man, or is "wrested" from phenomena, in experience, is present to him in his own being and in the being of the phenomena manifested in the world in which he finds himself. Knowledge, for Heidegger, is not restricted to tautologies, analytic statements, or the propositions of the natural sciences (propositional truth is only *one* mode of truth and, at that, not the most significant one). Rather, knowledge is relative to the existential situation of man, to his *praxis*, to his states of mind, to his concrete concerns with his own existence and the existence of others. It is not an end in itself which is epistemically neutral or purely impersonal; rather, it is for the realization of human possibilities. The emphases of Heidegger upon the affective, individuating aspects of human life are alien to the logical analyses of the Wittgenstein of the *Tractatus*. Indeed, it could be said that much of what is central in Heidegger's fundamental ontology would be relegated, by Wittgenstein, to the realm of *das Mystische*—the "mystical" about which nothing can be said. Heidegger insists that the ontological existential analysis of *Dasein* has its roots in ontic or factual being. This means, in effect, that it is rooted in, or related to, what is individual and particular in the complex specificity of personal existence. Such an emphasis, it need hardly be said, is wholly lacking in Wittgenstein's account of the "world" as the totality of facts. It is perhaps for this reason that an existential phenomenology, as opposed to a linguistic phenomenology, tends to be expressed in a rhetorical dimension.

The fact that this is the case, however, does not mean that an existential phenomenology can "say" nothing. For, as Aristotle pointed out in his *Rhetoric*, the art of rhetoric is fundamentally concerned with things about which we deliberate, and is the counterpart of dialectic (a process of criticism and analysis of *archai*). That is, it is concerned with what is not dealt with in any special "science," but which is within the cognizance of individual men. Rhetoric, despite the perverse uses to which it has been put by historical individuals and groups, is essentially the language of possibility. Philosophical communication, on the other hand, is the language of actuality (e.g., it attempts to describe what is the case) and of analytic truth. Logical analysis is in the realm of necessity; empirical inquiry in the realm of the probable. But a rhetorical philosophy (or one which could be so characterized) is concerned with the realm of the possible—thus, it is not surpising to see Heidegger referring to the "silent power of the possible." Rhetorical language is oriented towards the future whereas the language of communication is orientated towards the past or the present—hence, Wittgenstein can say that philosophy changes nothing.

In attempting to relate the thought of Heidegger to that of Wittgenstein it must be borne in mind that, for Wittgenstein, philosophy is primarily self-critical—it involves the prevention and destruction of error by virtue of a critical analysis of language. In this sense, it may be said that philosophy, as Wittgenstein understands it, has a negative, finite task. For Heidegger, on the other hand, philosophy is intimately related to the existence of man, to his self-reflective activity. Philosophy will *be* as long as there is history, as long as man *exists* (in Heidegger's sense of the word). Personally, I do not feel that there is any possible rapprochement between the fundamental method, orientation, and conception of philosophy of Wittgenstein and that of Heidegger. In the *Investigations* Wittgenstein suggests that linguistic activity is an expression of a form of life (*einer Lebensform*). And it is with a "form of life," rather than with a critique of language, that Heidegger is primarily concerned. Ironically, a linguistic phenomenology should also provide us with some understanding of man and his world even though it rarely does so. Wittgenstein stops before *das Mystische*, whereas the later Heidegger, in his *Seinsmystik*, attempts to describe and express the ineffable. But one need not follow Heidegger into the cloud of unknowing in order to value the insights, the descriptive power, of his fundamental ontology of human existence.

On one general point I would be in full agreement with Johnstone —that is, the view that whether a philosopher aims at precision of analysis and clarity of communication or a transformation of one's ontological orientation, he does indeed tend to be urging the acceptance of a new reorientation of attitudes. The rather large question I would like to raise is, why is this the case? In a tentative answer I would suggest that the historical situation of man obviously changes and so, too, do his philosophical perspectives and models—in effect, his way of thinking about himself, his world, and his language. It is for this reason that philosophy is fundamentally hermeneutic. But the problem here is that the criteria of interpretation change in relation to the material, technical, psychological, and intellectual changes which have affected the mode of being of man. In this sense, man cannot transcend history or his particular historical situation. But, inevitably, intellectual and practical commitment must take place. Hence, the ineluctability of persuasive or emotive uses of language is closely linked with the means and techniques which man employs in order to attain his perspectival goals.

Until man achieves universal hegemony of thought about what ought to be or what practical or cognitive values ought to prevail or until philosophy perishes there will be an unending dialectical conflict of opposing cognitive models, ends, theories, or *praxes*. In human thought as in human experience there is no ultimate resolution. Just as there will probably always be some opposition between theory and practice (or, in Kierkegaard's terms, an opposition between actuality and ideality), there will probably be a reciprocal dialectical relationship between rhetoric and communication. In this sense, and for the reasons stated, I would be fundamentally opposed to the kind of reconciliation Johnstone has proposed. Wholesale and universal agreement in philosophy or even such agreement in regard to the nature of philosophy would surely lead to sterility. If, as I have said, philosophical inquiry is fundamentally hermeneutic, it is clear that the exclusive reliance upon only one method or mode of interpretation would bring about the apotheosis of *one* aspect of human experience or thought. The rhetorical dimension in philosophy is useful and necessary in order to express or describe those aspects of human existence which fall outside the boundary limits of analytic truth or the natural sciences. The philosopher who excludes the rhetorical dimension from philosophy denies that he possesses and acts upon a form of "knowledge" which plays a significant role in his life.

SOME PHILOSOPHIC STRANDS
IN POPULAR RHETORIC

Harold Zyskind

I: 1

Contemporary philosophers inquiring into their basic problems often discover strands or echoes of rhetoric in their methods and subjects, whether in the persuasive definitions of ethics; in the circumstantial and shifting meanings of terms in philosophic semantics; or in the problems of influence and engagement in existentialisms. But as others have begun to show, there is another significant question which sounds much like this question of rhetoric in philosophy, but is in fact different; namely, the question of the philosophy in rhetoric. It is this which I wish to explore.

I should, however, specify the topic more sharply; for even among some who seek philosophy in rhetoric, there is a tendency to play down a direct confrontation with rhetoric in its actual workings among its normal audiences. Professor Maurice Natanson in his paper on "The Limits of Rhetoric" shows that rhetoric taken as an art of popular persuasion is indeed a subject for philosophers. But for him their interest is not in its techniques, its methods of persuasion, but in its deeper implications. Rhetoric is the counterpart of dialectic and accordingly has dialectical underpinnings. These give it a *theoretical* nature and it is this nature, more than rhetoric's practical devices and functions, which, for Professor Natanson, constitute its interest to philosophers.[1] I do not seek to controvert his thesis that there are critical presuppositions of universal import. Plato inaugurated that tradition, but it does not preclude the possibility of basic significances in popular rhetoric as such, as practiced.

Similarly, for Professor Chaim Perelman rhetoric is philosophic. But it is notably so in an exceptional case; namely, when the audience to which it is oriented is a universal one: the audience constituted of rea-

373

sonable men as the philosopher conceives them.[2] So far as this condition may exclude consideration of situation-bound audiences, my interest here is not in it; but of course Professor Perelman's new rhetoric explores the practical workings of the means of increasing adherence, and it is there also that I wish to focus. My subject, that is, is popular rhetoric treated at the level at which it operates actually, not transcendentally, or dialectically, and treated in the form in which it speaks to men as they are, not as they ought to be—except in so far as it can bring them closer to what they ought to be. This narrows the subject to the persuasive discourse itself, taken in its immediate context. In this context rhetoric could be considered as discourse which does not present universal concepts and truths but which functions rather as a language game, free of any essentialistic philosophy. If so, the philosophic task for the game would be to show that the rhetorician's apparent universals are not even intended as essences; that his appeals to eternal justice, for example, are in fact particular usages which make sense only in their immediate practical context.

I do not wish to be limited to interpretations of surface usage, however, any more than to ultimate theoretical implications. Rather, I shall confine myself to the area between the extremes just noted. At one pole the tendency, as in Natanson, is to bypass the immediate discourse for its deep structure; at the other the tendency is to see a particular language game without universal import or pervasive philosophic principles. My subject is the middle ground between these two: i.e., popular rhetoric examined for the philosophic strands which function within its immediate workings.

I would place this subject close to David Hume's easy philosophy. For him it consisted of essentially rhetorical devices of example, precept, and imagination, and in distinction from the accurate and the abstruse philosophy it dealt, not with underlying (or perhap he would have said not with remote analytic) principles but with the workings of discourse at the surface or immediate level of experience; it was adapted to man as an *active being*. Hence it was easy or obvious. But although it was in the region of experiential immediacies, it was nonetheless a kind of *philosophy*. It is true that he did not explore it as such, but neither did he turn exclusively to the abstract philosophy. Rather he tempered the latter with perspectives gained from the former.

Similarly I believe that the easy and obvious but nonetheless basic principles and methods of popular rhetoric have a contribution to make to the much broader philosophy of communications and the arts set forth by Professor Richard McKeon.[3] They at least have a place in the system of interrelations he describes, though they form only a phase of the new rhetoric of novelty there envisaged.

2

Like philosophy, rhetoric has many mansions. One of them may be called the rhetorician's rhetoric. Not only does its practitioner employ his devices openly but he talks the language of such devices. Not only does he make things manifest; he stresses the importance of doing so rather than of demonstrating necessities. His language elevates experience, concreteness, power—disparaging theory isolated from practice, the ideal from the real.

To be specific: He leans toward arguing, not that the nature of an office determines what its occupant must do, but that the man makes the office; not that judges apply law to cases, but that they make law in deciding cases. His style is not, say, that of the Declaration of Independence, when it asserts that all men are created equal and endowed with certain inalienable rights. Modern philosophy's pragmatisms and linguistic analyses have contributed to an atmosphere not overly hospitable to such rhetoric of inherent and invariable properties. Thus when Theodore Roosevelt reported the Declaration's statements, he said they asserted the "ideal that each man shall have an equal opportunity to show the stuff that is in him." [4] This was not an interpretation but a paraphrase. Yet in the linguistic turn he gave the statement, he converted what in the Declaration is an *ethical* concept (the right) into its operational condition (the opportunity), and similarly replaced the *natural ground* of the right with its *rhetorical* counterpart (showing).

Similarly the contemporary arguments which make the extreme political right wing as radical and revolutionary as the left reflect a tendency to treat such movements not in terms of whether their abstract principles rest on the assumption of supposedly eternal values—but in terms of what their actional intentions are toward existing institutions, and in that perspective the right and the left are both radical so far as they persuade men to reverse current opinions and practices.

3

In the context of such language usage, with its flavor of man as the measure, rhetoric tends not to require cognitive or dialectical certitudes as props for persuasion. Such so-called underpinnings may themselves be treated as inventions of more or less persuasive speakers. Hence rhetoric relies on herself as a self-sufficient and ultimate arbiter, thereby usurping philosophy's office.

Our initial question is: what *kind* of things would philosophic ingredients be in such rhetoric? The first point is a negative one—that unlike traditional philosophic principles they are not adequately meaningful apart from concrete communication contexts in which they occur. In its mild form this is only the familiar claim that words have circumstantially contextual rather than universal meanings. In its extreme form this point makes even the words await their full meaning in the *deeds* they promise or inspire; in which case action, though seen through a verbal frame, constitutes the most authentic communication. Practice makes preaching meaningful. When even the verbal frame is disavowed, a stark activism results: one can learn more from a night in jail than from a year's reading. But the second point is that certain elements within these concrete communications perform basic functions which image some of those of traditional philosophy: these elements, first, do the work of first *principles*, they are not merely terms with meanings or rules of a game; second, they constitute basic *methods* for ordering experience; and third, they connect the subject matter of rhetoric with the fundamental facts or subjects of the *world* by generating a rhetorical continuity of past, present, and future. To restate the two points: the bases of the easy and obvious philosophy lack accuracy and perhaps meaning if considered in abstraction from their particular uses, and in that sense are contingent or operational. But second, they are best understood if seen as doing the work, in the concrete, of (i) first principles, (ii) philosophic methods, and (iii) fundamental subject matters. My paper is an inquiry into each of these functions in turn.

II: 1

First then to basic principles: rhetoric employs and reveals them in their most literal and manifest form—as "start-up" beginnings—as what comes first in the order of operations directed at an issue. As such they are suggestive of the next step—initiatory motions made to carry a persuasive sense of progressive momentum, as when Kennedy urged acceptance of the test-ban treaty as a first step towards as yet still vague goals by way of uncharted steps. One does not make logical deductions of a scheme of stages from such beginnings, nor can one employ them as criteria in a cognitively or formally warranted way. But they are principles in a most authentic sense: novel and generative firsts, or rather, firsts because novel and generative. They can be as vast as Heidegger's Being being disclosed or thrusting itself violently into the world for the reshaping of history, or as restricted as a first-step reference to one linguistic usage of a term such as "game" or "the novel" to suggest in a second step that the same term be applied to similar but different actions or writings, thus producing a different and new meaning of the term by decision. But it is more to my purpose to remain with cases of intermediate scope.

Since it is obvious that a last step cannot be taken if the first is not, the ancient paradox of motion becomes grounds of action now. (Appropriately the rhetorical refutation of the paradox would be simply to catch the tortoise.) It is not enough of course that the first step be simply what does occur first; it must be seen *as* a beginning, as initiating a process in the sense of being its cause or direction-finder for subsequent steps moving towards completion.

Rhetoric's implicit claim is accordingly that principles are essentially incomplete actions, apprehended as such. Obviously they can be employed in any field. In the theater, genuinely creative audience participation depends on the play's being indeterminate, itself a first step requiring completion or at least extension of a sort which no routine can prescribe but which its suggestiveness generates in an appropriate audience. Sartre carries the point all the way in saying that in literature the author requires the freedom of his reader "in order to make his work exist." [5]

Similarly Thomas Kuhn in *The Structure of Scientific Revolutions* is concerned with the paradigms which constitute the first signs of new flowerings. The choice of such a paradigm, he argues, the grounds of its acceptance, is a rhetorical problem. The opposition is between an old paradigm which has been followed up exhaustively and a new one of remarkable promise. The feature relevant to my purpose here is that the paradigm is an exemplary, particular scientific inquiry rather than the full theoretical structure or underpinning of the new movement. The paradigm on which a normal research tradition is based is distinguishable from, and *prior* to, the rules and assumptions (not always agreed on) which constitute that tradition. It is a first step, spectacularly suggestive, and this suggestiveness rather than a determinate demonstration of the superiority of its resolution of a scientific problem enters into what persuades scientists to adopt it in preference to the old paradigm. This adoption is a decision that can be made, Kuhn says, only on faith.[6]

The rhetorical insight into principle focusses a universal problem present in all fields of action and thought; that of judging the value of an idea or line of action *prior* to full inquiry into it or to knowledge of its consequences, when it is still a seed, a hunch, a possible hypothesis—a sign of what may come to be. To fall in love at first sight, as it happens in *Phaedrus,* for example, is to be persuaded by the sign and promise, not the reality, of the beloved's qualities. Rhetoric always has been an art of reading or posting signs, and its contemporary value in this regard could lie in its insistence on treating some of them as principles which, as such, need to be examined in the large rather than to be passed over immediately into what they signify. For example, in the case of paradigm or virtuous actions, of the sort which Hume talks about, rhetoric would not pass rapidly into the core qualities of human nature which the action is a sign of, nor into the ethical or behavioral theory of which it is an application, but first would dwell at length on the features which give it this power of signifying personality or instantiating theory.

2

What is the ontological status of these first-step principles? They do not owe their being to the nature of things, in this sense: that whatever the nature of things may be, the step in question would not emerge and function as a principle were it not *laid down*. If not laid down, it exerts no force, and in rhetoric what exerts no force is not real. Its content may be drawn from guidelines supplied by the past, of course, but the operational emergence of the step is what its ontological status consists in; and this connects it more immediately with the agent who performs it than with a universal of one kind or another. To say this is not even to assume a cognitively certified separable existence for the agent: rather he is part of what is meant in talking of the phenomenon as an operation. To say this much—i.e., to tie the act to its agent rather than to its grounding in a universal—is only to treat the operation in isolation, however. Important consequences are bound up in the additional fact that the original act is projective, initiatory, persuasive—for this immediately implicates a *broader arena of action* into which it could be extended. The initial act then has the status only of a particular and the agent that of an *individual*—both being identifiable by their location within the larger space-time context or an analogue of it. Such is the framework within which rhetorical principles emerge and function.

No matter how diverse these principles may be, all require this framework, for it is an operational arena and they are operations. In this respect it suggests itself as a possible underpinning—akin to what Professor Strawson would call a descriptive metaphysics—for the activity of persuasion. If so, it is peculiarly adapted to the office. One does not have to invoke a speculative metaphysics or other prescriptive schema from which to derive it; the conceptions of agent, individual, particular act and context, which are bound up with it, are part of what is grasped in grasping a rhetorical principle as such, as I have sought to show. In that sense its ontological status and content are tied to the particularistic character of persuasive acts. At the same time it *does* do the traditional philosophic work of providing an abiding matrix for the location, career, and judgment, of acts. Rhetoric has always been an art of topics: these are *places* (topoi) within which to find and locate things; the framework I have elicited is rhetoric's *place of places*.

It is already apparent, I hope, that, given the importance in Strawson's descriptive metaphysics of the particular in a spatio-temporal setting, his work is of immense significance to those interested in the philosophy of rhetoric, and that, perhaps, an analysis of philosophic strands in rhetoric has a bearing on such metaphysics. It would not be surprising were this true in view of the traditional and necessary intimacy between arts of persuasion and of language.

I will recur to rhetoric's "metaphysics" later, for the question of just the sense in which its place of places is maintained has not been discussed. But as I have drawn this framework from the persuasive character of rhetoric's beginnings, so I wish to proceed by following rhetoric's characteristic direction of interest—namely, the interest in a framework's consequences prior to interest in its conceptual base. To return then to the consequences of principles.

3

What I have argued thus far tends to make a persuasive beginning a way of establishing an individual perspective, a point of view. Its consequences may be explored simply in its own terms, as Wayne Booth, for example, has done with such insight in *The Rhetoric of Fiction*, or as American political figures did with less depth in the 19th century when they looked at history and the future as the setting for America's manifest destiny.

But perhaps the more interesting consequences grow out of the *interplay* of rhetorical perspectives. Because these lines of destiny are not grounded in a rational structure and do not predetermine or embrace the structure of thought or action to which they are basic, there is nothing theoretical either to restrict their multiplicity, or antecedently to require a dialectical harmony among them. Indeed rhetoric looks without surprise on clashes among them, and it is frequently in terms of some indeterminate confrontation of individual perspectives that we discuss such concepts as the market-place of ideas (as in one theory of a university), transformations of fact (as in Durrell's Alexandria Quartet), the jarring of factions, the struggle for power, etc. Problems even may be resolved as well as generated by such interplay without the introduction of natural of dialectical principles of harmony, as when Madison argues that the dangers of democracy are lessened by the multiplication of factions, or a government proceeds by checks and balances—or one line of destiny destroys another.

Because of the peculiar character of rhetorical principles, then, it is native to this art more than any other to know and treat as ultimate, the "fact" that there is more than one side to every question. In this context perhaps the model actional principle—certainly a fundamental one—is successful self-defense. My point here is related to, though not identical with Professor H. W. Johnstone, Jr.'s analysis of the maintenance of the self in philosophic argument.[7] Rhetoric makes a prime virtue and philosophic necessity of *self-defense*—not as the mechanical working of an instinct but as the act of constituting the agent seen as such in his capacity to establish a place in his environment. This act is literally prior to and a condition of any others, and it *occurs without the necessity of a clear definition or even determination of what the self is*. On both counts the act can be taken as a peculiar first step needed for, but not determinative of what follows. Indeed self-defense *begins* defining or redefining as much as it succeeds in preserving one's identity.

Because of the priority of self-defense in a rhetorical world, further specifications of character are often derived from qualities displayed in that fundamental act (and aspect of every act). The meaning of "character" we have in mind in referring to a "man of character" is such a derivation; for we take the term as relating less immediately to the man's moral (just, honest, etc.) qualities than to his possession of strong will power, drive, vigor. These latter qualities are the *operational conditions*, not the constitutive determinants, of moral (or immoral) action.

I have specified how principles act in rhetoric when viewed relative to the agent. They may also be viewed relative to the field within which they constitute a beginning and line of development. The priority of operations when seen thus in relation to environmental circumstances causes the situation to be seen, not as of this or that abstractable kind, but as a greater or lesser opportunity or peril. This is, in part, because a self-evident assumption of a first-step principle is just that it is a way of making something in the immediate circumstances; i.e., it is the start of a process of taking advantage of the chances that offer themselves. This is the consequence or corollary of its not being determinate. Rhetoric is necessarily opportunistic. As a result it cannot dissolve the individual perspective which generates it; it cannot occur at any moment except the present.

4

The rhetorician has long been accused of the evils of the pursuit of power and the superficiality of *ad hoc* treatments. A prime basis for such charges is evident from what we have noted of self-defense, opportunism, and the competitive interplay in a rhetorical world. But if power is not treated as a determinate end, and if an *ad hoc* encompassment of a problem is not treated as a terminal solution—and according to our analysis they should not be—but if both are treated as *initiating* steps, as rhetorical beginnings, then their significance is intrinsically incomplete initially and alters in the subsequent steps they suggest conceptually or make possible actionally. The notion that in times of upheaval, order established by power must come first (whether by the success or suppression of the revolution), and that only then can justice be attended to, articulates an operational 2-step sequence in which *ends* themselves *shift* from power to justice. The steps are linked actionally of course, since a concrete institutional authority with requisite power is usually a condition for doing justice. The steps may also be linked conceptually or even philosophically since, in their context as a sequence, justice is not seen as a universal norm or relation but as a construction of—in a technical sense as an invention of—that institutional power. Indeed the rhetorical focus within this operational sequence furnishes a gloss on Kant's view that inclination is not a moral motive of duty, even when the gratification comes from benefitting others, and that, since no one ever can be certain he acts independently of such inclination, no one can be certain of his *disinterestedness*. A rhetorician of course would agree that the same behavior (say it is a concession which serves peace) can be diversified according to the motive. But in the operational sequence, the test of this diversification is not inclination but power. If the man who concedes has nothing to fear—if his power base is secure— it argues his disinterestedness in the practical sense that counts (he knowingly gains nothing). But if he is weak—if he is first-step deficient —then the same overtly generous act is probably an act of cowardice or meanness of soul.

The case is the same with *ad hoc* or opportunistic policy if it is seen as—and subsequently made—a significant move in a long-term trend. Policies need not themselves revolutionize a system as such to warrant our saying that they make a fundamental change. What is required rather is that the policy have a projective—even if symbolic—bearing based on the existent relations of power. The tremendous expansion in the reach of the office of the U.S. President is a major trend built up by a series of specific acts each of which involved a wider use of authority. It is true that much contemporary rhetoric of dissent presents itself as attacking the system as such. But even in these cases the restructuring of the system is envisaged in the distance as developments from such beginnings as the occupation of Hamilton Hall, and the individual in the audience is told that the only way he can really understand what the total system is, is to feel it at the end of a policeman's club. (The *Federalist* is of course the rhetorical defense of a system: my point is not alien to that fact, since, in its context the system is something to be instituted now as a single act, the performance of which now, in these conditions, is the matter at issue.)

To summarize: In the way that self-defense, order, etc., can work in operation sequences, they cause, without being or without even articulating, determinate structures; but this causal efficacy they have gives them the scope of traditional principles, while the indeterminate aspect avoids the supposed fallacies of essentialism and strict logics.

III:1

I turn now to the method of rhetoric. In a sense rhetoric is *all* method, if the term refers to what speaker or audience do to the subject matter—to how they treat it; for in persuasion, treatment is everything, and everything is treatment, to paraphrase Marshall McLuhan. The most factual of facts in this art is an assertion someone employs as an instrument to affect someone else (or himself). For rhetoric generally, moreover, the emotions aroused in the audience by persuasion are quite unlike the allegedly bracketed emotions aroused in them by supposedly self-sufficient poems; for the rhetorical emotions are by definition devices by which the audience alters the appearances or significance of the subject. The subject of rhetoric is thus exhausted within the processes of constructing, presenting, and responding to it.

Conversely, rhetoric may be looked at in a way which makes its method extremely content-dependent; for any attempt to specify the method distinctly but apart from a particular subject or content usually reduces to vague generalities of alleged logic. Aristotle analyzed the syllogism at length in isolation, but explained enthymematic forms mainly by concrete examples of them drawn from speeches. Rhetoric's logic taken purely by itself as a system of implication is pallid indeed.

I do not purport here to cover this paradox, by which rhetoric now seems to be all method, and now seems to be chiefly content; but I have selected three topics each of which shows a different ratio of the two elements. The three topics are (1) definitions or constitutions of single terms or objects, (2) the relations of opposites as an example of a two-term relation, and finally (3) the general problem of inferential patterns or complexes of terms.

Wittgenstein and such men as N. R. Hanson, Virgil Aldrich, and Paul Ziff have emphasized the variability of concepts which can be generated as a result of seeing something *as* this or that, or of imposing a pattern of discovery, or aspecting an object. I will try to show that rhetoric with its emphasis on the inventive skill of the speaker echoes in practice this relaxation of rigid criteria but, in addition, that it adapts the processes of persuasion in such a way as *to restore a philosophic function to such relativistic concept formation.* Consider for example the question of the "character" appropriate to a national leader. The Eisenhower character and that of Kennedy were sharply different, but both had considerable impacts. They were not two wholly different leader-images, however. If you begin *naming* the traits of each, many of the same terms apply: courage, for example, and strength of will were major elements in both. And even Eisenhower's tendency to cite moral generalities, which at the time was cited by some as an unfavorable feature peculiar to him, since everyone is against sin—this tendency to appeal to general morality was subsequently adopted in application to Vietnam by some of the same persons who had looked upon it so unfavorably in Eisenhower. Courage, morality, strength of will, were all found in both the youthful image of Kennedy and the paternal image of Eisenhower.

If one had asked beforehand—say through a public opinion poll—what was the Americans' concept of what a national leader should be, the collective answers would probably not have excluded one of these and adopted the other. This fact would be even clearer in a comparison of Lincoln and Douglas. Besides, these four images are but some of many possibilities: The assumption of rhetoric must therefore be that to some extent public opinion is formative—as in the content of a concept such as this. The audience has various but more or less plastic notions of courage, morality, will, leader. What each rhetorician does is to crystallize the notions in his image, so that for the time being he becomes what these indeterminate notions are determinately seen as. The philosopher-king is as variable a concept as the number of rhetoricians.

The feature which rhetoric highlights, and which I wish to stress here, however, is one that raises, as it were, the old philosophic question of the *stability* of such concepts or manifested definitions. Thus far we have emphasized only the variability of the concepts. Is there here, as there was with first principles, a substitute for the philosophic function served by definitions—that of marking off an area of at least some constancy? Rhetoric does not respond with a single voice of course, but *one* of the voices with which it responds is particularly appropriate to the character of the art. We can speak of seeing a diagram now as this, then as that *without* particular concern about the see-er. But the fact that the pattern is a visible *discovery* bespeaks is relativity to the see-er; and rhetoric always implicitly considers and often explicitly just this question of relativity in the case of the character of a speaker. He presents his character as this or that; but in recognition of a possible conception of himself as unstable, he also reflexively presents *a degree of commitment to that character*. We judge him not only as having the character but also as the *source of its stability*; will he continue, as it were, to see and be seen the same way? Indeed one can and does ask in rhetoric: Is his the kind of character—the kind of concept—which tends to sustain, stabilize, and reinforce itself? In the answer to this as in the relevance of the question is the continuity with philosophy. It is just this importance of the stability of a relativistic concept which analysts tend to neglect.

Once this focus on who sees—as the determinant of what is seen—is given sufficient attention, a further crucial importance it has in concept formation becomes apparent. Consider, for example, the concept of a state: It is often conceived not in terms of what it is or even what it is seen as, but in terms of the desire for its stability or change on the part of the groups who do the "seeing": the revolutionaries, moderates, and conservatives—i.e., groups classified in terms of their commitments to defend or to attack. We hear much today of The System; and the system is conceived in good measure as that whose Establishment is designed to perpetuate itself. In the concept of a conservative state or The system, seen in this light, the distinction between what the state is seen as, and who does the seeing, moves towards a vanishing point.

2

To turn now to 2-term relations: Rhetoric exploits the tendency of the mind to organize terms into pairs of contraries or to move in thought from a given term to its contrary—from an extreme to its opposite. Why this is so is not in question. Indeed it would be inappropriate to philosophic rhetoric to assume a fixed structure of the mind. All that rhetoric assumes is that audiences will follow and respond to such a movement of the mind. Accordingly, much of the art is devoted to the discovery of how to acquire or retain the value of both of the contraries: We want *both* freedom and authority, justice and power, theory and practice, guns and butter, idealism and realism, courage and gentleness, resistance and obedience, reason and experience, and so on down an indefinite list. If I wish to praise a man and say his mind is quick, I must immediately add that he is nonetheless deliberate, not impulsive or superficial. The focus on relating extremes goes back at least to Platonic rhetoric—I do not mean to Plato's theory of rhetoric but to his actual rhetoric in the *Apology*: Socrates has the virtues of confessing ignorance and of being wise, of prudence and fearlessness, of absolute defiance and total obedience (on the battlefield), of being a gadfly and a benefactor of the state, a patriot and a nonconformist, a nonprofessor and a logician with disciples etc. He goes to the extremes in getting or exhibiting the best of both worlds.

My theme on this point will be the same that it has been throughout: There are rhetorical treatments of this problem which have the *contingency* and *openness* suited to the invention and persuasiveness of rhetoric, and at the same time, in the development of such treatments, philosophic continuity is maintained; the work of philosophic principles is being done. This can be illustrated here by reference to three traditional ways of dealing with contraries philosophically; and then by juxtaposing each traditional way with its rhetorical counterpart.

First there is of course the dialectical treatment, in which in its simple form the opposition is sharpened into a contradiction or apparent contradiction, followed by their reconciliation in an overarching concept embracing both. The rhetorician's counterpart to this reconciling *concept* is the discovery of a reconciling *agent*—man or state or action—in whom the contraries *coexist*. Rhetoric pulses with indications of the men who were both strong and just, intellectual and at the same time men of action, logical and yet imaginative, and similarly with nations or situations in which power and justice are combined, and so on. Thus instead of dialectic's contradiction transcended by a fixed pattern, rhetoric seeks the *co-existence of contraries* in the same concrete existence. Notice that in the *Apology*, the paradoxes are not explained by higher formulas but rather they are embodied in Socrates' character in such a way that he can say of *himself*, not of a pure idea, "I have been always the same." (33B)

Second, an alternative traditional solution is the Aristotelian mean between the extremes. This I think is a formalistic solution. What must be noted about it is that the mean is not a mean *of* the extremes but of something else, as the extremes are not excesses and deficiencies of the mean but of something else; i.e., rashness is not an excess of the mean, courage, but an excess of confidence; and courage itself, as the mean between rashness and cowardice, cannot *itself* be carried to extremes. Courage, temperance, etc., are not things you can have too much of. The mean therefore is a *separate form* of some matter (fear, pleasure, etc.) located between the extremes.

Rhetoric would be inhibited by such formalism: for rhetoric, you *can* have too much of a good thing. Rhetoric in this case praises *moderation*, and in fact in this mode what courage is often set against is *not* cowardice but gentleness, another virtue, just as power or strength is set against justice. The two pairs are parallel and in each case you seek the best of both worlds, coexistence, not a *separate* form, but moderate versions of any form.

The particular device which rhetoric here substitutes for the formal mean is that of using each extreme as a *limiting case* of the other: i.e., freedom is good to the extent that it does not eliminate authority, quickness of mind to the extent that it does not eliminate depth, and vice versa. The danger which rhetoric sees in concrete cases is that a value such as freedom may be applied universally to every case, for "universally" would here mean "indiscriminately." Rhetoric avoids this danger by using the contrary value (order) to set up *counterclaims* and thereby excludes cases or aspects of cases from freedom (license). The system of checks and balances works among terms as among factions, for in rhetoric, *contrary terms are verbal factions.*

Finally, a third traditional way of making the combined values possible would be by such sharp and univocal definitions of freedom and of authority, of justice and of power, that the boundaries around each would be clear, thus precluding jurisdictional disputes. For abstract universals such jurisdiction could be clear; the separation precise. But this univocal clarity requires the isolation of the concept from a concrete context or from admixture with its contrary. To rhetoric this necessarily or ordinarily reduces its persuasiveness, for it seems to be *in fact* excluding its opposite. Rhetoric, accordingly, would reasonably prefer a view of freedom in which the moderation or combination is still manifest. At any rate, there is a commonly used rhetorical method which achieves this—namely, the device of merging the two contraries *in the perspective of whichever one is being emphasized.* Consider its illustration in the relation of theory and practice as the contraries. The practical becomes the region of action not which is nontheoretical but which *embodies* and enlarges theory, and thereby puts theory in its perspective; while conversely, political theory is not "pure" but sticks to description and analysis of the practical workings of *actual* states, and thus brings the practical into *its* perspective. Thus rhetoric here moves towards the center but does so by making each extreme term an *inclusive* perspective. Some of rhetoric's greatest achievements rest in part on this method of assimilating theory to practice. It is fundamental to the whole style of some rhetoricians, for example, Churchill.

3

Much discussion today in critical theory concerning fruitful tensions and paradox mirror rhetoric's contraries. In classical terms, however, the question falls simply under the ordinary topic of the more and the less—the enthymeme is simply that two goods are better than one.

This is a relationship which of course is to some extent abstractable from particulars of a subject matter, but yet not wholly so. It still is a matter of content rather than pure logical form. A logical relation that in itself *can* be considered apart is, for example, that which Hume describes: since on its first appearance A led to B and on its next appearance too, then on the third appearance of A, we infer B: i.e., we make a rhetorical induction, moving from particular to particular. Hume showed that the conclusion is not necessarily entailed in the premises, and accordingly he attributed the drawing of the inference to psychological acts—to expectations, to the habits set up of the mind's moving from A to B.

This instance epitomizes the bearing of rhetoric on logic: rhetoric is not purely emotive, a simple feeling that something is the case; there is reasoning in the sense that an inference is based on a *formal* pattern of relations, a pattern abstractable from the content and expressible as a relation of terms rather than purely mental impulses. At the same time the drawing of the inference is inseparable from psychological dispositions: logic and psychology are inseparable in the actual workings of the mind. This claim often excites curt dismissal today. But rhetorical theory can make it in two senses, one of which tends to take account of the objection by *embracing* its position as it were. Isocrates, for example, praised disciplines which, while not strict logics perhaps, were made up of relations of implication—geometry, astronomy, eristic; he defended them against the charge of being "hair-splitting," by citing their value as "a gymnastic of the mind." [8] In such praise he thus both allowed for formal structures of implicative relations and yet maintained his focus on their status as a mental activity. The dependence of the inference pattern on the psychological is more sharply assumed even in the etymology of the classical rhetorical syllogism—the enthymeme—i.e., "in mind."

If I write 2, 4, 6, blank, you will probably fill in with 8, although if you filled in with 12, you could extend the series in a way to make it an equally satisfactory proportion. Rhetorical logic is like that: *it is the tendency to discover and complete emerging patterns.* There is no a priori set of conditions defining the sorts of relations which constitute a pattern; and accordingly, the way is open in processes of observation and experience for the discovery and testing of new modes of relation as bases of probabilistic inference.

The critical distinction ceases to be that between logical and psychological, and becomes that between reasoning as a formal system of implications and reasoning as a process of making one's way in the effort to organize or discover a useful pattern in concrete problems of belief and action. Rhetoric's modes of inference are variously discoverable in or relative to the patterns of relation which emerge in our efforts to construct objects of communication—to bring the raw data of experience and existence under the sort of control and definiteness which enables them to be bridges among men, the content of community. The new rhetoric should seek ways, in this effort, not only of adapting logics but also of employing or adapting, and even perhaps of stimulating, psychological theories as diverse as those of Jerome Bruner's stratagems and B. F. Skinner's schedules.

IV: 1

Up to this point I have treated rhetoric's content only glancingly. There is less clarity or agreement in this than in most rhetorical topics, however; so I will lead into it by reverting to its silent role in the preceding discussion of method. In that discussion I avoided any effort to determine *the* relation between subject and method in rhetoric (in that sense of subject or content which refers to such things as people, facts, etc., not to things within logic such that philosophers might argue whether they constitute a logical content or are totally formal). I avoided the question by treating three phases of method in each of which the sense of what method means shifts (concept formation, confrontation of contraries, and pattern of inference), with parallel shifts in subject matter implied (empirical concepts and entities, perspectivally determined theories and practices, the instances of things in a formal relation).

Let us suppose the last term gave the "real" picture; i.e., that formal patterns of inference make up the method, and instances of them the subject matter. In that case one presumably could write a rhetoric like a logic, with "real life" content coming in only as external aids to grasping the formal relations it instantiates.[1] Most rhetoric handbooks fall into this category (adding emotional and stylistic techniques to forms of argument). They tend to fix on only this *one* of the graduated modes of relationship.

Because as there are these graduated shifts, it is possible that there is no final answer to the question of which is generally dominant. If I may be reflexive, the character of rhetorical principles, discussed in the first section, makes a diversity of perspectives possible within the same framework (in this case rhetoric itself); and this suggests the possibility that subject matter could have *its* turn as the dominant perspective from which to approach the problems and understand the power of rhetoric. In what follows I try to prove this to be the case. For this purpose I will make a new beginning, asking first whether it falls within the art of the rhetorician as such to decide which side of a dispute he will support—this being the first subject matter question.

In his *Elements of Rhetoric* Bishop Whately distinguishes rhetoric as the art of proving a proposition given to it (the art of the advocate) from the art of investigation (the art, ideally, of the philosopher). If the philosopher should take a rhetorical role

> the process of *investigation* must be supposed completed, and certain conclusions arrived at by that process, *before* he begins to impart his ideas to others.[9] (Whately's italics)

Whately accordingly criticizes those ancient writers who, unlike Aristotle, "introduced into their systems, Treatises on Law, Morals, Politics, &c." [10] Rather he argues that:

> the knowledge of the subjects on which the orator is to speak, constitutes no part of the art of rhetoric.[11]

In brief rhetoric as the advocate's art is subservient to ethics and other subect matter disciplines. They provide the finding, and rhetoric promotes it; they provide the product, and rhetoric sells it.

But suppose Whately and his version of Aristotle had the matter backwards. Suppose science and ethics were or should be subservient to rhetoric, and the manufactures told by the advertising world what products to make because the advertiser knows what will sell. This is far from unrealistic—nor is it absurd. Goods which no one will buy will not be used, and political advice which no one listens to is irrelevant. To possess means of influence, in this view, is not to be able to wrap things attractively but to cause them to *be* attractive and valuable. The rhetorician cannot be reduced to the mere advocate.

A comparison of the two views—that of Whately's advocate and that of the usurpatory rhetorician—shows diverse consequences for the scope of the art. For the advocate the question is, What arguments or actions will best support *this given* position on the issue? But in the rhetorical perspective the question is rather, What position on the issue will have the most advantageous influence? You normally adopt the stronger position. In the Whately context a man could well be an excellent rhetorician and yet fail to persuade; for qua rhetorician he is like an attorney assigned to the case; he thus may be defending too weak a cause. But in the full rhetorical context it is a sign that one is isolated from the mainstream of the nation if he is in a losing, and ever dwindling, minority. It is true that the effective rhetorician can argue on either side of a case, but to him the chief significance of this power is that it enables him to choose the stronger case and to anticipate the arguments of his opponent.

Further, the rhetorician's skill in combining within himself coexistent contraries, which we noted above in the discussion of method, has often been turned to the formulation of a position which *embraces* what others thought were the two opposing sides. The reason this can be done is that the rhetorician may take within his province not only the function of choosing his position on an issue but, more significant, *of determining what the issue is.*

Whately's advocate begins with the question, How do I prove this point on the issue? The full rhetorician begins with the question, What shall I cause the issue to be so that I may adopt an advantageous position? In 1952 one remembers Adlai Stevenson saying that Communists in government was not the issue; but some Republicans made it so. In rhetoric issues and problems are made, not born. Nor is such making confined to local issues. It can swell up to the task of the times, as in 19th-century America it swelled to our manifest destiny to advance to the Pacific. Similarly, today, leaders of resistance movements in the ghettos, at the Pentagon, and in the universities may or may not have a theoretically defensible view of what are the issues of the time and what should be the priorities among them. But there can be little doubt that they have gone a long way towards determining what has been and is to be at the top of the national agenda. To the degree that rhetoric has thus centered history on our destiny or our social ills, it has begun, in the sense indicated, to generate the world (its subject matter).

The world so generated is not a changed one only in issues, positions, and the focus of historical forces. Still another part of the usurpatory rhetoricians's power is that of redefining basic values and rules relative to the rhetoric of immediate issues. It needs no proof to note that in the actions of resistance there has been a tendency to reconceive and revalue in a fundamental way such things as violence, property, the system, etc. in terms of the rhetorical effects of those actions.

This world that rhetoric builds is marked by two primary features already suggested. First, it is ever in the making, and advances accordingly in terms of frontiers, old and new. Second, men and groups are measured in terms of their influence and power, and presumably their effective use is what makes a society great.

2

It will illustrate the radical character of the novelty of this world if we consider what from its standpoint has been a defect in some of the historical treatments of the frontier. At the extreme the American frontier was analysed as an *environmental* feature of such determinate character that its effects could be seen in turn as the natural adaptation of man to the stimulus of free land.[12] This kind of interpretation makes it the historian's business to determine what the nature of the frontier was as a basis for interpreting events.

Rhetoric on the other hand sees history as itself making this determination. The very processes historians go through in reaching their divergent interpretations of the meaning of the frontier may *mirror* the past just as they are *indeed part of the present historical process*. The history of the frontier is the story of the interplay of emergent groups each trying to discover a favored meaning for "the frontier" and to impose that meaning on history by word or deed so far as possible: The nature of the frontier in fact was generated in that process.

Still other historians see the advance of the frontier as part or manifestation of some basic American quality; e.g., mobility.[13] But rhetoric would emphasize the need for conceiving national traits in terms, not of a substrate unchanging *core* quality, but of the *overt* or manifest-powers and character the nation takes on when seen in terms of its achievements in conceiving and coping with the frontier.

In brief: Rhetoric is able to perceive the novelty and contingency of the world by seeing the *environment* not as a fixed stimulus but as relative to men and groups who interact with it; and by identifying those *agent-groups*—not by referring to natural or theoretic bases of classification, such as the "economic factor," but rather by discovering what groupings have in fact emerged as the power centers of the times, and by noting the operative rivalries and unities which variously tend to preserve or threaten to remake the very classificatory scheme itself.

3

A traditional function of philosophy is not, however, only to make way for novelty but to seek unity and sameness. Is there a counterpart in rhetoric of a philosophically grounded unity? Our discussion thus far indicates that, so far as this function may be served within rhetoric, it must appear not in the regularities of human nature or the transcendent unity of an idea, but in the *shape of the world itself*. The philosophic question becomes: Amidst all this novelty is it the same world, one world? To see the answer to this is at the same time to see the multiple meanings or natures which the genius of rhetoric can give to unity and sameness. At this point, I will consider only two of them, as exemplary; there are more.

One sort of unified world, say that of a Machiavelli, is not expressed primarily in terms of the organic character of the structure but of the centering of control over the disparate elements in *one* will and skill. Similarly, in reference to a historical development a rhetorical concept of unity would be that events interrelate in accordance with the plans of some far-seeing leader. These are operational unities, relative to the leading agent—the great man theory, in the form argued by William James, for example.[14] But, while operationally or rhetorically intelligible, they slight the actual multiplicity of agents and events as sources themselves of structure and relation as well as of novelty.

The unity of the rhetorical world conceived more realistically is adapted just to that multiplicity; for the parts constitute, as we noted initially, individual perspectives on the whole or on other parts; and, accordingly, the unity derives from the rhetorical truth that each part or agent, each group, *being* a perspective, *must proceed by taking the others into account.* For rhetoric nothing is more elemental than taking others into account. Indeed nations know themselves, as any rhetorician knows himself, by the *impress they or he can make on other minds.* E. M. Forster in *A Passage to India*, says this in a way which shows how rhetoric transforms the philosophic question of whether other minds exist. Forster says that "we exist not in ourselves but in terms of each others' minds." [15] The great evil is the "echo"—what you say bounces back without having sunk in anywhere. The first rhetorician must of course have seen *that.* It is why in *A Passage to India* communication, i.e., one's passage into another mind, is itself the value and basis of one world. As the material causes of interaction multiply, the problem of that kind of unity becomes more urgent. Unity of this sort—in terms of *coexisting* persons and groups—depends on the spatial dimension.

A second question of the unity or sameness of the rhetorical world in its novelty turns on temporal continuity. New frontiers which reorient principles as well as facts would seem to cut off from the past. (Similarly new generations cut off from old.) It becomes a new world. The relation between past and present for rhetoric cannot be saved by finding regularities or laws considered as *abstractable* from their times. The continuity of the world, rather, is embedded in the ongoing stream of successive times. *It derives in fact from the presence here and now of persuasive records of the past.* This of course does not mean that in order to be the same, the present must perform the identical operations of the past. The past persists as an instrument of action that can be used variously. Great men may be imitated *in spirit*, involving literally very different operations, as when a President asks himself what Lincoln *would* have done. Patterns of action and achievement in the past similarly enter the present by diverse modes of influence: We may imitate the pattern or model literally, or combine it in new unities, or imitate it only in spirit, or indeed we may use it as a foil *against* which to conceive our progress in breaking away; even here when we rebel, the past is still a present measure. The very diversity of the modes rhetoric provides of exploiting and extending the past is part of what makes the *new* world *one* with its past. The new world in turn is the *first step* in the charting of the future.

This push and power of rhetoric to locate unity and identity temporally in the extensions of history and spatially in the interplay of achieved groupings brings the discussion back by a different route to the actional time-space matrix derived, at the beginning of this paper, from the analysis of rhetorical principles. It was seen then that every rhetorical beginning implicates a here-and-now operational arena of individuals with singular perspectives in interplay. But in that analysis all that could be seen was that the arena in each case was *of the same kind* or structure. The analysis was in fact only of the grammar or elements of an arena. Our present analysis in terms of subject matter, of the unity and identity in the world of history, which rhetoric generates, adds an essential dimension to the conception of the arena as the philosophic basis of rhetoric; for, since in the earlier analysis the identity of the arena was formal, there existed the theoretical possibility of a plurality of unrelated albeit similar arenas, if one wished to be speculative. But in the subject matter analysis this "danger" is minimized in the operational continuity among the particulars of the whole matrix—it is numerically one—the place of places, the metaphysics of rhetoric.

Even though it is possible (I will not consider the point here) that this matrix is noncontingent, its character, as this has emerged in the preceding study, generally follows the pattern for whose pervasive existence I have been arguing throughout: Both grammatically and dynamically the matrix provides a structural underpinning for popular rhetoric, and thus does the work of a philosophic foundation. But it is peculiarly adapted to the needs and character of the contingent focus of rhetoric's principles and methods. (i) The agents in the matrix are related, but these relations are not self-subsistent; they are rather relations which the agents impose or at least themselves constitute by the characteristically rhetorical act of taking account of each other (reminding one of Bacon's treatment of even inanimate things as perceiving others, and making plausible Strawson's concern with the question of monads in his descriptive metaphysics). (ii) The stages in the matrix's unfolding constitute a continuity, but it is ontologically precarious since each passing stage depends on its successor to sustain its reality. (iii) In brief: While the matrix in its totality is numerically one, it is visible and graspable only from individual perspectives, with these themselves in continual change in space and time.

V

I should like to make sure that the intended scope of this paper is not overstated. I have dealt not with philosophy generally, but with philosophic strands in rhetoric, and not with such strands in any rhetoric but only in that kind which is in the tradition of Isocrates, Quintilian, and Winston Churchill. Their rhetoric is usurpatory in its effort to make their art basic to all subjects. In men such as Aristotle, Whately, and Lincoln rhetoric is made more modest—though it is not possible even for them to take away rhetoric's power to say *something* about any subject whatever. I have not at all sought to set up one sort as the "real" rhetoric; my position is pluralistic, and I believe that significant philosophic points attach to the devices employed by men such as Lincoln to make rhetoric modest and that these points carry into the content of their persuasions.

But I have here focused on usurpatory rhetoric for two reasons: (1) A philosophy *of* communications, which is part of our general subject, ought to be concerned not with just the principles which *underlie* communications but with those which *enter the fabric* of the communication as well; this is a subject much neglected in an age of communications when, for example, they are examined as made up only of propagandistic devices, or modes of experience, or metaphors, etc. and too often are thought to be the products perhaps, but rarely the bearers of philosophic content. I have chosen therefore to attempt to redress this imbalance, seeking such content in effective communications and *in such form as to help explain their effectiveness as communications.*[16] (2) So far as the philosophic content *is* of a kind to belong to such effective communications, it tends to be tied to their immediate, existential concerns—which I hope I have shown to be the case—and accordingly is adapted to the contemporary focus on existence and experience rather than the nature of things or the structure of the mind as the subject matter of philosophy.[17]

NOTES

1. "The Limits of Rhetoric," *Philosophy, Rhetoric and Argumentation*, ed. Natanson and Johnstone (University Park, Pa., Penn. State University Press, 1965), pp. 95–96.
    2. "Reply to Henry W. Johnstone, Jr.," *op. cit.*, p. 137.
    3. R. McKeon, "Philosophy of Communications and the Arts," in H. Kiefer

and M. Munitz, eds., Vol. III, *Perspectives* (Albany, State University of New York Press, 1970).

4. Theodore Roosevelt, *Works: Memorial Edition* (New York, Charles Scribner's Sons, 1955), XV, 368.

5. J.-P. Sartre, *What Is Literature?* tr., B. Frechtman (New York, The Citadel Press, 1962), p. 51.

6. T. S. Kuhn, *The Structure of Scientific Revolution* (Chicago, University of Chicago Press, 1965), pp. 23–24, 42, 43–46, 157.

7. "Some Reflections on Argumentation," *op. cit.*, p. 4.

8. "Antidosis," George Norlin, tr., in *Isocrates* (Cambridge, Loeb Classical Library, 1929), II, pp. 331, 333.

I believe that in such cases the relation between the form of inference and its empirical illustration in logic is quite different from the relation between the two in rhetoric. The syllogism and truth tables can be elaborated and their reasonableness grasped merely symbolically, without the illustration. But I doubt whether most enthymematic forms can be thought of as clearly apart from any concrete illustration; e.g., to prove something by enumerating parts. I do not defend this doubt here, but if it is defensible, it would support my effort in this section to give subject matter its needed turn as providing the dominant perspective of rhetoric.

9. *Elements of Rhetoric* (Boston, James Munroe and Co., 1855), pp. 21–22.

10. *Ibid.*, p. 19.

11. *Ibid.*, p. 20.

12. F. J. Turner, *The Frontier in American History* (N.Y., Holt, Rhinehart, & Winston, 1920), p. 15.

13. John Higham, "The Old Frontier," *N.Y. Review of Books*, X 8 (April 15, 1968), p. 13.

14. "Great Men and Their Environments" (1880), *The Will to Believe and other Essays* (New York, Dover Publications, Inc., 1956), p. 227.

15. E. M. Forster, *A Passage to India* (New York, Harcourt, Brace and Co., 1924), p. 250.

16. If such content exists, the point can be of critical importance, for it throws suspicion on the rigid distinction so often drawn today between rational or logical communication on the one hand and manipulative, emotive engineering of consent or confusions compounded on the other. Rhetoric can of course be degraded but its nature makes possible effective popular communication which is substantive in content and purpose alike. The push of my argument would imply also that in many situations such rhetoric would be more successful, more persuasive, than the type of propaganda which Ellul, say, describes.

17. I wish to express my gratitude for valuable discussion of this paper to Merrill Rodin, Robert Sternfeld, Victor Tejera and Walter Watson.

PHILOSOPHY AND RHETORIC

(A RESPONSE)

Harold Greenstein

Professor Zyskind's paper once more brings to our attention the growing sophistication of philosophers as they have become more sensitive to the multiform functions of language, hence, the apparent reunification of philosophical inquiry and rhetoric. Under the influence of writers such as Austin, Wittgenstein and Stevenson, philosophers have become as concerned about the performative, evocative and declarative uses of language, for example, as they had formerly been concerned about its descriptive, indicative and other cognitive uses. Needless to say, this concern has generated much needed light in such areas as ethics and the philosophy of mind, as well as in the philosophy of language itself. As Professor Zyskind notes, Wittgenstein, much in the manner of the Gesetalt psychologists, has pointed out to us the relativity of the pattern to the see-er, that is, that patterns, for example, in science and in language, which formerly seemed to be "in the nature of things," or which were thought of as comprising "fixed essences," can be reinterpreted from different points of view, in accordance with different interests. As Professor Zyskind also points out, depending upon one's politics, the state, as an existing political entity may be examined from different points of view, and the concept of "the state" may be explicated in accordance with those views and interests. Marx, as I recall, both sees and defines the state as an instrument for the repression of one class by another. We should hardly expect the same analysis to flow from the pen of a Burke or de Maistre. A great step forward is taken from an attempt to see things as they somehow ultimately are, to the attempt to see things in the light of "as if." In other words, we have become more sensitive to the important roles played by analogy, metaphor and simile. If we reflect on the impact of the Einsteinean and Quantum revolutions, what has just been said is seen to be equally applicable to the hardest of

396

sciences. And we may allow to both Professors Zyskind and Kuhns, that with respect to winning the acceptance of new paradigms in science, the choice of paradigms is at least partially a rhetorical problem having to do more with initial suggestiveness rather than "determinate demonstration of its superiority over the old paradigm."

But beyond this, perhaps I am still too much under the spell of Plato not to be cautious of any reconciliation between philosophy and rhetoric. Surely, with respect to political as well as other types of heroes, there is still a distinction to be made between the image and the man, between how the image makers present him to us (let us call them the sophists) and what he is really like. To use what is perhaps an archaic idiom, there is still a distinction to be made between reality and appearance, though not one which necessarily need lead us to a world of forms or unalterable essences. Surely, there is still a distinction to be drawn for instance between Marx's *persuasive* analysis of both the functions and concept of the state on one hand, useful as it may be in the light of special interests, and unbiased empirical accounts which purport to tell us how states have, do and can function, and emotively uncharged (or relatively uncharged) attempts to articulate a conception of the state on the other hand. In short, there still appears to be an important distinction to be drawn between persuasion and proof, declamation and demonstration, even though the lines may sometimes be drawn rather fuzzily.

Similarly, it seems to me that we may gratefully acknowledge the insights of writers such as Stevenson into the emotive and persuasive uses of moral terms and yet also allow that for critical minds there are more or less adequate grounds for accepting moral arguments that have nothing to do with the persuasive ability of the moralist. For some, far less than proof or demonstration will often persuade, while for others, no proof or demonstration will ever persuade. So the old bifurcation between logic and rhetoric seems to remain, even though we reject the idea of a changeless world of forms and become more aware of context. Lastly, in this vein, whatever may be the original promise that leads to the acceptance of new scientific paradigms and the rejection of old ones, no matter how eloquently those promises are presented, the new paradigms must sooner or later deliver their goods. Witness the sorry state of the behavioral sciences, rich with the promises of the rhetoric of scientific method, but so poor in their results.

Professor Zyskind states, "In a sense rhetoric is *all* method, if the term refers to what the speaker or audience do to the subject matter—to how they treat it; for in persuasion treatment is everything, and everything treatment." Along with Marshall McLuhan, Professor Zyskind contends, "The means of presentation is itself the message . . . For rhetoric generally moreover the emotions aroused in the audience . . . are devices by which the audience alters the appearances of the subject."

This is surely a dark saying. If I understand all this, what has just been said is mistaken prima facie. It appears to entail that whether a speech is made on television or in the lecture hall or is included in a textbook, affects its truth or meaning, and surely this is false. This is not to deny that time, place and circumstance may affect what is *read* into a speech or statement, or that different sorts of declamation may enhance or detract from what the audience takes from a presentation. But it does seem possible, at least sometimes, to distinguish between what is read into a speech and what the speech says. To have it otherwise would require maintaining that the transmission of information and meaning is impossible.

Interpreted in another sense the McLuhan-Zyskind thesis also seems mistaken. If it is possible to distinguish between reality and appearance, the way the rhetorician would like us to see and feel about things and the way things are, the medium is surely separable from the message, though often, to our own detriment, we may fail to separate them. I disagree with just about everything William Buckley has to say, nonetheless, I admire his style.

If I am not mistaken, Professor Zyskind argues that logic and psychology are inseparable. I am not quite sure whether this means that logic is a branch of psychology, which would make the former an empirical discipline, the main concern of which would presumably be to determine how in fact people do think, and to attempt to formulate descriptive generalizations about its subject matter; or whether it means that psychology is a branch of logic, which would make psychology an a priori discipline, concerned neither with attempting to determine how people do think, nor how they ought to think, but concerned instead with formulating criteria for the adjudication of inference claims. Again, I am not quite sure—if neither alternative is intended—whether it is claimed that the subject matter of the two disciplines are to be taken as coextensive. I am troubled about this because none of the options appear to be especially palatable. It is general and common knowledge that people reason in all sorts of ways yet few logicians, to my knowledge would want to maintain that the principle of contradiction or the law of the excluded middle are merely statistical generalizations, not applicable to all argument forms, the evidence for that claim being just those examples of argumentation and inference which violate them. Whatever the "proof" of the principles of logic, they still stand independently of any empirical information as to how people do in fact reason. The second option seems especially unconvincing, simply in the light of what it is that psychologists do. And if both options are unacceptable the third option must also be unacceptable.

It may be pointed out that non-essentialist philosophers, especially linguistic philosophers have been going to the forms of life of which language is a part to determine the sorts of reasoning processes embedded in them; that they no longer set up a priori ideals to which the inference processes found associated with different activities, such as making moral and aesthetic judgements, explaining historical events, etc. *must* conform. It might even be emphasized that the fashionable expression "logical geography" marks just this change from the older essentialist philosophies.

This would seem to make philosophical analysis a form of psychological or sociological analysis. The philosophical analysis of scientific discourse would now be regarded as the psychological and sociological analysis of the reasoning processes of scientists, meta-ethics would be construed as a psychological and sociological analysis of the reasoning processes of moralists and philosophical psychology regarded as the psychological and sociological analysis of the reasoning processes of psychologists.

But if this is what Professor Zyskind has in mind by the reunification of logic and psychology, there seems to me to be both a dangerous atomism and fideism implied. Which pieces of scientific, ethical and psychological reasoning shall be prized as paradigms for mapping logical geographies, and for what philosophical purposes? If we simply want to describe scientific reasoning, aren't we better off going to the historians and sociologists of science? If we want to know how and why the methods of the sciences work, why not simply enroll in a course of study in one of the sciences?

Similarly, to which specimens of moral reasoning shall philosophers direct their attention? Shall it be those of Billy Graham, Albert Schweitzer or Lyndon Baines Johnson? Philosophers, I think, know quite well how moralists reason, and they know fairly well what sorts of criteria moralists actually do employ in assessing their colleagues' arguments. But what are we to make of all this when the logical geographies have been mapped? Presumably, not every example of reasoning is as good as every other one, even when purposes and interests are taken into account.

Professor Zyskind asserts that from the point of view of the rhetorician, "Determinate natures and cognitive certitudes do not loom so large as purported props for persuasion. So-called dialectical underpinnings may themselves be treated as only the inventions of more or less persuasive speakers, relative to the particular discourses in which they appear." If I understand this correctly, it would appear that even the canons of the logician are to be taken as just so many props to be used for the persuasion of particular sorts of persons with certain sorts of training and interests. Thus, man is the measurer, not only in the obvious and innocuous sense that it is men who argue, make judgments and seek knowledge, but also in the sense that proof is relevant only to agreed upon predilection. If demonstration *does* collapse into declamation, then what I have said about the distinction between them is false. And if there is no distinction to be made, are we then persuaded by Professor Zyskind? For I am not sure that he has proved his point. Doesn't the plea for rhetoric, collapse into its own rhetoric?

POETICS AND COMMUNICATION

Kenneth Burke

It so happens that the concerns of this paper also tie in with a time when I was a fellow-student with one Dick McKeon, who was majoring in mediaeval philosophy, at Columbia. No, not quite a fellow-student. For I had become a "drop-out," but on a fateful day dropped *in* to pay McKeon a visit. He took me to a seminar where, for the first time, I encountered the notable scholastic formula, *fides quaerens intellectum*. I was already much interested in ways whereby theological and metaphysical patterns of thought might be adapted analogically to the analysis of sheerly secular literature. And those three words overwhelmed me, by suggesting a whole labyrinth of vaguely glimpsed possibilities, or implications. In a sense, one might say that I was "converted." I had seen the light, if not theologically then at least as regards the direction in which I would proceed, by adapting thoughts connected with the "Creator" to secular modes of speculation on the nature of what in current cant is called "creativity." The point is introduced to explain some steps leading to the conviction, at least as regards Poetics, that the term "Communication" needs a second term to supplement it; or more accurately, a third term, since McKeon's article (see Richard McKeon, above, pp. 329–350) already reveals clear traces of one companion-term.

Thus, in his paper, we read: "The subject of the present conference has been indicated and marked off" by combining two "familiar ambiguous terms: On one side, "experience" and "existence"; on the other, "language" and "communication." Though his paper explicitly features the term "communication," there are passing references (italics mine) to "arts of *expression* and communication" (p. 336), "arts of communication and construction, of *expression* and experimentation" (p. 336), "of things embodied and conveyed by *expression* and action" (p. 337), of subject-matter that "slips from experience and existence by

eluding *expression*" (p. 337). I quote these various incidental statements since they all include the word I have italicized.

In earlier decades of our century, the "most familiar ambiguous
general term" for the discussion of literary matters was "expression"
(sometimes "self-expression"), largely under the influence of Crocean
aesthetics. I got from aesthetics to poetics roundabout, first by a rhetorical concern with form as the "psychology of the audience," and through
later developments in a book, *Permanence and Change*, which I had
originally thought of calling a "Treatise on Communication." At times
the step from "expression" to "communication" was taken to involve a
kind of apostasy, the abandoning of one term for the other. Or there
were occasions when the two could be placed in a reflexive relationship,
as terms for motives that mutually reenforce and correct each other.
(I'd now want to consider both as "modes of symbolic action.")

When first encountering the succinct formula for a questing (and
questioning?) relationship between the realms of *fides* and *intellectus*, I
began in a loose and fluctuant way to equate *fides* with the kind of
motivational priority that would correspond to an order of intuitive,
spontaneous "expression"; and *intellectus* seemed to involve kinds of deliberate planning (even sophisticated scheming) that would fall roughly
under the head of "communication" (as with the devices of persuasion
that Aristotle's *Rhetoric* treats in terms of "topics").

Whether the third term in Anselm's fertile formula was mentioned
during that seminar, I cannot say. If it was, I didn't notice it. As has
been notably the case throughout much of its history, the dualistic version became the center of attention. However, even while analogically
building on the dualistic version, I began in ways of my own to confront
the need for a third term. For instance, in essays published during the
thirties (and reprinted in my *Philosophy of Literary Form*), I offered
such tentatively haphazard designations as:

> the phoenix-out-of-the-ashes category
> purification by excess
> the "to the end of the line" modes
> books that would seek Nirvana by burning something out
> withinness-of-withinness
> the aesthetic of the Poe story (insofar as Poe aimed at a "mono-
> tonic" art designed to "leave the spell upon us")

And in my *Attitudes Toward History* (1937) I had tried to get at
the matter in terms of "efficiency," as with certain "theories of 'pure
beauty' " in aesthetic movements of the nineteenth century:

Art was supposed to contain an element of "beauty," present in varying degrees of density and diffusion. All that one should do, apparently, was find a way of straining off this "beauty," and then construct a work of this element alone. Hence, the search for "pure form"—beauty "in the abstract."

Since *Alice in Wonderland* always has a place to cite whenever some such recondite twist is involved, I cited the passage where "the smiling cat vanishes, leaving only her smile. It was 'pure' smile, the most 'efficient' smile possible." But, still holding to the dualistic pattern at that time, I inclined to place all such trends on the "expression" slope, without inquiring further.

All told, just as Anselm offered a third stage, *contemplatio* (not unlike what Spinoza would later call *scientia intuitiva*) not reducible to the first two terms, I gradually began working towards a third term that would prevail in its own right, and that would involve a motive not reducible to either "expression" or "communication." Though not at first, I eventually came to think of it as a kind of creative yielding to potentialities which are seen by the given seer to be implicit in the given set of terms (and thus intrinsic to their species). A good example would be Beethoven's last quartets, at the time when they were written. He presumably discerned ultimate possibilities in the medium at which he had become adept; and he tracked them down as thoroughly as possible even though, as regards the state of musical traditions in his day, the actualizing of such potentialities in the musical medium, as he saw it, somewhat interfered with the act of communication as such.

James Joyce's later works were another example of such thoroughness, though a whole army of academic myrmidons has enlisted its services in the Cause of Commentary, thereby carrying out a campaign of doughty, scholarly research with such exceptional prowess that not a single line has failed to be trampled and retrampled from every direction.

Or, for that matter, much expert enterprise in any field (mathematics, physics, philosophy, what you will) may tug at the edges of communication, as the enterpriser (not unlike McKeon) strains to track down with thoroughness whatever possibilities are found to be implicit in any given subject matter, when it is strenuously viewed in terms of some particular symbol system that also contributes to its definition and location. And we dare feel sure that, again and again in this series, such conditions have been confronted, and the corresponding terministic possibilities have been actualized.

If there is such an incentive, its manifestations must range far. In fact, my first fumbling approach to it was through such pleonastic conceits as with a passage I had run across in Melville, and had discussed thus, in my *Philosophy of Literary Form*:

In *Moby Dick* there is an especially "efficient" passage of this sort, pro-
phetically announcing the quality of Ishmael's voyage: after walking
through "blocks of blackness," he enters a door where he stumbles over
an ash box; going on, he finds that he is in a Negro church, and "the
preacher's text was about the blackness of darkness."

It all can be done even more quickly than that, as with Coleridge's
line, "Snow-drop on a tuft of snow," or as with a statement of De Quin-
cey's, cited in Ogden and Richards' *Meaning of Meaning,* to the effect
that the name of Atrius Umber was a "pleonasm of darkness."

Although in pleonasm we find this pattern (or should I say, this
terministic *motive?*) reduced to its simplest, most direct rhetorical
manifestation, I assume that the principle can be as intrinsic to an epic
as to an epigram. A philosophy is unified only insofar as, however vast
the range of things it deals with, it is ultimately tautological, inspirited
by some one generating principle that is implicit in all its parts.

Though such a principle is not wholly capable of explicit location,
it is usually indicated in reduction to some such equations as Berkeley's
"esse is percipi" or Spinoza's *"Deus sive Natura."* A similar but slightly
different approach to such an indication is to be found in such pairs as
the Cartesian distinction between *res cogita* and *res extensa,* for which
Santayana's equivalent was "dialectics" and "physics"; or there is the
traditional *res-verba* pair, for which I would offer as a variant the distinction between "motion" and "action," "motion" being possible without "action," but "action" being neither possible without "motion" nor
reducible to "motion."

*   *   *

At this point I must make a bit of a leap, and at no small risk, particularly in view of the fact that, as regards the step beyond "communication" which I wanted to call "consummation," I subsequently decided
to give it the name of the "entelechial" principle. The dangers are obvious inasmuch as McKeon of all people is to be my judge—and none is
more expert that he in spotting those who would platonize Aristotle.
But his own paper ends on a statement to the effect that the "new"
rhetoric, grammar, logic, and dialectic "may be broadened." So perhaps
I can get by with the plea that my usage is but a "broadening" of the
term in Aristotle. In any case, whether or not the particular *term* "entelechy" is judged admissible here, I dare hope that the situation to
which I apply it will be accepted as real. And I must admit: I am using
the word in a way that would apply only to the realm of symbolic action, not to the realm of sheerly physical motion. I am concerned with
dialectical resources whereby, once you have such a word as "ruler," you

can advance to the idea of a "perfect ruler," thereafter viewing any particular ruler in terms of this idea, and although that design is as Platonic as could be, *the account of its terministic possibilities can be completely literal.*

In any case, I dare hope I shall not be deemed guilty of what McKeon has called "controversial oppositions" caused by some one art's "imperialistic pretensions to unique sovereignty in treating all problems." For though Poetics, when considered "dramatistically," in terms of "symbolic action," is found to involve a principle beyond "communication," I would decidedly not conclude that Poetics is adequate to cover the whole realm of motives (a kind of terministic imperialism to which Northrop Frye inclines.)

But perhaps the handiest way to present my point is to begin with transformations that Leibniz had introduced in *his* concept of the entelechy. Whatever one may think of Leibniz's monadology as a metaphysical system, its analogue, as applied to the idea of a well-formed poetic structure, is splendidly relevant. Consider the cast of characters in a drama, for instance. Each role is like a monad that fulfills the identity proper to its nature. And the poet's "creation," in fitting these roles together, thereby embodies an overarching principle of "preestablished harmony" among the parts. Thus, if character A is intrinsically a victim, and character B is intrinsically a victimizer, each will go through the sequence of developments proper to his nature; but the two lines of development will be so "harmonized" with each other that the victim is victimized precisely at the moment proper to the actualizing of his nature as an entelechy, and the victimizer perpetrates the act of victimage precisely at the moment proper to the fulfillment of his nature. For instance, if both of these "monads" are of such a nature that their characteristic actions and passions are dignified, then their different relations to the moment of victimage will involve such conditions as enable each, in his way, to be his characteristic dignified self. In that respect, each is a monad fulfilling its particular nature as an entelechy, quite as an acorn will embody, intrinsic to it, a development different from that intrinsic to a pine cone; yet it is the whole scheming of the poet's plot that preestablishes such individual fulfillments, which are "harmonious," as viewed from the standpoint of the drama as a whole. In sum, though each character is an "entelechy" that fulfills the possibilities intrinsic to his nature, he can do so only because not just all the other characters, but also all the other poetic elements (of plot, diction, and so on) likewise fulfill their possibilities appropriately, all in effect thus fitting together, to a common harmonious end that is in principle "preestablished."

Then, looking back at the concept of "imitation" in Aristotle's *Poetics*, I felt that it was spontaneously permeated with such an "entelechial" principle (later often called *decorum, to prepon*, as when Chapter XV sums up the characteristics that make the hero of a tragedy a perfect fit for his role). Here we confront norms of poetic "imitation" that are quite different from those of the "representative" in the sense of the statistical average.

As regards this motivational complexity: First, there is the obvious fact that proper internal adjustments among the parts of a drama involve precisely such resources as are necessary to its nature as a communication. But is this all? Is there not also the fact that the attempt to evolve such a marvel of internal poetic adjustments is a kind of *symbolic action for its own sake*, an exacting enterprise willingly undertaken by poet, performers, and audience through sheer love of the art, the delight in thus imaginatively exercising the full resources of our humanity as symbol-users? Thus, the more closely one examines the internal consistencies in a work of art, the more interrelationships and developments one discovers that seem accountable, not on the basis of sheer communication, but as a kind of consummation existing in its own right, sheerly as fulfillment, somewhat as one might count a number of objects, not to use the resultant sum, but simply because such an operation completes certain possibilities intrinsic to the nature of arithmetic.[1]

Let us approach the problem from another angle. Any structure, although designed for some particular end, also has a nature that transcends its use for this end. To say otherwise (as regards our kind of quandaries) would be to commit what might be dubbed the "pragmatic fallacy," about the edges of which a reduction of symbolic action to terms of "communication" always necessarily hovers. For instance, one could make many observations about the structure of a hammer, without any reference at all to its structure as a hammer. (In terms of sheer chemistry, it might be at least partially classifiable under the same heading as human geniuses and human imbeciles.) And it could be used for other purposes (as a pile of hammer-handles could be used for firewood, or as our scrupulous tax-paying is now used for firepower).

Similarly, though language unquestionably owes much of its *development* to its function as an instrument of persuasion and dissuasion in the everyday practical world of cooperation and competition, the *aptitude* for language cannot be *derived* from such a function. Its nature is such that it can serve such a purpose; and speculations along orthodox Darwinian lines would justify the assumption that, however this aptitude arose, at least up to now in the evolution of mankind this particular aptitude has flourished because the animal that happened to be endowed with it has found it helpful to the survival of the species (along with other properties, and corresponding possibilities, alas! that have become institutionalized, to the point where they threaten the survival of man and *a fortiori* of human symbolic action). But by its very nature as language, language is necessarily embodying principles intrinsic to itself. For the vocabulary, grammar, and syntax of any one language necessarily contain ultimate poetic possibilities not inherent in any other language.

To be sure, I am not telling you anything that you did not already know. But I must hang on. Perhaps the simplest way to illustrate the point I am trying to make (namely: my feeling that "communication" as key term can throw us off the track, not drastically, but somewhat) is to think of what is involved in an humble untranslatable pun. The fact that a certain pun is available only to a given language (or symbol-system) does not imply that such a possibility is derivable from the communicative uses to which any such pun may be put. Rather, the fact that two words happen to set up the possibilities of a pun in one particular idiom also sets up a lot of other likelihoods, any of which may be utilized, with varying degrees of skill, for some one particular (communicative) effect. The possibility of any particular pun's discovery necessarily depends upon the nature of the given linguistic idiom, regardless of what one might do with it, for specifically *communicative* purposes. On the edge of paradox we might say: The resource itself is a kind of accident that is essential to the given idiom (hence in most cases untranslatable), regardless of its adaptability for some particular mode of appeal (as when the particular pun is used against this Awful Person rather than that, or in one's or the other's favor).

When, in *Liberalism and Social Action*, John Dewey celebrated this particular ism on the grounds that it provides an opportunity for the "development of the inherent capacities of individuals," he was in his way dealing with the same principle that I would call "entelechial," in the sense that he envisioned the possibility of fully actualizing human potentialities. True, he also relied somewhat on an ambiguity helpful to his cause; for obviously his word "capacities" was secretly modified by the adjective "good." But underneath this fluctuant aspect of his instrumentalist gospel there lay the notion of a certain *nature* attaining its *consummation*, probably the mode of thinking implicit in the traditional preference for equating art with the "natural."

Santayana treated the same principle with ironic gallantry in his tributes to the Realm of Spirit, as grounded in the Realm of Matter (a scheme for which Dramatism's equivalent would be the distinction between "action" and sheer "motion"). How imaginatively he makes gleam the splendor of pure symbolic enterprise, even while believing, if he believed in anything beyond the exactions of his diction, that we live and die inexorably in the Realm of Matter—and that's that! Insofar as a bird gets gratification from flying because it is the kind of animal to which flight comes natural, so for man the Realm of Spirit would be on the "entelechial" slope, as contrasted with the pragmatics of flight or symbolic action for the particular purpose of getting some practical result, such as outwitting an enemy. But presumably, among creatures to which the "second nature" of symbolic action is alien, the realms of pragmatic and entelechial motivation would approach identity, as shrews, that presumably consume their own weight in a fantastically short time, doubtless do so under *compulsions* natural to their rate of metabolism, yet could also be thought of as merely gratifying their appetite like human gourmands that gorge for the fun of it.

Granted, such anecdotes prove nothing. But they might help clarify my attempts at a definition, like a parable. For the *particular* kind of entelechial motive with which I am concerned involves a species of symbolic action that, to our knowledge, is characteristic only of man. Also, whereas I have treated it as a step "beyond communication" so far as the realm of Poetics is concerned, the implications of the term take me much farther afield. For instance, when McKeon (p. 336) refers to "deep-seated cravings for generality and universality," we may look upon such "cravings" as "entelechially" grounded in the culminative possibilities of language itself, which points "naturally" towards ever more inclusive namings, while there is a kind of unity-in-diversity that characterizes even a single sentence. I'd want to put such "cravings" in the same class as Ernst Bloch's *Ergänzungs-Bedürftigkeit* (if I may quote a term from a Marxist-tinged philosopher whom, we are told, some German Protestant ministers are now inclined to favor, as an antidote to the "God is dead" school of theology). I assume that all terms for total "unity" and "unification" (such as invariably turn up somewhere in the various brands of Kantian and post-Kantian transcendentalism) are manifestations of the entelechial "craving" implicit in the dialectical ability (and/or incentive) to encompass ever higher "levels of generalization."

Physiologically, one kind of unity would be implicit in the centrality of the nervous system, with its tendency to experience whatever kind of "wholeness" there is in an attitude (as when pronounced pain or well-being saturates for us the whole world with its quality). Put this together with the genius of the sentence, and there is the "craving" for the culminative statement of an attitude towards "everything," as though a *Weltanschauung* could be ideally summed up in one emotionally tinged formula, which might in turn be systematically subdivided into a universal, infinitely variable tautology. The same trend is embodied in the "imperialistic pretensions" that are an innate temptation to any nomenclature (since it can be analogously extended beyond the area for which it was specifically fit).

But McKeon's own ingeniously pluralistic survey of the different ways in which the subject matter of philosophy can be transformed, or projected, depending upon its ontological, epistemological, or logological *Ausgangspunkt*, suggests the possibility that the very domains of the literal and analogical might correspondingly undergo shifts. Indeed, since "things" can exist for us only by reason of their place in "situations," our names for things may be but shorthand names for situations —and existentially, situations can but be *analogous* to one another, never identical.[2] So there is a reasonable sense in which, if I apply the same word to the same kind of object in two quite different situations, I am not quite cleansed of analogy, insofar as our words for even the most "concrete" individual objects are in essence classificatory, and abbreviations (omitting explicit reference to whatever particular context the object is necessarily a part of.)

But I am getting in deep here, and had better hurry on. My main point is: Let us suppose that I might be said to "analogously" extend the concept of the entelechy to include many kinds of "thoroughness." I would still want to contend that I am not merely extending a term beyond its rightful field. For instance: Frequently in times of conflict, people would attribute to the enemy no less than "perfect" viciousness (thereby reducing the situation to but a crude choice between the enemy's destruction and their own, with words like "freedom" and "slavery" bandied about absolutely, for the *rhetorical* sloganizing of their resistance). In such a situation, I am trying to suggest, whereas the "entelechial" principle that is embodied in such "perfect" imputing of motives can be seen to operate in the "communicative" realm of rhetoric (and above all, in connection with the typical resources of antithesis), there is a sense in which it can be said to center in the realm of poetics. For as considered from the "Dramatistic" point of view, such "perfection" can be seen to embody, though in a reprehensible way, terministic resources that are utilized with far greater perfection, in the realm of poetics, which is the realm of symbolic action "naturally" exercised for its own sake.

Though, as I have said, there is a sense in which papers on rhetoric and poetics could simply complement each other, there is also an area shared in common. Longinus *On the Sublime* is perhaps the grandest early text that illustrates this point, since selections from poets and orators serve equally well as examples. Similarly, Sister Miriam Joseph's delightful compendium on *Shakespeare's Use of the Arts of Language* illustrates by quotations from a poet the kind of stylistic devices classified in Quintilian's books on rhetoric. But as we have seen, the overlap of rhetoric and poetics turns up in another way, too. For insofar as the Dramatistic point of view equates the realm of poetics with symbolic action for its own sake, and "communication" as an aim would not completely cover this field, I must find us somewhat at odds.

True, my position is not without embarrassments. For instance, when a certain demonstration in mathematics is admired for its sheer "elegance," to that extent we'd be considering how it looked, as viewed in terms of Poetics. And the mere tracking down of the implications in any specific scientific nomenclature would be an example of such a poetic or entelechial "compulsion"—and all the more insistently so when any such "craving" has been massively potentiated by the accumulation of technological resources constructed in its image, a fateful duplication whereby many men of great skill and enterprise must strive like demons to track down the manifold implications of Technologism, with its labyrinthine entanglements of progress, pollution, and war. (We here move towards an indeterminate area where symbolic action in the neutral sense can become symbolic action in the pathological sense.)

But let us turn now to a different consideration. Although the entelechial principle, as here conceived, is not wholly reducible to the realm of the specifically rhetorical (or strictly to terms of "communication" in any form), there is still the fact that rhetorical pressures exert a major influence in their own right. I can best make my point by discussing a course I had planned, but did not give, on "Rhetoric—and the Social Comedy."

I had collected notes on a set of devices, some verbal, some "administrative," that people employ in their fluctuantly cooperative and competitive dealings with one another, or sometimes even with themselves. A citation from Demetrius *On Style*, contrasting how a subject would be presented by Aristippus of Cyrene, by Xenophon, and "in the 'Socratic' manner," would be an example of the purely verbal. A summary of the devices in Machiavelli's *The Prince* would illustrate the "administrative" sort.[3] I felt that all these could be classed under the head of "Rhetoric" in a broad sense of the term; and to this end I thought of considering the lot by reference to some overall discussion of what might be called in general the "Rhetorical Situation."

Inasmuch as any such "Rhetorical Situation" must be composed of both universal and transient (or local) elements, obviously an attempt to characterize it systematically would involve some considerations that would fall under the heading of traditional rhetoric, while others will necessarily be "new." And a discussion of any such "RS factor" requires a kind of circumstantiality not available to McKeon's modes of generalization.

Were this circumstantiality to be studied solely from the standpoint of rhetoric, it might be omitted from a *philosophy of language*, quite as McKeon omits it from his observations on the *language of philosophy*. But what if the given philosophy of language holds, among its major tenets, that the philosophic approach to "reality" itself must be through the piously and/or shrewdly close inspection of man's rhetorical quirks, as they color his relation to "reality?" At the very least, a philosophy so designed should, if only to the ends of clear exposition, give a sampling of the major particulars in the wordly situation towards which the philosophy would adopt appropriate attitudes. Central to its definition of man would be its concern with the principles of the Rhetorical Situation that so strongly marks the human condition.

The Rhetorical Situation, as it looks from this angle, centers in a bewilderingly interwoven nodus of elements, both symbolic and nonsymbolic. The beginning is almost absurdly simple. It can be stated as quickly as in the traditional formula, "the problem of the one and the many," as experienced by an animal whose prowess with symbols is capped by the genius of the negative. But everywhere one turns, its simplicity just as quickly frays into a complexity, so there's nowhere to begin. Hence, for want of a better way, I'll begin with an anecdote.

Some time back I attended a conference that included a wide and varied range of experts involved in questions of communication, which was specifically the subject of the conference. There were physiologists, sociologists, depth psychologists, behaviorists, psychiatrists, specialists in the newer developments of linguistics, computerologists, and one or two out-and-out devotees of traditional books on rhetoric (among which I count myself). As regards the "problem of the one and the many," the general tendency was to dissolve the individual in some larger kind of context, either social or physical, on the grounds that there is no dividing line between individual and context.

Adapting for secular purposes the Thomistic view of matter as a *principium individuationis*, I "dramatistically" contended that, along with our necessary merger in some universal context, there is an adequate empirical consideration whereby we can and must be differentiated as individuals; namely: "the centrality of the nervous system," the innate physiological condition whereby, though one man's pleasures and pains may be *like* another's, and can to varying degrees arouse our sympathies, the structure that is natural to the human organism after parturition allows any such pleasures and pains to be *immediately* experienced only by the given individual. I refer to the simple difference between your feeling sorry for my suffering from an accident, and your having actually suffered the accident while I went unscathed.

The principle of individuation, as so conceived, would be grounded in the realm of sheer motion (the motions of the organism's bodily processes, in a centralized biological system that is destroyed with the death of the body.) However, once such an organism somehow becomes endowed with an aptitude for symbolic action (adequately exemplified by the learning of a conventional symbol system such as prevails in any tribal idiom), a bewildering variety of essentially *symbolic* "identifications" becomes possible. For instance, the individual can become *identified* as a member of this clan rather than that, and so on. Add proper names, private property, the complicated division of labor, money, taxes, profusion of corporations (with corresponding corporate law), movements, causes, isms even unto the ends of the earth—and we necessarily confront in ever-changing guise that "paradox of substance" whereby, the more closely you examine the "individual," the very accentuating of his individuality dissolves into all sorts of *contextual* attributes that could not possibly be confined to the realm of his individual identity as a centralized nervous system. However, within the realm of symbolism proper, he takes on a new kind of individuality in the sense that, though he merges at every point into social rather than individual contexts (though his "personality" dissolves into *roles* that themselves merge with situations of much wider scope), his particular combination of experiences, with corresponding memories and associations (or "equations") is *unique*.

Here, then, is the tangle that we'd work from, in trying to characterize for philosophic purposes the Rhetorical Situation: As regards sheer dialectic, we confront the perennial problem of the One and the Many, in keeping with what Socrates celebrates as the prime resource of dialectics; namely: the distinction between generalization and specification, or in later terms, composition and division. Such a purely symbolic range is matched and modified by an empirical grounding in the distinction between the kind of nonsymbolic individuality intrinsic to the centrality of the nervous system (the realm of sheer motion) and the various modes of *identification* (in the realm of action) that the resources of symbol systems make possible. Such identifications involve a "paradox of substance" in the sense that one's intrinsic nature as a person dissolves into contextual properties extrinsic to the individual.

Aristotle calls attention to the special value of *antithesis* as a rhetorical device. It could in turn be considered as an aspect of man's peculiar genius, in adding the negative to nature, a "perfection" that comes to a head in the flat opposing of Yes and No. As regards *administrative* matters, the principle attains its clearest or sharpest embodiment in contrasting modes of congregation and segregation, with a "natural" ever-present tendency, or temptation, to demarcate a congregation by some device of segregation. Repeatedly, in the rhetoric of social relationships, this proclivity manifests itself in schemes whereby the rhetorician, to organize his group, focusses attention upon some enemy shared in common (an essentially dialectic subterfuge that also has the "conspiratorial" or rhetorical advantage of deflecting criticism from flaws in the given exhorter's arguments or conduct.)

To the extent that a spokesman is identified as the person who most fully represents the essence and aims of his group, there are set up the symbolic conditions needed for *charisma*, whereby the congregation can love itself through fanatic devotion to its leader (a gratification that may be all the stronger to the extent that there are secret self-doubts to be silenced.) And on the other side of the antithesis, the segregational, there is identification in terms of the enemy, who serves a unifying function as *scapegoat*.

The rhetorical principle of antithesis (as accentuated by tribal, national, or racial modes of identification) figures also in purely spontaneous forms of "conspiracy." For instance, "we" as a *nation* may fight a war, all of "us" sharing in one identification, though at one extreme there are the soldiers killing and being killed, while at the other extreme there are the gamblers who hope to make a killing in war stocks. And, when the Supreme Court ruled that a legal corporation should be given rights Constitutionally guaranteed to the human person, corresponding new tricks of identification became possible. These too should be considered, in a Dramatistic philosophy of human motives, as related to the Rhetorical Situation.

Nor should our troubled thought on the subject of identification be confined to the specifically socio-political realm. Our spontaneous identification with the powers of our technology can lead to quite a range of bluntness. Thus, a person with no greater technological aptitude than the ability to buy something if you give him the money to buy it with, can consider himself intrinsically superior to the members of a primitive tribe which, by its exceptional skills and sensitivities, can eke a livelihood out of a wilderness. There is much of this tendency in our typical view of things. Almost without thinking, we incline to be like the fellow who had delusions of grandeur because, each time he approached the door of a supermarket, it of itself opened to let him pass.

Dramatistic admonitions suggest: It would be much better for us, in the long run, if we "identified ourselves" rather with the natural things that we are progressively *destroying*—our trees, our rivers, our land, even our air, all of which we are a lowly ecological part of. For here, in the long run, a pious "loyalty to the sources of our being" (Santayana) would pay off best, even in the grossly materialistic sense. For it would better help preserve the kinds of natural balance on which, in the last analysis, mankind's prosperity, and even our mere existence, depend. But too often, in such matters, our attitudes are wholly *segregational,* as we rip up things that we are not—and thus can congratulate ourselves upon having evolved a way of life able to exhaust in decades a treasure of natural wealth that had been here for thousands of years.

I believe that no philosophy can better warn us of the limitations besetting the goals of purely symbolic motives than one that pays them maximum attention. And all such considerations, I submit, are major aspects of what I would want to class under the head of the Rhetorical Situation (in keeping with my notion that, along with the traditional stress upon "persuasion" as the central term of rhetoric, there is a kind of post-Marxist, post-Freudian place for the term "identification," as it relates to the antithetic quandaries of congregation and segregation).

Perhaps one further aspect of the subject should be considered. I have in mind the dialectical fact that the term "identification" also implies the need for some such corrective companion-term as "autonomy." In an age of highly specialized sciences, there are obviously good grounds for upholding the proposition that each such discipline is *autonomous* (since each has its own first principles and corresponding modes of expertise.) We necessarily confront a technical fallacy, a case of terministic imperialism, if ever any such realm proclaims hegemony over any other, by expanding its nomenclature to cover an area over which it has no proper jurisdiction. (I am aware that I am now simply talking good post-Aristotelian McKeon, so I feel safer than a church.) But the "RS factor" enters insofar as specialized activities happen willy-nilly to be *identified* with other activities outside their field.

For instance, the chemist, *qua* chemist, can properly invoke the principle of "autonomy," when contending that he wants no politician to dictate how he should define and teach chemistry. But, purely in his role as citizen, said chemist may happen to be *identified with* a concern that is producing chemicals for a malign purpose. He may, if he so chooses, propound arguments to justify his engaging in such behavior. But he cannot properly justify his actions in the name of sheerly technical "autonomy."

In my "Response" to McKeon's paper, I touched upon this subject, which I would now like to develop one step further. As regards our current interest in "interdisciplinary" projects, the principle of "autonomy" makes it obvious that no one among a set of "integrated" specialties could serve as architectonic basis for the lot. For if any one such specialty is made central, by the same token it would be a usurper, in attempting to impose its terms upon other "autonomous" fields. But there's a further problem.

Inasmuch as there are differences of opinion among specialists in any given field, one must also choose from among the contestants within that field. And one must somehow do so *ab extra*, whereas the principle of autonomy would require judgment *ab intra*. The only way I can see to deal with this problem of inter*disciplinary integration is to offer a general philosophy, on the basis of which any choice among intra*disciplinary contestants is decided upon. The given specialty would thus be as though "derived" from the overriding philosophy. And any reader who would judge the decision would thus at least be able to weigh the arguments on which it was based. This isn't a very heroic solution. But it's the best I can think of. (On the side, we might note: Certain intra*disciplinary decisions might be immaterial to a given philosophy. For instance, though specialists might quarrel as to just exactly where human culture began and exactly how it spread, many such decisions would be quite irrelevant to a philosophy of language which takes as its starting point a definition of man as he is, everywhere all over the world, regardless of how he came to be that way.)

There is one respect in which McKeon's approach to the language of philosophy grievously endangers a major Dramatistic property. I refer to Dramatism's investment in what (in my *Grammar of Motives*) I called the "temporizing of essence," and which I have later developed further.[1]

I might approach the issue thus: Recall, in Chapter VII of the *Poetics*, where Aristotle propounds the proposition that "A whole is what has a beginning, middle, and end." There are few statements that are more platitudinous, and even fewer that are more fertile. In particular, owing to my study of dramatic and narrative forms, I became involved in somewhat paradoxical considerations whereby, if a work is integrally formed, then whereas a beginning, middle, or end must be *explicitly* exactly as it is, each such stage must *implicitly* contain the other two, in anticipation (as regards a beginning), in retrospect (as regards an end), while the middle would somehow contain the "substance" of both.

Thus, when the literary critic, Frank Kermode, recently published a book entitled *The Sense of an Ending* (and using the Biblical Apocalypse as his *starting* point), one almost automatically thinks of possible companion titles, *The Sense of a Beginning* and *The Sense of a Middle*.

But whereas Kermode stresses the *narrative* aspect of the terms, a closer look at them brings up other possibilities. For there is a notable difference between temporal sequence (yesterday-today-tomorrow) and logical sequence (as with first premise, second premise, conclusion.) We could say that the man began something yesterday, and he will end it tomorrow. But one could not interpret the syllogism as saying: All men were mortal yesterday, Socrates is a man today, therefore Socrates will be mortal tomorrow. There is no *temporal* sequence in the premises and conclusion of a syllogism though the *stating* of the propositions involves the passing of time.

Furthermore, along with the ambiguities between temporal conclusions and logical conclusions, there is also the terministic situation whereby the "sense of an ending" involves the sense of an *end*, as a *purpose*, or overriding ultimate of some sort (in brief, the sense of the work as entelechial actualization). And there is the terminal nature of terms, in demarcating a universe of discourse.

Similarly, a concern with "middle" splits, not just as regards the narrative middle's janus-like relation to beginning and end, but also in the sense that a *medium* can permeate the whole with its essence. As Kermode points out, all thoughts of our being in a time of crisis or transition (as every age is) stress the temporal sense of a middle. Yet as he proceeds you find his speculations overlapping upon theories of artistic production as in its essence transitional. Harold Rosenberg's title, *The Tradition of the New*, paradoxically suggests how the concept of "permanent revolution" could thus shift back and forth between temporal middle and artistic means.

In various places (such as my essay on "The First Three Chapters of Genesis" in *The Rhetoric of Religion*) I have laid stress upon resources of nomenclature whereby *logical principles* (or "firsts") can be stated *mythically* in quasi-narrative terms. Plato's archetypes are a case in point. And when reading Kermode's book I realized that I had missed an excellent example of ways whereby middles, while overlapping upon beginnings, can serve as the temporizing of essence. Though he does not thus interpret his observations about Aquinas on angels, he does note that, in making essential distinctions between God, man, and angels, the *Summa* introduces for angels a third kind of duration (identical with neither God's realm of eternity nor man's existence in time). For all his stress upon endings, Kermode here helpfully observes that this issue "is ultimately an argument about origins."

In keeping with such speculations, I would interpret Joseph Frank's concern with "spatial form" in literature as basically motivated by the fact that, although the various parts of a narrative are progressively "revealed" to the reader in temporal sequence, their interrelationships "just *are*" (having the same fixity in their bearing upon one another as the parts of a sculpture or a painting).

Perhaps because my philosophy of language is based so largely upon dramatic *action* as model (in contrast with "scientistic" approaches that place their primary stress upon matters of *knowledge* or *information*) I find it particularly engrossing to study the transformations involved in the shuttling between the temporal sequence of narrative fictions and the logical sequence of philosophic fictions, along with their bewildering overlaps (as, for instance, in psychologies like Freud's or Jung's). So I was somewhat aggrieved to see McKeon riding smooth-shod over such speculations thus: "Conclusions are, with a change in the mode of analysis, denouements, consummations, ends, fulfillments, climaxes, or achievements." There goes the best part of my life, down the drain in one sentence. But just before disappearing, I cry out: "He would leave unplumbed the depths of the problems to which Spinoza helped give rise, when his equating of God with Nature so fertilely brought together the modes of temporal and logical sequence. Or, going farther back, I'd see precisely such considerations of similarity and difference implicit in Aristotle's reference to the close kinship between poetry and philosophy."

In sum, then: Though a Dramatistic philosophy of language entertains doubts as to whether the Aristotelian concept of the entelechy works well, or usefully, in the realm of physics (the realm of sheer motion), and though in any case it does not need the concept there, it would urgently ask for the refurbishing of the term as regards the kinds of "perfection" that are intrinsic to symbol systems. And such a motive would be assigned to the realm of Poetics insofar as it, like poetry, is grounded in sheer love of the art. And by the same token, any other art would share in such a motive, to the extent that, whatever its usefulness, it was pursued purely in and for itself.

Such "perfection" shows up almost compulsively, as regards the *Rhetorical* uses of "antithesis," with its corresponding modes of "identification" (and corresponding paradoxes of substance.)

Such paradoxes of substance attain *their* perfection, so far as the quandaries of symbol systems are concerned, in problems to do with terministic ways of shifting between temporal and logical modes of sequence.

It all gets down to this: Since a Dramatistic theory of terminology begins by definition with terms for "action" rather than terms for knowledge, factuality, "truth," it is necessarily involved, from the very start, in a kind of "Cartesian split" between "motion" and "action." It is built atop the proposition that *things move* and *persons act.* "Persons" are defined by their ability and/or compulsion to act in terms of such identifications as owe their existence to the human body's innate capacity for learning conventional symbol systems. And the lack of an ability or opportunity to so develop would so bring it about that the given body would not be deemed "normal" by its fellow bodies.

Since such resources also involve corresponding temptations, a Dramatistic philosophy of language (or of symbolicity in general) must feature such conditions, which come to a focus in what could well be called The Rhetorical Situation—and particularly when, as with this particular panel, we are approaching our problems from the standpoint of McKeon's expert ways of deriving an alignment from "Communication" as the key term.

NOTES

1. In this connection I recall, many years back, meeting a lightning calculator who could add ten-digit numbers as fast as they were read off to him. I asked him if some combinations of numbers appealed to him more than others. Usually, he said, he was asked questions that had to do only with the speed of his calculating; but as a matter of fact, he did have a kind of attitude such as I was asking about. As he walked along the street, for instance, certain numbers on street cars (there were many more of them then than now) were spontaneously *pleasing* to him because of their internal relationships. Of a certain number, for instance, if you multiply the middle two digits, the product is the same as the sum of the outer two, and as the remainder got by subtracting the smaller from the larger of the other two. (Unless I made a mistake, the conditions are met by the otherwise quite uninteresting number, 712491.) It is my notion that such "aesthetic" observations emerge purely through love of the art. To be sure, they arise out of the operative possibilities intrinsic to arithmetic as a "communicative" idiom. But they exist in their own right, too. And in this sense they serve as illustration of the third stage with which I am here concerned (analogous to the kind of *comtemplatio* that Anselm would interweave with the term *species*).

2. I got considerably entangled in this problem in my essay, "What Are the Signs of What?—A Theory of 'Entitlement,' " *Language as Symbolic Action,* (Berkeley, U. of California Press, 1966), pp. 359 ff.

3. These and other instances are mentioned in my article, "Rhetoric—Old and New," originally published in the *Journal of General Education,* April 1951; recently reprinted in *New Rhetorics,* edited by Martin Steinmann, Jr. (New York, Charles Scribner's Sons, 1967).

4. As in my *Rhetoric of Religion,* and the essay "Myth, Poetry, and Philosophy," originally published in *Journal of American Folklore,* October–December 1960, and reprinted in my *Language as Symbolic Action.*

NOTES ON CONTRIBUTORS

HAROLD TAYLOR   Former President, Sarah Lawrence College. Publications include: *Essays in Teaching*, (1952); *On Education and Freedom* (1953); *Art and Intellect* (1960); and contributions to *American Scholar*, *Journal of Philosophy*, *Saturday Review*, and *The New York Times Sunday Magazine*.

WILLIAM K. FRANKENA   Professor of Philosophy at University of Michigan; President of the American Philosophical Association, Western Division, Guggenheim Fellow (1948–1949). Publications include: *Ethics* (1963); *Philosophy of Education* (1965); *Three Historical Philosophies of Education* (1965).

HENRY AIKEN   Professor of Philosophy, Brandeis University; Guggenheim Fellow (1960–1961). Publications include: *The Age of Ideology* (1957); *Reason and Conduct* (1962); Coauthor, *Philosophy in the Twentieth Century* (1962).

MARVIN FARBER   Distinguished Professor of Philosophy at State University of New York at Buffalo, President of the International Phenomenological Society, Editor of *Quarterly Journal* and *Philosophy and Phenomenological Research*. Publications include: *The Foundation of Phenomenology* (1943); *The Aims of Phenomenology* (1966); *Phenomenology and Existence* (1967).

SAMUEL B. GOULD   Chancellor, State University of New York. Publications include: *Knowledge is Not Enough* (1959); and contributions to *Antioch Review*, *Science*, and *School and Society*.

JOHN MACQUARRIE   Professor of Systematic Theology at Union Theological Seminary. Lecturer in Systematic Theology at University of Glasgow, 1953–1962. Publications include: *An Existentialist Theology* (1955); *The Scope of Demythologizing* (1960); *Twentieth-century Religious Thought* (1963); *Principles of Christian Theology* (1966); *God-Talk* (1967).

KAI NIELSEN Professor of Philosophy at New York University. Publications include: "Justification and Moral Reasoning," *Methodos* (1957); "On Speaking of God," *Theoria* (1962); "Religion and Commitment," (in W. T. Blackstone and R. H. Ayers, eds., *Problems of Religious Knowledge and Language*); "On Fixing the Reference Range of 'God'," *Religious Studies* (1966).

WINFIELD E. NAGLEY Chairman, Department of Philosophy, University of Hawaii; Fellow, American Scandinavian Foundation, 1964–1965. Publications include: "Kierkegaard's Irony as Controlled Moment," UNESCO; "Kierkegaard on Liberation," *Ethics* LXX (1), (1959); "Kierkegaard's Irony in the 'Diapsalmata,'" *Kierkegaardiana* (1966); and numerous reviews in *Philosophy East and West*.

MORRIS WEITZ Professor of Philosophy at Brandeis University; Fullbright Research Fellow, 1951–1952; Guggenheim Fellow, 1959–1960. Publications include: "Analysis and the Unity of Russell's Philosophy" (in P. Schilpp, ed. *The Philosophy of Bertrand Russell*, 1944); *Philosophy in Literature* (1963); *Hamlet and the Philosophy of Literary Criticism* (1964); *Philosophy of the Arts* (1964).

MONROE C. BEARDSLEY Professor of Philosophy at Temple University; Vice-President of the American Society for Aesthetics; member of the Editorial Board of the *Monist; Guggenheim Fellow*, 1950–1951. Publications include: Coauthor (with Elizabeth Beardsley), *Philosophical Thinking: An Introduction* (1965). Author, *Aesthetics: Problems in the Philosophy of Criticism* (1958); *Aesthetics From Classical Greece to the Present: A Short History* (1965).

W. E. KENNICK Professor of Philosophy at Amherst College. Publications include: *Art and Philosophy* (1964); Coeditor (with Morris Lazerowitz), *Metaphysics: Readings and Reappraisals.* (1965).

JACK GLICKMAN Instructor in Philosophy, State University of New York College, Brockport, New York. Publications include: "Hoffman on Ziff's 'About "God",'" *Sophia* (1965).

JEROME STOLNITZ Chairman, Department of Philosophy, Herbert Lehman College of the City University of New York. Editor, *Aesthetics* (1965). Publications include: *Aesthetics and Philosophy of Art* (1960).

H. W. JANSON Professor of Fine Arts, New York University. Publications include: *History of Art* (1962); *Key Monuments in the History of Art* (1962); *Sculpture of Donatello* (1963).

CLIFTON FADIMAN   Former Regents Lecturer, University of California at Los Angeles, Former Member, Board of Editors, *Encyclopedia Britannica*. Publications include: translation of Frederich Nietzsche's *The Birth of Tragedy* and *Ecce Homo* (1926).

RICHARD McKEON   Charles F. Grey Distinguished Professor of Philosophy and Greek, the University of Chicago. Publications include: *Thought, Action and Passion* (1954); ed., *Medieval Philosophers, Selections* (1959); ed., *Aristotle, Basic Works* (1941).

H. W. JOHNSTONE, JR.   Professor of Philosophy, Pennsylvania State University; Fulbright Lecturer at Trinity College, Dublin, Ireland. Publications include: *Elementary Deductive Logic* (1954); *Philosophy and Argument* (1959); coauthor (with J. Anderson) *Natural Deduction* (1962).

GEORGE J. STACK   Associate Professor of Philosophy at State University of New York College at Brockport. Publications include: *Berkeley's Analysis of Perception* (1969); and numerous articles and reviews in *The Personalist, Modern Schoolman, Journal of the History of Philosophy, Philosophy and Phenomenological Research, Journal of Value Inquiry, Philosophische Rundschar, Studium Generale*.

HAROLD ZYSKIND   Professor of Philosophy, State University of New York at Stony Brook. Publications include: "A Case Study in Philosophical Rhetoric," *Philosophy and Rhetoric* (1968).

HAROLD GREENSTEIN   Assistant Professor of Philosophy at State University of New York College, Brockport, New York. Publications include: "Biologists as Philosophers," *Bioscience* (1966); and contributions to *Methodos, Philosophy and Phenomenological Research*, and *Australasian Journal of Philosophy*.

KENNETH BURKE   Former Visiting Professor at Harvard University, Literary Critic, and Poet. Publications include: *Philosophy of Literary Form: Studies in Symbolic Action* (1967); *Language as Symbolic Action: Essays on Life, Literature and Method* (1966); *Collected Poems, 1915–1967* (1968).